AF725876

Grants FOR Medical Research

A Guide to Federal and Private Funding

Robin Jones, Editor

Capitol Publications Inc.
1101 King Street, Suite 444
Alexandria, VA 22314
www.grantscape.com

Copyright © 1997 by Capitol Publications Inc.
Marjorie Weiner, Publisher
Robin Jones Williams, Manager, Ancillary Products

All rights reserved. No part of this book may be reproduced or used in any form without permission in writing from the publisher. Address inquiries to Permissions Editor, Capitol Publications Inc., P.O. Box 1453, Alexandria, Va. 22313-2053.

Printed in the United States of America

ISBN: 1-56925-095-2

Table of Contents

Table of Contents (Cont.)

Introduction

Typically, health funding directories contain a wealth of information on all types of health-related projects. Having to weed through these to find medical research funders can be labor-intensive and tedious. For this reason, ***Grants for Medical Research: A Guide to Federal and Private Funding*** was developed. Profiling more than 400 funders that give to medical research organizations, individuals, or medical schools, for example, ***Grants for Medical Research*** provides the first critical step in the research process by identifying funders that give to specific medical research causes.

Compiled from Capitol Publication's ***GrantScape*** fundraising databases of foundation, corporate and federal funders, each profile includes the funder's giving priorities; contact information; application procedures; geographic restrictions; recent grants; a listing of the funder's directors, officers, and trustees; and more. Figure 1 illustrates a sample foundation profile and describes the type of information contained in each field. Keep in mind that some profiles may be missing a category of information because it was either not available from the funder or it is not applicable to the grant program.

Some rules of thumb to follow when using ***Grants for Medical Research:***

- If the geographic scope rules out your organization as a direct applicant, remember that where a single application might fail to win a grant, a geographically diverse consortium of organizations might have a better chance of success. Consider teaming with an organization in the geographic area in which the funder awards grants.

- Don't overlook a grant opportunity just because the deadline has passed. Many grant programs are cyclical, with deadlines falling at about the same time each year. Starting to prepare now can give you the jump on the next competition.

- Read each profile carefully to determine the nature of the funder's giving priorities. Make note of any restrictions that may prevent a foundation from funding your organization.

- Review the listing of directors, officers, and trustees for each funder and look for personal connections with your organization. Remember, people make the funding decisions, and having a personal contact at a foundation or corporate giving program is a good place to start your prospect research.

It's important to remember that a successful grant, in terms of project funding and implementation, is one that has the *right project idea* matched to the priority of the *right funder* and is submitted in a well-written proposal. ***Grants for Medical Research*** will serve as a starting point for finding the right funders for your research project. But don't stop here. Continue your research by contacting the funders you select and gathering more in-depth information from them, such as annual reports, application guidelines, and 990-PF tax fillings (for foundations).

I hope you find ***Grants for Medical Research*** a useful addition to your research library.

Sincerely,
Robin Jones
Editor

FIGURE 1. SAMPLE PROFILE

Orthopaedic Research and Education Foundation

c/o Katherine Walker, Dir., Grants
6300 N. River Rd., Suite 700
Rosemont, IL 60018-4261
(847) 698-9980
Source Date: 12/95

Geographic Restrictions:
Limited to U.S. and Canada.

To Whom:
Research Grants: encourage new investigators by providing seed money and start up funding.

Career Development Awards: encourage commitment to scientific research in orthopaedic surgery.

Prospective Clinical Research Proposals: provide funding for promising prospective clinical research projects.

Resident Research Awards: encourage development of research interests for residents in approved orthopaedic programs.

OREF Clinical Research Award: recognizes outstanding clinical research related to musculoskeletal disease or injury.

AAOS/OREF Fellowship in Health Services Research: develop orthopaedic surgeons with research skills to undertake and manage health services and outcomes research.

Bristol-Myers Quibb/Zimmer Unrestricted Orthopaedic Research Grant for Excellence in Research in Orthopaedic Treatment: proposal under the direction of a principal investigator, for epidemiologic, clinical, or laboratory based research, designed to positively affect the treatment of orthopaedic disease processes or conditions leading to better patient care.

Educational Awards: provide 1 year support for education programs developed in conjunction with a recognized, national organization for programs that evaluate the effectiveness of orthopaedic education at all levels, clinical consensus conferences, workshops and symposia. **Research and development of educational electronic media and innovative approaches to education will also be considered.**

Fred W. Hark, M.D. and William A. Hark, M.D. Lectureship: honorarium for a lectureship on a topic of interest o orthopaedic surgeons.

State Orthopaedic Society Lectureship: for speakers at state society annual meetings.

Financial info:
Assets: $7,913,700.
Giving: $2,714,300 for grants.

Application info:
Applications accepted. Application form required. Deadline is Aug. 1. Publishes annual report.

Recent Grants:

- Medical College of Wisconsin. "Relationship Between Disc Degeneration and Spinal Instability."
- McGill University. "Intervertebral Disc Composition and Integrity Assessed by Quantitative Magnetic Resonance."
- Case Western Reserve University School of Medicine. "Slow Gradual Spinal Cord Compression: Effects on Regional Spinal Cord Blood Flow and Neural Conduction."
- Columbia University College of Physicians & Surgeons. "MRI and Physicochemical Studies on the Load-Carrying Characteristics of Human Intervertebral Disc."
- University of California, San Francisco, School of Medicine. "Characterization of the Human Intervertebral Disc with High Resolution and Diffusion Weighted Magnetic Resonance Imaging."
- Biochemistry and Molecular Biology Case Western Reserve University School of Medicine. "Regulation of Cell-Cycle Progression in Growth Plate Chondrocytes by Thyroid Hormone."
- Duke University Medical Center. "Biological Modulation of Proliferation, Differentiation, and Cytokine Gene.
- Expression of Human Cartilage-Forming Tumors" University of California, San Diego, School of Medicine "Muscle Response to Tenotomy and Tendon Repair."
- University of California, Los Angeles, School of Medicine. "Recombinant Human Bone Morphogenetic Protein (rh-BMP-2) Enhancement of Bone Growth Across a Gap into a Porous Coated Implant."
- University of North Carolina at Chapel Hill School of Medicine. "Characterization of Drug Resistance Patterns in Osteosarcoma Cell Lines Treated with Taxanes and Camptothecins."
- Creighton University School of Medicine. "Prostaglandin in the Mediation of Mechanical Load Induced Bone Formation."
- Washington University School of Medicine. "Molecular Mechanisms of Implant Osteolysis."
- University of Chicago Pritzker School of Medicine. "Investigating Synovial Anti-Proteoglycan Activity as a Possible Auto-Immune Etiology for Osteoarthritis."
- University of Arkansas College of Medicine. "Global Regulatory Elements of Staphylococcus Aureus as Therapeutic Targets in the Treatment of Osteomyelitis."

Foundation name and contact information
This section contains all of the contact information that the funder provides, including foundation name, contact person, foundation address, phone number, and website or e-mail information, when available. The Employer Identification Number (EIN) and Source Date are also in this section. The EIN is the number listed on the funder's tax return. This number is useful when gathering information on a funder. The Source Date reflects the date of the source material used to update the profile. (This could be the date a questionnaire was completed, the date of an annual report, etc.)

Geographic Restrictions
This section specifies which regions of the United States the funder gives to. Keep in mind that although some funders emphasize giving in a particular area of the country, they may make grants elsewhere as well. Check the **Recent Grants** listings to see where the funder has made grants in the past.

Restrictions
This area covers any giving restrictions the funder may have. Pay close attention to this area so that you do not apply to funders that do not fund your type of project or organization.

To Whom
This section contains the funder's giving priorities. The medical research giving priority is boldfaced in each profile for easy recognition. Make sure your request for funding directly applies to the funder's priorities.

For What
This section lists the types of funding that the funder provides, for example, operating budgets or seed money.

Financial info
This section contains the funders most recent total giving figure, their range of funding—for foundations—and their total assets. You should use the profile Source Date to determine the year of the financial information.

Application info
This section provides you with any deadline or application information needed to contact the funder. Adhering to the funder's instructions is extremely important. Read this section carefully.

Recent Grants
This section lists past recipients of the funder's awards. Depending on the funder, this section could include award amount, recipient name and brief description of the funded project.

Director, Officers and Trustees
This section lists of all of the directors, officers and trustees associated with the foundation.

Acknowledgments

Many thanks are due to people who contributed to this book. Thanks are due to Rosette Graham, Director of Production; and Linda McDonald, Art Director.

Section I
Funder Profiles

Alabama

Herman & Emmie Bolden Foundation

P.O. Box 360028
Birmingham, AL 35236
(205) 988-8989
Source Date: 12/95

Geographic Restrictions:
Primarily in AL.

To Whom:
Health associations, health, social services, **cancer research**, Protestant religion.

Financial info:
Assets: $3,110,100.
Giving: $528,900 for 30 grants (high: $150,000; low: $250).

Application info:
Applications accepted. Submit letter. No deadline.

Directors, Officers, Trustees:
Bolden, Emmie C., Officer
Bolden, Herman D., Donor, Officer
Bolden, Stanley C., Officer
Southern Coach Manufacturing Company, Donor

Brock Foundation

701 S. 20th St.
Birmingham, AL 35233
(205) 933-4880
Source Date: 12/95

Geographic Restrictions:
Primarily in Birmingham, AL.

To Whom:
Higher and other education, community funds, hospitals, religion, social services, child welfare, youth, recreation, conservation, environment, **cancer research.**

For What:
Annual campaigns, capital campaigns, endowment funds.

Financial info:
Assets: $3,550,300.
Giving: $103,700 for 40 grants (high: $25,000; low: $100).

Application info:
Applications accepted. Submit letter. Deadline is Dec. 1. Board meets in Dec.

Directors, Officers, Trustees:
Brock, Harry B., Jr., Donor, Director, Officer
Brock, Jane H., Director, Officer
Brock, Stanley M., Director, Officer

Child Health Foundation

c/o Leah Webb, Exec. Coord.
P.O. Box 530964
Birmingham, AL 35253
(205) 592-9322
Source Date: 12/96

Geographic Restrictions:
Limited to South and Central America.

To Whom:
Fellows for the purpose of refining pediatric medical skills as well as **research** to establish services for Spanish speaking pediatric patients in South and Central America.

For What:
Fellowships, individuals, **research.**

Financial info:
Assets: $1,261,400.
Giving: $68,000 for grants.

Application info:
Applications accepted. Application form required (3 copies). Deadline is Aug. 31. Board meets annually. Publishes annual report.

Directors, Officers, Trustees:
Harwell, Donny, Advisor
Johnson, Joseph D., Director
Jorquiera, Carlos, Director
Loeb, Betty, Advisor
Robbins, Ed, Advisor
Ronderos, Alvaro, Advisor
Ryan, Peter, Director
Serrano, Rosa, Director
Stagno, Sergio, Dr., Director, Officer
Trafford, John, Director, Officer
Wagnon, Nancy, Advisor

Dixon Foundation

c/o Joy Levio, Operations Manager
Financial Center, Suite 1625
Birmingham, AL 35203
(205) 252-2828
Source Date: 12/95

Geographic Restrictions:
Primarily in AL.

To Whom:
Ministers of the United Methodist Church for continuing study and programs [religion], **fellowships in pediatrics research**, prescription medicines and health supplies through local welfare departments.

For What:
Individuals, fellowships.

Financial info:
Assets: $9,073,400.
Giving: $399,300 for grants and $40,400 for 10 grants to individuals (high: $10,000; low: $2,000).

Application info:
Applications accepted. Submit letter. No deadline.

Directors, Officers, Trustees:
Dixon, Carol D., Officer
Dixon, David E., Officer
Dixon, Edwin M., Director, Officer
Dixon, Margaret Y., Director, Officer
Grotnes, Alice D., Officer

Florence Foundation

c/o G. Sage Lyons, Trustee
P.O. Box 2727
Mobile, AL 36652
(334) 432-4481
Source Date: 12/95

Geographic Restrictions:
Primarily in AL.

Restrictions:
No grants to individuals.

To Whom:
Diagnosis, treatment, and medical research concerning pulmonary diseases, lung disorders, no smoking education.

For What:
Annual campaigns.

Financial info:
Assets: $2,679,400.
Giving: $146,000 for 10 grants (high: $50,000; low: $1,000).

Application info:
Applications accepted. Submit letter. No deadline. Board meets in Nov. or Dec.

Directors, Officers, Trustees:
Bodie, William C., M.D., Trustee
Luce, Dwain G., Trustee
Lyons, G. Sage, Trustee
Staples, Florence (d), Donor

Charles & Esther Lee Kimerling Charitable Foundation

2208 University Blvd.
Birmingham, AL 35233
(205) 322-8636
Source Date: 12/95

Geographic Restrictions:
Primarily in AL.

To Whom:
Jewish giving and welfare, education, social services, health associations, **medical research.**

Financial info:
Assets: $1,187,000.
Giving: $53,900 for 75 grants (high: $5,000; low: $100).

Application info:
Applications accepted. Submit letter. No deadline.

Directors, Officers, Trustees:
Kassouf, David P., Trustee

Ben May Charitable Trust

c/o AmSouth Bank
P.O. Drawer 1628
Mobile, AL 36629

Application address:
P.O. Box 123
Mobile, AL 36601
Source Date: 12/95

Geographic Restrictions:
Primarily in AL.

Restrictions:
No grants to individuals.

To Whom:
Higher education, community development, **cancer research.**

For What:
Research, special projects.

Financial info:
Assets: $8,707,600.
Giving: $546,200 for 5 grants (high: $350,000; low: $5,000).

Application info:
Applications accepted. Submit letter. No deadline.

Directors, Officers, Trustees:
AmSouth Bank, N.A., Trustee
Hand, William Brevard, Committee
Johnston, Vivian G., Jr. Committee
Perlman, Martin, M.D., Commitee

Barbara Ingalls Shook Foundation

206 Hart Fell Crescent
Birmingham, AL 35223-2905
(205) 970-0062
Source Date: 12/95

Geographic Restrictions:
Primarily in AL and CO.

Restrictions:
No grants to individuals.

To Whom:
Hospitals, **medical research**, higher and secondary education, cultural programs, arts.

For What:
Research, special projects.

Financial info:
Assets: $4,771,500.
Giving: $213,400 for 45 grants (high: $75,000; low: $100).

Application info:
Applications accepted. Application form required. No deadline.

Directors, Officers, Trustees:
Ingalls Testamentary Trust II, Robert I., Donor
Merck, Adele Shook, Trustee
Shook, Barbara Ingalls, Officer, Trustee
Shook, Elesabeth Ridgely, Trustee
Shook, Ellen Gregg, Trustee
Shook, Robert P., Officer, Trustee
White, William Bew, Trustee

J. Craig & Page T. Smith Foundation

P.O. Box 1566
Birmingham, AL 35201

Application address:
2500 Virginia Ave., N.W., Apt. 704S
Washington, DC 20037
Source Date: 12/94

Geographic Restrictions:
Primarily in Birmingham, AL.

To Whom:
Medical research, religion, family planning, environmental, general charitable giving.

Financial info:
Giving: $64,300 for 15 grants (high: $50,000; low: $100).

Application info:
Applications accepted. Submit letter. No deadline.

Directors, Officers, Trustees:
Dudley, C. Ray, Jr., Trustee
Smith, Mignon C., Donor, Trustee
White, William Bew, Trustee

Arizona

Flinn Foundation

c/o Mary Sue Middleton, Exec. Assistant
3300 N. Central Ave., Suite 2300
Phoenix, AZ 85012-2513
(602) 274-9000
E-mail: flinn@enet.net
Internet: http://aspin.asu.edu/flinn/index.html
EIN: 860421476
Source Date: 12/95

Geographic Restrictions:
Limited to AZ.

Restrictions:
No grants to individuals, annual campaigns, capital or endowment funding, operating or deficit needs, film or video projects, equipment, publications, or workshops and conferences.

To Whom:
Leadership, leadership in health, career development fellowship in medicine, **biomedical research**, medical education, rural hospitals and health care in rural communities, higher education, artistic growth and development, arts stabilization fund, health care for children, seniors, and Native Americans, programs for pregnant and parenting teens, health education in the public elementary and secondary schools, abused and neglected children, AIDS.

For What:
Special projects, **research**, seed money, scholarship funds, fellowships.

Financial info:
Assets: $129,989,300.
Giving: $5,576,300 for 165 grants (high: $250,000; low: $1,000).

Application info:
Applications accepted. Submit letter. No deadline. Publishes application guidelines.

Recent Grants:

$30,000	Arizona AIDS Foundation, Phoenix, AZ. Care consortium.
$100,000	Actors Theatre of Phoenix, AZ. Improve management-information system.
$10,000	Yavapai College, Prescott, AZ. Mentorship program for at-risk gifted students.
$10,000	ALS Association, Phoenix, AZ. Salary support of services coordinator.
$49,579	Yuma Regional Medical Center, AZ. School-based health care program for the Crane School District.

Directors, Officers, Trustees:
Brooks, Robert A., M.D., Trustee
Buffmire, Donald K., M.D., Officer, Trustee
Flinn, Irene (d), Donor
Flinn, Robert S., M.D. (d), Donor
Frazer, David R., Officer, Trustee
Gullen, David J., M.D., Trustee
Kampfer, Merlin W., M.D., Officer, Trustee
Murphy, John W., Officer
O'Malley, Edward V., Jr., Officer, Trustee
Pfister, A. J., Trustee
Ruffner, Jay S., Officer, Trustee

Hudson Foundation

c/o Margaret Bloom, Secretary
80 W. Franklin St.
Tucson, AZ 85701
(520) 623-6416
EIN: 860385802
Source Date: 12/95

Geographic Restrictions:
Limited to Tucson, AZ.

Restrictions:
No grants to individuals.

To Whom:
Health, higher education, seniors, community development, **medical research.**

Financial info:
Assets: $1,217,900.
Giving: $53,200 for 25 grants (high: $10,000; low: $500).

Application info:
Applications accepted. Submit proposal. No deadline.

Recent Grants:

$3,000	Primavera Foundation
$4,000	Mobile Meals
$1,000	Tucson Loan Chest
$3,000	Educational Enrichment

Directors, Officers, Trustees:
Bloom, Cliffton E., Officer
Bloom, Margaret, Officer
Lohse, Ashby I., Officer
Lohse, Florence, Officer

J. W. Kieckhefer Foundation

c/o John I. Kieckhefer, Trustee
P.O. Box 750
Prescott, AZ 86302
(520) 445-4010
Source Date: 12/95

Restrictions:
No grants to individuals, seed money, deficit financing, scholarships, fellowships, or demonstration projects.

To Whom:
Medical research, hospice, health, family planning, disabled, social services, higher, medical, and other education, youth, child welfare, conservation, community funds, public policy, cultural programs.

For What:
Operating budgets, continuing support, annual campaigns, emergency funds, building funds, equipment, land acquisition, endowment funds, matching funds, **research**, publications, conferences and seminars, special projects.

Financial info:
Assets: $15,468,800.
Giving: $870,800 for 70 grants (high: $50,000; low: $500).

Application info:
Applications accepted. Submit letter between May and Nov. Board meets in Nov. and Dec.

Directors, Officers, Trustees:
Kieckhefer, John I., Trustee
Kieckhefer, John W. (d), Donor
Kieckhefer, Robert H., Trustee
Polk, Eugene P., Trustee

Marshall Foundation

c/o Elizabeth Sugges, Board Member
P.O. Box 3306
Tucson, AZ 85722
(520) 622-8613
EIN: 860102198
Source Date: 12/95

Geographic Restrictions:
Limited to Pima County, AZ.

Restrictions:
No grants to individuals.

To Whom:
Higher and secondary education, **medical research**, social services, health.

For What:
Scholarship funds.

Financial info:
Assets: $9,856,700.
Giving: $353,400 for 20 grants (high: $150,000; low: $100).

Application info:
Applications accepted. Submit letter. No deadline. Board meets in Dec. Publishes application guidelines.

Directors, Officers, Trustees:
Castelan, Debra, Director
Jackson, Charles, Director
Marshall, Louise F. (d), Donor
Molloy, John F., Director

Margaret T. Morris Foundation

c/o Eugene P. Polk, Trustee
P.O. Box 592
Prescott, AZ 86302
(520) 445-4010
Source Date: 12/95

Geographic Restrictions:
Primarily in AZ.

Restrictions:
No grants for religious purposes or individuals.

To Whom:
Performing arts, arts, cultural programs, higher and other education, youth, child welfare, family planning, **medical research and education,** environment, animal

welfare, social services, disabled, disadvantaged, mental health, marine sciences, music, family planning, youth, hospice.

For What:
Land acquisition, general purposes, building funds, scholarship funds, deficit financing, endowment funds, operating budgets, special projects.

Financial info:
Assets: $26,361,000.
Giving: $1,365,000 for 65 grants (high: $100,000; low: $500).

Application info:
Applications accepted. Submit letter or proposal in May through Nov. Board meets in Aug. and Dec.

Directors, Officers, Trustees:
Menschel, Richard L., Trustee
Morris, Margaret T. (d), Donor
Polk, Eugene P., Trustee

Southern Arizona Foundation, Inc.

(Formerly Dialysis Foundation of Southern Arizona, Inc.)
P.O. Box 13047
Tucson, AZ 85732-3047
(520) 886-5495
EIN: 510157715
Source Date: 6/95

Geographic Restrictions:
Primarily in AZ.

Restrictions:
No grants to individuals.

To Whom:
Kidney research.

For What:
Research.

Financial info:
Assets: $2,494,000.
Giving: $129,300 for 15 grants (high: $30,000; low: $1,000).

Application info:
Applications accepted. Submit letter. No deadline.

Recent Grants:
Anthropology Department-University Of Arizona-Hopi Dictionary Project
Arizona Historical Society-Historic Research, Publishing Support
Arizona Sonora Desert Museum-Construction Of New Exhibits, Educational Equipment
Arizona State Museum-Conference Support And Scholarships
Cline Library-Northern Arizona University-Grand Canyon River Guide Oral History
Confluence Press Inc-Documentary, Louise Serpa
Desert Survivors-Documentary, Horticultural Therapy
Diocese Of Tucson-Beautification Of Father Eusebio Francisco Kino
Foundation Of Campus Ministry-University Of Arizona-Operating Support
Jesuit Fathers Of Southern Arizona-Publishing Support, Kino Guide
Kerala Jesuit Society-School In Kerala, India
Kuat - University Of Arizona-Operating Support
Late Medieval And Reformation Studies-University Of Arizona- Scholarships
Mexican American Studies And Research Center-University Of Arizona - Historic Research, Archival Documentation
Newman Catholic Center-Operating Support
Patronato San Xavier-Restoration Of San Xavier Mission
S.E.A.R.C.H.-Native Seeds Project
St. Gregory College Preparatory School-Scholarships, Capital Campaign

Directors, Officers, Trustees:
Ben-Asher, David, Director
Bondell, Frederick, Director, Officer
Donfeld, Robert, Director, Officer
Evanhoff, George, Director, Officer
Fried, Mary, Director, Officer

Talley Industries Foundation, Inc.

c/o William Bonnell, Dir., Human Resources
2702 N. 44th St., Suite 100A
Phoenix, AZ 85008-1592
(602) 957-7711
EIN: 066090371
Source Date: 12/95

Geographic Restrictions:
Primarily in Phoenix, AZ.

Restrictions:
No grants to individuals.

To Whom:
Arts, cultural programs, museums, zoos, youth, higher education, **medical research.**

For What:
Scholarship funds, **research.**

Financial info:
Assets: $229,400.
Giving: $86,200 for 25 grants (high: $10,000; low: $500).

Application info:
Applications accepted. Submit proposal by Oct. of current year for contribution in the following year.

Directors, Officers, Trustees:
Crim, Jack C., Director
Dickerson, Mark S., Director, Officer
Mallender, William H., Director, Officer
Mullen, Daniel R., Officer

Del E. Webb Foundation

c/o Majorie Klinefelter, Secretary/Dir.
2023 W. Wickenburg Way
P.O. Box 20519
Wickenburg, AZ 85358
(520) 684-7223
EIN: 866052737
Source Date: 12/95

Geographic Restrictions:
Primarily in AZ, NV, and CA.

Restrictions:
No grants for government agencies, sectarian or religious organizations, pass-through organizations, individuals, deficit financing, or indirect costs.

To Whom:
Medical research, health, hospitals.

Financial info:
Assets: $52,569,500.
Giving: $2,007,900 for 25 grants (high: $1,500,000; low: $5,000).

Application info:
Applications accepted. Application form required (4 copies). Deadline is Mar. 31 and Oct. 31. Board meets in May and Dec. Publishes application guidelines.

Recent Grants:
$5,000,000 University of Nevada School of Medicine, Reno, NV. Construct a medical education and patient care center in Las Vegas, NV.

Directors, Officers, Trustees:
Childress, Owen F., Officer
Johnson, Robert H., Officer
Klinefelter, Marjorie, Officer
Milliken, W. D., Director
Webb, Del E. (d), Donor
Werderman, Del V., Officer

Arkansas

Frank D. Hickingbotham Foundation

c/o Frank D. Hickingbotham, Trustee
425 W. Capitol, Suite 1100
Little Rock, AR 72201
(501) 688-8204
Source Date: 12/94

Geographic Restrictions:
Primarily in AR.

Restrictions:
No grants to individuals.

To Whom:
Higher education, social services, **cancer research**, health, Protestant religion.

Financial info:
Giving: $289,000 for 10 grants (high: $250,000; low: $1,000).

Application info:
Applications accepted. Submit proposal. No deadline.

Directors, Officers, Trustees:
Hickingbotham, Frank D., Donor, Trustee

William C. & Theodosia Murphy Nolan Foundation

200 N. Jefferson, Suite 308
El Dorado, AR 71730
(501) 863-7118
Source Date: 12/95

Geographic Restrictions:
Primarily in AR.

To Whom:
Medical education and research, cultural programs, social services, youth, historic preservation, secondary education, Protestant religion.

For What:
Building funds, operating budgets, general purposes, **research**, scholarship funds.

Financial info:
Assets: $1,260,700.
Giving: $60,000 for 20 grants (high: $10,000; low: $100).

Application info:
Applications accepted. Submit letter. No deadline.

Directors, Officers, Trustees:
Nolan, Robert C., Officer
Nolan, Theodosia Murphy, Donor, Officer
Nolan, William C., Donor, Officer

Ottenheimer Brothers Foundation

c/o E. Grainger Williams, Chairman Projects Committee
Union Nat'l Plaza, Suite 1400
124 W. Capitol Ave.
Little Rock, AR 72201
(501) 376-4531
Source Date: 12/95

Geographic Restrictions:
Primarily in the Pulaski County, AR, area.

Restrictions:
No grants to individuals.

To Whom:
Higher education, cancer, **medical research**, hospitals, libraries.

For What:
Building funds, renovation projects.

Financial info:
Assets: $5,008,700.
Giving: $227,500 for 10 grants (high: $100,000; low: $500).

Application info:
Applications accepted. Submit letter. No deadline.

Directors, Officers, Trustees:
Bauman, Steve, Director, Officer
Blass, Noland, Director, Officer
Grundfest, Judy, Director
Penick, Edward M., Director
Rosen, Louis, Director, Officer
Selz, Fred, Director
Strauss, Sam, Jr., Director
Williams, E. Grainger, Director

California

A-T Medical Research Foundation

5241 Round Meadow Rd.
Hidden Hills, CA 91302
(818) 704-8146
EIN: 953882022
Source Date: 9/94

Geographic Restrictions:
International and U.S. giving.

To Whom:
Ataxia telangiectasia medical research.

For What:
Research, seed money.

Financial info:
Giving: $101,000 for 5 grants to individuals.

Application info:
Applications accepted. Submit letter. No deadline.

Jenifer Altman Foundation

c/o Elise Miller, Pgm. Off.
P.O. Box 1080
Bolinas, CA 94924
(415) 868-0821
E-mail: altman123@aol.com
EIN: 943146675
Source Date: 6/95

Geographic Restrictions:
U.S. and international giving for environment and health including Mexico, Europe, England, Uganda, Ecuador, India, Cambodia, and China, CA with an emphasis on San Francisco for child care and at risk youth.

To Whom:
Socially just and ecologically sustainable future: emphasis concerns the impact of endocrine disrupting chemicals on human health and the preservation of the environment, raising the level of citizen and scientific dialogue on this issue in the U.S. and internationally, support the global citizens' movement for a just and sustainable future in relation to international governmental decision-making forums.

Parent Voices: improve the quality of childcare with emphasis on Bay Area childcare resource and referral networks and childcare networks in CA; rarely fund unsolicited proposals.

Innovative research and demonstration programs in mind-body health, especially those focused on cancer.

Local initiatives that contribute to the quality of life in our small community of Bolinas.

For What:
Conferences and seminars, continuing support, general purposes, special projects.

Financial info:
Assets: $14,675,400.
Giving: $1,506,400 for 45 grants (high: $500,000; low: $1,000).

Application info:
Applications accepted. Application form required with proposal. No deadline. Publishes application guidelines.

Directors, Officers, Trustees:
Almond, Peter O., Director, Officer
Altman, Jenifer (d), Donor
Altman, Jonathan, Director
Dustan, Jane, Director
Lerner, Michael, M.D., Director, Officer
Silk, Thomas, Officer
Wells, Albert, Officer

Ameritec Foundation

760 Arrow Grand Cir.
Covina, CA 91722
(818) 915-5441
EIN: 954147156
Source Date: 12/95

Geographic Restrictions:
Limited to southern CA.

To Whom:
Individuals to promote medical research toward the goal of finding a cure for spinal cord functional impairment (paralysis).

Health, hospitals.

For What:
Research, endowment funds, seed money, special projects.

Financial info:
Assets: $1,368,600.
Giving: $70,000 for 10 grants (high: $20,000; low: $1,000).

Application info:
Applications accepted. Prize not available to individuals conducting clinical research. Submit one page abstract. Deadline is Oct. 15. Board meets quarterly.

Directors, Officers, Trustees:
Ameritec Corp., Donor
Hollfelder, Tom, Director, Officer
McDaniel, Leroy, M.D., Director
Newman, Michael P., Director, Officer
Watson, John R., Director, Officer
Windham, Van, Director

Antonini Foundation

11374 Tuxford St.
Sun Valley, CA 91352
EIN: 954094278
Source Date: 6/95

Geographic Restrictions:
Primarily in Los Angeles, CA [southern].

Restrictions:
No grants to individuals.

To Whom:
Health associations, social services, Catholic giving, blind, **medical research**, early childhood and adult education, hospitals, health, mental health, domestic violence, nutrition, youth, women, voluntarism.

For What:
General purposes.

Financial info:
Assets: $1,196,400.
Giving: $61,500 for 35 grants (high: $20,000; low: $50).

Application info:
Applications accepted. Submit letter. No deadline. Board meets May 15.

Directors, Officers, Trustees:
Antonini, Mario E., Officer
Antonini, Marisa A., Officer

Arata Brothers Trust

c/o Renato R. Parenti, Co-Trustee
P.O. Box 430
Sacramento, CA 95812-0430
(916) 451-5358
EIN: 237204615
Source Date: 12/95

Geographic Restrictions:
Primarily in northern CA, with emphasis on Sacramento area.

Restrictions:
No grants to individuals.

To Whom:
Catholic giving, religion education, health associations, social services, arts, cultural programs, hospitals, disadvantaged children, hunger, **medical research.**

For What:
General purposes.

Financial info:
Assets: $2,165,400.
Giving: $424,100 for 60 grants (high: $35,000; low: $500).

Application info:
Applications accepted. Submit letter. No deadline.

Directors, Officers, Trustees:
Dillon, Francis B., Trustee
Lavezzo, Nellie, Trustee
Parenti, Renato R., Trustee

AT & T Pebble Beach National Pro-Am Youth Fund

(Formerly Bing Crosby Youth Fund, Inc.)
c/o Carmel C. Martin, Jr., Secretary
490 Calle Principal
P.O. Box 112
Monterey, CA 93942
(408) 375-3151
EIN: 946050251
Source Date: 12/94

Geographic Restrictions:
Primarily in Monterey and Santa Cruz counties, CA [northern].

Restrictions:
No grants to individuals.

To Whom:
Retarded and physically disabled children, private secondary and elementary education, boys' and girls' athletic teams, youth symphony, youth music festivals, youth theater groups, opera performances geared to youth, arts classes for youth, hospitals, Boy Scouts, Girl Scouts, YMCA, YWCA, Salvation Army, social services, **medical research**, drug counseling, blind children, municipalities for special youth programs.

For What:
Building funds, equipment, scholarship funds, consulting services, matching funds.

Financial info:
Giving: $456,300 for 150 grants (high: $15,000; low: $500).

Application info:
Applications accepted. Submit letter (2 page limit). No deadline. Board meets in July, Aug., Sept., Oct., and Dec.

Directors, Officers, Trustees:
Brown, Marsha Searle, Trustee
Burns, John, Officer
Coniglio, Peter J., Trustee
Crosby, Bing (d), Donor
Durein, Ted, Officer
Edner, Leon E., Trustee
Keeley, Warner, Trustee
Martin, Carmel C., Jr., Officer
Thacker, Frank, Trustee
Vout, Murray C., Trustee

Solomon R. & Rebecca D. Baker Foundation, Inc.

1900 Ave. of the Stars, Suite 630
Los Angeles, CA 90067
(213) 552-9822
EIN: 237152503
Source Date: 4/94

Geographic Restrictions:
Primarily in CA.

Restrictions:
No grants to individuals.

To Whom:
Medical research in autism, related fields, and the care and therapy of autistic individuals, education for disadvantaged, mental health, Jewish welfare, social services, animal welfare.

Financial info:
Giving: $150,800 for 5 grants (high: $100,000; low: $250).

Application info:
Applications accepted. Submit letter. No deadline.

Directors, Officers, Trustee:
Baker, Rebecca D., Officer, Trustee
Baker, Solomon R., Donor, Officer, Trustee
Barker, Richard H., Trustee
Marsella, Al, Trustee
Plourde, Robert J., Officer, Trustee

Bank of America-Giannini Foundation

Bank of America Ctr., Dept. 3246
Box 37000
San Francisco, CA 94137
(415) 953-0932
EIN: 946089512
Source Date: 12/94

Geographic Restrictions:
Limited to CA.

Restrictions:
No grants to individuals, endowment funds, or matching gifts.

To Whom:
Medical research fellowships for advanced applicants sponsored by accredited medical schools in CA, higher education, health, child welfare, youth.

For What:
Fellowships, **research.**

Financial info:
Assets: $11,805,300.
Giving: $701,200 for grants.

Application info:
Applications accepted. Submit letter, telephone, or proposal. Application form required for fellowships. Deadline is Aug. 1 for grants; Dec. 1 for fellowships. Board meets in Apr. and Nov. Publishes application guidelines.

Directors, Officers, Trustees:
Boitano, Caroline O., Director
Bowman, Jerry L., Director
Deane, James C., Director
Fancher Trust, Fred B., Donor
Giannini, A. P. (d), Donor
Hoffman, Claire Giannini, Director, Officer
Knowles-Sorokin, Cheryl, Director, Officer
Miscoll, James P., Director
Mullane, D. A., Director
Nishioka, Janet, Director, Officer
Paioni, A. T., Director
Smeby, Kyhl S., Director, Officer

Donald R. Barker Foundation

P.O. Box 936
Rancho Mirage, CA 92270
(760) 324-2656
EIN: 930698411
Source Date: 11/95

Geographic Restrictions:
Primarily in CA and OR.

Restrictions:
No grants for sectarian religious purposes, agencies that rely on federal or tax dollars for their principal support, individuals, endowment funding, conferences, or operational deficits.

To Whom:
Higher and secondary education, disabled, hospitals, youth, health, community funds, arts, environment, mental health, **medical research**, cultural programs, family services, community development.

For What:
Operating budgets, scholarship funds, building funds, equipment, special projects.

Financial info:
Assets: $4,733,200.
Giving: $212,200 for 30 grants (high: $50,000; low: $1,000).

Application info:
Applications accepted. Application form required. Deadline is Mar. 1 and Aug. 1. Board meets in May and Oct. Publishes application guidelines.

Directors, Officers, Trustees:
Barker, Donald R. (d), Donor
Lamb, John R., Trustee
McGowan, Coeta Barker, Trustee
McGowan, J. R., Trustee
Moore, Joseph A., Trustee

Bireley Foundation

130 N. Brand Blvd. 4th Flr.
Glendale, CA 91203
(818) 500-7755
EIN: 956029475
Source Date: 12/95

Geographic Restrictions:
Primarily in Los Angeles County, CA [southern], Lee County, FL, and north central UT.

Restrictions:
No grants to individuals.

To Whom:
Medical research affecting children and adolescents, cancer research, youth, child abuse, hospitals, health.

For What:
Annual campaigns, build funds, equipment, general purposes, matching funds, operating budgets, renovation projects, seed money.

Financial info:
Assets: $6,488,500.
Giving: $310,100 for 35 grants (high: $50,000; low: $500).

Application info:
Applications accepted. Submit letter or proposal (2 copies), between Jan. and June. Board meets 4 times a year.

Directors, Officers, Trustees:
Baldwin, Ernest R., Director, Officer
Bireley, Christine Harriet, Director, Officer
Bireley, Frank W. (d), Donor
Bireley, Frank W., Director, Officer
Bireley, William Robert, Director
Gire, Leroy M., Officer
Oliver, Christine Bireley, Officer

Borrego Fund

100 Mason St.
San Francisco, CA 94108
Source Date: 12/94

Geographic Restrictions:
Primarily in Borrego Springs and San Francisco, CA.

To Whom:
Education, religion, child development, youth, **medical research.**

Financial info:
Giving: $35,900 for 25 grants (high: $15,000; low: $50).

Application info:
Applications accepted. Submit letter. No deadline.

Directors, Officers, Trustees:
McGuire, Thomas G., Trustee

Bright Family Foundation

1620 N. Carpenter Rd., Suite B
Modesto, CA 95351
(209) 526-8242
EIN: 770126942
Source Date: 3/97

Geographic Restrictions:
Primarily in Stanislaus County, CA.

Restrictions:
No grants to individuals.

To Whom:
Youth, higher, business, medical and other education, health, Native Americans, religion, **medical research,** social services.

For What:
Operating budgets, renovation projects, special projects, scholarship funds, building funds.

Financial info:
Giving: $258,000 for 35 grants (high: $39,000 low: $500).

Application info:
Applications accepted. Submit letter. No deadline.

Recent Grants:

$10,000	Community Housing and Shelter Services
$25,000	California State University, Stanislaus. Scholarships.
$11,000	Children's Crisis Center
$2,500	M.O.M. Project. Doctors Medical Center Foundation.

Directors, Officers, Trustees:
Bright, Calvin E., Donor, Director, Officer
Bright, Lyn E., Director, Officer
Bright, Marjorie H., Donor, Director, Officer
Tougas, Carol B., Director, Officer

Brotman Foundation of California

c/o Robert D. Hartford, Treasurer
16830 Ventura Blvd., No. 236
Encino, CA 91436
EIN: 956094639
Source Date: 12/94

Geographic Restrictions:
Primarily in southern CA.

Restrictions:
No grants to individuals.

To Whom:
Child welfare, health, **medical research, AIDS research**, arts, environment, museums, seniors, education, cultural programs, blind.

For What:
Conferences and seminars, continuing support, **research.**

Financial info:
Assets: $6,535,000.
Giving: $300,000 for 45 grants (high: $50,000; low: $1,000).

Application info:
Applications accepted. Submit letter. No deadline. Board meets monthly.

Directors, Officers, Trustees:
Brotman, Toni, Director
Hartford, Robert D., Director, Officer
Marks, Lowell, Director, Officer
Sherman, Michael B., Director, Officer

Fritz B. Burns Foundation

c/o Joseph E. Rawlinson, Pres.
4001 W. Alameda Ave., Suite 201
Burbank, CA 91505
(818) 840-8802
EIN: 943218106
Source Date: 9/95

Geographic Restrictions:
Primarily in Los Angeles, CA, area [southern].

Restrictions:
No grants to individuals or private foundations.

To Whom:
Education, hospitals, Catholic giving, **medical research**, social services.

For What:
Building funds, equipment, endowments, scholarships, loan funds, faculty fellowships.

Financial info:
Assets: $123,858,400.
Giving: $18,017,200 for 95 grants (high: $1,500,000; low: $2,500).

Application info:
Applications accepted. Submit proposal. No deadline. Board meets quarterly. Publishes application guidelines.

Directors, Officers, Trustees:
Burns, Fritz B. (d), Donor
Freeberg, Don, Director
Rawlinson, Joseph E., Director, Officer
Skinner, W. K., Director, Officer
Slattery, Edward F., Director
Vaughan, J. Robert, Director

California Foundation for Biochemical Research

10901 North Torrey Pines Rd.
La Jolla, CA 92037
(619) 452-7268
Source Date: 12/96

Geographic Restrictions:
Primarily in southern CA.

Restrictions:
No grants to individuals.

To Whom:
Biochemical research fellowships.

For What:
Fellowships, **research**.

Financial info:
Giving: $2,089,000 for 20 grants (high: $2,000,000; low: $2,000).

Application info:
Applications accepted. Submit letter. Deadline is Jan. Board meets semi-annually.

Directors, Officers, Trustees:
Drell, William, Officer, Trustee
Roberts, Eugene, Officer, Trustee
Smith, Emil L., Officer, Trustee

Frank A. Campini Foundation

c/o Paul J. Ruby, President
220 Montgomery St., Suite 1000
San Francisco, CA 94104-3419
(415) 421-4171
EIN: 946107956
Source Date: 12/93

Geographic Restrictions:
Primarily in San Francisco Bay area, CA [northern].

Restrictions:
No grants to religious organizations or individuals.

To Whom:
Social services, education, performing arts, museums, **medical research**, AIDS, **cancer research**, museums.

Financial info:
Giving: $585,000 for 70 grants (high: $70,000; low: $1,000).

Application info:
Applications accepted. Submit letter. Deadline is Oct. 31. Board meets in Dec.

Directors, Officers, Trustees:
Campini, Frank A. (d), Donor
Neys, M. Alan, Director, Officer
Neys, Patricia M., Officer
Ruby, Paul J., Director, Officer

Candle Foundation

c/o Carol Lewis, Admin.
2425 Olympic Blvd.
Santa Monica, CA 90404
(310) 582-4041
EIN: 953796620
Source Date: 12/95

Geographic Restrictions:
International and U.S. giving, with emphasis on CA in areas of company operations.

Restrictions:
No grants to individuals or building funds.

To Whom:
Medical research, education/information dissemination, hunger and homeless relief, preventive health services, community investment.

For What:
Research, seed money, special projects, general purposes.

Financial info:
Assets: $183,900.
Giving: $141,000 for 60 grants (high: $10,000; low: $50).

Application info:
Applications accepted. Application form required (original and 2 copies) and proposal (10 page limit). Deadline is July 15.

Directors, Officers, Trustees:
Candle Corp., Donor
Chernick, Aubrey G., Donor, Director, Officer
Minnick, Owen, Director, Officer
Smith, Margaret, Director, Officer

Caruso Family Foundation

c/o Rick J. Caruso, Pres.
100 Wilshire Blvd., 14th Flr.
Santa Monica, CA 90401-1112
(310) 458-0202
EIN: 954317077
Source Date: 12/96

Geographic Restrictions:
Limited to CA.

To Whom:
Higher and other education, hospitals, music, **medical research,** Catholic giving, youth.

For What:
Building funds, continuing support, general purposes, operating budgets, renovation projects.

Financial info:
Assets: $1,436,300 (from 1995 990PF).
Giving: $124,800 for 20 grants (high: $5,000; low: $50).

Application info:
Applications accepted. Submit letter. Deadline is Nov. 1. Board meets in Dec.

Directors, Officers, Trustees:
Caruso, Christina, Donor, Officer, Trustee
Caruso, Gloria G., Trustee
Caruso, Henry J., Trustee
Caruso, Marc, Donor, Officer, Trustee
Caruso, Rick J., Donor, Officer, Trustee
Caruso, Tina, Trustee
Gladstone, Len, Officer

Chapman Research Fund

c/o Richard F. Chapman, M.D., Pres.
P.O. Box 438
Carmel Valley, CA 93924
(415) 326-0701

Application address:
780 Welch Rd., Suite 201
Palo Alto, CA 94304
EIN: 946115496
Source Date: 12/95

Geographic Restrictions:
Primarily in CA.

Restrictions:
No grants to individuals.

To Whom:
Medical, economic, religion **research** with a view of making new discoveries. Research must be conducted at a higher educational institution, hospitals, or other research facilities.

For What:
Research, original, not applied.

Financial info:
Assets: $212,600.
Giving: $21,200 for 5 grants (high: $10,000; low: $2,000).

Application info:
Applications accepted. Submit proposal (4 copies). Deadline is Dec. 15. Board meets in Feb.

Directors, Officers, Trustees:
Chapman, Edward, Officer
Chapman, Richard F., M.D., Officer
Chapman, Robert G., M.D., Trustee

Richard H. Chartrand Eye Research Foundation

1720 El Camino Real, No. 7
Burlingame, CA 94010
(415) 697-1324
EIN: 930951517
Source Date: 12/93

Geographic Restrictions:
Primarily in San Francisco, CA.

To Whom:
Eye disease, **medical eye research**.

For What:
Research.

Financial info:
Giving: $31,100 for 10 grants (high: $15,000; low: $50).

Application info:
Applications accepted. Application form required. No deadline.

Directors, Officers, Trustees:
Schwartz, Ariah, M.D., Officer
Schwartz, Daniel M., M.D., Officer
Schwartz, Pauline, Officer

Christensen Fund

c/o C. Diane Christensen, Pres.
145 Addison Ave.
Palo Alto, CA 94301
(415) 462-8600
EIN: 946055879
Source Date: 11/92

Geographic Restrictions:
Primarily in San Francisco Bay Area, CA, area [northern].

Restrictions:
No grants to individuals.

To Whom:
Science and technology, **medical research**, higher, elementary and secondary education, arts, museums, Australia, environment, libraries.

For What:
Fellowships, matching funds, publications, **research**, seed money, special projects, scholarship funds, general purposes.

Financial info:
Giving: $165,000 for 5 grants (high: $50,000; low: $2,500).

Application info:
Applications accepted. Submit proposal (2 page limit). No deadline.

Recent Grants:
Smithsonian Institution-Natural History Museum
Australian-American Foundation for the Arts
Palo Alto Medical Foundation
Christensen Research Institute-Papua New Gunea
Honolulu Academy of Arts

Directors, Officers, Trustees:
Benevento, William R., Director, Officer
Christensen, Allen D. (d), Donor
Christensen, C. Diane, Director, Officer
Christensen, Carmen M., Donor, Director, Officer
Christensen, Karen K., Director, Officer

Carrie Estelle Doheny Foundation

c/o Shirley Bernard, Grants Coord.
911 Wilshire Blvd. Suite 1750
Los Angeles, CA 90017
(213) 488-1122
EIN: 952051633
Source Date: 12/95

Geographic Restrictions:
Primarily in Los Angeles, CA [southern].

Restrictions:
No grants for tax supported organizations, radio, television, individuals, publications, travel, advertising, political purposes, or scholarships.

To Whom:
Advancement of Roman Catholic religion, **medical research**, hospitals, advancement of education, family services, health and welfare of children, seniors, disabled, disadvantaged.

For What:
General purposes.

Financial info:
Assets: $110,491,000.
Giving: $5,555,000 for 125 grants (high: $1,000,000; low: $1,500).

Application info:
Applications accepted. Submit letter. No deadline. Board meets monthly. Publishes annual report with application guidelines and grants list.

Recent Grants:

$100,000	Archdiocesan Educational Foundation
$5,000	Bishop Amat Memorial High School
$15,000	Bishop Mora Salesian High School
$20,000	Don Bosco Technical Institute
$45,000	Flintridge Sacred Heart Academy
$65,000	Independent Colleges of Southern California
$28,319	Institute for Catholic Leadership
$15,000	Junipero Serra High School
$20,000	La Reina High School
$295,000	Loyola Marymount College
$400,000	Mount St. Mary's College
$20,000	Our Lady of Loretta-Bishop Conaty
$265,000	Puente Learning Center
$300,000	Roman Catholic Archbishop of LA
$5,000	Cancer Foundation of Santa Barbara
$25,000	Hospitaller Foundation of California
$7,000	House Ear Institute
$15,000	LA Heart Institute
$260,000	Archdiocese of Los Angeles
$6,000	Carmel of St. Joseph
$10,000	Catholic Charities USA
$5,000	Center for Renewed Life
$127,000	CED Trust for St. Vincent's Church
$3,000	Epiphany Lutheran Church
$11,500	Fadica
$1,500	First United Methodist Church
$10,000	Jesuit Volunteer Corp Southwest
$20,000	Marianists
$2,000	Monastery of Our Lady of Mount Carmel
$6,000	Monastery of the Angels
$50,000	Our Lady of Miraculous Medal
$2,000	Paulist Communications
$15,000	PICO
$10,000	Right to Life League
$6,000	San Carlos Mission
$5,000	Blind Children's Center
$5,000	Children's Hospital of LA
$10,000	Covenant House
$1,500	Crippled Children's Society
$150,000	Dolores Mission/Proyecto Pastora
$5,000	Downtown Ketchum YMCA
$5,000	Braille Institute
$5,000	Caregivers
$10,000	Downtown Women's Center
$1,500	Epilepsy Society
$165,000	Esperanza Community Housing
$5,000	Foodbank of Southern California
$15,000	House of Ruth
$5,000	John Tracy Clini
$10,000	LA Conservation Corp

Directors, Officers, Trustees:
Doheny, Edward L., Mrs. (d), Donor
Erburu, Robert F., Director
Gavin, Austin F., Director
Gibbs, George, Director
Nally, Joseph, Director
Pansini, F. David, Rev., Director
Seidler, Terry, Mrs., Director
Smith, Robert A., III, Director, Officer
Thunell, Arthur E., Officer

Joseph Drown Foundation

c/o Wendy Wachtell Schine, VP
1999 Ave. of the Stars, Suite 1930
Los Angeles, CA 90067
(310) 277-4488
EIN: 956093178
Source Date: 12/94

Geographic Restrictions:
Primarily in CA.

Restrictions:
No grants to individuals, conferences, religious programs, fundraising events, endowment or building funding.

To Whom:
Education: private secondary and higher education for financial assistance, public and private elementary and secondary education for education reform.

Medical Research: initiated by foundation only.

Community, Health and Social Services: drop-out prevention, families, teen pregnancy, lack of sufficient health care, drug and alcohol abuse, poverty issues, economically and physically disabled.

Arts and Humanities: outreach and education programs.

For What:
General purposes, **research**, operating budgets, special projects, scholarship funds.

Financial info:
Giving: $3,341,700 for 125 grants (high: $200,000; low: $3,000).

Application info:
Applications accepted. Submit proposal. Deadline is Jan. 15, Apr. 15, July 15, and Oct. 15. Board meets in Mar., June, Sept., and Dec. Publishes application guidelines.

Directors, Officers, Trustees:
Coit, Benton C., Director
Drown, Joseph W. (d), Donor
Fillius, Milton F., Jr., Director, Officer
Magaram, Philip S., Director, Officer
Mahoney, Elaine, Director
Marshall, Thomas C., Director, Officer
Obrow, Norman C., Director, Officer
Schine, Wendy Wachtell, Officer

Carl Gellert & Celia Berta Gellert Foundation

(Formerly The Carl Gellert Foundation)
c/o Peter J. Brusati, Secretary
1169 Market St., #808
San Francisco, CA 94103
(415) 255-2829
EIN: 946062858
Source Date: 11/95

Geographic Restrictions:
Primarily in the San Francisco Bay Area, CA [northern].

Restrictions:
No grants to individuals, seed money, emergency funds, land acquisition, matching gifts, or conferences.

To Whom:
Seniors, recreation, **medical research**, drug and alcohol abuse, hospitals, Catholic giving, public and private higher, secondary and elementary education, engineering education, community development, social services, family planning, animal welfare.

For What:
Operating budgets, continuing support, annual campaigns, deficit financing, building funds, equipment, endowment funds, scholarship funds, **research**, publications, special projects, renovation projects, capital campaigns, general purposes.

Financial info:
Assets: $11,471,600.
Giving: $784,800 for 100 grants (high: $100,000; low: $1,000).

Application info:
Applications accepted. Submit proposal by Oct. 1st. Board meets in Nov. Publishes annual report.

Recent Grants:

$2,500	Archbishop Alemany Scholarship Fund, San Francisco, CA. Tuition Assistance For Sacred Heart and St. Paul of the Shipwreck students.
$5,000	Archbishop Mitty High School, San Jose, CA. For Equipment in their Computer Program.
$7,000	Association For Retarded Citizens, San Francisco, CA. To Provide Professional Training and Consultation to Staff from a Behavior Management Consultant.
$7,500	Bellarmine College Preparatory. San Jose, CA. Campus Ministry Endowment Fund.
$2,500	Big Brothers/Big Sisters Of San Francisco. San Francisco, CA. To Strengthen and Educate Single-Parent Families.
$1,000	Blind Babies Foundation. San Francisco, CA. To Pay for Services of One Blind Child.
$10,000	Canine Companions For Independence. Santa Rosa, CA. Towards the Cost of Funding a Team Sponsorship for a Disabled Person to Receive an Assistance Dog to Live a More Independent Life.
$10,000	Catholic Charities. San Francisco, CA. Home Care Program.

$4,500 Catholic Youth Organization. San Rafael, CA. Towards Large-Scale Renovation Work to 6 Group Homes on CYO/St. Vincent's Campus in San Rafael.

$3,000 Center For Handicapped Children And Teenagers. San Francisco, CA. The Handicapped Children and Teenagers Program.

$2,500 Centro Latino De San Francisco. San Francisco, CA. Eliminating Mortgage and Providing Meals for the Elderly.

$1,000 Christian Counseling Services. Danville, CA. Maintaining Counseling Facilities.

$12,500 City Of Daly City. Daly City, CA. Maintenance/Improvement of City's Recreational Facilities/Equipment/Senior Center Operating Funds.

$22,500 College Of Notre Dame. Belmont, CA. Financial Aid to Deserving Students.

$5,000 Coyote Point Museum, San Mateo, CA. School Services Program.

$5,000 Daly City Host Lions Club White Cane Drive. Daly City, CA. To Meet the Growing Eye Care Needs of the Community.

$2,500 Diocese Of Oakland. Oakland, CA. To Connect to the Teacher Training Lab and 2 Schools to the Internet for One Year.

$3,500 Dominican College Of San Rafael. San Rafael, CA. Full Presidential Scholarship.

$5,000 Dominican Sisters Of Mission San Jose. Oakland, CA. Development of 23 Parochial Schools Staffed by Dominican Sisters.

$2,000 Early Childhood Education Center Of San Mateo County. Redwood City, CA. Towards Computer Equipment and Software for a Special Day Class to Develop Student's Language.

$5,000 Edgewood Children'S Center. San Francisco, CA. Grandparents Who Care Program at the New Center.

$2,000 El Camino House Organization. San Mateo, CA. Upkeep and Maintenance of Redwood House.

$3,500 Family Aid Catholic Education. Oakland, CA. Tuition Assistance for 7 Low-Income Families in Oakland Diocese

$5,000 Freewheelers Association, Inc. San Francisco, CA. Continuance and Expansion of Freewheeler Program.

$6,000 Friends For Youth. Redwood City, CA. For Continued Program Expansion and Development of New Services.

$2,000 Friends Of The Veterans Home Of California. Pebble Beach, CA. Improving the Welfare of the Elderly at the Veterans Home in Yountville, California.

$5,000 Golden Gate University. San Francisco, CA. Library Network Improvement and Expansion of the General Library.

$10,000 Good Shepherd Gracenter. San Francisco, CA. Operating Expenses to Ensure Recovery from Addiction for Chemically Dependent Women.

$5,000 Holy Angels School. Colma, CA. Financial Assistance to Meet the Educational Needs of Families Whose Children Attend the School.

$3,000 Holy Family Convent. Mission San Jose, CA. Pre-retirement Program.

$10,000 Holy Name Of Jesus Church. San Francisco, CA. Repairs and Renovations Needed in the Parish.

$20,000 Immaculate Conception Academy. Scholarship Endowment Fund. San Francisco, CA

$2,500 Independent Living Resource Center. Elder Independence Program. San Francisco, CA

$7,000 Interplast, Inc. Mountain View, CA. Surgical end educational Program in Equador.

$7,500 Jesuit Retreat House. Los Altos, CA. Repair Retaining Wall Along Road Leading to Upper Property.

$2,500 Jesuit School Of Theology At Berkeley. Student Scholarships. Berkeley, CA

$5,000 John's Closet. Daly City, CA. Provide Clothing for Needy Ben Franklin Junior High School Children.

$2,500 Larkin Street Youth Center. San Francisco, CA. Program to Inspire Homeless Youth to Move Beyond the Streets.

$5,000 Little Brothers-friends Of The Elderly. San Francisco, CA. To Support the Year-Round Friendly Visits Program.

$25,000 Little Sisters Of The Poor. San Francisco, CA. Toward Operations at St. Anne's Home for the Aged.

$5,000 Loyola University For Mundelein College. Chicago, IL. Weekend College Program.

$5,000	Make A Circus. San Francisco, CA. Clown Therapy Program.
$5,000	The Marianists. Cupertino, CA. Recruitment Program.
$5,000	Marin Catholic High School. Kentfield, CA. To Augment and Replace Video Collection in the Science Department.
$3,000	Mater Dolorosa School. South San Francisco, CA. Towards Updating the Computers and Replacing Audio Visual Equipment.
$2,000	Medical Mission Sisters. Mountain View, CA. Towards Teaching, Medicine, Technology, Nursing and Social Work for the Poor, Sick & Lonely.
$12,500	Mercy High School. Burlingame, CA. Tuition Assistance for Students.
$10,000	Mercy High School. San Francisco, CA. Scholarships and Financial Aid for Students.
$10,000	Old St. Mary's. San Francisco, CA. Retrofit the Church to Restore and Preserve San Francisco's #2 Landmark.
$1,000	Operation Santa Claus. Daly City, CA. Toys and Food Coupons for Christmas.

Directors, Officers, Trustees:

Atlas Realty Company, Donor
Bahrt, Fred R., Director
Brusati, Peter J., Director
Cresci, Andrew A., Director
Gellert, Carl (d), Donor
Gellert, Celia Berta, Donor
Gellert, Gertrude E. (d), Donor
Grassilli, Robert J., Jr., Director
Pacific Coast Construction Company, Donor
Pauly, Robert L., Director

Genentech Foundation for Biomedical Sciences

c/o Marty Glick, Secretary
460 Point San Bruno Blvd.
S. San Francisco, CA 94080-4490
(415) 225-3202
EIN: 943083018
Source Date: 12/96

Geographic Restrictions:
Limited to northern CA.

Restrictions:
No grants to individuals.

To Whom:
Education and **research in biomedical sciences,** including programs emphasizing under-represented minorities in elementary, secondary, and higher education or research organizations.

For What:
Equipment, **research**, scholarship funds, fellowships.

Financial info:
Assets: $310,600 (from 1995 990PF).
Giving: $644,000 for 15 grants (high: $80,000; low: $10,000).

Application info:
Applications accepted. Application form required. Deadline is Mar. 15. Board meets in May.

Recent Grants:

- ARCS (Achievement Rewards for College Scientists)
- Mills College. Mid-career math and science teacher preparation program.
- The Gene Connection. San Mateo County High School biotech program.
- Expanding Your Horizons. One day math and science conference for 6-12th grade girls in the Bay Area.

Directors, Officers, Trustees:

Alberts, Bruce, Ph.D., Director
Boyer, Herbert W., Ph.D., Director
Delacote, Goery, Director
Genentech, Inc., Donor
Glick, Marty, Officer
Harris, Edward, M.D., Director
Smith, Lloyd, M.D., Director
Swanson, Robert A., Director

Samuel Goldwyn Foundation

10203 Santa Monica Blvd., Suite 500
Los Angeles, CA 90067
(213) 552-2255
EIN: 956006859
Source Date: 12/95

Geographic Restrictions:
Limited to the Los Angeles, CA, area [southern].

Restrictions:
No grants to individuals or building funding.

To Whom:
Libraries, higher and other education, cultural programs, youth, child development, **medical research,** health, social services.

For What:
Annual campaigns, seed money, scholarship funds, **research**, special projects.

Financial info:
Assets: $23,721,900.
Giving: $347,700 for 40 grants (high: $100,000; low: $200).

Application info:
Applications accepted. Submit proposal. Deadline is Mar. 30 and Sept. 30. Board meets quarterly.

Directors, Officers, Trustees:
Goldwyn, Anthony, Director
Goldwyn, Frances H. (d), Donor
Goldwyn, John, Director
Goldwyn, Peggy E., Director, Officer
Goldwyn, Samuel (d), Donor
Goldwyn, Samuel, Jr., Director, Officer
Gottlieb, Meyer, Director, Officer

Grousbeck Family Foundation

Attn: Wycliffe Grousbeck, Secretary
c/o Stanford University
Graduate School of Business, Rm. L-336
Palo Alto, CA 94305-5015
EIN: 770267061

Restrictions:
No grants to individuals.

To Whom:
Ophthalmic research, children's mental and physical health, higher education, tutoring and psychological treatment for crack babies and learning disabled children, training of medical students to respond more effectively to at-risk children, funding for food banks, emergency prescription medicine funding serving disadvantaged children, blind.

Financial info:
Assets: $36,497,300.
Giving: $1,502,700 for 45 grants (high: $75,000; low: $1,000).

Application info:
Applications accepted. Submit letter. No deadline.

Directors, Officers, Trustees:
Grousbeck, Anne H., Officer
Grousbeck, H. Irving, Donor, Officer
Grousbeck, Susanne B., Officer
Grousbeck, Wycliffe K., Officer

Hedco Foundation

c/o Mary Goriup, Fdn. Mgr.
1221 Broadway, 21st Flr.
Oakland, CA 94612-1837
(510) 451-3300
EIN: 237259742
Source Date: 11/95

Geographic Restrictions:
Primarily in CA.

Restrictions:
No grants to individuals, general support, operating funds, endowments, scholarships, fellowships, special projects, research, publications, or conferences.

To Whom:
Higher education, health, social services, arts, music, theater, libraries, cultural programs, **medical research,** youth.

For What:
Building funds, equipment, land acquisition, matching funds, renovation projects.

Financial info:
Assets: $11,036,800.
Giving: $2,216,200 for 20 grants (high: $250,000; low: $1,500).

Application info:
Applications accepted. Submit proposal. No deadline. Board meets in Nov.

Directors, Officers, Trustees:
Ainsworth, Laine, Director
Appleton, James, Director
Catalina Associates, Donor
Dobbins, Allen L., Director
Dornsife, David H., Director, Officer
Dornsife, Ester M., Director, Officer
Dornsife, Harold W., Director, Officer
Goriup, Mary A., Mgr.
Herrick Corp., Donor
Jernstedt, Dorothy, Director, Officer
Little, James S., Director
Picard, William, Director

George E. Hewitt Foundation for Medical Research

c/o George E. Hewitt, Pres.
137 Jasmine Creek Dr.
Corona del Mar, CA 92625-1422
(909) 760-0554
EIN: 953711123
Source Date: 12/95

Geographic Restrictions:
Primarily in CA.

To Whom:
Medical research.

For What:
Fellowships.

Financial info:
Assets: $4,102,000.
Giving: $133,100 for 10 grants to individuals (high: $35,000; low: $500).

Application info:
Applications accepted. Submit letter and resume. No deadline.

Directors, Officers, Trustees:
Hewitt, George E., Donor, Officer
Woolsey, Roy B., Officer

George Hoag Family Foundation

2029 Century Park East, Suite 4392
Los Angeles, CA 90067
(213) 683-6500
EIN: 946086766
Source Date: 12/95

Geographic Restrictions:
Limited to CA with emphasis on Orange County [southern].

Restrictions:
No grants for government agencies, tax-supported projects, sectarian or religious organizations for the benefit of their own members, individuals, deficit financing, or operating expenses.

To Whom:
Medical research, health, hospitals, religion, youth, science and technology, wildlife, libraries, museums, hunger, cultural programs.

For What:
Capital campaigns.

Financial info:
Assets: $47,115,700.
Giving: $738,200 for 45 grants (high: $75,000; low: $1,000).

Application info:
Applications accepted. Application form required. Deadline is Mar. 31 and Sept. 30. Board meets in Apr. and Oct.

Recent Grants:

$10,000	Los Angeles Regional Foodbank, CA. Solicit and obtain food donations.

Directors, Officers, Trustees:
Auer, Albert J., Director
Curci, John L., Jr., Director
Hoag, George Grant (d), Donor
Hoag, George Grant, II, Donor, Director, Officer
Hoag, Grace E., Donor
Hoag, Patty, Director, Officer
Milliken, W. Dickerson, Director, Officer
Parry, Gwyn P., Director
Smith, Melinda Hoag, Director
Werderman, Del V., Director, Officer

Hofmann Foundation

(Formerly K. H. Hofmann Foundation)
P.O. Box 907
Concord, CA 94522
(510) 682-4830
EIN: 946108897
Source Date: 12/96

Geographic Restrictions:
Primarily in northern CA, with emphasis on San Francisco Bay Area organizations with emphasis in Contra Costa County; limited support for national organizations U.S. No grants for general purposes, capital funding, routine operating expenses, or deficit financing.

Restrictions:
No grants to individuals, general purposes, capital funding, deficit financing, or operating funds.

To Whom:
Acquisition, preservation, and conservation of wildlife lands especially the wetlands and marshlands that are

sanctuaries to waterfowl and related wildlife, education of the community to preserve wildlife without undermining related sports and recreation, local educational institutions that demonstrate a profound need to challenge and improve the hearts and minds of its students, cultural expansion, local community and religion organizations which address the general citizens' welfare and education, hospitals, health, **nationally recognized medical research that strives to overcome physical and mental suffering.**

For What:
Building funds, **research**, scholarship funds (not individuals), special projects, emergency funds, endowment funds, matching funds.

Financial info:
Giving: $1,029,700 for 135 grants (high: $500,000; low: $100).

Application info:
Applications accepted. Submit inquiry letter (3 page limit). No deadline. Board meets quarterly. Publishes annual report with application guidelines.

Directors, Officers, Trustees:
Alta Mortgage Company, Donor
Hofmann, Kenneth H., Donor, Officer
Hofmann Company, Donor
Hofmann-Seeno, Lisa Ann, Officer
New Discovery, Inc., Donor
Shaw, Albert T., Officer
Shurtz, Lori Hofmann, Officer

Lucile Horton Howe & Mitchell B. Howe Foundation

c/o Mitchell B. Howe, Jr., Pres.
180 S. Lake Ave.
Pasadena, CA 91101-2619
(818) 792-0514
EIN: 956081945
Source Date: 12/96

Restrictions:
No grants to individuals.

To Whom:
Youth, social services, **medical research**, hospitals, religion, child welfare, drug abuse, education, family services.

For What:
Continuing support, general purposes, operating budgets, **research**.

Financial info:
Giving: $90,1900 for 4 grants (high: $75,000; low: $3,000).

Application info:
Applications accepted. Submit letter (3 page limit). Deadline is Feb. 15.

Recent Grants:

$75,000	Huntington Medical Research Institute.
$12,000	Children's Hospital, Pasadena Auxillary. Los Angeles, CA.
$3,000	Lake Forest Academy.

Directors, Officers, Trustees:
Cushman, John C., Director, Officer
Howe, Mitchell B. (d), Donor
Howe, Mitchell B., Jr., Director, Officer
Hunter, Hugh V., Director
Myers, Lynn Howe, Director, Officer
Taylor, Martha, Director

Irvine Health Foundation

c/o Edward B. Kacic, Exec. Dir.
18301 Von Karman Ave., Suite 440
Irvine, CA 92715-1009
(714) 253-2959
E-mail: 102336.2265@compuserve.com
Internet: http://www.ihf.org
EIN: 330141599
Source Date: 6/95

Geographic Restrictions:
Limited to Orange County, CA [southern].

Restrictions:
No grants for religious purposes or individuals.

To Whom:
Community health care for education, AIDS, **basic and applied research**, health and the delivery of health care services, mental health, alcohol and drug abuse, youth, seniors, women, health promotion and research.

Financial info:
Assets: $22,254,600.
Giving: $431,000 for 35 grants (high: $200,000; low: $500).

Application info:
Applications accepted. Submit brief letter of inquiry (3-5 pages). No deadline. Board meets regularly throughout the year. Publishes annual report with application guidelines.

Recent Grants:

$45,220	AIDS Services Foundation
$224,750	CI Attention Deficit Disorder Program
$79,000	Irvine Temporary Housing
$100,000	Laguna Beach Community Clinic
$61,230	California Health Decisions
$466,310	Choices for a Healthier Lifestyle
$10,000	KOCE-TV "Women's Health"
$30,000	Irvine Children's Fund
$16,768	AIDS Walk Orange County
$2,500	Child or Parental Emergency Services

Adam Walsh Child Resource Center
Advanced Resources for Foster Kids
AIDS Services Foundation
AIDS Walk Orange County
American Heart Association
American Red Cross - L.A. - Kids Care Fair
American Red Cross, O.C. Chapter
American Women's Economic Development
Beckman Laser Institute
Beta Foster Care
Blind Children's Learning Center
C.O.P.E.S.
California Health Decisions
Canyon Acres Residential Center
Casita de San Jose
Center for Creative Alternatives
Chapman University
Choices for a Healthier Lifestyle
Coalition of O.C. Community Clinics
Crippled Children's Society
CSP Domestic Violence Program
Dayle McIntosh Center - Mariposa Villa
Eli Home
Exchange Club Center for Prevention of Child Abuse
Food Distribution Center
Friendship Shelter
H.O.M.E.S.
High Hopes Head Injury Program
Human Options
Institute of Medicine
Irvine Health Foundation Adult Day Health Services Ctr.
Irvine Chemical People
Irvine Childrens Fund
Irvine Temporary Housing
Irvine Valley College Fdn.
KOCE -TV
Laguna Beach Community Clinic
Laguna Shanti
Lillipop Lodge
Make-A-Wish Foundation
Mardan Center for Educational Therapy
Maternal Outreach Management System
Mental Health Association
NAMES Project, O.C. Chapter
Navy-Marine Corps Relief Society
New Directions for Women
O.C. Bar Foundation
Orange County Rescue Mission
Pegasus School
Share Our Selves Free Medical Clinic

Directors, Officers, Trustees:
Gaffney, John C., Director, Officer
Hoffman, Carol A., Director, Officer
Hunt, Gary H., Director
Irvine Medical Center, Donor
Kacic, Edward B., Director
Peltason, Jack W., Director
Sills, David G., Director, Officer
Sinykin, Gerald B., M.D., Director
Strader, Timothy L., Director, Officer

William G. Irwin Charity Foundation

c/o Michael R. Gorman, Executive Director
711 Russ Bldg.
235 Montgomery St.
San Francisco, CA 94104
(415) 362-6954
EIN: 946069873
Source Date: 12/95

Geographic Restrictions:
Limited to HI and CA.

Restrictions:
No grants to individuals or scholarships.

To Whom:
Hospitals, **medical research**, secondary and higher education, social services, cultural programs, community development, arts.

For What:
Building funds, equipment, general purposes, land acquisition, **research**.

Financial info:
Assets: $73,127,900.
Giving: $3,497,000 for 30 grants (high: $400,000; low: $10,000).

Application info:
Applications accepted. Submit letter. Deadline is 4-6 weeks prior to board meeting. Board meets every 2 months.

Directors, Officers, Trustees:
- Cronin, George T., Trustee
- Fagan, Helene Irwin (d), Donor
- Gorman, Michael R., Director
- Grant, Fred R., Trustee
- Irwin, Fannie M. (d), Donor
- Olds, William Lee, Jr., Officer, Trustee
- Olds, William L., III, Trustee
- Ritchie, Jane Olds, Officer

J. W. & Ida M. Jameson Foundation

c/o Les M. Hugn, Pres.
P.O. Box 397
Sierra Madre, CA 91025
(818) 355-6973
EIN: 956031465
Source Date: 12/96

Geographic Restrictions:
Primarily in CA.

To Whom:
Higher and theological education, hospitals, **medical research**, cultural programs, Protestant and Catholic religion.

For What:
Research, general purposes, operating budgets.

Financial info:
Giving: $975,000 for 75 grants (high: $50,000; low: $2,000).

Application info:
Applications accepted. Submit proposal. Deadline is Jan. 31.

Directors, Officers, Trustees:
- Betz, Bill B., Director
- Croxton, William M., Director, Officer
- Huhn, Les M., Director, Officer
- Jameson, Ida M. (d), Donor
- Leydorf, Fred L., Director
- Vetrovec, Pauline, Director, Officer

W. M. Keck Foundation

c/o Joan F. DuBois, Pgm. VP
555 S. Flower St., Suite 3230
Los Angeles, CA 90071
(213) 680-3833
EIN: 956092354
Source Date: 12/95

Geographic Restrictions:
Eligible institutions are accredited universities, colleges, medical schools and major, independent medical research institutions in U.S.

Restrictions:
No grants for conduit organizations, individuals, routine expenses, general endowments, deficit reduction, fund-raising events, dinners, mass mailings, conferences, seminars, publications, films, or public policy research.

To Whom:
Science and engineering higher education (13% of funding), **medical research/education (21% of funding)** and liberal arts (4% of funding), Earth sciences (8% of funding), involving development of natural resources, southern CA grant program (8% of funding) (arts, cultural programs, community development, health care, elementary and secondary education, seniors, at-risk youth, social services).

For What:
Building funds, seed money, equipment, special projects, **research**, renovation projects, fellowships, scholarship funds, endowment funds, professorships.

Financial info:
Assets: $27,088,700.
Giving: $34,293,000 for 60 grants (high: $2,000,000; low: $20,000).

Application info:
Applications accepted. Submit letter of inquiry only. No deadline for letters. Foundation selects applicant institutions to submit a complete proposal. Application form required. Accepted invited proposals only between Sept. 16th and March 15th for June board meeting and between March 16th and Sept. 15th for the Dec. board meeting. Publishes annual report with application guidelines.

Recent Grants:
- Alfred University, Alfred, NY. To provide chemical analysis instrumentation for a bioceramics laboratory.
- Bard College, Annandale-on-Hudson, NY. To renovate chemistry laboratories.
- Boston College, Chestnut Hill, MA. To establish a new laboratory for student research projects in molecular neurobiology.

Boston University, Boston, MA. To construct a scanning tunneling microscope for the Department of Physics.

Bowdoin College, Brunswick, ME. Toward construction of a laboratory for instruction and research in molecular biology and biochemistry.

Carnegie Institution of Washington, Washington, DC.Toward purchasing an ion microprobe for geochemical research in the Department of Terrestrial Magnetism.

Colby College, Waterville, ME. To reconfigure space for a molecular and cellular biology research laboratory.

Colorado College, Colorado Springs, CO. To purchase equipment for the Department of Geology.

Connecticut College, New London, CT.To purchase an ion accelerator for the Department of Physics and Astronomy.

Gallaudet University, Washington, DC. To provide science program support and equipment for educating deaf and hard of hearing students

Georgia Institute of Technology, Atlanta, GA. To equip an Integrated Process and Facilities Laboratory for industrial and systems engineering.

Grinnell College, Grinnell, IA.Toward modernizing physics laboratories.

Gustavus Adolphus College, Saint Peter, MN. To create a cluster of research and teaching laboratories for plant biology in the new science wing.

Harvey Mudd College, Claremont, CA. To centralize and equip the Academic Computing Center.

Linfield College, McMinnville, OREG. To purchase scientific equipment for physics laboratories.

Oklahoma State University, Stillwater, OK. To establish a regional facility for spectroscopy research.

Reed College, Portland, OR. For equipment to incorporate computer-assisted instruction into biology and chemistry laboratories.

Saint John's University, Collegeville, MN. For instrumentation for the Departments of Chemistry at Saint John's University and the College of Saint Benedict.

San Diego State University, San Diego, CA. To construct and equip a clean room for the isotope geochemistry program in the Department of Geological Sciences.

Scripps Institution, La Jolla, CA. Toward construction of an Oceonography and of Oceanography Atmospheric Sciences Building.

St. Norbert College, De Pere, WI. To equip laboratories for biology, chemistry, geology, and environmental science programs.

St.Olaf College, Northfield, MN. To equip and renovate space for a microscopy center for the Departments of Chemistry and Physics.

Syracuse University, Syracuse, NY. To establish an Advanced Materials and Prototyping Laboratory.

Texas Christian University, Fort Worth, TX. To purchase equipment for biochemistry research.

Transylvania University, Lexington, KY. To equip a multimedia, computer-networked teaching center for the Division of Natural Sciences.

University of Arizona, Tucson, AZ. To purchase instrumentation for the Center for Thermochronology and Noble Gas Studies.

University of California, Santa Barbara, CA. To provide instrumentation and program support for Santa Barbara marine sciences research.

University of Chicago, Chicago, IL. To support research in high pressure geophysics using the Advanced Photon Radiation Source at Argonne National Laboratory.

University of Illinois, Champaign, IL. To provide research instrumentation for the Center for Complex Structures.

University of Kansas, Lawrence, KS. To establish an inductively coupled plasma facility for geochemical research and teaching.

University of Maryland, Adelphi, MD. To purchase an imaging system for research at the Biotechnology Institute Institute's Center of Marine Biotechnology.

University of Nevada, Reno, Reno, NV. Support for equipment and programs at Mackay School of Mines

University of New Mexico, Albuquerque, NM. To renovate and equip laser imaging laboratory for optical science research.

University of New Orleans, New Orleans, LA. To provide research instrumentation for the Department of Chemistry.

University of Portland, Portland, OREG. To equip new computer laboratories for science instruction.

University of Texas at Austin, Austin, TX. Toward instrumenration for a high-resolution x-ray computed tomography facility in the Department of Geological Sciences.

Washington and Lee University, Lexington, VA. Toward construction of a geology laboratory for teaching and research in the new science center.

Wellesley College, Wellesley, MA. Continuing support for the Reck Northeast Astronomy Consortium.

Willamette University, Salem, OREG. To establish three laboratories in the Department of Earth Science.
Claremont McKenna College, Claremont, CA. To support curricular development, research, and networking for campus-wide academic computing.
Skidmore College, Saratoga Springs, NY. To endow a student/faculty collaborative research program in the liberal arts.
University of Richmond, Richmond, VA. Support for an undergraduate faculty-student research program.
Cleveland Clinic Foundation, Cleveland, OH. To purchase equipment for the Clinic's Research Institute.
National Academy of Sciences, Washington, DC. For a national study by the Institute of Medicine on the status and future directions of substance abuse research.
Rockefeller University, New York, NY. To support research and a fellows program at the Center for Studies in Physics and Biology.
University of California, Berkeley, CA. Continued support for the WM. Reck Program in Berkeley Biomedical Research.
University of California, San Francisco, San Francisco, CA. To renovate and expand a laboratory for research in neurodegeneration at the School of Medicine.
University of California, Santa Cruz. Santa Cruz, CA. For equipment for research in biomolecules relevant to controlling and understanding human diseases.
University of Colorado, Boulder, CO. To support the mammalian biology program in the Department of Molecular, Cellular and Developmental Biology.
University of Utah, Salt Lake, UT. To support the Program in Molecular Biology City, and Genetics at the University's Institute of Human Genetics.

Directors, Officers, Trustees:
Allen, Lew, Jr., Director
Barker, Norman, Jr., Director
Cooper, Marsh A., Director
Cummings, Naurice G., Director
Day, Howard M., Director, Officer
Day, Robert A., Director, Officer
Day, Tammis M., Director
Day, Theodore J., Director
Dorsey, Bob Rawls, Director
Ford, Thomas P., Director
Gerken, Walter B., Director, Officer
Harris, Dorothy A., Officer
Keck, Erin A., Director
Keck, Howard B., Director, Officer
Keck, Howard B., Jr., Director
Keck, W. M., II, Director, Officer
Keck, William M. (d), Donor
Kolb, John E., Director
Lents, Max R., Director
Lower, James Paul, Director
Mott, Kerry K., Director
Ramo, Simon, Director
Ryan, Gregory R., Officer
Smith, Arthur M., Jr., Director
Stone, Edward C., Jr., Director
Thomas, David A., Director
Verity, C. William, Jr., Director
von Kalinowski, Julian O., Director, Officer

Karl Kirchgessner Foundation

c/o Karl F. Kramer, Jr.
2101 Crestview Dr.
Laguna Beach, CA 92651
EIN: 953439716
Source Date: 6/95

Geographic Restrictions:
Limited to the southern CA area.

Restrictions:
No grants to individuals or fundraising campaigns.

To Whom:
Medical research, health care to disadvantaged, with emphasis on seniors, youth, blind. Applicants should be involved with research and/or clinical programs connected with eyesight, eye care, or helping the blind and partially-sighted to be more self sufficient.

For What:
Research, continuing support, endowment funds, equipment, general purposes, matching funds, operating budgets, professorships, publications, scholarship funds, seed money, special projects, technical assistance.

Financial info:
Assets: $15,220,400.
Giving: $473,600 for 20 grants (high: $100,000; low: $5,000).

Application info:
Applications accepted. Submit brief letter of intent. Deadline is Jan. 1 for preliminary applications. Grants made once a year, in June. Publishes application guidelines.

Directors, Officers, Trustees:
Cahalan, Patrick, Jr., Rev., Director
Kramer, Karl (d), Donor
Kramer, Karl, Jr., Officer

Kramer, Nina (d), Donor
Mills, Amelia Louise, Director, Officer
Webster, Martin H., Director, Officer
Whitney, Lewis, Director, Officer

Thomas & Dorothy Leavey Foundation

c/o J. Thomas McCarthy, Trustee
4680 Wilshire Blvd.
Los Angeles, CA 90010
(213) 936-4147
EIN: 956060162
Source Date: 12/95

Geographic Restrictions:
Primarily in southern CA.

To Whom:
Hospitals, **medical research**, higher and secondary education, Catholic giving, scholarships to children of employees of Farmers Insurance Group, Inc.

For What:
Employee-related scholarships, special projects, general purposes, operating budgets.

Financial info:
Assets: $170,911,200.
Giving: $9,306,100 for 75 grants (high: $1,000,000; low: $1,000) and $272,700 for 95 grants to individuals.

Application info:
Applications accepted. Submit letter. No deadline.

Directors, Officers, Trustees:
Castruccio, L., Trustee
Leavey, Dorothy E., Donor, Trustee
Leavey, Joseph James, Trustee
Leavey, Thomas E. (d), Donor
McCarthy, J. Thomas, Officer, Trustee
McCarthy, Kathleen Leavey, Trustee
Tyler, Kenneth, Trustee

Richard M. Lucas Cancer Foundation

Bldg. 3, Suite 210
3000 Sandhill Rd.
Menlo Park, CA 94025
(415) 854-4223
EIN: 942781117
Source Date: 6/94

Geographic Restrictions:
Primarily in Stanford, CA [northern].

Restrictions:
No grants to individuals.

To Whom:
Medical research for prostate cancer.

For What:
Research.

Financial info:
Giving: $1,046,100 for 5 grants (high: $400,000; low: $25,000).

Application info:
Applications accepted. Submit letter. No deadline.

Directors, Officers, Trustees:
Lucas, Donald L., Director
Lucas, John W., Director
Lucas, Mary G., Director

Della Martin Foundation

c/o Sheppard, Mullin, Richter & Hampton
333 S. Hope St., 48th Flr.
Los Angeles, CA 90071
(213) 620-1780
EIN: 237444954
Source Date: 12/95

Geographic Restrictions:
Primarily in southern CA.

Restrictions:
No grants to individuals, general support, capital funds, scholarships, fellowships, or matching gifts.

To Whom:
Study and discovery of cures for all forms of mental illness through grants for research.

For What:
Research.

Financial info:
Assets: $4,966,800.
Giving: $200,000 for 1 grant.

Application info:
Applications accepted. Submit letter (7 copies). No deadline. Board meets quarterly.

Directors, Officers, Trustees:
Flynn, Edward J., Trustee
Garrett, Alton B., Trustee
Gould, Lawrence K., Jr., Trustee
Martin, Della (d), Donor
Morgan, Barbara B., Trustee
Roberts, John D., Trustee
Sheppard, Thomas R., Trustee

Maurice J. Masserini Charitable Trust

c/o Wells Fargo Bank
101 W. Broadway, Suite 301
San Diego, CA 92101
(619) 238-6504
EIN: 956812685
Source Date: 3/94

Geographic Restrictions:
Limited to San Diego, CA [southern].

Restrictions:
No grants to individuals.

To Whom:
Higher education, marine sciences, community development, cultural programs, social services, **medical research**, music.

For What:
Research, scholarship funds, special projects.

Financial info:
Giving: $299,900 for 35 grants (high: $25,000; low: $500).

Application info:
Applications accepted. Submit letter. No deadline. Board meets in Mar., June, Sept., and Dec.

Directors, Officers, Trustees:
Wells Fargo Bank, N.A., Trustee

Maxfield Foundation

12930 Saratoga Ave., Suite B-3
Saratoga, CA 95070
(408) 253-0723
EIN: 770099366
Source Date: 12/95

Geographic Restrictions:
Limited to U.S.

Restrictions:
No grants for capital funds.

To Whom:
Institutions and individuals doing research in fields related to understanding and treating cancer, with emphasis on Leukemia.

For What:
Operational research, individuals.

Financial info:
Assets: $5,452,800.
Giving: $415,500 for 10 grants (high: $200,000; low: $1,000).

Application info:
Applications accepted. Submit proposal. Deadline Sept. 30. Publishes annual report and application guidelines.

Recent Grants:

$5,000	Cold Spring Harbor Laboratory, Cold Spring Harbor, NY Cancer Research.
$212,500	Rice University, Houston, TX Education.
$20,000	Wistar Institute, Philadelphia, PA Cancer Research.
$5,000	EconBeat, Saratoga, CA Education.
$50,000	Santa Fe Institute, Santa Fe, NM Systems Research.
$2,000	Hoover Institution, Stanford University, CA Social Research.
$1,000	Ctr for Economic Policy Res., Stanford University, CA Economic Research.
$20,000	Foundation for Shamanic Studies, Norwalk CT Healing Research.
$15,000	Univ of Rochester, Rochester, NY Cancer Research.
$20,000	Fox Chase Cancer Center, Philadelphia, PA Cancer Research.
$10,000	University of Colorado, Denver, CO Cancer Research,
$55,000	Angeles Arrien Foundation, Palo Alto, CA Healing Research.

Directors, Officers, Trustees:
Ferrari, Clarence J., Jr., Officer
Maxfield, Melinda, Officer
Maxfield, Robert R., Donor, Officer

McCarthy Family Foundation

c/o Jane D. McCarthy, President
P.O. Box 270051
San Diego, CA 92198-2051
Internet: http://fdncenter.org/grantmaker/mccarthy/index.html
EIN: 954182410
Source Date: 12/96

Geographic Restrictions:
Limited to CA, with emphasis on San Diego county [southern].

Restrictions:
No grants to individuals, scholarship funds, sectarian religious activities, political activities, or general fundraising drives.

To Whom:
Secondary school science education: foster increased study of science by high school students and to promote further scientific study and careers by qualified students; **AIDS research**, education, and support, **research to determine the pathogenisis of AIDS and HIV and to develop new experimental therapies**, provide support to AIDS patients and public education regarding the disease.

Homeless.

Children and Families: help abused and abandoned children or children with special emotional and/or physical disabilities.

Environmental Protection: promote the preservation and restoration of natural areas and biological species in their natural habitat and the maintenance of biodiversity.

For What:
Matching funds, seed money, special projects, **research.**

Financial info:
Assets: $4,377,400 (from 1995 990PF).
Giving: $195,500 for 30 grants (high: $40,000; low: $1,000).

Application info:
Applications accepted. Submit letter of inquiry (2 page limit). Deadline is May 15 and Nov. 15 for full proposals. Board meets in June and Dec. Publishes annual report and application guidelines.

Recent Grants:

$3,000	AIDS Foundation San Diego. General Support.
$5,000	Aunt Bee's, Los Angeles. Housekeeping Services.
$10,000	Desert Hospital, Palm Springs. Comprehensive HIV Services.
$6,000	Matri AIDS Hospice, San Francisco. Relocation Project.
$6,000	Project Open Hand, San Francisco. Children's Meal Program.
$10,000	San Diego AIDS Collaboration. Grantmakers affiliated with National AIDS Fund.
$2,000	San Francisco Suicide Prevention. AIDS Nightline for Southern California.
$5,000	Dolores Street, San Francisco. Shelter Night Supervisor Training.
$2,000	Faith & Love Ministries, Vista. Operating Expenses.
$2,000	Fresh Start Farms, San Francisco. Salary Expenses.
$3,500	Harbor Interfaith Shelter, San Pedro. Emergency Food Services.
$10,000	Larkin Street, San Francisco. Youth Center Job Developer Position.
$4,000	North County Chaplaincy, Encinitas. Post-Natal Services.
$3,500	St. Mary's I/F Dining Room, Stockton. Children's Play Therapy Room.
$7,500	Shelter for Homeless, Westminster. Washington Street Shelter Services.
$7,500	YWCA of San Diego County. Stabilization Program.
$2,500	Big Sister League, Inc., San Diego. Educational Program.
$4,000	Child Abuse Prev. Fndn., San Diego. Outreach Program.
$4,000	Family Service Assn., San Diego. Counseling Groups.
$5,000	Home Staff, San Diego. Reach for Heights Program.
$5,000	Kids' Turn, Inc., San Francisco. Rally Project (Family Visitation).
$3,500	Lutheran Social Services, San Diego. Prison Children Visitor Program.
$5,000	Mainstream Fndn. Pacific Palisades. Housing Expenses.
$5,000	San Bernardino Child Advocacy, Inc. Family Preservation Program.
$5,000	San Diego Volunteer Lawyer Program. Computer Equipment.
$4,000	Sharp Healthcare Fndn., San Diego. Parenting Program.

$10,000	United Way of San Diego County. Children's Initiative Collaboration.
$5,400	Voices for Children, San Diego. Court appointed children's advocacy.
$5,000	Wild Iris, Mammoth Lakes. Mono County Staffing.
$4,000	Surfrider Fndn., San Clemente. Film Editing.
$6,000	Arts Alive! Fndn., Poway. Fourth year of 5 year capital campaign grant.
$5,000	United Way of San Diego County. Information Superhighway Project.
$5,000	Eureka Communities, Washington, DC. Eureka San Diego Fellows.

Directors, Officers, Trustees:

McCarthy, James T., Donor, Director, Officer
McCarthy, Jane D., Donor, Director, Officer
McCarthy, Kristin L., Director, Officer
McCarthy, Rachel K., Director, Officer

Milken Family Foundation

c/o Foundations of the Milken Families
Attn: Dr. Julius Lesner, Exec. VP
1250 Fourth St., 6th Flr.
Santa Monica, CA 90401
(310) 998-2800
Internet: http://www.mff.org/index.html
EIN: 954073646
Source Date: 11/95

Geographic Restrictions:
Primarily in the Los Angeles, CA, area and NY.

To Whom:
Education: strengthen the profession by recognizing and rewarding outstanding educators, by expanding their professional leadership and policy influence, encourage talented young people to become educators, stimulate creativity and productivity among educators, foster the involvement of both the family and the community in schools.

Health Care and **Medical Research: basic and applied medical research, especially in the areas of cancer and epilepsy**, improve and protect the health of people of all ages.

Community Services: help build vibrant communities that connect people with each other, respond to basic human needs.

For What:
Research, conferences and seminars, scholarship funds, building funds, renovation projects, general purposes.

Financial info:
Assets: $311,326,600.
Giving: $20,039,500 for 90 grants (high: $1,000,000; low: $200).

Application info:
Applications accepted. Submit letter of intent (3 page limit). No deadline. Publishes annual report and application guidelines.

Recent Grants:

Constitutional Rights Foundation, Los Angeles, CA. Youth Community Service program.
Junior Achievement, Los Angeles, CA. Business Basics program.
Pasadena Unified School District: Kindergarten for Four Year Olds, Pasadena, CA. General operating support.
University of Judaism, Los Angeles, CA. Making Marriage Work program.
Westminster Neighborhood Association, Los Angeles, CA. Bradley/Milken Family Youth Center and general operating support.
Greater Los Angeles Zoo Association, Los Angeles, CA. Construction of Adventure Island and general operating support.
Juvenile Diabetes Foundation, Culver City CA. Underwrite two summer research interns and general operating support.
The Los Angeles Free Clinic, Los Angeles, CA. Numerous special projects and general operating support.
Center for the Partially Sighted, Santa Monica, CA. Therapy programs and general operating support.

Directors, Officers, Trustees:

Finerman, Ralph, Director
Flans, Allen, M.D., Director
Guzman, Mariano, Director
Hackel, Murray, Director
Hoffstein, Lisa, Director
Lesner, Julius, Director, Officer
Milken, Ferne, Director
Milken, Lori A., Donor, Director
Milken, Lowell J., Donor, Director, Officer
Milken, Michael R., Donor
Milken, Sandra E., Donor, Director
Salka, Evelyn, Director
Sandler, Ellen, Director
Sandler, Richard, Director
Silbert, Harvey L., Director
Solmon, Lewis C., Director
Ueberroth, Peter V., Director
Victor, Edward G., Director

Moldaw Family Foundation

c/o Gymboree Corp.
700 Airport Blvd., Suite 200
Burlingame, CA 94010
EIN: 942450734
Source Date: 11/95

Geographic Restrictions:
Primarily in CA, with emphasis on San Francisco and Stanford [northern].

To Whom:
Jewish welfare, social services, AIDS, **medical research**, health associations, mental health, heart disease, public affairs, foreign policy and international studies, arts, minority education, race relations, gays and lesbians.

Financial info:
Assets: $1,961,900.
Giving: $1,049,800 for 80 grants (high: $10,000; low: $50).

Application info:
Applications accepted. Submit letter. No deadline.

Directors, Officers, Trustees:
Moldaw, Phyllis, Officer
Moldaw, Stuart, Officer

Kenneth T. & Eileen L. Norris Foundation

c/o Nancy Boyer, Grants Mgr.
11 Golden Shore, Suite 450
Long Beach, CA 90802
(310) 435-8444
EIN: 956080374
Source Date: 11/96

Geographic Restrictions:
Primarily in Los Angeles County, CA [southern].

Restrictions:
No grants to individuals.

To Whom:
Hospitals, health, private higher and other education, **medical research**, public broadcasting, theater, **cancer research**, science and technology, arts, music, cultural programs, social services, child welfare, youth, disabled.

For What:
Building funds, equipment, **research**, scholarship funds, continuing support, endowment funds, professorships, matching funds, special projects, general purposes.

Financial info:
Giving: $5,074,500 for 185 grants (high: $1,000,000; low: $1,000).

Application info:
Applications accepted. Submit letter (2 page limit). Deadline is Nov. 1-Feb. 15 for Medical and Education; Feb. 15-June 30 for Youth, Social Services, and Cultural Programs.

Recent Grants:
$10,000 Los Angeles Regional Foodbank, CA. Operating support.
Boys & Girls Clubs of Long Beach, CA.
East Los Angeles College Foundation, CA.
Beyond Shelter.
Peninsula Symphony Assoc.
USC/Norris Cancer Research Institute.

Directors, Officers, Trustees:
Barnes, Ronald R., Director, Officer, Trustee
Corey, William G., M.D., Trustee
Gordon, George M., Trustee
Hansen, Lisa D., Trustee
Norris, Eileen L. (d), Donor
Norris, Harlyne J., Trustee
Norris, Kenneth T. (d), Donor
Norris, Kenneth T., Jr., Officer, Trustee
Zanino, Walter J., Officer, Trustee

Oxnard Foundation

c/o Stephen W. Veitch, President
505 Sansome St. Suite 1001
San Francisco, CA 94111
(415) 981-3455
EIN: 237323007
Source Date: 12/94

Geographic Restrictions:
Primarily in CA, NY, TX, NM, and southwestern U.S.

Restrictions:
No grants to individuals, general support, capital funds, endowments, scholarships, fellowships, special projects, publications, or conferences.

To Whom:
Medical research, emphasis on cancer and surgical research.

For What:
Matching funds, **research**.

Financial info:
Giving: $246,200 for 10 grants (high: $50,000; low: $10,000).

Application info:
Applications accepted. Submit letter. Deadline is Feb. 15. Board meets quarterly with final notification in 3 months. Current and ongoing commitments in present projects account for nearly 90% of the foundation's budget.

Directors, Officers, Trustees:
Meade, Caroline, Director, Officer
Meade, Gary J., Director, Officer
Oxnard, Thomas Thornton (d), Donor
Thieriot, Charles H., Jr., Director, Officer
Veitch, Christopher, Director, Officer
Veitch, Stephen W., Director, Officer

Parker Foundation

c/o Robbin C. Powell, Asst. Sec.
4365 Executive Dr., Suite 1600
San Diego, CA 92121-2189
(619) 677-1431
EIN: 510141231
Source Date: 9/95

Geographic Restrictions:
Limited to San Diego County, CA [southern].

Restrictions:
No grants for sectarian religious purposes, individuals, endowments, scholarships, or fellowships.

To Whom:
Cultural programs, health, **medical research**, youth, education, community development, AIDS.

Adult and youth services (39% of funding), visual and performing arts, museums and zoos (36% of funding), education (10% of funding), community activities (7% of funding), medical (8% of funding.

For What:
Seed money, matching funds, operating budgets, annual campaigns, emergency funds, building funds, equipment, land acquisition, research, program-related investments, continuing support, special projects, publications, general purposes, renovation projects.

Financial info:
Assets: $17,335,000.
Giving: $599,000 for 65 grants (high: $100,000; low: $500).

Application info:
Applications accepted. Submit letter. No deadline. Board meets monthly with final notification in 2 months. Publishes an annual report and application guidelines.

Recent Grants:

$10,000	California Association, salaries for '95'96 major productions.
$15,000	KPBS, a challenge matching grant for computer software.
$2,500	La Jolla Stage Company, a challenge matching grant to support production costs.
$25,000	Lamb's Players Theatre, a challenge matching grant for construction of new theater in Coronado.
$25,000	Old Globe Theatre, for partial underwriting of production of Mr. Roberts.
$50,000	San Diego Symphony Orchestra, a conditional grant for salary for assistant conductor, Jung-Ho.
$5,400	Spreckels Organ Society, a conditional grant for one-half of cost to install tibia pipes in the organ.
$10,000	Museums of San Diego History, to support the Pacific Coast League exhibit.
$50,000	San Diego Aerospace Museum, for construction of new hangar facility.
$30,000	San Diego Museum of Man, a challenge matching grant to support building of the Children's Discovery Center.
$5,000	Access Center of San Diego, to support independent living program for disabled persons.
$7,500	Alpha Project for the Homeless, for tools and equipment for Take Back the Streets program.
$10,000	Christian Social Concerns, to support manager for Rainbow House a shelter for women and children with AIDS.
$7,500	Disabled Businesspersons Association, a challenge matching grant for salary for assistant.
$5,000	EYE Counseling and Crisis Services, to support Family Recovery Center.
$12,000	Freedom Ranch, to support purchase of pickup truck for its alcohol recovery for men program.

$6,000 George G. Glenner Alzheimers Family Center, to support purchase of carpet and window coverings for new Escondido facility.

$5,000 Mama's Kitchen, for general operating expenses in support of AIDS patients.

$5,000 Promising Futures, for development costs for adult daycare program.

$2,000 Salvation Army, for Christmas baskets.

$3,000 San Diego Safe Harbor, Inc., to support rent toward transitional housing for homeless persons.

$10,000 San Diego Service Center for the Blind, a challenge matching grant to support North County Transition Counselor program.

$15,000 San Diego Urban League, Inc., to support the African Outreach Worker Project.

$5,000 Senior Adult Services, to support purchase of copier.

$5,000 Senior Community Centers of San Diego, for breakfast program.

$10,000 Western Institute Foundation for Mental Health, to support building renovation in San Marcos for Alzheimer's patients.

$2,200 Assistance League of San Diego, for Operation Schoolbell to provide clothing for needy schoolchildren.

$2,500 Boy Scouts of America, for camperships for boys from low-income families.

$2,500 Boy Scouts of America, a challenge matching grant for cost to resurface pool at Mataguay Scout reservation.

$10,000 Boys & Girls Club of Escondido, a challenge matching grant for Street Safe program.

$10,000 Boys & Girls Club of Imperial Beach, a $5,000 outright grant and a $5,000 challenge matching grant to support construction of multipurpose gymnasium.

$4,500 Boys & Girls Club of Oceanside, salary for part-time coordinator of volunteers.

$25,000 Children's Initiative (United Way), financial commitment for '95'96 fiscal year.

$5,000 High Five America, a challenge matching grant to support one midnight basketball team.

$10,000 Home Start, a challenge matching grant for family and community development program to prevent child abuse.

$2,500 Kidzartz, for administrative support.

$5,400 San Diego Armed Services YMCA, to support self-esteem program for teenage girls.

$2,000 San Diego Children's Choir, for scholarship fund.

$16,000 San Diego Rescue Mission, to support purchase of van.

$2,000 San Dieguito Boys & Girls Hubs, for Jobs for Teens program.

$10,000 South Bay Community Services, Inc., seed money for KIDS BIZ project for teens.

$8,333 St. Vincent DePaul, a challenge matching grant to support remodeling of Children's Center.

$9,540 YMCA Border View, to support summer camp and soccer league.

$7,500 YWCA, $3,750 outright grant and $3,750 challenge matching grant for purchase of computers and related equipment for San Ysidro teen leadership program.

$1,500 County of San Diego, for purchase of six digital baby weight scales.

$5,000 Mental Health Association of San Diego County, a challenge matching grant to support its membership campaign.

$10,000 San Diego Blood Bank Foundation, a challenge matching grant to support purchase of a new bloodmobile.

$10,000 San Diego Family Care (Linda Vista Health Care Center), for computer software and copier.

$16,000 National Conference, for City Heights Community Diversity Education Program.

$1,000 Aseltine School, to support purchase of a computer.

Directors, Officers, Trustees:

Beamer, William E., Director, Officer
McDonald, Judy, Director, Officer
Mosher, Paul F., Director, Officer
Parker, Gerald T. (d), Donor
Parker, Inez Grant (d), Donor
Pay, Sandra, Director
Powell, Robbin C., Officer
Rios, Sylvia, Director
Trotter, Mark C., Director

Gustavus & Louise Pfeiffer Research Foundation

c/o George R. Pfeiffer, Pres.
1048 Doral Ct.
Banning, CA 92220
EIN: 136086299
Source Date: 12/95

Geographic Restrictions:
Limited to U.S.

Restrictions:
No grants for national fund raising organizations, publicly financed projects, individuals, building, travel, conferences, general purposes, or political groups.

To Whom:
Bio-Medical and pharmacological research in: predictive factors in cardiovascular disease, cancer, limited to prostate, breast and ovarian tumors, and gerontological immunology. Pilot projects involving relatively small amounts of money are preferred.

For What:
Research, matching funds, seed money.

Financial info:
Giving: $1,132,100 for 25 grants (high: $50,000; low: $10,000).

Application info:
Applications accepted. Submit letter of inquiry. Deadline is Jan. 15. Board meets annually, usually in April. Publishes biennial report with application guidelines.

Recent Grants:

$30,000	**California Institute of Technology. Research projects in Division of Biology.**
$30,000	**National Center for the Study of Wilson's Disease. Research study on prevalence of Wilson's disease in selected populations of psychiatric in-patients.**
$37,635	**Pennsylvania State University, PA. Research study on ovarian tumor treatment.**
$25,000	**University of AZ, College of Medicine. Research in cardiac arrhythmias.**
$20,000	**Yale University, School of Medicine. Research study on antigenic suppression of transplanted organs in Department of Surgery.**
$10,000	**University of VT. Research study in molecular biology in Department of Microbiology.**
$19,352	**University of NC. Research study on regulation of cell growth by platelet-derived growth factor.**

Directors, Officers, Trustees:
Bakaly, Kimberly Herold, Director
Chapman, Lise P., Director
Herold, H. Robert, II, Director, Officer
Herold, Matthew G., Jr., Director, Officer
Nagle, Patricia Herold, Director
Pfeiffer, George R., Director, Officer
Pfeiffer, Gustavus A. (d), Donor
Pfeiffer, Louise F. (d), Donor
Pfeiffer, Robert H., Director
Rose, Milton C., Director

Rasmussen Foundation

c/o Ruby Law, Chief Financial Officer
2360 Shasta Way
Simi Valley, CA 93065
(818) 991-3024
EIN: 770166925
Source Date: 12/95

Geographic Restrictions:
Primarily in CA.

Restrictions:
No grants to individuals.

To Whom:
Private higher and other education, recreation, **medical research**, health associations, youth, child abuse.

Financial info:
Giving: $232,800 for 25 grants (high: $100,000; low: $100).

Application info:
Applications accepted. Submit letter. No deadline.

Directors, Officers, Trustees:
Law, Ruby, Officer
Rasmussen, Dean, Director, Officer
Rasmussen, Larry, Officer
Rasmussen, Inc., C. A., Donor

Ellen Browning Scripps Foundation

c/o Union Bank of CA, N.A.
Attn: E. Douglas Dawson, VP
P.O. Box 85060
San Diego, CA 92186-5060
(619) 230-4709
EIN: 951644633
Source Date: 12/96

Geographic Restrictions:
Primarily in San Diego County, CA [southern].

Restrictions:
No grants to individuals.

To Whom:
Medical and oceanographic **research**, marine science, higher education, conservation, recreation, arts, youth, child welfare.

For What:
Equipment, program-related investments, **research**, scholarship funds.

Financial info:
Giving: $762,000 for 45 grants (high: $100,000; low: $1,000).

Application info:
Applications accepted. Submit proposal (2 page limit). Deadline is May 1. Board meets in June.

Directors, Officers, Trustees:
Davis, Ellen Scripps, Trustee
Goddard, Deborah, Trustee
Meanley, Edward S., Trustee
Scripps, Ellen Browning (d), Donor
Scripps, Paul K., Trustee
Scripps, Robert Paine (d), Donor

Albert Soiland Cancer Foundation

18500 Von Karman Ave., No. 600
Irvine, CA 92715
(714) 474-8995
EIN: 956027828
Source Date: 6/95

To Whom:
Needy cancer patients, fellowships in radiological therapy, **institutions for cancer research.**

For What:
Research, fellowships.

Financial info:
Assets: $367,100.
Giving: $75,800 for 1 grant.

Application info:
Applications accepted. Submit letter. No deadline.

Directors, Officers, Trustees:
Henderson, Brian E., M.D., Director
Meserve, J. Robert, Director
Soiland, Albert, M.D. (d), Donor
Van Den Nort, Stanley, M.D., Director

Charles H. & Anna S. Stern Foundation

c/o Melitta Fleck, Secretary
4365 Executive Dr., Suite 1600
San Diego, CA 92121
(619) 677-1488
EIN: 956878433
Source Date: 12/94

Geographic Restrictions:
Primarily in San Diego County, CA, area.

Restrictions:
No grants to individuals, continuing support, conferences or symposia.

To Whom:
Medical research into the cause, cure, treatment and prevention of disease and disability from cancer, diabetes, emphysema, psoriasis, and arthritis.

For What:
Research.

Financial info:
Giving: $142,200 for 3 grants.

Application info:
Applications accepted. Submit proposal (original and 5 copies). Deadline is Feb. 1 and Sept. 1. Board meets in Mar. and Oct. Publishes annual report and application guidelines.

Recent Grants:

$47,661 **Scripps Institution of Oceanography Research Study. New anti-inflammatory agents from marine organisms: development of new drugs for arthritis.**

$46,500 **University of California San Diego School of Medicine. Cancer research studies on newly-discovered Human Ras Protein.**

$48,000 Salk Institute for Biological Studies. Cell cycle control and cancer: role of P53 tumor suppressor gene in cellular response to DNA damage.

Directors, Officers, Trustees:

Calkins, Christopher C., Director
Dell, Pat, Officer
Durbin, Barbara, Director
Fleck, Melitta, Officer
Gordon, William W., Director, Officer
Hasterlik, Robert J., M.D., Director
Nielsen, Frank, Director, Officer
Stern, Anna S., Trust, Donor

Harold R. Swanton & Winifred R. Swanton Foundation

c/o The Bank of California, Trustee
Attn: Gina Southgate, 550-3
P.O. Box 60477
Los Angeles, CA 90060
(213) 243-3158
EIN: 954019288
Source Date: 1/96

Restrictions:
No grants to individuals or political purposes.

To Whom:
Respiratory ailments, particularly asthma and allergies, hospitals, **medical research**.

For What:
Research, equipment, outreach program support.

Financial info:
Assets: $1,562,200.
Giving: $61,500 for 5 grants (high: $25,000; low: $2,000).

Application info:
Applications accepted. Submit letter. Deadline is Nov. 1. Board meets in Jan.

Directors, Officers, Trustees:

Bank of California, N.A., The, Trustee
Swanton, Harold R. (d), Donor
Swanton, Winifred (d), Donor

Flora L. Thornton Foundation

c/o Flora L. Thornton, Trustee
4444 Lakeside Dr., Suite 300
Burbank, CA 91505
(818) 842-1645
EIN: 953855595
Source Date: 11/94

Geographic Restrictions:
Primarily in Los Angeles and San Francisco, CA.

To Whom:
Cultural programs, with emphasis on music, elementary and higher education, **medical research**, cancer, public broadcasting.

Financial info:
Giving: $1,417,200 for 45 grants (high: $250,000; low: $1,000).

Application info:
Applications accepted. Submit letter. No deadline.

Directors, Officers, Trustees:

Landry, Edward A., Trustee
McDaniel, Glen P., Trustee
Thornton, Flora L., Donor, Trustee
Thornton, William Laney, Trustee

Towbes Foundation

c/o Susan Sheller, Secretary
P.O. Box 20130
Santa Barbara, CA 93120-0130
(805) 962-2121
EIN: 953519577
Source Date: 6/96

Geographic Restrictions:
Primarily in Santa Barbara, CA, area [southern].

Restrictions:
No grants to individuals.

To Whom:
Education, **medical research, especially in the area of neurological disease**, performing arts, and promotion and preservation of the free enterprise system.

For What:
Scholarship funds, fellowships, capital campaigns, conferences and seminars.

Financial info:
Assets: $900.
Giving: $207,900 for 40 grants (high: $30,000; low: $1,000).

Application info:
Applications accepted. Application form required (original and 5 copies). Deadline is Dec. 31, Apr. 30, and Aug. 31. Board meets in Feb., June, and Oct.

Directors, Officers, Trustees:
- Gerarel, Sheridah, Director, Officer
- Jarvis, Charles H., Director
- Sheller, Susan S., Director, Officer
- Towbes, Gail, Donor, Director, Officer
- Towbes, Michael, Donor, Director, Officer

Nora Eccles Treadwell Foundation

239 Joaquin Ave.
San Leandro, CA 94577
(510) 351-8626
EIN: 237425351
Source Date: 12/93

Geographic Restrictions:
Limited to UT and CA.

Restrictions:
No grants to individuals, research in areas not related to the cardiovascular system, diabetes, or arthritis.

To Whom:
Cardiovascular, diabetes, and arthritis medical research.

For What:
Professorships, **research**, general purposes, equipment.

Financial info:
Giving: $3,617,500 for 35 grants (high: $800,000, low: $500).

Application info:
Applications accepted. Submit letter. No deadline.

Directors, Officers, Trustees:
- Canepa, Patricia, Director, Officer
- Eccles, Spencer F., Director
- First Security Bank of Utah, N.A., Trustee
- Harrison, Lawrence M., Director
- Harrison, Nora Eccles Treadwell (d), Donor
- Harrison, Richard A., Director, Officer
- Hilger, William D., Director, Officer
- Prepouses, Nicholas T., Director, Officer
- Watson, Alonzo W., Jr., Director

Western Cardiac Foundation

436 N. Roxbury Dr., No. 222
Beverly Hills, CA 90210
(310) 276-2379
EIN: 956116853
Source Date: 12/93

Geographic Restrictions:
Primarily in Los Angeles, CA [southern].

Restrictions:
No grants to individuals.

To Whom:
Medical research, hospitals, higher and medical education.

For What:
Fellowships, **research**.

Financial info:
Giving: $131,000 for 5 grants (high: $100,000; low: $5,000).

Application info:
Applications accepted. Submit letter. No deadline.

Directors, Officers, Trustees:
Cavagnaro, Rae, Officer
Kennamer, Rexford, M.D., Director, Officer
Mercader, George, Director, Officer
Vance, Katherine R. (d), Donor

L. K. Whittier Foundation

c/o Linda J. Blinkenberg, Dir. of Fdns.
625 Fair Oaks Ave., Suite 360
South Pasadena, CA 91030
(818) 441-5188
EIN: 956027493
Source Date: 12/96

Geographic Restrictions:
Limited to Los Angeles, CA, area [southern].

Restrictions:
No grants to individuals.

To Whom:
Hospitals, **medical research**, youth, higher and other education.

For What:
Endowment funds, matching funds, special projects, seed money, **research.**

Financial info:
Giving: $1,279,900 for 15 grants (high: $500,000; low: $5,000).

Application info:
Applications accepted. Submit letter of inquiry. No deadline. Board meets annually. Foundation prefers to initiate it's grants.

Directors, Officers, Trustees:
Blinkenberg, Linda J., Officer
Sorensen, Arlo G., Officer
Whittier, Leland K. (d), Donor
Woods, Laura-Lee Whittier, Officer

W.W.W. Foundation

1260 Huntington Dr., Suite 204
South Pasadena, CA 91030-4561
(213) 259-0484
EIN: 953694741
Source Date: 7/95

Geographic Restrictions:
Primarily in CA.

Restrictions:
No grants to individuals.

To Whom:
Animal welfare, youth, hospitals, **medical research**, arts, zoos, music, civic affairs, higher, early childhood, secondary, and other education.

For What:
Renovation projects, matching funds, building funds, endowment funds, special projects.

Financial info:
Assets: $19,222,600.
Giving: $1,244,400 for 15 grants (high: $1,000,000; low: $200).

Application info:
Applications accepted. Submit letter of inquiry. No deadline.

Directors, Officers, Trustees:
Bea, Winifred W. Rhodes, Officer
Blinkenberg, Linda J., Officer
Constance, Marcia W., Officer
Sorensen, Arlo G., Officer
Woodward, Helen W. (d), Donor

Zaffaroni Foundation

Attn: Dr. Alejandro Zaffaroni, CEO
950 Page Mill Rd.
Palo Alto, CA 94304
EIN: 946100109
Source Date: 12/95

Geographic Restrictions:
Primarily in CA.

To Whom:
Higher education for biomedical research, nutritional research for developing countries.

For What:
Research.

Financial info:
Assets: $957,100.
Giving: $191,700 for 5 grants (high: $50,000; low: $3,000).

Application info:
Applications accepted. Submit letter. No deadline.

Directors, Officers, Trustees: CA696a

Colorado

American Foundation for Surgery of the Hand

c/o Jeryl Hough, Acting Exec. Dir.
6060 Greenwood Plaza Blvd., Suite 100
Englewood, CO 80111-4801
(303) 771-9236
Source Date: 12/96

To Whom:
Research and investigation of and teaching on the methods for preventing, correcting, and treating disorders of the hand arising from congenital, developmental, nutritional, traumatic, or other causes, fund worthy education services and programs concerning hand surgery for surgeons and others in the medical profession as well as patients and their families.

For What:
General purposes.

Financial info:
Assets: $1,420,900.
Giving: $96,900 for 7 grants.

Application info:
Applications accepted. Submit letter. Deadline is Aug. Publishes annual report.

Recent Grants:
- "Reproducible Positioning of the Wrist for Precision Measurements of Ulna Variance an Intercarpal Angles: in vivo Validation of the Extensor Carpi Ulnaris Groove and the Scapho-piso-capitate Relationship for Radiographic Recognition of Standard Neutral Posteroanterior and Lateral Views of the Wrist as Regards Their Surgical Implications" Louis A. Gilula, MD, Principal Investigator.
- "Protection of Microcirculatory Function From Surgical Trauma" Maria Siemionow, MD, Principal Investigator.
- "Thumb Osteotomy in Thumb CMC Osteoarthritis" Robert S. Richards, MD, Principal Investigator.
- "Flexor Tendon Repair: An in vitro Analysis of Suture Techniques Subjected to Cyclic Loading" Graham King, MD, Principal Investigator.
- "A Quantitative Mechanical Analysis of the Interosseous Membrane in the Forearm: Pathomechanics of Injury and Implications for Reconstruction" Emmie S. Hsu, MD, Principal Investigator.
- "Biomechanical Behavior of the Median Nerve in and About the Carpal Tunnel" Neil A. Sharkey, PhD, Principal Investigator.
- "The Experimental Study of Vein Graft Wrapping Nerves for Chronic Nerve Compression in Rats" Matthew M. Tomaino, MD.

Directors, Officers, Trustees:
Cooney, William P., M.D., Trustee
Froimson, Avrum I., M.D., Officer, Trustee
Hentz, Vincent R., M.D., Officer, Trustee
Hough, Jeryl, Director
Lister, Graham D., M.D., Trustee
Peimer, Clayton A., M.D., Trustee
Phelps, Dennis B., M.D., Officer, Trustee
Taleisnik, Julio, M.D., Officer, Trustee
Weiland, Andrew J., M.D., Trustee
Zook, Elvin G., Trustee

Community Foundation Serving Northern Colorado

(Formerly Fort Collins Area Community Foundation)
c/o Diane Hogerty, Exec. Dir.
The Nicol Bldg., 528 S. College
Fort Collins, CO 80524
(303) 224-3462
Source Date: 12/95

Geographic Restrictions:
Limited to northern CO, with emphasis on Larimer and Weld counties.

To Whom:
Civic Affairs and Community development: housing, seniors, libraries, animal welfare, youth, literacy, religion.

Arts and Humanities.

Education: literacy, higher, science, and other education.

Health: hospice, hospitals, family planning, health associations, **medical research**.

Human Services: disabled, women, seniors, community funds, at-risk families and youth.

For What:
Individuals, scholarship funds, seed money.

Financial info:
Assets: $1,527,700.

Giving: $162,700 for 60 grants (high: $5,000; low: $100).

Application info:
Applications accepted. Application form required. Deadline is Feb. 1, May 1, Aug. 1, and Nov. 1. Distribution committee meets the first Tuesday of June, Sept., Dec. and Mar.

Recent Grants:
Humane Society of Larimer County
St. Luke's Episcopal Church
Housing Task Force
Fort Collins Symphony
Poudre Valley Art League
Longs Peak Science Foundation
Adult Literacy
Hospice of Larimer County
Swedish Medical Center

Directors, Officers, Trustees:
Anderson, Greg, Trustee
Ballah, Wayne, Trustee
Bennett, Sarah, Trustee
Birky-Kreutzer, Pauline, Trustee
Bischoff, Brad, Director
Burton, Don, Director
Cada, Dot, Director
Devereaux, Harry, Director
Edwards, Paula, Director
Farnham, Pat, Director
Farnham, Steve, Director
Ferguson, Sue, Director
Fischer, Gene, Director
Frazier, Tom, Director
Frederick, Larry, Director
Freeman, John, Director
Gaspar, Dan, Director
Gunn, Bill, Director
Hansford, Bruce, Director
Hauser, Mike, Director
Havener, Gary, Director
Heth, Mo, Director
Hoffman, Marty, Director
Hogerty, Diane M., Officer
Hoogendyk, Tom, Director
Hopkins, Don, Director
Kirkpatrick, Susan, Director
Nesbitt, Harv, Director, Officer
Nicol, Elsie, Director
Reeves, Peggy, Director
Rennels, Cheryl, Director
Sargent, Trudy, Director
Schatz, Jill, Director
Tool, Steve, Director
Wear, Nancy, Director
Wolfe, Lorrie, Director
Yates, Ann, Director

HealthONE

c/o Khanh T. Nguyen, Grants Admin.
600 S. Cherry St., Suite 217
Denver, CO 80222-1704
(303) 322-3515
Source Date: 12/94

Geographic Restrictions:
Limited to CO and the Rocky Mountain region of U.S.

Restrictions:
No grants for ongoing operating expenses, scholarships, endowments, real estate acquisitions, capital expenses for building construction or renovation, fundraising events, or religious or political purposes.

To Whom:
Research: new clinical research efforts, health services research.

Professional Education: promote continuing education and training for health care professionals.

Community Health Care: seniors, support services for persons with long-term illness, educate the public about health concerns and issues, maintenance of good health through health promotion, screening, and prevention of illness.

For What:
Individuals, seed money, **research**.

Financial info:
Assets: $20,528,000.
Giving: $265,900 for 10 grants (high: $50,000; low: $2,500) and $200,100 for 5 grants to individuals (high: $100,000; low: $5,000).

Application info:
Applications accepted. Application form required (3 copies). Deadline is Jan. 8, Apr. 9, July 9, and Oct. 8. Board meets in Mar., June, Sept., and Dec. Publishes annual report and application guidelines.

Recent Grants:

$12,467	Home HealthONE. Joint program with Hospice of Metro Denver to provide hospice services to HealthONE patients.
$50,000	Community Health Services-Commerce City. Place P/SL physician in school-based clinic program.
$32,397	Senior Citizen Health Center, Aurora Presbyterian Hospital. Form partnership between Senior Citizen's Health Center and Morning Star Senior Day Program.

$2,650	Medical Care and Research Foundation. Hire community volunteer coordinator for intergenerational project at Park Manor.
$50,000	Office of Research and Development, HealthONE. Outcomes Research projects within system.
$28,460	Urban Peak and P/SL Family Health Clinic. Prenatal care and health services to homeless pregnant teenagers.
$21,442	Warren Village and P/SL Family Health Clinic. On-site health education program for single-parent families.
$31,000	Western Heart Institute. Continuing medical education for specialists and rural primary care physicians.

Kettering Family Foundation

c/o Charles Kettering, III, Pres.
2833 S. Colorado Blvd., Suite 2415
Denver, CO 80222
Internet: http://www.kettering.org
Source Date: 12/96

Geographic Restrictions:
U.S. giving.

Restrictions:
No grants for foreign purposes, religious organizations, individuals, scholarships, or fellowships.

To Whom:
Higher and secondary education, cultural programs, fine arts, environment, conservation, disabled, **specialized medical research**.

For What:
Operating budgets, annual campaigns, seed money, deficit financing, building funds, equipment, land acquisition, endowment funds, special projects, **research**, publications, capital campaigns, continuing support, general purposes, matching funds.

Financial info:
Assets: $9,933,000.
Giving: $309,700 for 25 grants (high: $50,000; low: $500).

Application info:
Applications accepted. Submit proposal (2 copies). Deadline is Mar. 1 and Sept. 1. Board meets in May and Nov. Publishes annual report with application guidelines.

Recent Grants:

$1,000	Boca Ballet Theatre Company, Boca Raton, FL. General operating support.
$25,000	Cassidy Endowment for Education, Santa Rosa, CA. Operating funds for "Project FAST."
$10,000	Center for Marine Conservation, Washington, D.C. Flonda Living Marine Resources Program.
$101,000	**Children's Seashore House, Philadelphia, PA. Research and general operating support.**
$50,000	Citizen Exchange Council, New York, NY. Environmental programs.
$3,200	Council on Foundations, Washington, D.C. General operating support.
$20,000	Dartmouth Hitchcock Medical Center, Lebanon, NH. Family & Child Trauma Center.
$16,400	David's House, Lebanon, NH. General operating support.
$20,000	Eco Education, St. Paul, MN. General operating support.
$20,000	Faculty of Color Program, New York, NY. "Teachers of Color" program.
$20,000	Foto Fest, Houston, TX. "Literacy Through Photography' program.
$25,000	Global Action Plan, Woodstock, NY. "National Youth Lifestyle Campaign" project.
$500	Good Neighbor Health Clinic, White River Junction, VT. General operating support.
$1,500	Jimmie Heuga Center, Avon, CO. General operating support.
$25,000	Kempe Children's Foundation, Denver, CO. Capital construction.
$1,000	Listen Foundation, Lebanon, NH. "Building for the Future" Campaign.
$500	Lyme Nursery School, Lyme, NH. General operating support.
$25,000	**Missouri Foundation for Medical Research, Columbia, MO. Lupus research.**
$50,000	Montshire Museum of Science, Norwich, VT. Construction of Trailside Pedestrian Bridge.
$10,000	National Center for Health Education, New York, NY. Educational handbook.
$25,000	Nature Conservancy, Boulder, CO. Carpenter Ranch.
$15,000	Outreach House, Hanover, NH. General operating support.

$1,500 St. Anne's Episcopal School, Denver, CO. Endowment.
$15,500 St. Luke's Community Services, Stamford, CT. Family Housing Program.
$10,000 Strings in the Mountains, Steamboat Springs, CO. General operating support.
$5,000 Universal Ballet Foundation, Washington, D.C. General operating support.
$30,000 **University of Alabama at Birmingham, Birmingham, AL. Research on pediatric pneumonia.**
$15,000 University of Chicago, Chicago, IL. "Genetic Alterations during Bladder Cancer and Progression" project.
$25,000 University of NH Center for Educational Field Services, Durham, NH. General operating support.
$500 Warren Village, Denver, CO. General operating support.
$500 Women's Information Service, Lebanon, NH. General operating support.

Directors, Officers, Trustees:
Beck, Susan K., Officer, Trustee
Kettering, Charles F., III, Donor, Officer, Trustee
Kettering, E. W., Donor
Kettering, Virginia W., Donor
Lombard, J. K., Donor
Lombard, Jane K., Officer
Lombard, Richard D., Donor
Verity, Jonathan G., Officer
Weiffenbach, B., Donor
Williamson, Debra L., Officer, Trustee
Williamson, Leslie G., Officer, Trustee
Williamson, Peter D., M.D., Donor
Williamson, S. K., Donor

Milheim Foundation for Cancer Research

c/o Colorado National Bank
Attn: Margaret M. Armstrong, Trust Admin.
P.O. Box 5168
Denver, CO 80217
(303) 394-4839
Source Date: 12/94

Restrictions:
No grants for travel to meetings, presentation of papers, or salaries of academic personnel.

To Whom:
Cancer medical research.

For What:
Individuals, **research**.

Financial info:
Assets: $1,475,700.
Giving: $137,700 for 20 grants to individuals (high: $15,000; low: $3,500).

Application info:
Applications accepted. Application form required (original and 6 copies). Deadline is Mar. 15. Board meets in May.

Directors, Officers, Trustees:
Aarstad, Norman, M.D., Advisor
Cohen, John, M.D., Advisor
Colorado National Bank, Trustee
Franco, Robert, Advisor
Jennings, R. Lee, M.D., Advisor
Major, Francis J., M.D., Advisor
Roberts, Walden K., M.D., Advisor
Wheeler, Clara (d), Donor

Bal F. & Hilda N. Swan Foundation

c/o Wells Fargo Bank
Attn: Hal R. Wofford, VP
P.O. Box 5825
Denver, CO 80217
(303) 293-5365
EIN: 742108775
Source Date: 12/95

Geographic Restrictions:
Limited to CO.

To Whom:
Disabled, **medical research**, child welfare, cultural programs, social services, higher education, youth.

For What:
Scholarship funds, fellowships, special projects, equipment, **research**, general purposes.

Financial info:
Assets: $1,019,000.
Giving: $203,300 for 50 grants (high: $25,000; low: $500).

Application info:
Applications accepted. Submit letter. No deadline.

Directors, Officers, Trustees:
First Interstate Bank of Denver, Trustee
Kimmett, James F., Trustee
Swan, Bal F. (d), Donor
Zarlengo, Richard A., Trustee

Ruth & Vernon Taylor Foundation

1670 Denver Club Bldg.
Denver, CO 80202
(303) 893-5284
EIN: 846021788
Source Date: 6/96

Geographic Restrictions:
Primarily in TX, CO, WY, MT, IL, and the Mid-Atlantic U.S.

Restrictions:
No grants to individuals.

To Whom:
Higher and secondary education, cultural programs, social services, youth, ecology, conservation, hospitals, **medical research**, arts.

For What:
Research, endowment funds, building funds, general purposes.

Financial info:
Assets: $32,715,100.
Giving: $1,407,900 for 130 grants (high: $100,000; low: $200).

Application info:
Applications accepted. Submit proposal. Deadline is Apr. 30. Board meets in May and Aug.

Directors, Officers, Trustees:
Campbell, Ruth Taylor, Trustee
Green, Friday A., Trustee
Swift, Sara Taylor, Trustee

Connecticut

Adler Foundation, Inc.

534 E. Putnam Ave.
Greenwich, CT 06830
(203) 622-9069
Source Date: 12/95

Restrictions:
No grants to individuals.

To Whom:
Medical education, **medical research in Diabetes, Leukemia, and Alzheimer's Disease.**

For What:
Research, seed money, conferences and seminars.

Financial info:
Assets: $7,058,400.
Giving: $328,500 for 15 grants (high: $50,000; low: $100).

Application info:
Applications accepted. Submit letter (2 copies). No deadline. Board meets in Apr.

Directors, Officers, Trustees:
Adler, John, Officer, Trustee
Adler, Morton M. (d), Donor
Astrove, Katherine A., Trustee
Berson, Joel I., Officer, Trustee
Felch, William C., Trustee
Kuhns, William G., Trustee
Leblang, Paul, Trustee
Ledonne, Edmond V., Trustee
Potter, Helen A., Officer, Trustee
Quickel, Kenneth E., Jr., Trustee
Rosenthal, Harry (d), Donor
Selkoe, Dennis J., Trustee
Vale, Wylie, Trustee

Jane Coffin Childs Memorial Fund for Medical Research

c/o Elizabeth H. Ford, Admin. Dir.
333 Cedar St.
New Haven, CT 06510
(203) 785-4612
EIN: 066034840
Source Date: 6/95

Restrictions:
No grants to individuals, building or endowment funding, matching gifts, or general purposes.

To Whom:
Medical research into the causes, origins, and treatment of cancer.

For What:
Fellowships, **research.**

Financial info:
Assets: $32,661,300.
Giving: $1,946,900 for 80 grants (high: $30,000; low: $3,000).

Application info:
Applications accepted. Application form required (original and 5 copies). Deadline is Feb 1. Board meets in May. Publishes application guidelines.

Directors, Officers, Trustees:
Barclay, John W., Manager
Boyer, Herbert W., Ph.D., Manager
Childs, Edward C., Manager
Childs, James E., Manager
Childs, John W., Officer, Manager
Childs, Richard S., Jr., Officer, Manager
Childs, Starling W. (d), Donor
Coffin, Alice S. (d), Donor
Lamm, Donald S., Manager
Lawrence, Anne Garrels, Manager
Lawrence, James F., Mrs., Manager
Lawrence, Starling R., Manager
Schmalz, Robert N., Officer
Steitz, Joan A., Director

Charles E. Culpeper Foundation, Inc.

c/o Mary Ellen Bucci, Pgm. Off.
Financial Centre
695 E. Main St., Suite 300
Stamford, CT 06901-2155
(203) 975-1240
Internet: http://www.culpeper.org/
EIN: 131956297
Source Date: 12/96

Geographic Restrictions:
Limited to organizations in the U.S.

Restrictions:
No grants to individuals, conferences, conduit organizations, operating funds, travel, endowment or building funding.

To Whom:
Health: **basic biomedical research, research in health care delivery,** study of social, ethical, and other issues in human health and disease, evaluation advancement and reform of American medical education, clinical services, including ambulatory and hospital programs.

Education: undergraduate education in the liberal arts and sciences at private higher education institutions, foreign language teaching programs, particularly those using new technologies, environmental studies, increase the use of technology in teaching and research.

Arts and Culture: educational outreach.

Administration of Justice: programs evaluating the state of education of criminal justice professionals and recommending improvements with the objective of ascertaining how best to prepare them for the challenges they fact, programs heightening public understanding of the workings and complexities of the criminal justice system in the conviction that an informed citizenry is the most efficient engine for needed change, programs considering how best to target scarce resources to achieve maximum results in the area of prevention and reduction of violent crime.

For What:
Research, general purposes, special projects, seed money.

Financial info:
Assets: $179,680,000.
Giving: $7,509,000 for 190 grants (high: $500,000; low: $500).

Application info:
Applications accepted. Submit letter. No deadline. Board meets quarterly. Publishes annual report and application guidelines.

Recent Grants:

$132,631	Dana-Farber, Inc., Boston, MA. Toward the research of Ezekiel Emanuel, MD, PhD, on the methods of allocating health care resources and the development of a model, "The Impartial Community Allocator Method."
$125,210	National Academy of Sciences, Washington, DC. Toward a study by the Institute of Medicine on decisionmaking about care at the end of life.
$45,872	University of Washington School of Medicine, Seattle, WA. Toward the research of Albert R. Jonsen, PhD, on a comprehensive cultural and intellectual history of bioethics in the United States.
$180,763	Acadia Institute, Bar Harbor, ME. Toward a study of the merger of the Hahnemann University and Medical College of Pennsylvania Schools of Medicine and its impact on medical education and health care delivery.
$75,000	Beth Israel Medical Center, New York, NY. Toward the development of institutional policies on medical ethics issues; the expansion of ethics education programs for physicians, nurses and other health care providers; and the establishment of an ethics resource center for patients and their families.
$105,006	Medical College of Pennsylvania and Hahnemann University, Philadelphia, PA. Toward the development and assessment of a model program of structured medical ethics training exercises for the improvement of future physicians' clinical competency.
$156,005	Northwestern University, Evanston, IL. Toward a new computer technician position and multimedia equipment to enhance the Medical School's program in student clinical skills evaluation.
$300,000	University of California, Los Angeles, Los Angeles, CA. Toward the development and the implementation of an interdisciplinary generalist doctoring curriculum over the third and fourth years of medical school.

$132,000 University of Missouri, Kansas City, MO. Toward the design of a core curriculum in Medical Humanities.

$60,000 Washington University, St. Louis, MO. Toward research by Kenneth Ludmerer, MD, entitled, "American Medical Education in the Twentieth Century."

$90,552 South End Medical Center, Inc., Stamford, CT. Toward improved medical care for the underserved, including a full-time registered nurse position and the prescription emergency fund.

$324,000 University of New Mexico, Albuquerque, NM. Clifford R. Lyons, MD, PhD, for research on mechanisms of host defense against Mycobacterium tuberculosis.

$324,000 University of Pennsylvania, Philadelphia, PA. Lewis A. Chodosh, MD, PhD, for research on the role of BRCA1 in differentiation pathways.

$324,000 Washington University, St. Louis, MO. Dwight A. Towler, MD, PhD, for research on the molecular genetics of osteoblast-specific gene expression.

$150,000 Gustavus Adolphus College, St. Peter, MN. Toward multimedia equipment for the teaching of foreign languages, the new position of Language Laboratory Coordinator, faculty development and foreign language assistants.

$121,000 Hamilton College, Clinton, NY. Toward upgrading the language laboratory and faculty training in the uses of multimedia technology.

$87,850 Kalamazoo College, Kalamazoo, MI. Toward the establishment of a joint faculty position in Chinese language and history.

$150,762 Pacific Lutheran University, Tacoma, WA. Toward equipping a Multicultural Language Learning Center to serve language programs, international studies programs across the curriculum and special needs of Asian, Hispanic and hearing-impaired students.

$153,508 Swarthmore College, Swarthmore, PA. Toward the establishment of a multimedia Language Learning Center including hardware/software and faculty training in the use of technologies.

$42,000 Association of Governing Boards of Universities and Colleges, Washington, DC. Toward the publication of a special issue of Trusteeship magazine dedicated to technology and its impact on higher education.

$115,840 Bennington College, Bennington, VT. Toward training faculty, students and local public school teachers in the use of multimedia and Internet technologies.

$165,500 Hartwick College, Oneonta, NY. Toward information technology hardware and software for applications throughout the curriculum, faculty training and dissemination of project results.

$174,000 Illinois Wesleyan University, Bloomington, IL. Toward the establishment of a faculty development and training program in the uses of instructional technologies.

$100,000 Marymount College, Tarrytown, NY. Toward the establishment of a multimedia teaching and resource center, including hardware/software and related faculty training.

$97,440 New England Board of Higher Education, Boston, MA. Toward a telecommunications initiative to help institutions develop distance learning strategies.

$100,000 Scripps College, Claremont, CA. Toward software for the application of state-of-the-art technologies to teaching and learning toward the end of increasing the use of computing technology throughout the curriculum.

$203,208 Trinity College, Hartford, CT. Toward the new position of Director of the Center for Technology-Assisted Learning, the establishment of a Center Associates Program to promote the objectives of the center and to foster faculty development.

$156,500 Washington College, Chestertown, MD. Toward multimedia hardware/software, the establishment of a multimedia Instructional Technologist position and faculty training.

$142,555 William Marsh Rice University, Houston, TX. Toward the establishment of the positions of Reference Librarian and Educational Specialist to help train faculty in adopting multimedia technology for their courses.

$126,000 Carleton College, Northfield, MN. Toward the interdisciplinary environmental studies program, including program administration, faculty and curricular development, the establishment of a visiting professorship and student internships.

$75,000 American Craft Museum, New York, NY. Toward an outreach initiative to increase the museums visibility and audience by promoting an understanding of craft.

$25,000 American Symphony Orchestra League, Washington, DC. Toward the Music Assistance Fund, a national scholarship program for talented, young, minority musicians.

$25,000 Asia Society, New York, NY. Toward a multidisciplinary exhibition-based educational program for New York City youth, including teacher workshops, artist-teachers and educational materials.

$100,000 Carnegie Hall Society, Inc., New York, NY. Toward Link Up!, an educational outreach program for New York City public elementary school students, including artist training, teacher training and classroom workshops.

$25,000 Chamber Music Society of Lincoln Center, Inc., New York, NY. Toward expansion of an educational concert series for New York City school children, ages 10-14, including teacher workshops and preparatory in-school artist visits.

$25,000 Civil War Trust, Washington, DC. Toward the creation of the Civil War Discovery System, an interactive, multimedia program for grades 6-12 that explores the life and times of the Civil War era.

$75,000 Connecticut Grand Opera and Orchestra, Stamford, CT. Toward the establishment of the position of Director of Education and Outreach to work toward the institutionalization of outreach efforts.

$67,570 Dallas Theater Center, Dallas, TX. Toward the establishment of the Dallas Theater Center Institute to prepare public school teachers to lead in the study of the arts using teaching artists and experiential methods.

$70,000 The Folger Shakespeare Library-Amherst College, Washington, DC. Toward the creation of the Shakespeare Gallery, an interactive multimedia information center for the library's general public visitors.

$300,000 Metropolitan Opera Association, New York, NY. Toward the expansion of the Metropolitan Opera Presents telecast series, the Met's national and international outreach programming on PBS.

$158,534 Museum of Fine Arts, Houston, Houston, TX. Toward a Place for all People, a program designed to increase the accessibility of the permanent collection and to cultivate a diverse audience.

$50,000 National Actors Theatre, New York, NY. Toward the expansion of the High School Outreach Program for New York City students, including enhancement of classic theatre production-based educational activities and curriculum materials.

$150,000 National Building Museum, Washington, DC. Toward the expansion of outreach/audience diversification initiatives, school programs K-6, programs for secondary students and programs for adults and families.

$138,313 The National Museum of Women in the Arts, Washington, DC. Toward a pilot program in Texas and Arkansas, in collaboration with Girl Scouts of the U.S.A., to promote an awareness of women in the arts and to foster individual creativity.

$25,000 The New Museum, New York, NY. Toward art programs for New York City high school students to encourage understanding of diverse cultures through contemporary art.

$100,000 New York City Ballet, New York, NY. Toward City Ballet Bridges, a pilot program to reach new, diverse audiences in Brooklyn, Queens and the Bronx.

$150,000 New York City Opera, New York, NY. Toward the expansion of education and community service staff and the institutionalization of the High School Partnership and the Opera is Elementary programs.

$49,900 New York Landmarks Conservancy, New York, NY. Toward an expanded edition of the Restoration Directory and an historic building workshop related to maintenance, repair, rehabilitation and restoration of landmark-quality structures.

$190,000 Old State House Association, Hartford, CT. Toward the establishment of an education department and the development of educational programs to foster citizen participation in and recognition of the democratic process as basic to American culture.

$50,000 Roundabout Theatre Company, New York, NY. Toward the expansion of outreach programs for New York City schools: From Page to Stage, a classroom-based theatre education program, and Teacher's Outreach Program, a seminar series for teachers.

$60,000 Spanish Theatre Repertory Company, Ltd., New York, NY. Toward the establishment of the position of Education Outreach and Development Director to advance outreach initiatives and relationships with area schools.

$25,000 The Stamford Symphony Society, Inc., Stamford, CT. Toward the establishment of an arts-based curriculum in partnership with Stamford public schools, including teacher and artist training.

$50,000 Vivian Beaumont Theater at Lincoln Center, New York, NY. Toward the Membership Expansion/Diversification Project, a subscription program targeting non-traditional audiences.

$147,000 Wadsworth Atheneum, Hartford, CT. Toward the development and implementation of a K-12 teacher training program and the establishment of a minority, education fellowship program.

$383,520 The Governance Institute, Washington, DC. Toward a study of how law enforcement can be better organized to meet the challenges of violent crime.

$100,000 The Governance Institute, Washington, DC. Toward research entitled, "Citizen Involvement in State Court Understanding and Support."

$100,000 American Inns of Court Foundation, Alexandria, VA. Expansion of Inn affiliations with law schools to enhance law school programming in practical lawyering, legal ethics and professional responsibility.

$100,000 Arena Stage, Washington, DC. Theater as Discovery, production-based program for high school students, including in-school play writing, workshops, teacher education and related humanities seminars.

$25,000 Ballet Theatre Foundation, Inc. New York, NY. Expansion of educational outreach initiatives for New York City school children and their families including lectures, demonstrations, workshops and performances.

$150,000 Haverford College, Haverford, PA. New position of Director of the Language Center and acquisition of multimedia equipment.

$186,802 Fairfield University, Fairfield, CT. Establishment of multimedia language resource center.

$89,929 Harvard University, Boston, MA. Research of Linda Emanuel, MD, PhD, entitled, "A Process Theory of Death: Medical Policy Implications".

$60,000 Case Western Reserve University. Cleveland, OH. Preservation of 60 collections of records on New Medical Curriculum for purposes of scholarly use.

Directors, Officers, Trustees:

Campbell, Colin G., Director
Culpeper, Charles E. (d), Donor
Drake, Philip M., Director, Officer
Fahey, Joseph F., Jr., Director
Jacobs, Linda E., Officer
Lynch, Ronald P., Director
McNamara, Francis J., Jr., Director, Officer
Morning, John, Director
Rose, John C., M.D., Director

Patrick & Catherine Weldon Donaghue Medical Research Foundation

85 Gillett St.
Hartford, CT 06105
(203) 525-2747
EIN: 066348275
Source Date: 12/95

Geographic Restrictions:
Limited to CT.

To Whom:
Medical research, cancer, heart disease.

For What:
Individuals, fellowships.

Financial info:
Assets: $67,420,700.
Giving: $2,528,100 for 60 grants (high: $150,000; low: $25,000).

Application info:
Applications accepted. Application form required. No deadline.

Directors, Officers, Trustees:
Andrews, Raymond S., Jr., Trustee
Donaghue, Ethel F. (d), Donor
Fleet Bank, N.A., Trustee

Carl J. Herzog Foundation, Inc.

c/o Bentley, Lane, Mosher, & Babson
P.O. Box 788
Greenwich, CT 06836-0788
(203) 629-2424
EIN: 510200524
Source Date: 12/95

To Whom:
Medical research, particularly in the field of dermatology, hospitals, education.

For What:
Research, general purposes, operating budgets.

Financial info:
Assets: $21,039,700.
Giving: $1,300,000 for 70 grants (high: $200,000; low: $1,000).

Application info:
Applications accepted. Submit letter. No deadline.

Directors, Officers, Trustees:
Alcock, Nancy M., Director, Officer
Babson, David F., Jr., Director, Officer
Bentley, Peter, Director, Officer
Cahusac, Sidney A. Wood, Director, Officer

National Emphysema Foundation, Inc.

c/o Chest Medicine, Norwalk Hospital
Maple St.
Norwalk, CT 06856
(203) 852-1009
EIN: 237124098
Source Date: 12/95

Geographic Restrictions:
Primarily in CT.

To Whom:
Pulmonary care and pulmonary medical research.
For What:
Conferences and seminars, **research.**

Financial info:
Assets: $1,717,300.
Giving: $65,900 for 10 grants (high: $25,000; low: $250).

Application info:
Applications accepted. Submit letter. No deadline.

Directors, Officers, Trustees:
Anthony, Lloyd, Trustee
Anthony, William, Trustee
Baum, Walter, Trustee
Hinds, B., Donor
Imbruce, Richard, Trustee
Lipton, Charles, Trustee
Nair, Sreedhar, M.D., Officer, Trustee
Nardi, Nicholas J., Trustee
Staunton, Muriel F. (d), Donor

Robert Leet Patterson & Clara Guthrie Patterson Trust

c/o Fleet Bank
Attn: Maggie Willard, VP
777 Main St., CTMOH18A
Hartford, CT 06115
(860) 986-4071
Source Date: 12/96

Geographic Restrictions:
Primarily in Continental U.S. with emphasis on CT and other eastern states.

Restrictions:
No grants to individuals, operating funds, or endowments.

To Whom:
Hospitals and organizations devoted to the advancement of medical science and **engaged in research relating to human diseases**. Improvements in clinical care.

For What:
Matching funds, **research**, seed money, special projects.

Financial info:
Assets: $13,000,800 (from 1993 990PF).
Giving: $410,400 for 5 grants (high: $100,000; low: $50,000).

Application info:
Applications accepted. Application form required (8 copies). Deadline is May 1 and Nov. 1. Board meets in June and Dec. Publishes application guidelines.

Directors, Officers, Trustees:
Fleet Bank, N.A., Trustee
Patterson, Clara Guthrie (d), Donor
Patterson, Robert Leet (d), Donor
Patterson Trust No. 2, Robert, Donor

Richard & Hinda Rosenthal Foundation

5 High Ridge Park
Stamford, CT 06905
(203) 322-9900
EIN: 136104817
Source Date: 12/95

Restrictions:
No grants to individuals.

To Whom:
Social sciences, **medical and scientific research**, hospice, and clinical medicine. Rosenthal Awards for Fiction and for Painting through the American Academy and National Institute of Arts and Letters, conceived and sponsors five national awards in clinical medicine through the American College of Physicians, American Heart Association, American Association for Cancer Research, and others. Has sponsored similar discovery awards in film.

For What:
Research, special projects, general purposes, continuing support, fellowships, matching funds, conferences and seminars.

Financial info:
Assets: $14,547,100.
Giving: $515,600 for 160 grants (high: $75,000; low: $500).

Application info:
Applications accepted. Submit letter. Deadline is Oct. 31. Board meets quarterly.

Directors, Officers, Trustees:
Rosenthal, Hinda Gould, Officer, Trustee
Rosenthal, Richard L., Officer, Trustee
Rosenthal, Richard L., Jr., Officer, Trustee
Wolf, Jamie G. R., Officer, Trustee

Tow Foundation, Inc.

c/o Emily Tow Jackson, Dir.
50 Locust Ave.
New Canaan, CT 06840
EIN: 061255825
Source Date: 12/96

Geographic Restrictions:
Primarily in NY, CT, and MA.

Restrictions:
No grants to individuals.

To Whom:
Medical research, youth, family services.

For What:
Seed money for new medical research, program support.

Financial info:
Assets: $14,000,000.
Giving: $717,000 for 140 grants (high: $50,000; low: $50).

Application info:
Applications accepted. Submit letter of inquiry. No deadline. Board meets in Mar., June, Sept. and Dec.

Recent Grants:

$10,000	Westchester Children's Assoc., White Plains, NY. Westchester Center for School/Community Partnership.
$25,000	New York Cares, Inc., New York, NY. Children's cultural and recreation programs.
$19,857	Kids in Crisis, Inc., Greenwich, CT. Safe haven for children at risk program.
$20,000	Long Wharf Theatre, New Haven, CT. New audience initiative (education program).
$50,000	Memorial Sloan-Kettering Cancer Center. Breast Cancer Research.
$50,000	**New England Medical Center. Research in pediatric pain management.**

Directors, Officers, Trustees:
Jackson, Emily Tow, Director
Rosensweig, David, Director, Officer
Schneider, Scott, Director, Officer
Tow, Andrew, Director
Tow, Claire, Donor, Director, Officer
Tow, Frank, Director
Tow, Leonard, Donor, Director, Officer

Delaware

Beneficial Foundation, Inc.

P.O. Box 911
Wilmington, DE 19899
(908) 781-3010
EIN: 516011637
Source Date: 12/95

Geographic Restrictions:
Primarily in DE, FL, NJ, and NY.

Restrictions:
No grants for endowments.

To Whom:
Higher and legal education, hospitals, **medical research**, cultural programs.

For What:
Employee-related scholarships, **research**, continuing support, annual campaigns, seed money, building funds, equipment, special projects.

Financial info:
Assets: $7,841,700.
Giving: $1,150,800 for 35 grants (high: $150,000; low: $1,000) and $239,800 for 185 grants to individuals (high: $2,500; low: $200).

Application info:
Applications accepted. Submit proposal. No deadline. Application form required for scholarship applicants. Board meets in May and Dec.

Directors, Officers, Trustees:
Beneficial Corp., Donor
Beneficial New Jersey, Donor
Caspersen, Finn M. W., Director, Officer
Gilliam, James H., Jr., Officer
McCardle, M. A., Officer
Neff, W. K., Director
Tucker, Robert A., Director, Officer
Williams, John O., Director

Fuller Foundation, Inc.

c/o J. P. Morgan Services, Inc.
P.O. Box 8714
Wilmington, DE 19899
Source Date: 12/94

Geographic Restrictions:
Primarily in New York, NY and Palm Beach, FL.

To Whom:
Hospitals, arts, **cardiac research**, cultural programs.

Financial info:
Assets: $2,937,100.
Giving: $125,800 for 45 grants (high: $10,000; low: $100).

Application info:
Applications accepted. Submit proposal. No deadline.

Directors, Officers, Trustees:
Bowen, Robert L., Officer
Fuller, Andrew P. (d), Donor
Fuller, Geraldine, Officer
Fuller, Gillian, Officer
Fuller, William M., Donor

Murray Foundation for Eye Research, Inc.

c/o J. P. Morgan Services, Inc.
P.O. Box 8714
Wilmington, DE 19899-8714
Source Date: 12/94

To Whom:
Medical eye research, blind.

For What:
General purposes, operating budgets, **research.**

Financial info:
Assets: $6,266,400.
Giving: $397,800 for 5 grants (high: $150,000; low: $2,000).

Application info:
Applications accepted. Submit proposal. No deadline.

Directors, Officers, Trustees:
Hosea, Elizabeth, Director
Kelsey, Ellen, Director
Murray, James M., Director, Officer

Murray, John P., Donor, Director, Officer
Murray, John P., III, Director, Officer
Murray, Mary T., Director, Officer
Murray, Matthew T., Director
Murray, Robert S., Director
Murray, W. Stephen, Director, Officer

District of Columbia

Paul & Annetta Himmelfarb Foundation, Inc.

c/o Lillian Kronstadt, Exec. Dir.
4545 42nd St., Suite 203
Washington, DC 20016
(202) 966-3795
EIN: 520784206
Source Date: 12/95

Geographic Restrictions:
Primarily in the Washington, DC, area and Israel.

Restrictions:
No grants to individuals.

To Whom:
Jewish welfare, Israel, early childhood and other education, seniors, disabled, homeless, health, **medical research**, AIDS, educational research, environment, **cancer research**.

Financial info:
Assets: $7,565,400.
Giving: $198,300 for 100 grants (high: $20,000, low: $50).

Application info:
Applications accepted. Submit letter. No deadline. Board meets monthly.

Recent Grants:

$200,000	Forward in the Fifth, Berea, KY. Support to design and pilot the Student Leadership Initiative Project (SLIP), a leadership, entrepreneurship, and workforce skills development curriculum to be implemented throughout eastern Kentucky through the involvement of teachers, students, local businesses, and community agencies.
$49,550	Kids Working/Peterstown Library, Peterstown, WV. Support to promote the incubution of social and economic entrepreneurship among youth through mentoring activities, apprenticeships, the establishment of the youth-run Job and Service Center, youth enterprise developmental, and youth leadership activities.
$199,968	South Bronx Community Coalition, New York, NY. Support to implement the Hunts Point Multi-Media Education/Leadership Initiative — a community economic development project for youth.
$200,000	Southend Community Services, Hartford, CT. Support to develop and implement Our Piece of thc Pie (O.P.P.), a program to provide young people with concrete work experiences and career enhancement activities and to assist teams of youth in starting and operating their own businesses in Hartford and Greater Hartford.
$201,905	Chugachmiut, Anchorage, AK. Support for the implementation of the Chugachmiut Career Development Project, which provides the youth of the Chugach region education and training including initial assessment, career exploration and planning, job shadowing and mentoring, and education or job placement assistance.
$200,000	Detroit One to One, Detroit, MI. Support to design and implement career awareness and mentoring "prototypes" to be piloted at Spain Elementary (beginning with talc eighth grade) and Central High (beginning with tenth grade) schools.
$187,500	Greater Washington Urban League, Washington, DC. Support to establish an intergenerational mentoring program linking middle school/junior high students and working or retired seniors, to help students increase academic and employment abilities, gain confidence, and increase awareness of employment options and how to pursue them.
$188,700	One to One Philadelphia, Philadelphia, PA. Support to enhance, expand, and link three programs - Shadowing Day, Business Education Goes Into Neighborhoods (BEGIN), and Work-Based Learning (WBL) - and to integrate and institutionalize them in schools and businesses.
$271,152	Impact Services Corp., Philadelphia, PA. Support for the implementation of the Community Blockbuilders Program, a community development training program that enhances the academic achievement and economic

	self-suffiiciency of disadvantaged youth in the Kensington area.
$294,340	Cornerstone Community Partnerships, Santa Fe, NM. Support to strengthen and coordinate the academic component of a job training program that builds job skills through historic and cultural preservation projects in Zuni Pueblo, Dona Ana, and two other sites.
$298,150	Girls, Inc. of Alameda County, San Leandro, CA. Support to enhance the workforce preparation component of the Eureka! Program by reconstructing, strengthening, and extending its summer internship and training component, performing an evaluation, and building long-term sustainability.
$275,062	Association of Science-Technology Centers, Washington, DC. Support to enhance the existing YouthAlive! Program with activities to help middle and high school students become aware of and develop the skill competencies they need and to create a workplace network that endorses those skills. Project work will involve ten museums as pilot sites.

Directors, Officers, Trustees:
Kronstadt, Annette, Director
Kronstadt, Lillian N., Director, Officer
Naiman, Ada, Director, Officer
Naiman, Norma Lee, Director
Parker, Carol Himmelfarb, Director, Officer
Preston, Carole, Director, Officer

Ella O. Latham Trust

c/o Crestar Bank
Attn: Jack Nichols, Trust Off.
1445 New York Ave., NW, 2nd Flr.
Washington, DC 20005
(202) 879-6335
Source Date: 12/95

Geographic Restrictions:
Limited to Washington, DC.

To Whom:
Medical research in the cure of diseases of women, medical, nursing, and hospital care of persons suffering from such diseases who are financially disadvantaged.

Financial info:
Giving: $95,300 for 10 grants (high: $40,000; low: $4,000).

Application info:
Applications accepted. Submit letter and proposal. No deadline. Board meets yearly.

Walter G. Ross Foundation

c/o ASB Capital Management Inc.
Attn: F. Scott Amling, Secretary
1101 Pennsylvania Ave., N.W., 3rd Flr.
Washington, DC 20004
EIN: 526057560
Source Date: 12/95

Geographic Restrictions:
Limited to the Washington, DC, area and FL.

Restrictions:
No grants to individuals, public higher education, or organizations who receive substantial support from the Federal Government.

To Whom:
Education, disadvantaged, physically disabled, **medical research**, seniors, health associations, hospitals, heart disease, higher education, family services, hospice, child development.

For What:
Research, general purposes, endowment funds, matching funds.

Financial info:
Assets: $4,842,800.
Giving: $990,000 for 10 grants (high: $500,000; low: $5,000).

Application info:
Applications accepted. Submit proposal (5 page limit). Deadline is Sept. 15. Board meets in Oct.

Recent Grants:

$500,000	George Washington University Medical Center, School of Medicine and Health Sciences, Washington, DC. Research and endowment.

Directors, Officers, Trustees:
Bernard, Eugene L., Trustee
Elliott, Lloyd H., Officer, Trustee
Zahn, J. Hillman, Trustee

Wallace Genetic Foundation, Inc.

4900 Massachusetts Ave., N.W., Suite 220
Washington, DC 20016
(202) 966-2932
Source Date: 12/95

Restrictions:
No grants to individuals, scholarships, or overhead expenses.

To Whom:
Agricultural research and preservation of farmland, higher education, **nutritional research**, populations studies, **cancer research**, conservation, environment.

For What:
Research, continuing support, seed money, special projects.

Financial info:
Assets: $133,986,000.
Giving: $3,276,500 for 80 grants (high: $250,000; low: $1,000).

Application info:
Applications accepted. Submit letter or proposal. No deadline.

Directors, Officers, Trustees:
Douglas, Jean W., Director
Wallace, Henry A. (d), Donor
Wallace, Henry B., Director
Wallace, Robert B., Director

Florida

Anthony R. Abraham Foundation, Inc.

6600 S.W. 57th Ave.
Miami, FL 33143
(305) 665-2222
Source Date: 12/95

Geographic Restrictions:
Primarily in Miami, FL.

Restrictions:
No grants to individuals.

To Whom:
Catholic welfare and giving, hospitals, youth, child welfare, **medical research.**

Financial info:
Assets: $8,500,000.
Giving: $400,000 for 70 grants (high: $100,000; low: $50).

Application info:
Applications accepted. Submit letter. No deadline.

Directors, Officers, Trustees:
Abraham, Anthony R., Donor, Director, Officer
Abraham, Norma Jean, Director
Abraham, Thomas G., Director, Officer
Malouf, Thomas, Director
Shaker, Anthony, Director

Ataxia Telangiectasia Children's Project

c/o Brad Margus, Pres.
398 W. Camino Gardens Blvd., Suite 104
Boca Raton, FL 33432
(561) 395-2621
Source Date: 12/95

To Whom:
Ataxia telangiectasia medical research.

For What:
Research.

Financial info:
Assets: $257,700.
Giving: $496,000 for 20 grants (high: $50,000; low: $20,000).

Application info:
Applications accepted. Submit proposal (10 page limit, 10 copies). Deadline is Apr. 1, July 1, and Oct. 1.

Recent Grants:
- George S. Wise Faculty of Life Sciences, Tel Aviv University, Tel Aviv, Israel. Translational Regulation of ATM Expression.
- University of California at Davis, Davis, CA. The Drosophila mei-41 gene: An animal model for A-T.
- Johns Hopkins Hospital, Baltimore, MD. Investigations of ATM Function.
- **Department of Genetics, St Jude Children's Research Hospital Memphis, TN. The Mechanism of Neurodegeneration in Ataxia Telangiectasia.**
- The Johns Hopkins University School of Medicine, Baltimore, MD. Assessment of the swallowing CCC/SIP problems of A-T patients.
- Departments of Genetics and Pediatrics, Yale University School of Medicine, New Haven, CT. Inhibiting and Rescuing ATM and Related Proteins.
- Department of Molecular Biology and Genetics, Johns Hopkins University, Baltimore, MD. Characterization of the Saccharontyces cerevisia homologues, HATI and MEC1 the human gene ATM mutated in Ataxia Telangiectasia.
- Department of Neuroscience and Cell Biology, Robert Wood Johnson Medical School, Piscataway, NJ. Purkinje cell development in a genetic murine model of ataxia telangiectasia: Effects of ATM gene knock out on Purkinje cell morphogenesis, survival and responsiveness to neurotrophic factors.
- Department of Human Genetics, Sackler School of Medicine, Tel Aviv University, Tel Aviv, Israel. Ataxia-Telangiectasia: From Genetics Back to Phenotype.
- University of Arizona, Tucson, AZ. MEC 1: Understanding its multiple functions in yeast and relevance to ATM.

Directos, Officers, Trustees:
Aicardi, Jean, M.D., Advisor
Cooper, M.D., Advisor
Cox, David, M.D., Director
DeVivo, Darryl C., M.D., Advisor
Friend, Stephen, M.D., Advisor
Heintz, Nathaniel, Advisor
Hempstead, Barbara L., M.D., Advisor
Hiebner, Jeffrey A., Officer

Johnson, Eugene, Advisor
Margus, Albert F., Jr., Donor, Officer
Margus, Bradley A., Donor, Officer
Menkes, John, M.D., Advisor

John E. & Nellie J. Bastien Memorial Foundation

100 E. Sample Rd., Suite B
Pompano Beach, FL 33064
Source Date: 12/95

Geographic Restrictions:
Primarily in FL.

To Whom:
Higher and other education, medical sciences, hospitals, youth, social services, performing arts, animal welfare, drug and alcohol abuse, health, **medical research, cancer research**, family services, hospice, seniors, Catholic giving, disadvantaged, marine science.

For What:
Scholarship funds, special projects, operating budgets.

Financial info:
Assets: $10,195,100.
Giving: $349,700 for 100 grants (high: $15,000; low: $200).

Application info:
Applications accepted. Submit letter. No deadline.

Directors, Officers, Trustees:
Bastien, Nellie J. (d), Donor
Kearns, Carol R., Trustee
Schneider, Gene F., Trustee
Wrightson, J. Wallace, Trustee

Batchelor Foundation, Inc.

950 S.E. 12th St.
Hialeah, FL 33010
Source Date: 5/97

Geographic Restrictions:
Primarily in FL.

Restrictions:
No grants to individuals.

To Whom:
Recreation, zoos, natural environment, **medical research**, child welfare, health associations, conservation, youth.

Financial info:
Assets: $3,326,100.
Giving: $610,200 for 50 grants (high: $200,000; low: $250).

Application info:
Applications accepted. Application form required. No deadline.

Directors, Officers, Trustees:
Batchelor, George E., Officer
Batchelor, Marianne, Officer
Batchelor Enterprises, Donor
Ferraresi, Daniel J., Officer
International Air Leases, Donor

Frank Stanley Beveridge Foundation, Inc.

301 Yamato Rd., Suite 1130
Boca Raton, FL 33431-4929
(561) 241-8388
Internet: http://www.beveridge.org/
Source Date: 12/96

Geographic Restrictions:
Primarily in Hampden and Hamshire counties, MA.

Restrictions:
No grants for tax-supported organizations, individuals, operating funds, endowments, deficit financing, travel, fundraising, or United Ways.

To Whom:
Community/Civic Issues: business development, civil rights, consumer education/protection, intercultural/race relations, leadership development, nonprofit development/technical assistance, public safety/crime prevention, transportation accessibility, volunteerism.

Culture: architecture/design, arts education, arts service organizations, dance, historic preservation/restoration, libraries, museums, music, public media, theater, visual arts.

Environment: air/water/noise pollution, animal welfare, conservation/protection of natural resources, energy/renewable resources, environmental education, hazardous wastes/waste management, urban environment/open space.

Health: community-based health care, consumer education/protection, equal opportunity/access, family planning, hospice/home care, hospitals, **medical research,** mental health/counseling, mental retardation/developmental disabilities, public health education, alcohol and drug abuse.

Religion.

Social Services: adoption/foster care, bereavement, corrections, counseling, day care, employment/job training, hunger, housing/shelter, information and referral, life skills training, long-term care, multi-services, recreation/fitness, summer camps, youth development.

For What:
Capital campaigns, seed money, equipment, building funds, renovation projects, scholarship funds, matching funds, special projects, publications, conferences or seminars, or films.

Financial info:
Assets: $37,489,900.
Giving: $2,043,300 for 85 grants (high: $700,000; low: $500).

Application info:
Applications accepted. Application form required. Deadline is Feb. 1 and Aug. 1. Board meets in Apr. and Oct. Applicants outside the Hampden and Hamshire counties, MA, areas must have support of 1 or more directors. Publishes application guidelines.

Recent Grants:

$32,500	Sharp HealthCare Corporation, San Diego, CA.
$50,000	Trustees of Westminster School, Simsbury, CT.
$37,500	American Red Cross, Tampa Bay Regional Chapter, Tampa, FL.
$5,000	Child Development Center, Inc., Sarasota, FL.
$2,500	Cork Elementary School, Plant City, FL.
$2,500	The DePaul School of Northeast Florida, Inc., Jacksonville, FL.
$2,500	George Snow Scholarship Fund, Boca Raton, FL.
$25,000	The Goodwill Suncoast Foundation, Inc., St. Petersburg, FL.
$17,400	Gulf Stream Council Boy Scouts of America, Inc., Palm Beach Gardens, FL.
$10,000	H. Lee Moffitt Cancer Center & Research Institute Foundation, Tampa, FL.
$25,000	Hospice of Hillsborough Foundation, Inc., Tampa, FL.
$25,000	Intracoastal Health Foundation, W. Palm Beach, FL.
$2,500	Jewish Community Center of the Palm Beaches, Inc., W. Palm Beach, FL.
$37,500	Lowry Park Zoological Society, Inc., Tampa, FL.
$1,000	North County Humane Society, Jupiter, FL.
$2,500	North Florida Botanical Society, Inc., Gainesville, FL.
$25,000	Palm Beach Atlantic College, Inc., W. Palm Beach, FL.
$5,000	Raymond F. Kravis Center for the Performing Arts, Inc., W. Palm Beach, FL.
$2,000	Saint John's Episcopal Church, Tampa, FL.
$1,500	Saint Mary the Virgin Anglican Church, Inc., Delray Beach, FL.
$1,500	Saint Mary the Virgin Anglican Church, Inc., Delray Beach, FL.
$2,500	Saint Mary the Virgin Anglican Church, Inc., Delray Beach, FL.
$1,000	Sarasota County Youth Foundation, Inc., Sarasota, FL.
$4,000	The South Florida Chopin Foundation Council, Miami, FL.
$5,000	South Florida Fellowship of Chruistian Athletes, Pompano Beach, FL.
$12,500	The Spring of Tampa Bay, Inc., Tampa, FL.
$2,500	Tampa Bay Chamber Orchestra, Inc., Tampa, FL.
$2,500	Tampa Bay History Center, Inc., Tampa, FL.
$2,500	Southeastern Council of Foundations, Inc., Atlanta, GA.
$10,000	Prevent Blindness Florida, Schaumburg, IL.
$50,000	Allen-Chase Foundation d/b/a Eaglebrook School, Deerfield, MA.
$2,000	American Red Cross; Hampshire County Chapter, Northampton, MA.
$2,400	American Red Cross; Pioneer Valley Chapter, Springfield, MA.
$4,200	American Red Cross; Westfield, Massachusetts Chapter, Westfield, MA.
$2,000	American Red Cross; Westfield, Massachusetts Chapter, Westfield, MA.
$5,000	Amherst Writers & Artists Press, Inc., Amherst, MA.
$25,000	Arcadia Nature Center & Wildlife Sanctuary, Lincoln, MA.

$1,000	The Association for Community Living, Inc., Springfield, MA.
$5,000	Babson College, Babson Park, MA.
$30,000	Baystate Health Systems, Springfield, MA.
$25,000	Brooks School, North Andover, MA.
$10,000	Center for Ecological Technology, Inc., Pittsfield, MA.
$15,000	Child & Family Service of Pioneer Valley, Inc., Springfield, MA.
$10,000	Children's Museum At Holyoke, Inc., Holyoke, MA.
$5,000	Church of the Atonement Preschool, Westfield, MA.
$25,000	Clara Barton Camp for Girls with Diabetes, Inc., North Oxford, MA.
$5,000	Community Foundation of Western Massachusetts, Springfield, MA.
$10,000	Connecticut River Watershed Council, Inc., Easthampton, MA.
$5,000	Dunbar Community Center, Inc., Springfield, MA.
$5,000	Dunbar Community Center, Inc., Springfield, MA.
$10,000	Easthampton Council on Aging, MA.
$5,000	The Episcopal Diocese of Western Massachusetts, Chalton Depot, MA.
$2,000	Fannie Stebbins Memorial Wildlife Refuge, Inc., Longmeadow, MA.
$25,000	First Congregational Church of Blandford, Blandford, MA.
$5,000	First United Methodist Church of Westfield, Westfield, MA.
$25,000	Hampshire Regional Young Men's Christian Association, Northampton, MA.
$25,000	Institute for Community Economics, Inc., Springfield, MA.
$2,000	Martin Luther King, Jr. Community Center, Inc., Springfield, MA.
$25,000	Metropolitan Springfield Y.M.C.A., Inc., Springfield, MA.
$5,000	North End Community Center, Inc., Springfield, MA.
$5,000	Open Door Nursery School, Westfield, MA.
$34,000	Open Pantry Community Service, Inc., Springfield, MA.
$25,000	Partners for a Healthier Community, Inc., Springfield, MA.
$5,000	Pioneer Valley Girl Scout Council, Inc., East Longmeadow, MA.
$20,000	Pioneer Valley Regional Education Alliance, Springfield, MA.
$20,000	Sevenars Concerts, Inc., Worthington, MA.
$35,000	Springfield College, Springfield, MA.
$5,000	Springfield Council for Cultural and Community Affairs, Springfield, MA.
$25,000	Springfield Day Nursery Corporation, Springfield, MA.
$2,500	Springfield Library and Museums Association, MA.
$25,00	Springfield Symphony Orchestra, Inc., MA.
$10,000	Springfield Symphony Orchestra, Inc., MA.
$50,000	Springfield Theatre Arts Association, MA.
$200,000	The Stanley Park of Westfield, Inc., Westfield, MA.
$589,000	The Stanley Park of Westfield, Inc., Westfield, MA.
$25,000	Trustees of Tufts College, Medford, MA.
$25,000	Visiting Nurse Foundation of Pioneer Valley, Inc., Springfield, MA.
$5,000	Visiting Nurse Services of Western Massachusetts, Inc., Holyoke, MA.
$12,500	WGBY TV/Channel 57, Springfield, MA.
$25,000	West Springfield Boys & Girls Club, Inc., MA.
$10,000	The Western Massachusetts Learning Tree, Inc., Springfield, MA.
$2,050	Westfield State College Foundation, Inc., Westfield, MA.
$7,500	Willie Ross School For The Deaf, Longmeadow, MA.
$5,000	World Affairs Council of Western Massachusetts, Inc., Springfield, MA.
$8,000	Young Men's Christian Association of Westfield, Westfield, MA.
$25,000	Mayo Foundation for Medical Education and Research, Rochester, MN.
$25,000	David's House, Inc., Lebanon, NH.
$15,000	Old Meeting House of Francestown, Inc., Francestown, NH.
$5,000	Samuel H. Wentworth Library, Center Sandwich, NH.
$40,000	Crohn's & Colitis Foundation of America, Inc., New York, NY.
$5,000	First United Methodist Church of Port Byron, Port Byron, NY.
$25,000	Baldwin-Wallace College, Berea, OH.
$2,000	The Company of the Redwood Library and Athenaeum, Newport, RI.
$17,250	The John Carter Brown Library, Providence, RI.
$2,000	Adopt-A-School of Beaufort County, Inc., Dataw Island, SC.
$5,500	InterVarsity Christian Fellowship of the United States, Madison, WI.

Directors, Officers, Trustees:
- Bartelt, Sarah Caswell, Director
- Beveridge, Frank Stanley (d), Donor
- Caswell, John Beveridge, Director
- Caswell, Philip, Director, Officer
- Caswell, Ward S., Director
- Gallup, John G., Director
- Griggs, Alfred L., Director
- Lenhart, Carole S., Officer
- Palmer, Joseph Beveridge, Director
- Stecher, Patsy Palmer, Director
- Touchton, J. Thomas, Director
- Woods, David F., Director, Officer

Lester I. Conrad Research Foundation, Inc.

c/o Muriel C. Reisner, Secretary
1801 S. Flager Dr., Suite 1203
West Palm Beach, FL 33401
Source Date: 12/94

To Whom:
Clinical and investigative dermatological medical research.

For What:
Research.

Financial info:
Giving: $38,000 for 5 grants (high: $5,000; low: $1,000).

Application info:
Applications accepted. Submit letter. No deadline.

Directors, Officers, Trustees:
- Conrad, Muriel F., Director
- Feinberg, Herbert D., Director
- Perlman, Andrew J., M.D., Director
- Reisner, Bernard J., Director
- Riskin, Bernard, Director

Cooper Institute for Advanced Studies in Medicine & the Humanities

(Formerly Naples Institute for Advanced Studies in Medicine & the Humanities)
c/o Kathy Gilson, Exec. Dir.
565 16th Ave., S.
Naples, FL 33940
(941) 261-3290
Source Date: 3/97

To Whom:
U.S. and international medical research, applying research intelligently and compassionately to human needs and aspirations, exchange of information between medical research, the professions, policy-makers and the public.

Financial info:
Giving: $52,100 for 10 grants (high: $50,000; low: $50).

Application info:
Applications accepted. Submit letter. No deadline.

Directors, Officers, Trustees:
- Biles, Fay, Trustee
- Bos, Sissel Cooper, Officer
- Cooper, Sissel H., Donor
- Heinemann, Denise, Trustee
- Kavanaugh, Frank, Officer
- Keller, Polly, Trustee
- MacDuffie, Linda, Officer
- McArdle, Ellen, Trustee
- Munz, Roger, Trustee
- Perlmutter, David, M.D., Officer
- Symposia, Donor

Tine W. Davis Family-W.D. Charities, Inc.

c/o T. Wayne Davis, Pres.
1910 San Marco Blvd.
Jacksonville, FL 32207
(904) 398-3986
Source Date: 12/95

Geographic Restrictions:
Primarily in southeastern U.S.

Restrictions:
No grants to individuals.

To Whom:
Higher education, youth, **medical research**, Christian religion, health, arts, cultural programs, social services.

Financial info:
Assets: $15,402,600.
Giving: $947,200 for 75 grants (high: $500,000; low: $1,000).

Application info:
Applications accepted. Application form required. No deadline. Board meets quarterly.

Directors, Officers, Trustees:
Baggett, Fred W., Director
Davis, Tine W., Donor
Davis, Tine Wayne, Jr., Officer
McNeil, Eunice Davis, Director
O'Donnell, James D., Director

Alfred I. duPont Foundation

c/o Rosemary C. Wills, Asst. Secretary
P.O. Box 1380
Jacksonville, FL 32201
(904) 396-6600
Source Date: 12/95

Geographic Restrictions:
Primarily in the southeast U.S.

Restrictions:
No grants to individuals.

To Whom:
Seniors in distressed situations requiring health, economic, or educational assistance, higher education, **medical research.**

For What:
Individuals, special projects.

Financial info:
Assets: $26,890,000.
Giving: $517,400 for 95 grants (high: $50,000; low: $100) and $394,600 for 200 grants to individuals (high: $10,000; low: $150).

Application info:
Applications accepted. Application form required. No deadline.

Directors, Officers, Trustees:
Ball, Braden, Director, Officer
Belin, J. C.m Director, Officer
duPont, Jessie Ball (d), Donor
Land, Lillie S., Director, Officer
Nedley, R. E., Director

Greenburg-May Foundation, Inc.

P.O. Box 54-5816
Miami Beach, FL 33154
(305) 864-8639
Source Date: 12/95

Geographic Restrictions:
Primarily in southern FL, IL, and NY.

Restrictions:
No grants to individuals, conferences, scholarships, or fellowships.

To Whom:
Medical research, cancer and heart disease, seniors, hospitals, Jewish giving, Jewish hospitals, Jewish temples, social services.

For What:
Operating budgets, continuing support, building funds, **research**, endowment funds, scholarship funds.

Financial info:
Assets: $4,363,300.
Giving: $191,400 for 50 grants (high: $50,000; low: $50).

Application info:
Applications accepted. Submit letter. No deadline. Board meets in Jan., Apr., July, and Oct.

Directors, Officers, Trustees:
Greenburg, Harry (d), Donor
May, Isabel, Director, Officer
May, Peter, Director, Officer
May, Samuel D., Director, Officer
Sklar, Linda, Director, Officer

Ethel & W. George Kennedy Family Foundation, Inc.

1 S.E. 15th Rd., Suite 250
Miami, FL 33129-1260
(305) 374-2455
Source Date: 12/96

Geographic Restrictions:
Limited to Miami, FL.

Restrictions:
No grants to individuals.

To Whom:
Rehabilitation and welfare for children, both physically and psychologically, **research**, education, and medical equipment in the areas of heart, brain, and eye diseases, diabetes, and cancer.

Financial info:
Assets: $13,097,500.
Giving: $650,000 for 65 grants (high: $50,000; low: $250).

Application info:
Applications accepted. Send brief letter describing program. Qualified organizations will receive an application form. Application form required (10 copies). Deadline is Feb. 1 and Sept. 1. Board meets in Mar. and Oct.

Recent Grants:

$50,000	Miami Youth Museum
$41,000	U/M M.T.S.L.
$30,000	Miami City Ballet
$25,000	All Saints Nursing Home
$10,000	Miami City Ballet
$10,000	Northland Community Church
$10,000	Troy
$10,000	Florida Shakespeare Festival
$9,614	Childrens Home Society Computors
$9,000	Key Biscayne Community Church
$6,930	Bay Point Schools Re Tax
$6,000	Temple Emanuel
$5,500	Whitwell High School
$5,202	Childrens Home Society Computors
$5,000	Calvary Baptist Church
$5,000	Childrens Home Society Deposit Computors
$5,000	Appalachian Summer Festival
$5,000	Fish & Game Unlimited Youth Fishing Tournament
$5,000	Miami Museum Of Science
$5,000	YPO
$5,000	Calvary Baptist Church
$5,000	Community Baptist Church
$5,000	Mercy Corps
$4,000	Temple Emanuel
$4,000	Ceralde School Of Art
$3,000	Community Baptist Church
$3,000	Boys Town Of Central Florida
$3,000	Ceralde School Of Art
$3,000	Resourcemobile
$3,000	I C A R E
$3,000	Marion County Rescue
$2,550	Greater Miami Jewish Federal
$2,500	American Red Cross Spectrum Awards
$2,500	Childrens Wish Foundation
$2,500	Key Life Network
$2,000	Boyd Buchanan High School
$2,000	Temple Emanuel
$2,000	Help Our State Parks
$2,000	M O C A
$2,000	Boys Town Of Italy
$1,750	Blowing Rock Schools
$1,650	Zoological Society Metro-Dade Zoo
$1,500	Childrens Home Society
$1,500	I C A R E Tux
$1,500	Whitwell Dixie Youth Program
$1,200	Miami City Ballet
$1,000	Blowing Rock Symphony
$1,000	Whitwell High School Baseball
$1,000	Blowing Rock Community Foundation
$1,000	Watauga Medical Center Foundation

Directors, Officers, Trustees:
Dobkin, Kendel Kennedy, Officer
Herterich, Karen Kennedy, Director, Officer
Kennedy, Kimberly, Director, Officer
Kennedy, W. George (d), Donor
Kennedy, Wayne G., Director, Officer
Olsen, Kathleen Kennedy, Director, Officer

Florence & Edgar Leslie Charitable Trust

3302 Aruba Way, Apt. K-3
Coconut Creek, FL 33066
(305) 973-7147
EIN: 136720542
Source Date: 12/95

Geographic Restrictions:
Primarily in NY.

Restrictions:
No grants to individuals.

To Whom:
Medical education and **research, cancer research**, rehabilitation, hospitals.

Financial info:
Assets: $1,587,300.
Giving: $70,000 for 10 grants (high: $10,000; low: $500).

Application info:
Applications accepted. Submit letter. No deadline.

Directors, Officers, Trustees:
Brucker, Andrew G., Trustee
Brucker, Edward G., Trustee

Joe & Emily Lowe Foundation, Inc.

c/o Bernard Stern, Trustee
249 Royal Palm Way, Suite 502
Palm Beach, FL 33480-4386
(561) 655-7001
Source Date: 12/95

Geographic Restrictions:
Primarily in the New York, NY, area, including NJ, and Palm Beach, FL.

Restrictions:
No grants to individuals.

To Whom:
Jewish welfare and giving, arts, museums, higher, medical, arts, and other education, hospitals, **medical research**, disabled, performing arts, health, hospice, AIDS, alcohol and drug abuse, social services, child welfare, disadvantaged, youth, homeless, women.

For What:
General purposes, building funds, equipment, endowment funds, matching funds, continuing support.

Financial info:
Assets: $19,048,400.
Giving: $1,180,300 for 385 grants (high: $75,000; low: $100).

Application info:
Applications accepted. Submit letter and proposal. No deadline. Board meets in Feb. and May or June.

Directors, Officers, Trustees:
Hauben, Bruce, Trustee
Hauben, David M., Officer, Trustee
Liman, Ellen, Officer, Trustee
Lowe, Emily (d), Donor
Lowe, Joe (d), Donor
Stern, Bernard, Officer, Trustee

NationsBank Community Foundation

c/o Lynn Smith, Trust Assoc.
P.O. Box 4295
Sarasota, FL 34230-4295
(941) 952-2710
Source Date: 12/95

Geographic Restrictions:
Limited to Sarasota County, FL.

Restrictions:
No grants to individuals, endowments, or operating expenses.

To Whom:
Arts, cultural programs, higher, secondary, early childhood, vocational, adult, elementary and other education, urban development, environment, conservation, community development, museums, performing arts, humanities, historic preservation, literacy, family planning, health, mental health, AIDS, **medical research**, juvenile delinquency, recreation, social services, youth, seniors, hospice, family services, disabled, women, homeless, disadvantaged.

For What:
Capital campaigns, building funds, matching funds, publications, seed money, renovation projects, special projects, equipment.

Financial info:
Assets: $4,844,900.
Giving: $290,100 for 35 grants (high: $345000; low: $100).

Application info:
Applications accepted. Submit proposal (10 copies). Deadline is May 1 and Nov. 1. Board meets in June and Dec.

Directors, Officers, Trustees:
NationsBank of Florida, Trustee

Mary E. Parker Foundation

P.O. Box 699
Bradenton, FL 34206
(941) 748-3666
Source Date: 12/95

Geographic Restrictions:
Primarily in FL.

To Whom:
Medical, nursing, and hospital care for the needy, assistance for the education and training of nurses and medical students in hospitals and medical schools, child abuse, animal welfare, care and training of guide dogs for the blind, wildlife, prevention, care, **research in heart and cancer disease**, oceanography, museums.

For What:
Endowment funds, general purposes, operating budgets.

Financial info:
Assets: $6,915,500.
Giving: $290,500 for 50 grants (high: $75,000; low: $500).

Application info:
Applications accepted. Application form required. Deadline is Nov. 15. Board meets in early Dec. Publishes application guidelines.

Directors, Officers, Trustees:
Blalock, Robert, Trustee
Parker, Mary E., Donor, Trustee
Pratt, Richard, Trustee
Wentzel, Willett E., M.D., Trustee
Wilmington Trust Company, Trustee
Young, Woodrow, Trustee

Mary Joanne Rand, Morris Rand & Michael Anthony Rand Memorial Charitable Foundation, Inc.

534 Bontana Ave.
Fort Lauderdale, FL 33301
Source Date: 12/94

Geographic Restrictions:
Limited to FL.

To Whom:
AIDS care and **AIDS research**.

Financial info:
Giving: $66,500 for grants.

Application info:
Applications accepted. Submit letter. No deadline.

Directors, Officers, Trustees:
Duffy, George, Fr., Director
Rand, Mary Joanne, Director, Officer
Rand, Morris M., Director, Officer

Stiefel Foundation for Dermatological Research, Inc.

c/o Bill Whitaker
255 Alhambra Cir., Suite 1000
Coral Gables, FL 33134-7412
(305) 443-3807
Source Date: 12/94

To Whom:
Medical research in dermatology.

For What:
Research.

Financial info:
Giving: $33,300 for 15 grants (high: $3,000; low: $50).

Application info:
Applications accepted. Submit letter. No deadline.

Directors, Officers, Trustees:
Steyer, Helen, Donor, Officer
Steyer, Stanley, Officer
Steyer, Thomas M., Donor, Officer

Joseph Weintraub Family Foundation, Inc.

200 S.E. First St., Suite 901
Miami, FL 33131
Source Date: 12/95

Geographic Restrictions:
Primarily in FL.

Restrictions:
No grants to individuals.

To Whom:
Higher education, social services, health associations, hospitals, **cancer research, heart research.**

Financial info:
Assets: $5,305,600.
Giving: $195,700 for 20 grants (high: $100,000; low: $100).

Application info:
Applications accepted. Submit letter. No deadline.

Directors, Officers, Trustees:
Beier, Thomas, Officer
Weintraub, Joseph, Donor
Weintraub, Michael, Officer

Arthur & Gullan Wellman Medical Research Trust

860 U. S. Hwy. One, Suite 210
North Palm Beach, FL 33408
Source Date: 12/94

To Whom:
Medical research.

Financial info:
Giving: $112,500 for grants.

Application info:
Applications accepted. Submit letter. No deadline.

Directors, Officers, Trustees:
Bullock, Marjorie W., Trustee
Stone, Alan F., Trustee
Wellman, Arthur O., Donor
Wellman, Gullan M., Trustee

Lillian S. Wells Foundation, Inc.

c/o Barbara W. Van Fleet, Pres.
P.O. Box 14338
Fort Lauderdale, FL 33302
(954) 462-8639
Source Date: 12/95

Geographic Restrictions:
Limited to Chicago, IL, Fort Lauderdale, FL, and the Garden County, NE, area.

To Whom:
Medical research, art education and appreciation.

For What:
Endowment funds, operating budgets, general purposes, **research**, scholarship funds.

Financial info:
Assets: $7,128,100.
Giving: $343,000 for 5 grants (high: $100,000; low: $3,000).

Application info:
Applications accepted. Submit letter. No deadline.

Directors, Officers, Trustees:
Malecek, Joseph E., Officer
Moulding, Mary B., Officer
Van Fleet, Barbara W., Donor, Officer
Wells, Preston A., Jr., Donor, Officer

Dr. Herbert A. Wertheim Foundation, Inc.

4470 S.W. 74th Ave.
Miami, FL 33155
(305) 264-4465
Source Date: 12/95

Geographic Restrictions:
Primarily in Miami, FL and Vail, CO.

Restrictions:
No grants to individuals.

To Whom:
Fine arts, public broadcasting, cultural programs, **medical research**, higher education, libraries, youth.

For What:
Research.

Financial info:
Assets: $4,515,900.
Giving: $208,000 for 20 grants (high: $50,000; low: $50).

Application info:
Applications accepted. Submit letter. No deadline.

Directors, Officers, Trustees:
Wertheim, Herbert A., Donor, Officer
Wertheim, Nicole J., Officer

Whitehall Foundation, Inc.

c/o Laurel T. Baker, Secretary
251 Royal Palm Way, Suite 211
Palm Beach, FL 33480
(561) 655-4474
Source Date: 9/96

Restrictions:
Applicant must have Ph.D. before applying. No grants for investigators who already have or expect to receive substantial support from other quarters, for the purchase of major items of permanent equipment, travel unless to unique field areas essential to the research, salary support, living expenses while working at home, travel to conferences or for consultation, or secretarial services. Grants-in-aid paid to assistant and/or senior professors. Research grants available to Ph.D.'s with established labs. Employee-related scholarships are awarded only through CPC International.

To Whom:
Research in the life sciences with emphasis on invertebrate and vertebrate (exclusive of human beings) neurophysiology. Specifically, investigations of neural mechanisms involved in sensory, motor, and other complex functions of the whole organism as these relate to behavior.

For What:
Research, seed money, technical assistance, special projects, equipment, publications, employee-related scholarships.

Financial info:
Assets: $54,467,700.
Giving: $2,489,000 for 65 grants (high: $50,000; low: $5,000) and $107,000 for grants to individuals.

Application info:
Applications accepted. Submit letter of intent (one page limit). Deadline is Jan. 15, Apr. 15, and Oct. 1. Deadline for full proposal is June 1, Sept. 1, and Feb. 15. Board holds three grant review sessions yearly. Publishes grants list and application guidelines.

Recent Grants:

$40,000	Cornell University. Central Nervous System Modulation of Reflex Pathways: three year grant totaling $120,000.
$39,000	Duke University. Influence of Early Motor Behavior on Tactile Processing by Neuronal Networks: three year grant totaling $117,000
$35,000	Eastern Virginia Medical School. Developmental Aspects of Pb2+ Neurotoxicity: three year grant totaling $91,000.
$35,000	Albert Einstein College. Positional Markers in the Mammalian Nervous System: three year grant totaling $109,000.
$40,000	Emory University. Oxytocin and the Neurobiology of Social Attachment: three year grant totaling $120,000.
$40,000	Emory University. Identification of Neurons Important for Male Copulation: three year grant totaling $124,000.
$40,000	Harvard Medical School. Mechanisms of Neuronal Injury and Neuroprotection in Limbic Seizures Induced by Kainate: three year grant totaling $120,000.
$39,000	Harvard Medical School. Transcriptional regulation of Forebrain-specific Gene Expression by Homeodomain Proteins: three year grant totaling $113,000.
$40,000	Hebrew University. Brainstem Mechanisms of Alertness: one year grant totaling $40,000.
$40,000	Johns Hopkins University. Molecular Mechanisms of Growth Cone Guidance: Semaphorin Function During Neurodevelopment: three year grant totaling $120,000.
$15,000	University Of Kansas. GRANT-IN-AID: Neurokinin Receptor Function During Nociception.
$26,000	Kenyon College. Central Processing of Gustatory Information in Larval Manduca sexta: three year grant totaling $79,000.
$40,000	Louisiana State University. RENEWAL: Functional Organization of Olfactory Bulb Circuits: two year grant renewal totaling $80,000: total project support: $223,130.
$39,000	Massachusetts Institute Of Technology. Neural Basis of Prospective Memory: three year grant totaling $90,000.
$27,000	University Of Massachusetts. The Role of Trophic Factors in the Generation of Neural Sex Differences: three year grant totaling $92,000.
$40,000	University Of Massachusetts. Cerebral Integration in the Primate Visual System: The Functional Significance of "Back-Projecting" Pathways: three year grant totaling $120,000.
$23,000	Massey University. In Vitro Studies on Neuronal Cell Death: three year grant totaling $87,000: final payment September 1997.

$34,000 McGill University. Auditory Receptors of Crickets: Physiology, Anatomy and Connectivity: three year grant totaling $102,000.

$40,000 University Of Minnesota. Characterization of a Mouse Immunoglobulin G-like Epitope Expressed by Behaviorally Important Identified Neurons in Invertebrates: three year grant totaling $120,000.

$40,000 University Of Missouri-St. Louis. Locating the Respiratory Rhythm Generator in the Brainstem of Larval Lampreys: two year grant totaling $80,000.

$25,000 University Of Nebraska. The Mechanism of Neural Tube Formation and Neural Tube Defects: two year grant totaling $50,000.

$35,000 New Mexico State University. Sensory Transduction in the Xenopus Internal Ear: three year grant totaling $105,000.

$35,000 New York University. Serotonin Brain Rhythms and the Chemistry of Memory: three year grant totaling $105,000.

$38,000 New York University. Role of Parietal Cortex in Attention and Saccade Preparation: three year grant totaling $113,000.

$40,000 New York University. Dissection of Short-term Memory Phase in Drosophila: two year grant totaling $82,000.

$16,000 North Dakota State University. In vitro Effects of Steroids on Oxytocin Release and Receptors: three year grant totaling $48,000.

$35,000 Northeastern University. Electrophysiology of Display Mononeurons in the Siamese Fighting Fish: three year grant totaling $108,000.

$31,000 University Of Notre Dame. Navigation in Bees: Cognitive Maps or Dead Reckoning: three year grant totaling $84,000.

$40,000 Ohio State University. D1-D2 Mediation of Striatal Efferents: Age-Dependent Plasticity Following Early Dopamine Depletions: three year grant totaling $120,000.

$33,000 Oregon State University. Neural Mechanisms of Pheromonally Mediated Reproductive Behavior: three year grant totaling $102,000.

$37,000 University Of Ottawa. Molecular Basis of Synaptic Transmission: Isolation of Components of the Secretory Machinery in Neurons: three year grant totaling $110,000.

$25,000 University Of Pennsylvania. The Relationship Between Neural Activity and Synaptic Plasticity in the Developing Nervous System: three year grant totaling $75,000.

$29,000 Queen's University. Sensorimotor Integration Underlying Avoidance Maneuvers in Flying Locusts: three year grant totaling $93,000.

$40,000 Rutgers University. RENEWAL: Interneuronal Networks in the Hippocampus: two year renewal grant totaling $80,000.

$40,000 Rutgers University. Imaging of Intracellular Activity in the Behaving Rat: two year grant totaling $80,000.

$14,000 Rutgers University. GRANT-IN-AID: Social and Acoustic Determinant of Vocal Development.

$39,000 San Diego State University. Olfactory Transduction in Drosophila melanogaster: three year grant totaling $116,000.

$10,000 Southwestern Louisiana State. Regulation of Cardiac Contractility in Bivalves by FMR Famide: three year grant totaling $32,000.

$16,000 University Of Texas. Top-Down Cortical Influences Upon Primary Sensory Processing: three year grant totaling $60,000.

$40,000 University Of Texas. Regulation of Brain Adrenergic Systems in Stress: three year grant totaling $120,000.

$39,000 Texas Tech University. The Biochemical and Cellular Basis of AMPA Receptor-induced Apoptosis of Cerebellar Purkinje Cells: three year grant totaling $116,000.

$38,000 University Of Toronto. The Role of the Cingulate Cortex in Pain Perception: A Functional Magnetic Resonance Imaging Study: three year grant totaling $111,000.

$15,000 University Of Toronto. GRANT-IN-AID: Search for a Possible FR-1 Homologue in C. elegans: Towards "Knockout" Worms.

$35,000 Tufts University. Second Messengers in an Insect Nervous System: Modulation of Motor Function: three year grant totaling $105,000.

$40,000 Virginia Commonwealth University. Cortical Regulation of Information Transfer in Visual Thalamus: three year grant totaling $119,000.

$40,000	Wayne State University. Control of the Development of Neural Patterns: three year grant totaling $120,000.
$39,000	Wellesley College. Sexual Dimorphism in Cortical Structure and Cognitive Function: three year grant totaling $119,000.
$43,000	Whitehead Institute. Neurogenesis in the Zebrafish, Danio: three year grant totaling $122,000.
$15,000	University Of Wisconsin. GRANT IN AID: The Functional Significance of Dopamine and Opiate Interactions in Mesolimbic Structures.
$50,000	Yale University. Higher Order Visual Contour Processing in Area V2 of the Primate: three year grant totaling $150,000.

Directors, Officers, Trustees:
Adams, Warren S., II, Trustee
Baker, Laurel T., Trustee
Beall, Kenneth S., Jr., Trustee
Brooks, Helen M., Trustee
Burger, Van Vetchen, Trustee
Dawes, Michael V., Trustee
Gibbons-Neff, Peter, Officer, Trustee
Moffett, George M. (d), Donor
Moffett, George M., II, Officer, Trustee
Rumbough, J. Wright, Jr., Officer, Trustee
Rumbough, Melissa M., Trustee

Whitehead Charitable Foundation

1001 North U. S. Hwy. 1, Suite 800
Jupiter, FL 33477
Source Date: 12/95

To Whom:
Biomedical research.

For What:
Endowment funds, **research.**

Financial info:
Assets: $8,941,400.
Giving: $1,367,000 for 10 grants (high: $1,000,000; low: $3,000).

Application info:
Applications accepted. Submit letter. No deadline.

Directors, Officers, Trustees:
Brill, Arthur W., Officer
Whitehead, Edwin C. (d), Donor
Whitehead, John J., Director, Officer
Whitehead, Peter J., Director, Officer
Whitehead, Susan, Director

Georgia

Georgia Health Foundation, Inc.

57 Executive Park, Suite 315
Atlanta, GA 30329
(404) 636-2525
Source Date: 12/94

Geographic Restrictions:
Primarily in GA.

To Whom:
Medical education, health associations, health, **medical research**, family planning.

For What:
Operating budgets, general purposes, equipment, seed money, **research**, special projects.

Financial info:
Giving: $288,500 for 15 grants (high: $50,000; low: $5,000).

Application info:
Applications accepted. Submit one page letter between Jan. 1 and May 1. Deadline for full proposal is Aug. 1. Publishes application guidelines.

Directors, Officers, Trustees:
Borek, John, Director, Officer
Cornelius, Henry D., Director, Officer
Elmer, Richard A., M.D., Director
Georgia Medical Plan, Donor
Gotlieb, Jaquelin, M.D., Director, Officer
Haverty, J. Rhodes, M.D., Director
Levison, S. Jarvin, Director
Maudlin, John T., M.D., Director
Posey, France, Director
Zwald, Robert, Director, Officer

Georgia Power Foundation, Inc.

333 Piedmont Ave., N.E., 20th Flr.
Atlanta, GA 30308
(404) 526-6784
Source Date: 12/96

Geographic Restrictions:
Primarily in GA.

Restrictions:
No grants to individuals.

To Whom:
Seniors, AIDS, cancer, community development, race relations, education, family services, health, homeless, rehabilitation, human rights, leadership development, legal services, libraries, **medical research**, museums, performing arts, theater, historic preservation, environmental conservation, social services, youth, civic affairs, arts, women, handicapped, minorities, fine arts.

For What:
Annual campaigns, building funds, capital campaigns, conferences and seminars, endowment funds, equipment, operating budgets, renovation projects, **research**, scholarship funds, seed money, special projects, deficit financing.

Financial info:
Assets: $65,000,000.
Giving: $6,000,000 for 700 grants (high: $150,000; low: $200).

Application info:
Applications accepted. Submit brief letter. No deadline. Board meets the 1st week of each month. Publishes application guidelines.

Directors, Officers, Trustees:
Anderson, Judy M., Director, Officer
Blalock, Rebecca A., Exec.Director
Boyer, R. L., Director
Dahlke, Wayne T., Director
Davis, James K., Director
Evans, Dwight H., Director
Georgia Power Company, Donor
Haubein, Robert H., Director
Hodges, Gene R., Director
Jobe, Warren Y., Director, Officer

Dennis C. Hayes Foundation, Inc.

750 Hammond Dr., Bldg. 17
Atlanta, GA 30328-5502

Application address:
c/o Hayes Microcomputer
P.O. Box 105203
Atlanta, GA 30348
(404) 449-8791
Source Date: 12/94

Geographic Restrictions:
Primarily in GA.

Restrictions:
No grants to individuals or scholarships.

To Whom:
Museums, hospitals, education, **medical research**, science and technology.

For What:
Research, building funds.

Financial info:
Giving: $65,000 for 5 grants (high: $50,000; low: $5,000).

Application info:
Applications accepted. Submit letter. No deadline.

Directors, Officers, Trustees:
Harlin, Robert R., Director
Hobby, Scott M., Director
Marzetti, Philip J., Director

Carlos & Marguerite Mason Fund

c/o Wachovia Charitable Funds Management
Attn: Kay McMaster, Asst. VP
191 Peachtree St., NE
Atlanta, GA 30303
(404) 332-5106
Source Date: 12/95

Geographic Restrictions:
Limited to GA.

Restrictions:
No grants to individuals.

To Whom:
Organ transplants and related medical research.

For What:
Building funds, equipment, renovation projects, **research**, seed money, special projects.

Financial info:
Assets: $49,600,800.
Giving: $2,960,000 for 30 grants (high: $500,000; low: $15,000).

Application info:
Applications accepted. Telephone to request meeting. Deadline is Aug. 1. Board meets in Dec.

Directors, Officers, Trustees:
Mason, Marguerite F., Donor
Wachovia Bank of Georgia, Trustee

Savannah Foundation

(Formerly The South Atlantic Foundation, Inc.)
c/o William W. Byram, Jr., Dir.
428 Bull St.
Savannah, GA 31401
(912) 238-3288
Source Date: 12/96

Geographic Restrictions:
Primarily in Savannah, GA.

Restrictions:
No grants to individuals, continuing support, deficit financing, foundation managed projects, matching or challenge grants, program-related investments, operating support, or endowment funding.

To Whom:
Focus area for 1997 is Literacy. Social services, welfare, religion, health, **medical research**, education, cultural programs.

Education (42% of funding), Social Services (21% of funding), Civic Affairs (16% of funding), Religion (12% of funding), Health (3% of funding), Art (6% of funding).

For What:
Building funds, conferences and seminars, emergency funds, employee-related scholarships, equipment, land acquisition, professorships, program-related investments, publications, renovation projects, seed money.

Financial info:
Assets: $3,533,100.
Giving: $729,200 for 225 grants (high: $20,000; low: $100).

Application info:
Applications accepted. Application form required. Call for deadline. Board meets in Jan., Apr., July, and Oct. Publishes annual report with application guidelines.

Recent Grants:

$5,000	Lucas Theatre for the Arts
$5,000	The Savannah Symphony, Inc.
$7,000	Arts Ashore, Inc.
$3,000	Ballet South
$15,000	City of Savannah-Olympic Cauldron
$2,500	Professional Reach-Out Program

Directors, Officers, Trustees:
Anderson, Frank T., Officer, Trustee
Baxter, Lewis D., Director
Critz, Dale C., Jr., Trustee
Edel, Julius, Trustee
Gongaware, Robert D., Mrs., Trustee
Kemp, Michael F., Trustee
Morrison, Mills Lane, Trustee
Morse, John, Trustee
Seymour, William, III, Trustee
Simpson, K. Russell, Trustee
Traynor, Michael C., Trustee
Wasden, Wiley A., III, Officer, Trustee
Williams, Richard, Mrs., Officer, Trustee
Young, David A., Trustee
Zoller, Michael, Mrs., Officer, Trustee

UPS Foundation

c/o Gary Lee, Exec. Dir.
55 Glenlake Pkwy, N.E.
Atlanta, GA 30328
(404) 828-6374
Source Date: 12/96

Geographic Restrictions:
Health Care is no longer a focus for the foundation.

Restrictions:
No grants to individuals (except for employee-related scholarships), building funding, operating funds, or religious purposes.

To Whom:
Human welfare in the U.S., including families and children in crisis, adult literacy, food distribution to the hungry, economic opportunity for minorities, disabled, community development, **medical research**, improved health care, higher education, including academic, public policy, and transportation/logistics research. Education (40% of funding), Social Services (35% of funding).

For What:
Continuing support, seed money, equipment, matching funds, employee matching gifts, professorships, internships, scholarship funds, employee-related scholarships, fellowships, special projects, research, general purposes.

Financial info:
Assets: $62,267,400.
Giving: $17,459,100 for 395 grants (high: $500,000; low: $5,000).

Application info:
Applications accepted. Submit letter (2 page limit) submitted Jan. through Aug. Board meets in June and Nov. Publishes annual report with application guidelines.

Directors, Officers, Trustees:
Clanin, Robert J., Officer
Fisher, Don, Trustee
Kelly, John J., Trustee
Lee, Gary, Exec.Director
Nelson, Kent C., Officer, Trustee
Tyler, Calvin E., Jr., Officer, Trustee
UPS, Inc., Donor
Yard, Bud, Trustee

Illinois

Abbott Laboratories Fund

c/o Cindy Schwab, VP
Dept. 379, Bldg. AP14C
100 Abbott Park Rd.
Abbott Park, IL 60064-3500
(847) 937-7075
EIN: 366069793
Source Date: 12/96

Geographic Restrictions:
Primarily in areas of company operations.

Restrictions:
No grants for social organizations, religious institutions, political activities, fundraising events, individuals, annual campaigns.

To Whom:
Higher, secondary, and elementary education, medicine, pharmacy, nutrition, nursing, and **medical research in physical and biological sciences**, health and welfare, disadvantaged youth, seniors, improve the socioeconomic status of women, minorities, immigrant population groups, arts and cultural programs, civic affairs for administration of justice, public service and social policy.
Health and Welfare (47% of funding), Education (22% of funding), Culture and Arts (10% of funding), Civic, Environment (6% of funding), Matching grants (15% of funding).

For What:
Operating budgets, continuing support, scholarship funds, **research**, employee matching gifts.

Financial info:
Assets: $48,448,400 (from 1993 990PF).
Giving: $8,900,000 for 5,410 grants.

Application info:
Applications accepted. Submit letter or proposal. No deadline. Board meets in Apr. and Dec. Publishes application guidelines.

Directors, Officers, Trustees:
Abbott Laboratories, Donor
Beck, Robert N., Director
Coughlan, Gary P., Director
Farmer, Kenneth W., Director, Officer
Roge, Paul E., Officer
Schwab, Cindy, Officer
Stasiek, Carol, Officer

Baxter Allegiance Foundation

c/o Patricia A. Morgan, Exec. Dir.
1 Baxter Pkwy.
Deerfield, IL 60015
(847) 948-4605
EIN: 363159396
Source Date: 12/95

Geographic Restrictions:
Nationally [U.S.] for health care organizations which address a broad national or regional need.

Restrictions:
No grants for religious, fraternal or veterans organizations, disease-specific organizations, capital and endowment campaigns, hospitals, educational institutions except where grant supports a health care goal, individuals, fundraising events.

To Whom:
Health Care (61% of funding): increasing access to health care services, small projects designed to act as models, immediate needs with emphasis on preventive or educational components, resources to help hospital managers and medical personnel become more effective. Prize programs include the Foster G. McGraw Prize, **the Baxter Health Services Research Award**, the Baxter International Faculty Fellowships, the Baxter Fellowships for Innovation in Health Care Management, and the Baxter Foundation Episteme award.
Civic (4% of funding), Culture (3% of funding), Education (19% of funding), and Social Service (13% of funding).

For What:
Employee matching gifts, employee-related scholarships, special projects, seed money.

Financial info:
Assets: $11,637,000 (from 1994 990PF).
Giving: $3,368,100 for 245 grants (high: $250,000; low: $100).

Application info:
Applications accepted. Submit proposal. No deadline. Board meets in Jan., Apr., July, Oct., and Dec. Publishes annual report with application guidelines.

Recent Grants:

$2,000	Adler Planetarium. Chicago, IL. General support.
$7,500	Art Institute of Chicago. Chicago, IL. General support.
$22,500	Association of University Programs in Health Administration. Arlington, VA. Baxter Health Services Research Prize.

$5,000	Association of American Medical Colleges. Washington. DC. Award for Distinguished Research.
$327,190	Citizens Scholarship Foundation of America, Inc., St. Peter, MN. Baxter Foundation Scholarship program.
$100,000	Commercial Club Foundation. Chicago, IL. General support.

Directors, Officers, Trustees:

American Hospital Supply Corp., Donor
Anderson, Timothy B., Director
Baxter Travenol Laboratories, Inc., Donor
Damico, Joseph F., Director
Graham, William B., Director, Officer
Lucas, Wilfred J., Director
May, Karen J., Director, Officer
Morgan, Patricia A., Officer
Mulligan, Terrence J., Director
Staubitz, Arthur F., Director, Officer
White, Tony L., Director

Blowitz-Ridgeway Foundation

c/o Robert N. DiLeonardi, Admin.
1 Northfield Plaza, Suite 230
Northfield, IL 60093-1213
(847) 446-1010
Internet: http://fdncenter.org/grantmaker/blowitz/index.html
EIN: 362488355
Source Date: 9/96

Geographic Restrictions:
Primarily in IL.

Restrictions:
No grants for government agencies, organizations which subsist mainly on 3rd-party funding, operating budgets, continuing support, religious or political purposes, writing or production of audio-visual materials, or individuals.

To Whom:
Medical, psychiatric, psychological and/or residential care of individuals who lack sufficient resources to provide for themselves, **research programs in medicine**, psychology, social science, mental health, and education.

For What:
Research, special projects, capital campaigns, continuing support.

Financial info:
Assets: $21,921,300.
Giving: $908,600 for 50 grants (high: $50,000; low: $5,000).

Application info:
Applications accepted. Application form required (5 copies). Deadline is Oct. 1, Feb. 1, and June 1. Board meets in Jan. 2, May 1, and Sept. 1. Publishes application guidelines.

Recent Grants:

$10,000	Aidscare, Inc. Towards the provision of food, clothing and shelter for indigent persons with AIDS.
$5,000	American Lung Association Of Metropolitan Chicago For support of its CAMP ACTION program of education and recreation for severely asthmatic children.
$15,000	Better Existence With HIV. In support of its direct service and education programming for persons with HIV/AIDS and their families.
$7,500	Chicago Area Chapter, Alzheimer's Association. To help fund its Support Group Network for families of persons with Alzheimer's.
$39,000	Chicago House. For support of nursing costs at its 24-hour care hospice program for persons with AIDS.
$10,000	EHS Bethany Hospital. For health screening and immunizations for children on Chicago's west side.
$2,000	Grantmakers In Health. General operating support.
$5,000	Heartland Community Health Clinic. To provide no-charge medications to medically underserved families in Peoria, Illinois.
$5,000	Horizons Community Services. In support of its awareness programs to help youth remain HIV negative.
$200,000	Illinois Facilities Fund. Capital needs of two healthcare agencies (PRI).
$20,000	Illinois Primary Health Care Association. For continued support of the Physician Referral and Linkage Project, which seeks to improve continuity of care for Chicago's medically indigent.
$10,000	Jayne Shover Easter Seal. To fund a Volunteer Coordinator position.
$50,000	Arthritis Foundation, Greater Chicago Chapter. To fund research to learn more about the cause and treatment of Adult-Onset Still's Disease.
$25,000	Massachusetts General Hospital. For research to examine the role of oxidative injury in the pathogenesis of Parkinson's Disease.

$40,000	National Organization For Rare Disorders. To fund clinical research on new treatments for rare disorders.
$28,000	Rush-Presbyterian-St. Luke's Medical Center. For research into the cultivation of cells which could be raised in the laboratory to provide a continuous source of tissue for transplantation into patients with Parkinson's Disease.
$31,831	University of California, San Diego. For research and analysis of mitochondrial DNA as it relates to Parkinson's Disease.
$20,900	University of Michigan. Comprehensive Cancer Center For research into means of targeting and killing testosterone-resistant prostate cancer.
$60,000	University of Wisconsin Medical School. For DNR-related research to aid in developing a therapeutic drug to prevent progression of prostate cancer.
$3,500	ARTS Unlimited. To provide cultural arts presentations and performances to those confined to nursing homes and institutions.
$5,000	Big Brothers/Big Sisters of Lake County. In support of initiative to recruit additional volunteers to match with at-risk children & youth.
$5,000	Big Brothers/Big Sisters of Metropolitan Chicago. Towards salary support for a professional case manager for its clients.
$7,500	Casa Lake County. To expand the Court-Appointed Special Advocate program for abused and neglected children in Lake County.
$7,000	The Center Of Concern. For its inter-generational program, which matches senior citizen clients with school-age pen-pals.
$7,500	Chicago Area Alternative Education League. To expand its program of sports- and recreation-based programs for behavior disordered and emotionally disturbed teens.
$7,000	Chicago Coalition For The Homeless. In support of its Homeless Youth Empowerment project.
$25,000	Child Abuse Prevention Services. Towards implementation Of its From Day One prenatal child abuse and neglect prevention program.
$16,800	Community Crisis Center. For treatment and support of abused women and their children.
$1,500	The Foundation Center. For general operating support of its information services for grantseekers.
$12,333	H.O.M.E. For support of its moving service and furniture distribution programs for low-income elderly.
$6,750	St. Gregory College Preparatory School. Towards scholarship fund.
$10,000	Science And Arts Academy. To allow four economically limited, gifted students to attend its school.
$5,000	Uptown Center Hull House. For continued support of its Grandma, Please program of telephone support (provided by senior citizen volunteers) for latchkey children.
$22,333	Lake County Council Against Sexual Assault. For its program of comprehensive services for abused children.
$15,000	The Night Ministry. For continued support of its Open Door youth emergency shelter.
$5,500	Peacock Camp. For support of its tuition-free summer camp program for physically disabled children.
$20,000	Rainbow House. To fund a Health Advocate staff position, to address in a comprehensive manner the health needs of women and children in its shelter.
$5,000	Recording for the Blind. To provide visually impaired, special education children in Chicago public schools with recorded textbooks.
$7,000	Rehabilitation Institute of Chicago. For support of its Pediatric free Care program of rehabilitation and treatment for disabled and severely injured children.
$10,000	St. Anthony Hospital. To help pay for laboratory costs associated with providing annual community health screenings to inner city residents.
$12,334	Suburban Primary Health Care Council. Towards health care access program for medically indigent residents of suburban Cook County.
$25,000	UCC South Side Health Project. For support of its Teens Interested in Positive Solutions program of peer counseling, mentorship and pregnancy prevention.
$16,667	University of Illinois-Chicago Craniofacial Center. Towards construction of a psychology suite.
$7,500	Girl Scouts Of Chicago. Towards its Shelter Troop program for homeless girls.

$5,000	Life Span. Towards its program of counseling and comprehensive services for children of battered women.
$5,000	R.E.S.T. For its programs serving the homeless in Chicago's uptown neighborhood.
$9,000	Northwest Institute for Medical Research. To support research into the action of cord blood and amniotic fluid in the development of certain carcinomas.
$28,404	North Side Community Health Resource Facility. For staff salaries and related service provision at this free to low-cost clinic for the impoverished and uninsured.
$10,000	Shelter Of God's Love. For salary support for administrative position at this agency providing housing for the disabled and elderly.
$17,500	National Lekotek Center. Towards a new program to help ensure easy access to the information superhighway for children with special needs and their families.

Directors, Officers, Trustees:

Collison, Arthur R., Trustee
Dean, Anthony M., Officer, Trustee
Jackson, James W., Rev., Officer, Trustee
Kline, Daniel L., Officer, Trustee
Lanigan, Joanne L., Officer, Trustee
LeBreton, Pierre R., Ph.D., Trustee
MacAlister, Patricia A., Trustee
Pastin, Max, Officer, Trustee
Pitluk, Marvin J., Ph.D., Trustee
Winston, Samuel G., Trustee

Charles H. & Bertha L. Boothroyd Foundation

c/o Lorraine Marcus, Secretary
120 W. Madison St., Suite 14-L
Chicago, IL 60602
(312) 346-8333
EIN: 366047045
Source Date: 6/94

Geographic Restrictions:
Primarily in IL.

To Whom:
Medical schools for research on Parkinson's disease, hospitals, higher education, social services, cultural programs.

For What:
Scholarship funds, **research**, continuing support, general purposes, operating budgets, special projects.

Financial info:
Assets: $3,421,900.
Giving: $214,000 for 25 grants (high: $20,000; low: $1,000).

Application info:
Applications accepted. Submit letter. No deadline. Board meets in June.

Directors, Officers, Trustees:

Alcock, Gudrun, Officer, Trustee
Gancer, Donald C., Officer, Trustee
Kaufman, Thomas C., Officer, Trustee
Marcus, Lorraine, Officer, Trustee
McAvoy Trust, Agnes K., Donor
Palzkill, Mary T. (d), Donor

Butz Foundation

c/o The Northern Trust Company
Attn: Tom Boyden, Admin.
50 S. La Salle St.
Chicago, IL 60675
(312) 630-6000
EIN: 366008818
Source Date: 12/92

Geographic Restrictions:
Primarily in IL.

Restrictions:
No grants to individuals.

To Whom:
Medical research, higher and secondary education, disabled, religion, hospitals.

For What:
Operating budgets, continuing support, equipment, **research**.

Financial info:
Assets: $3,012,700.
Giving: $130,300 for 25 grants (high: $10,000; low: $250).

Application info:
Applications accepted. Submit letter. Deadline is Oct. 1. Board meets quarterly.

Directors, Officers, Trustees:
Butz, Barbara, Director, Officer
Butz, Elvira M., Director
Butz, Robert B., Director, Officer
Butz, Theodore C. (d), Donor
Butz, Theodore H., Director, Officer
Butz, Thompson H., II, Director, Officer
Dover, Vera, Officer
James, Jean Butz, Donor, Director

Coleman Foundation, Inc.

(Formerly The Coleman/Fannie May Candies Foundation, Inc.)
c/o John E. Hughes, Exec. Dir.
575 W. Madison, Suite 4605-II
Chicago, IL 60661
(312) 902-7120
EIN: 363025967
Source Date: 12/95

Geographic Restrictions:
Primarily in the Chicago, IL, area and some support in Midwest U.S.

Restrictions:
No grants to individuals, deficit financing, or ticket purchases.

To Whom:
Social services, housing, civic affairs, elementary, secondary, entrepreneurial, and other education, **medical sciences, hospitals, cancer research and treatment, scientific research**, rehabilitation, handicapped.

For What:
Operating budgets, general purposes, special projects, **research**, conferences and seminars, building funds, equipment, land acquisition, professorships, internships, scholarship funds, fellowships, capital campaigns, renovation projects, endowment funds, emergency funds, continuing support, matching funds, program-related investments.

Financial info:
Assets: $91,776,700.
Giving: $1,227,500 for 45 grants (high: $400,000; low: $250).

Application info:
Applications accepted. Submit letter. Submit proposal only at the request of the foundation. Deadline is Sept. 30 for full proposals. Publishes annual report with application guidelines.

Directors, Officers, Trustees:
Albers, C. Hugh, Director
Coleman, Dorothy W. (d), Donor
Coleman, J. D. Stetson (d), Donor
Davies, Trevor C., Director, Officer
Furlong, R. Michael, Director
Hennessy, Michael W., Director, Officer
Hughes, John E., Director, Officer
Jones, James H., Director
Peritz, Richard M., Director

Dr. Ralph & Marian Falk Medical Research Trust

c/o Bank of America
Attn: M. Catherine Ryan
231 S. LaSalle St.
Chicago, IL 60697
(312) 828-2345
EIN: 366975534
Source Date: 11/93

Geographic Restrictions:
Primarily in U.S. with emphasis on IL.

Restrictions:
No grants to individuals.

To Whom:
Medical research.

Financial info:
Assets: $93,645,000.
Giving: $3,200,000 for 10 grants (high: $1,000,000; low: $100,000).

Application info:
Applications accepted. Submit letter. No deadline.

Directors, Officers, Trustees:
Bank of America Illinois, Trustee,
Falk Trust, Marian Citron, Donor

Max Goldenberg Foundation

c/o Harris Trust & Savings Bank
111 W. Monroe St., Trust Dept.
Chicago, IL 60603
(312) 461-2613
EIN: 362471625
Source Date: 12/95

Geographic Restrictions:
Primarily in IL.

To Whom:
Medical research in areas of cancer, heart disease, multiple sclerosis, and eye disorders, hospitals, higher education, social services, with emphasis on Jewish welfare.

Financial info:
Assets: $4,951,500.
Giving: $162,000 for 30 grants (high: $10,000; low: $1,000).

Application info:
Applications accepted. Submit proposal (3 copies). Deadline is Aug. 31. Board meets in Oct.

Directors, Officers, Trustees:
Goldenberg, Max (d), Donor
Goodman, Marion, Trustee
Harris Trust & Savings Bank, Trustee

Harris Foundation

c/o Irving B. Harris, Chairman
2 N. LaSalle St., Suite 605
Chicago, IL 60602-3703
(312) 621-0566
EIN: 366055115
Source Date: 12/94

Restrictions:
No grants to individuals, continuing support, emergency or endowment funding, deficit financing, land acquisition, renovations, scholarships, or fellowships.

To Whom:
Demonstration and research programs in prevention of family dysfunction, prevention of teenage pregnancy, infant mortality and morbidity, infant mental health and early childhood development, Jewish giving, arts, educational broadcasting.

For What:
Annual campaigns, seed money, special projects, **research,** publications, conferences and seminars, general purposes, operating budgets, scholarship funds.

Financial info:
Assets: $27,646,000.
Giving: $2,422,800 for 425 grants (high: $150,000; low: $100).

Application info:
Applications accepted. Submit letter. No deadline. Deadline for arts and arts education proposals is Apr. 1 and Sept. 1. Board meets semiannually.

Directors, Officers, Trustees:
Barrows, Sidney, Officer
Harris, Irving B., Officer, Trustee
Harris, Joan W., Officer, Trustee
Harris, William W., Officer, Trustee
Meyer, Daniel, Trustee
Wolff, Benno F., Officer, Trustee

Harris Family Foundation

c/o Neison Harrison, Pres.
P.O. Box 2279
Northbrook, IL 60065-2279
(847) 498-1261
EIN: 366054378
Source Date: 12/96

Geographic Restrictions:
Primarily in Chicago, IL, area.

Restrictions:
No grants to individuals.

To Whom:
Medical research, family services, family planning, mental health, health, rehabilitation, social services, child development, early childhood, secondary, higher and other education, Jewish giving, race relations, cultural programs.

For What:
General purposes, building funds, annual campaigns, internships.

Financial info:
Assets: $13,208,100 (from 1993 990PF).
Giving: $1,404,400 for 135 grants (high: $500,000; low: $50).

Application info:
Applications accepted. Submit letter. No deadline. Board meets in May and Nov.

Directors, Officers, Trustees:
Harris, Bette D., Director, Officer
Harris, Katherine, Director
Harris, King W., Director
Harris, Neison, Donor, Director, Officer
Paul, Toni H., Director

Grover Hermann Foundation

c/o Schiff, Hardin & Waite
7200 Sears Tower
Chicago, IL 60606
(312) 876-1000

Application address for Monterey County, CA, programs:
P.O. Box 596
Pebble Beach, CA 93953
EIN: 366064489
Source Date: 12/95

Geographic Restrictions:
Limited to Chicago, IL, and Monterey County, CA [northern], for social services and community development. Other programs funded nationwide [U.S.].

Restrictions:
No grants for fraternal, political, athletic, or foreign organizations, individuals, operating funds, except for national health organizations.

To Whom:
Higher education, limited support for elementary and secondary education. Preference is private higher education.

Health: Hospitals, **basic medical research, disease specific organizations.**

Public Policy: strengthen and improve our governmental and economic systems.

Community: community development, libraries, youth, seniors, disadvantaged, cultural programs.

Religion.

For What:
Renovation projects, equipment, building funds, seed money, endowment funds, annual campaigns, scholarship funds, special projects, general purposes.

Financial info:
Assets: $4,005,100.
Giving: $730,500 for 135 grants (high: $350,000, low: $1,000).

Application info:
Applications accepted. Submit letter. No deadline. Board meets quarterly. Publishes application guidelines.

Directors, Officers, Trustees:
Hermann, Grover M., Donor
Hermann, Sarah T., Director, Officer
Rhoads, Paul K., Director, Officer
Thurmond, Harriet R., Director, Office

A. D. Johnson Foundation

1 N. LaSalle St., Suite 3000
Chicago, IL 60602
(312) 782-7320
EIN: 366124270
Source Date: 12/92

Geographic Restrictions:
Primarily in IL and FL.

Restrictions:
No grants to individuals.

To Whom:
Medical research, hospitals, education, child welfare, hospice, arts, social services, youth.

For What:
General purposes, **research**, endowment funds, building funds.

Financial info:
Assets: $2,345,700.
Giving: $145,000 for 20 grants (high: $25,000; low: $2,000).

Application info:
Applications accepted. Submit letter. No deadline.

Directors, Officers, Trustees:
Johnson, A. D. (d), Donor
Johnson, Diane T., Officer
Johnson, Wayne J., Officer

L. C. Klenk Charitable Foundation

P.O. Box 584
Glen Ellyn, IL 60138
EIN: 752192617
Source Date: 12/92

Geographic Restrictions:
Primarily in TX, IL, and MI.

To Whom:
Lutheran religion, hospitals, **medical research**.

For What:
General purposes, equipment, **research**.

Financial info:
Assets: $2,137,000.
Giving: $116,100 for 15 grants (high: $15,000; low: $2,000).

Application info:
Applications accepted. Application form required. No deadline.

Directors, Officers, Trustees:
JMK International, Donor
Klenk, Ardena L., Officer
Klenk, Don L., Officer
Klenk, Lester C. (d), Donor
Phillips, Edward J., Officer
Pope, Elaine Klenk, Officer

Suzan R. Mackler Fund

135 S. LaSalle St., Suite 2011
Chicago, IL 60603
EIN: 366049232
Source Date: 12/95

To Whom:
Jewish giving, performing arts, **medical research**, higher education, general charitable giving.

For What:
General purposes, **research**.

Financial info:
Giving: $25,000 for 15 grants (high: $15,000; low: $50).

Application info:
Applications accepted. Submit proposal. No deadline.

Directors, Officers, Trustees:
Becker, Robert H., Director, Officer
Head, Murdock, Director, Officer
Mackler, Suzan R., Director, Officer
Rothschild, A. Frank, Director, Officer

Memorial Medical Center Foundation

c/o Cary Colwell, Exec. Dir.
1 Memorial Plaza
Springfield, IL 62781-0001
(217) 788-4700
Source Date: 12/96

Geographic Restrictions:
Primarily in Springfield, IL, area.

To Whom:
Develop and maintain a high quality, fully integrated health system managing the full range of health related services.

Contain the costs of health services through operational improvements and application of cost saving technology.

Maintain a highly skilled, well trained staff and a modern physical facility with advanced equipment and technology.

Support research and education leading to improvement of health services.

Application info:
Applications accepted. Application form required. Deadline is Apr. 30. Publishes application guidelines.

Recent Grants:
- MMC Regional Cancer Center - for a free Colon Cancer Screening program to be offered to the community.
- SIU Division of Urology - for the development of a Continence Center in Central Illinois.
- SIU Diabetes Outreach Program - SAVE (Salvage All Viable Extremities Foot Clinic) - for the education and prevention of foot ulcers.
- HealthFirst Community Clinic - for clinic expansion and medication for patients.
- Chatham Fire Department - to assist with the purchase of an automatic external heart defibrillator.
- New Berlin Emergency Services, Inc. - to assist with the purchase of a semi-automatic external heart defibrillator.

Healing the Children - to underwrite the expenses of sending a team of local surgeons and MMC staff abroad to provide surgery for pediatric patients in Central and South America.
MMC Educational Resources - to provide computer training classroom multimedia upgrade for nursing staff personnel.
MMC 2B Pulmonary Rehabilitation & Enterostomal Therapy - for pre-printed materials, models, videos, etc. in Patient Education Center.
Memorial Child Care - for purchase of computer, monitor/screen, printer, and pre-school programs.
MMC Volunteer Service - for Outreach Volunteer Program.
MMC Educational Resources and Nursing - to cover expenses for the Fifth Annual Nursing Research Conference.
MMC Educational Resources (Schnepp Library) - to purchase additional books for the Schnepp Professional Library.
Mental Health Centers of Central Illinois - for development of a Resource Center.
Iles Elementary School - Discover Skills for Life Program . . . learning life skills for personal and environmental health program.
Planned Parenthood - for prenatal counseling.
MMC Cardiology - for implementation of post-discharge patient outcomes research project for cardiology patients.
SIU Division of Pulmonary Medicine - for support of pulmonary research fellowship.
SIU Department of Surgery - for research/examination of rejection following organ transplant.
SIU Division of Orthopaedics - to study identification of novel metastasis associated genes in RIF- 1 clones with different metastatic potentials.
SIU Department of Surgery - for research on estrogen receptor expression in breast cancer metastases.

Orthopaedic Research and Education Foundation

c/o Katherine Walker, Dir., Grants
6300 N. River Rd., Suite 700
Rosemont, IL 60018-4261
(847) 698-9980
Source Date: 12/95

Geographic Restrictions:
Limited to U.S. and Canada.

To Whom:
Research Grants: encourage new investigators by providing seed money and start up funding.

Career Development Awards: encourage commitment to scientific research in orthopaedic surgery.

Prospective Clinical Research Proposals: provide funding for promising prospective clinical research projects.

Resident Research Awards: encourage development of research interests for residents in approved orthopaedic programs.

OREF Clinical Research Award: recognizes outstanding clinical research related to musculoskeletal disease or injury.

AAOS/OREF Fellowship in Health Services Research: develop orthopaedic surgeons with research skills to undertake and manage health services and outcomes research.

Bristol-Myers Quibb/Zimmer Unrestricted Orthopaedic Research Grant for Excellence in Research in Orthopaedic Treatment: proposal under the direction of a principal investigator, for epidemiologic, clinical, or laboratory based research, designed to positively affect the treatment of orthopaedic disease processes or conditions leading to better patient care.

Educational Awards: provide 1 year support for education programs developed in conjuntion with a recognized, national organization for programs that evaluate the effectiveness of orthopaedic education at all levels, clinical consensus conferences, workshops and symposia. **Research and development of educational electronic media and innovative approaches to education will also be considered.**

Fred W. Hark, M.D. and William A. Hark, M.D. Lectureship: honorarium for a lectureship on a topic of interest o orthopaedic surgeons.

State Orthopaedic Society Lectureship: for speakers at state society annual meetings.

Financial info:
Assets: $7,913,700.
Giving: $2,714,300 for grants.

Application info:
Applications accepted. Application form required. Deadline is Aug. 1. Publishes annual report.

Recent Grants:

Medical College of Wisconsin. "Relationship Between Disc Degeneration and Spinal Instability."
McGill University. "Intervertebral Disc Composition and Integrity Assessed by Quantitative Magnetic Resonance."
Case Western Reserve University School of Medicine. "Slow Gradual Spinal Cord Compression: Effects on Regional Spinal Cord Blood Flow and Neural Conduction."
Columbia University College of Physicians & Surgeons. "MRI and Physicochemical Studies on the Load-Carrying Characteristics of Human Intervertebral Disc."
University of California, San Francisco, School of Medicine. "Characterization of the Human Intervertebral Disc with High Resolution and Diffusion Weighted Magnetic Resonance Imaging."
Biochemistry and Molecular Biology Case Western Reserve University School of Medicine. "Regulation of Cell-Cycle Progression in Growth Plate Chondrocytes by Thyroid Hormone."
Duke University Medical Center. "Biological Modulation of Proliferation, Differentiation, and Cytokine Gene.
Expression of Human Cartilage-Forming Tumors" University of California, San Diego, School of Medicine "Muscle Response to Tenotomy and Tendon Repair."
University of California, Los Angeles, School of Medicine. "Recombinant Human Bone Morphogenetic Protein (rh-BMP-2) Enhancement of Bone Growth Across a Gap into a Porous Coated Implant."
University of North Carolina at Chapel Hill School of Medicine. "Characterization of Drug Resistance Patterns in Osteosarcoma Cell Lines Treated with Taxanes and Camptothecins."
Creighton University School of Medicine. "Prostaglandin in the Mediation of Mechanical Load Induced Bone Formation."
Washington University School of Medicine. "Molecular Mechanisms of Implant Osteolysis."
University of Chicago Pritzker School of Medicine. "Investigating Synovial Anti-Proteoglycan Activity as a Possible Auto-Immune Etiology for Osteoarthritis."
University of Arkansas College of Medicine. "Global Regulatory Elements of Staphylococcus Aureus as Therapeutic Targets in the Treatment of Osteomyelitis."

Phillips-Green Foundation, Inc.

5800 Blackstone Ave.
Chicago, IL 60637
EIN: 133334090
Source Date: 8/94

To Whom:
Nursing and medical education, **medical research, cancer research**, domestic violence, civil rights, women, Jewish giving, Native Americans, minorities, seniors, AIDS, disadvantaged.

For What:
Annual campaigns, capital campaigns, endowment funds, general purposes, operating budgets, **research**.

Financial info:
Assets: $5,864,100.
Giving: $688,500 for 100 grants.

Application info:
Applications accepted. Submit letter. No deadline. Board meets in Nov.

Directors, Officers, Trustees:

Green, Carol P., Donor, Director, Officer
Green, Cathy J., Director, Officer
Green, Douglas M., Director
Mikkelsen, Janet A., Director, Officer
Phillips, David L., Director
Phillips, Laura, Director
Phillips, Lawrence, Donor, Director, Officer
Phillips, Madelyn, Donor
Phillips, Seymour (d), Donor

Redhill Foundation-Samuel & Jean Rothberg Family Charitable Trust

700 Commercial National Bank Bldg.
Peoria, IL 61602-1574
(309) 685-3240
EIN: 371217165
Source Date: 12/95

Geographic Restrictions:
Primarily in IL and NY.

To Whom:
Higher education, Jewish education, Jewish giving, hospitals, **medical research**.

For What:
Scholarship funds, general purposes, **research**.

Financial info:
Assets: $1,862,700.
Giving: $1,178,300 for 10 grants (high: $100,000; low: $3,000).

Application info:
Applications accepted. Submit letter. No deadline.

Directors, Officers, Trustees:
Barnett, Kathleen M., Donor, Trustee
Munday, Heidi B., Donor, Trustee
Rothberg, Jean C., Trustee
Rothberg, Lee Patrick, Donor, Trustee
Rothberg, Michael, Trustee
Rothberg, Samuel, Donor, Trustee

Regenstein Foundation

c/o Joseph Regenstein, Jr., Pres.
8600 W. Bryn Mawr Ave., Suite 705N
Chicago, IL 60631
(312) 693-6464
EIN: 363152531
Source Date: 12/94

Geographic Restrictions:
Primarily in the Chicago, IL, area.

Restrictions:
No grants to individuals, scholarships, fellowships, annual campaigns, seed money, emergency funds, deficit financing, land acquisition, publications, conferences, matching gifts, or operating support.

To Whom:
Music, arts, higher, medical and early childhood education, cultural programs, **medical research**.

For What:
Building funds, equipment, **research**, endowment funds, special projects, renovation projects.

Financial info:
Assets: $92,425,200.
Giving: $2,644,500 for 30 grants (high: $500,000; low: $500).

Application info:
Applications accepted. Submit brief letter. No deadline. Most grants made on the initiative of the trustees. Board meets in May. Publishes application guidelines.

Directors, Officers, Trustees:
Eggum, John, Director, Officer
Hartman, Betty R., Director, Officer
Mecca, Robert A., Officer
Regenstein, Helen (d), Donor
Regenstein, Joseph (d), Donor
Regenstein, Joseph, Jr., Director, Officer

Schweppe Foundation

c/o Gary H. Kline, Esq., Treasurer
500 W. Madison St., Suite 3700
Chicago, IL 60661
(312) 715-5019
EIN: 366014667
Source Date: 12/95

Geographic Restrictions:
Limited to Chicago, IL, area.

To Whom:
Medical research fellowships for training at Chicago area medical schools or university-affiliated hospitals.

For What:
Fellowships.

Financial info:
Assets: $389,800.
Giving: $135,000 for 9 grants to individuals of $15,000 each.

Application info:
Applications accepted. Application form required. Deadline is Sept. 1.

Directors, Officers, Trustees:

Anderson, Truman O., M.D., Director
Armour, A. Watson, IV, Director
Bell, Walter W., Director, Officer
Bone, Roger C., M.D., Director
Kline, Gary H., Director, Officer
Llewellyn, Parker B., Director, Officer
Schweppe, John S., M.D., Donor, Director, Officer
Schweppe, Lydia E., Donor

Siragusa Foundation

c/o John R. Siragusa, Pres.
919 N. Michigan Ave., Suite 2701
Chicago, IL 60611
(312) 280-0833
EIN: 363100492
Source Date: 12/95

Geographic Restrictions:
Primarily in the Midwest U.S., with preference to the Chicago, IL, area.

Restrictions:
No grants to individuals, operating funds, capital funds, or endowments.

To Whom:
Higher education, medical research, cultural programs, child development, education of the disabled, elderly [seniors].

For What:
Equipment, matching funds, research, special projects, general purposes, scholarship funds.

Financial info:
Assets: $11,937,100 (from 1994 990PF).
Giving: $601,900 for 75 grants (high: $30,000; low: $250).

Application info:
Applications accepted. Submit letter of inquiry. No deadline. Board meets in Mar. Publishes application guidelines.

Recent Grants:

$5,000	The Art Institute of Chicago
$10,000	Five Hospital Homebound Elderly Program
$7,500	The Fund for the Children of the Americas
$12,500	Hospice of Northeastern Illinois, Inc.
$5,000	The Wetlands Initiative
$7,500	Rehab. Institute of Chicago, IL.
$10,000	University of Chicago, IL.

Directors, Officers, Trustees:

Driscoll, George E., Director
Hicks, John E., Director
Schneider, Melvyn H., Director
Siragusa, John R., Director, Officer
Siragusa, Martha P., Director
Siragusa, Richard D., Director
Siragusa, Ross D. (d), Donor
Siragusa, Ross D., Jr., Director
Siragusa, Sinclair C., Director
Wilson, James B., Director

Wadsworth Memorial Fund

c/o The Northern Trust Company
50 S. LaSalle St., Trust Dept.
Chicago, IL 60675
EIN: 366426753
Source Date: 12/95

Geographic Restrictions:
Primarily in Chicago, IL.

Restrictions:
No grants to individuals.

To Whom:
Cancer medical research.

For What:
Research.

Financial info:
Assets: $2,404,700.
Giving: $100,000 for 1 grant.

Application info:
Applications accepted. Submit letter. No deadline.

Recent Grants:

$100,000	Rush-Presbyterian St. Lukes Medical Center, Chicago, IL.

Directors, Officers, Trustees:

Northern Trust Company, The, Trustee

Washington Square Health Foundation, Inc.

c/o Howard Nochumson, Exec. Dir.
875 N. Michigan Ave., Suite 3516
Chicago, IL 60611
(312) 664-6488
EIN: 361210140
Source Date: 9/96

Geographic Restrictions:
Primarily in the Chicago, IL, area.

Restrictions:
No grants for general operating, administrative expenses, individuals, political activities, construction, capital funds, or land acquisition.

To Whom:
Health (37% of funding), **medical research (15% of funding),** medical equipment (28% of funding), AIDS, and medical and nursing education scholarships (20% of funding).

For What:
Research, equipment, scholarship funds, special projects.

Financial info:
Assets: $27,376,500.
Giving: $1,114,800 for 60 grants (high: $50,000; low: $100).

Application info:
Applications accepted. Application form required. Deadline is June 1 and Dec. 1. Publishes annual report and application guidelines.

Recent Grants:

AIDS Alternative Health Project
AIDS Foundation of Chicago
Allendale Association
Bethany Hospital
Chicago Women's Health Center
Christ Hospital and Medical Center
Columbia University School of Nursing
Council on Foundations
Donors Forum of Chicago
Funders Concerned About AIDS
Grantmakers In Health
Greek American Nursing Home Committee
Holy Family Medical Center
Howard Brown Health Center
Illinois Foundation of Dentistry for the Handicapped
Jane Addams Hull House Association Lake County Center
Keshet
La Rabida Children's Hospital and Research Center
Lake County Council Against Sexual Assault
Little City Foundation
Louis A. Weiss Memorial Hospital
Loyola University Chicago Marcella Niehoff School of Nursing
Loyola University Medical Center Stritch School of Medicine
Lutheran General Hospital
Mount Sinai Hospital Medical Center
Northwestern Memorial Hospital's Hospice Program
Northwestern University Medical School
PCC Community Wellness Center
Ravenswood Hospital Medical Center
Rosalie Dold Center for Children
Roseland Christian Health Ministries
Rush-Presbyterian-St. Luke's Medical Center/Rush College of Nursing
Rush-Presbyterian-St. Luke's Medical Center/Section of Immunology/Microbiology/Infectious Disease
Scholl Chicago Foot Health Centers
Scholl College of Podiatric Medicine
Schwab Rehabilitation Hospital and Care Network
South Shore Hospital
St. James Hospital and Health Centers
STOP AIDS
Swedish Covenant Hospital
The ARK
The Children's Memorial Foundation
The Night Ministry
Thresholds
University of Chicago Pritzker School of Medicine
University of Illinois School of Public Health Center for Health Services Research
University of Illinois College of Medicine
University of Illinois College of Nursing
Virginia Wadsworth Wirtz Sports Program Rehabilitation Institute of Chicago

Directors, Officers, Trustees:

Creticos, Angelo P., M.D., Director, Officer
Friedeman, William B., Director, Officer
Henrotin Hospital, Donor
Kirby, Robert S., Director, Officer
Nochumson, Howard, Exec.Director
Patterson, Richard B., D.P.M., Director
Werner, William N., M.D., Director, Officer
Wiley, Bill G., Director
Wirtz, Arthur M., Jr., Mrs., Director, Officer
York, John C., Director, Officer

Indiana

Health Foundation of Greater Indianapolis, Inc.

Formerly The Metropolitan Health Council of Indianapolis, Inc.)
c/o Betty H. Wilson, Exec. Dir.
401 Marott Ctr., 1st Flr.
342 Massachusetts Ave.
Indianapolis, IN 46204-2132
(317) 630-1805
EIN: 356203550
Source Date: 12/96

Geographic Restrictions:
Limited to Marion County, IN, and contiguous 7 counties in IN.

Restrictions:
No grants to individuals, religious purposes, continuing support, or deficit financing.

To Whom:
Current Focus is adolescent health, and HIV/AIDS. Encourage health related projects and programs which would advance and support effective, efficient, and innovative service to the community, particularly to the medically disadvantaged, **promote research and development in the provision and delivery of health care,** support the development of health careers, be a catalyst in developing dialogue and cooperative effort between health professionals, individuals, and organizations within the community.

Adolescent Health (29% of funding), Maternal and Child Health (16% of funding), Neighborhood Based Health Service Centers (14% of funding), General Programs (20% of funding), AIDS (21% of funding).

For What:
Scholarship funds, technical assistance, equipment, matching funds, seed money, special projects.

Financial info:
Assets: $24,545,000 (from 1995 990PF).
Giving: $810,000 for 50 grants (high: $75,000; low: $100).

Application info:
Applications accepted. Call for information. Submit letter (20 copies). No deadline. Publishes annual report with application guidelines.

Recent Grants:

$14,082	Community Action of Greater Indianapolis. AIDS education program.
$3,000	Dayspring Center. AIDS Awareness for Youth.
$17,000	Indiana AIDS Fund. Fund development.
$2,500	Indiana AIDS Walk. Contribution.
$11,798	Indiana Cares. AIDS education and prevention.
$18,750	Indiana Cares. Stop AIDS program.
$5,000	Jameson Camp. Tataya Mato consultant.
$500	Marion County Health Department. World AIDS Day conference.
$45,000	Metro Advocate Ministry, Minority Affairs. Health education.
$10,000	American Lung Association. Camperships.
$1,100	The Assistance League of Indianapolis. Operation School Bell.
$50,000	Today's Partners for Tomorrow's Health. Media campaign on HIV/AIDS.
$1,000	I.P.S. Daniel Webster School #46. La Shonna Bates Memorial Swimming Pool.
$10,000	Diabetes Youth Foundation of Indiana. Camperships.
$5,000	Dynamo F.C. Soccer Teams of Indianapolis. Program development.
$40,000	Family Advocacy Center. Program support.
$18,000	Girls Inc.. Preventing adolescent pregnancy program.
$520	M.S.D. Warren Township, Hawthorne Elementary School. CPR instructor program.
$8,000	Hemophilia of Indiana. Camperships.
$8,000	Jameson Camp. Camperships.
$55,162	Kaleidoscope Church and Community Partnership. After school prevention/intervention program.
$300	M. L. King Multi-Service Center. Youth forum.
$2,000	Marion County Health Department. Camp S.C.A.T. camperships.
$24,933	People's Health Center. School-based health services.
$15,000	Planned Parenthood. Teen pregnancy prevention program.
$2,500	M.S.D. Warren Township, Raymond Park Middle School. "Baby Think It Over" dolls.
$27,815	Southside Youth Council Inc.. Adolescent sexual offender treatment program.

$50,000	United Way/community Service Council. Bridges to Success.
$25,000	Vivian Smith House. Teen parenting program.
$4,000	Crooked Creek Community Council. Environment.
$1,000	Gleaners Food Bank, Southside Community Pantry. Establish food bank.
$1,450	The Hispanic Center. Health fair.
$2,500	HealthNet Community Health Center. Audio-visual equipment.
$2,000	HealthNet Community Health Center. Equipment.
$2,000	HealthNet Community Health Center. Program support.
$2,000	Huntington's Disease Society of America. Conference support.
$900	Indiana Literacy Foundation. Tutor training.
$2,640	Indiana Minority Health Coalition, Inc.. Communication linkage among state coalitions.
$10,000	Indiana University school of Dentistry. Minority student scholarships.
$3,550	Julian Center. Increased educational services.
$2,000	The Access Network - C.I.C.O.A.. Fans for low-income senior citizens.
$10,000	American Red Cross. Healthy babies program.
$23,205	At-Your-School Child Services Inc.. Childcare staff training.
$2,480	Breaking Free Inc. Domestic violence.
$20,000	Children's Express. Adolescent Health Alert: The Kids' Perspective.
$17,500	Ruth Lilly Center for Health Education. Fifth grade human growth programs.
$1,345	M.S D. Perry Township, Southport Middle School. "Baby Think It Over" dolls.
$3,000	Pathway to Recovery Inc.. Client services.
$1,000	Poor People's Action Council. Food pantry.
$50,000	Rainbow of Hope, Inc.. Transitional housing for homeless families.

Directors, Officers, Trustees:

Baker, Beverly A., Director, Officer
Conner, Betty A., Director, Officer
Feeney, Thomas, Director
Holmes, Cynthia B., Director, Officer
Holt, Buford C., Director
Huse, Elmer, Director
Kahn, Terence P., Director
Love, C. Phillip, Director
Ludwig, George E., Director
North, Robert L., Director
Olive, G. Scott, Jr., Director, Officer
Radecki, Martin J., Director
Robinson, Robert, M.D., Director
Ryan, Lawrence M., Director, Officer
White, Reuben L., D.D.S., Director
Wilson, Betty H., Director, Officer

Iowa

Roy J. Carver Charitable Trust

c/o Troy K. Ross, Ph.D., Exec. Admin.
P.O. Box 76
Muscatine, IA 52761-3733
(319) 263-4010
EIN: 421186589
Source Date: 4/96

Geographic Restrictions:
Primarily in IA.

Restrictions:
No grants for annual campaigns, operating funds, individuals, religious activities, advertising, or political activities.

To Whom:
Education, **medical research**, science and technology, youth.

Medical/Scientific Research (14% of funding),
Science, Math, Technology (35% of funding), Education (24% of funding), Youth General (6% of funding), Youth Recreation (6% of funding).

For What:
Research, seed money, special projects, scholarship funds.

Financial info:
Assets: $186,100,000 (from 1995 990PF).
Giving: $7,942,500 for 65 grants (high: $1,000,000; low: $1,000).

Application info:
Applications accepted. Submit letter. Deadline is Nov. 15, Feb. 15, May 15, and Aug. 15. Board meets in Jan., Apr., July, and Oct. Publishes biennial report with application guidelines.

Recent Grants:

$25,000	Iowa State University Institute for Physical Research, Technology, Ames, IA. Postdoctoral research in synthetic reality constructs.
$4,419,351	Augustana College, Rock Island, IL. Construct new science building.
$20,000	Bellevue Public Library, Bellevue, IA. Renovation.
$100,000	Arrowhead Ranch, Coal Valley, IL. Educational center.
$300,000	Quad City Sports Center Association, Davenport, IA. Skating and soccer facility.

Directors, Officers, Trustees:
Boyd, Willard L., Trustee
Carver, Lucille A., Officer, Trustee
Carver, Roy J., Sr. (d), Donor
Carver, Roy J., Jr., Officer, Trustee
Cory, William F., Trustee
Dahl, Arthur E., Officer, Trustee
Griffith, J. Larry, Trustee
Hughes, Roger A., Exec.Director
LeGrand, Clay, Trustee

Iowa Pharmacy Foundation

8515 Douglas Ave., Suite 16
Des Moines, IA 50322
EIN: 426075767
Source Date: 12/93

Geographic Restrictions:
Limited to IA.

To Whom:
Pharmaceutical education and research.

For What:
Individuals, **research**, scholarship funds.

Financial info:
Assets: $2,095,700.
Giving: $16,000 for 2 grants and $20,600 for 5 grants to individuals.

Application info:
Applications accepted. Submit letter. No deadline.

Directors, Officers, Trustees:
Griffiths, Bob, Officer
Karbiling, Terry, Officer
Marion Laboratories, Inc., Donor
McKesson Foundation, Inc., Donor
PNI, Inc., Donor
Temple, Thomas R., Officer
Upjohn Company, The, Donor

Kansas

Kansas Health Foundation

(Formerly Wesley Foundation)
c/o Jana L. Konek, Grants Mgr.
309 E. Douglas
Wichita, KS 67202-9947
(316) 262-7676
EIN: 480873431
Source Date: 12/96

Geographic Restrictions:
Limited to KS.

Restrictions:
No grants to individuals.

To Whom:
Primary health care education: Increase the number and capacity of primary care providers in order to enhance the access to and increase the quality of primary health care.

Rural health: enhance access to health services for rural Kansans by serving as a catalyst for the development and support of innovation and systemic changes.

Health promotion and disease prevention: promote healthy behaviours and enhance preventive services to reduce health problems that are primarily preventable.

Public health: reinstate a public health agenda within the state in order to better address community needs.

Health policy and research: increase the quality and quantity of health services research to influence health decisions in KS.

For What:
Fellowships, general purposes, operating budgets, special projects, technical assistance.

Financial info:
Assets: $5,144,100.
Giving: $12,892,000 for 160 grants.

Application info:
Applications accepted. Application form required. Deadline varies.

Recent Grants:

$6,000,000	Initiate Kansas Health Institute, a health policy and research institute in Topeka, KS.
$100,000	Pilot Medicaid managed care program in Wichita and western Kansas that includes Wichita hospitals, Sedgwick County Medical Society and hospitals in Garden City and Independence through grant to St. Joseph Health Corporation, Wichita, KS.
$6,500	Symposium for Kansas Hospital Association in Topeka to encourage healthier communities through integrated health care systems in KS.
$352,858	Develop mini-grant program, administered by Kansas State University, for communities throughout state, which would encourage health promotion activities within existing programs for seniors.
$167,405	Additional technical assistance through University of Kansas in Lawrence for teen pregnancy prevention projects in Junction City, Ottawa and Wichita, KS.

Directors, Officers, Trustees:
Chandler, C. Q., Director, Officer
Davis, A. B., Jr., Director, Officer
Focht, Jack, Director
Henney, Jane E., M.D., Director
Hicks, Kenneth W., Bishop, Director
Meyers, Evan A., Officer
Stewart, Donald M., Officer
Stewart, John T., III, Director, Officer
Tacha, Deanell Reece, Judge, Director
Vliet, Marni, Officer
Vogt, Jerold W., Rev., Director
Wedel, Kermit G., M.D., Director

Flossie E. West Memorial Trust

c/o Shirley Moon, Trustee
P.O. Box 607
Augusta, KS 67010
(316) 775-2675
EIN: 486125209
Source Date: 12/95

Geographic Restrictions:
Limited to Wichita, KS, area.

To Whom:
Medical cancer research.

For What:
Research.

Financial info:
Assets: $1,457,400.
Giving: $46,800 for 2 grants.

Application info:
Applications accepted. Submit letter. No deadline.

Directors, Officers, Trustees:
Bisagno, Robert, Trustee
Brooks, Eugene, Trustee
Moon, Shirley, Trustee

Kentucky

Humana Foundation, Inc.

c/o Virginia K. Lewman, Pub. Affairs Mgr.
The Humana Bldg.
500 W. Main St.
P.O. Box 1438
Louisville, KY 40201
(502) 580-1000
EIN: 611004763
Source Date: 12/95

Geographic Restrictions:
Primarily in KY.

To Whom:
Performing arts, health, **medical research**, higher and secondary education, community development.

For What:
Employee related scholarships.

Financial info:
Assets: $74,383,200.
Giving: $6,171,800 for 85 grants (high: $1,000,000; low: $500).

Application info:
Applications accepted. Submit letter. No deadline. Board meets quarterly.

Directors, Officers, Trustees:
Bauernfeind, George G., Officer
Doucette, James W., Officer
Drury, W. Roger, Sr., Director, Officer
Humana, Inc., Donor
Jones, David A., Director, Officer
Murray, James E., Officer
Neely, Walter E., Officer
Smith, Wayne T., Director, Officer

Louisiana

Edward G. Schlieder Educational Foundation

431 Gravier St., Suite 400
New Orleans, LA 70130
(504) 581-6179
Source Date: 12/92

Geographic Restrictions:
Limited to educational institutions in LA.

Restrictions:
No grants to individuals, general purposes, building or endowment funding, scholarships, fellowships, or operating expenses.

To Whom:
Higher and other education, **medical research** at universities.

For What:
Research, equipment, capital campaigns.

Financial info:
Assets: $23,101,200.
Giving: $1,105,000 for 15 grants (high: $250,000; low: $10,000).

Application info:
Applications accepted. Submit letter (3 copies). No deadline.

Directors, Officers, Trustees:

Nalty, Donald J., Director, Officer
Parker, Blanc A., Officer
Schlieder, Edward G. (d), Donor
Westfeldt, George G., Jr., Director, Officer
Westfeldt, Thomas D., Director

Maine

Maine Medical Assessment Foundation

c/o Ellen Jane Schneiter, Assoc. Dir.
P.O. Box 249
Manchester, ME 04351
(207) 622-9342
EIN: 010440180
Source Date: 12/96

Geographic Restrictions:
Limited to ME.

Restrictions:
No grants to individuals.

To Whom:
Medical research:
The Obstetrics/Gynecology Study Group: focused study of factors influencing Maine's cesarean section rate.

The Urology Study Group: for dissemination of information from the completed prostatectomy outcomes study.

The Orthopaedic/Neurosurgical Study Group: research on variations in lumbar disc surgical procedures; refinement and dissemination of practice guidelines for the care of patients with acute low back problems.

The Pediatric Study Group: research on variations in pediatric medical admissions, the treatment of asthma in children and in the treatment of otitis media with effusion.

The Ophthalmology Study Group: research on variations in the use of YAG laser procedures following cataract surgery.

Cardiology Study Group: development and dissemination of Maine-specific pracice guidelines for the use of stress testing with imaging.

Primary Care Study Group: refinement and dissemination of practice guidelines for the treatment of patients with heart failure.

Financial info:
Assets: $331,400 (from 1995 990PF).
Giving: $606,000 for 5 grants (high: $200,000; low: $40,000).

Application info:
Applications accepted. Submit letter. No deadline. Board meets quarterly.

Maryland

Eugene B. Casey Foundation

800 S. Frederick Ave., Suite 100
Gaithersburg, MD 20877-4102
(301) 948-4595
EIN: 526220316
Source Date: 8/94

Geographic Restrictions:
Primarily in MD and Washington, DC, area.

To Whom:
Higher education, Catholic giving, **medical research**, hospice, fine arts, hospitals, community development, social services.

For What:
General purposes, **research**.

Financial info:
Assets: $86,825,800.
Giving: $4,336,800 for 40 grants (high: $2,500,000; low: $100).

Application info:
Applications accepted. Submit proposal. No deadline.

Directors, Officers, Trustees:
Casey, Betty Brown, Officer, Trustee
Casey, Douglas R., Trustee
Jones, Stephen N., Officer, Trustee
Price, W. James, Trustee

Howard Hughes Medical Institute

c/o Joseph G. Perpich, M.D., VP
4000 Jones Bridge Rd.
Chevy Chase, MD 20815-6789
(301) 215-8890
EIN: 590735717
Source Date: 12/95

Restrictions:
No grants for the direct conduct of biomedical research (except to scientific investigators employed by the Institute). No grants or fellowships except to individuals or institutions competing under established science education programs.

To Whom:
Institute is a qualified medical research organization, predoctoral fellowships in biological sciences, **research training fellowships for medical students, postdoctoral research fellowships for physicians, undergraduate research and science education programs**, faculty development in the sciences, curriculum and laboratory development and equipment, elementary and secondary science education and outreach programs, elementary and secondary science teacher training and curriculum enhancement, children and youth, family and community-oriented programs, health sciences, science museums, **international research scholars programs.**

For What:
Research, fellowships, special projects.

Financial info:
Assets: $8,179,282,100 (from 1994 990PF).
Giving: $52,500,000 for 300 grants (high: $2,000,000; low: $5,000), $11,549,000 for 440 grants to individuals (high: $50,000; low: $20,000), and $273,210,000 for 1 foundation-administered program.

Application info:
Applications accepted. Submit letter of inquiry. Board meets in Feb., May, Aug., and Nov. Applicants should consult guidelines in the Institute's publication prior to application. Fellowships are awarded on the basis of U.S. and international competition and peer review. Publishes application guidelines.

Recent Grants:

$600,000	Allegheny College, Meadville, PA.
$600,000	Bard College, Annandale-on-Hudson, NY.
$1,100,000	Barnard College, New York, NY.
$600,000	Bates College, Lewiston, ME.
$1,200,000	Beloit College, Beloit, WI.
$600,000	Benedictine University, Lisle, IL.
$1,000,000	Bryn Mawr College, Bryn Mawr, PA.
$650,000	Canisius College, Buffalo, NY.
$650,000	Carleton College, Northfield, MN.
$600,000	Centenary College of Louisiana, Shreveport, LA.
$1,200,000	City University of New York, Brooklyn, NY.
$600,000	City University of New York-Queens, Flushing, NY.
$1,000,000	Colby College, Waterville, ME.
$650,000	Colgate University, Hamilton, NY.
$1,100,000	College of the Holy Cross, Worcester, MA.
$750,000	Colorado College, Colorado Springs, CO.
$650,000	Davidson College, Davidson, NC.
$600,000	Earlham College, Richmond, IND.
$700,000	Florida Agricultural and Mechanical University, Tallahassee, FL.
$1,300,000	Hampshire College, Amherst, MA.

$700,000 Hope College, Holland MI.
$750,000 Haverford College, Haverford, PA.
$650,000 Humboldt State University, Arcata, CA.
$1,500,000 Kenyon College, Gambier, OH.
$800,000 Lawrence University, Appleton, WI.
$1,000,000 Macalester College, St. Paul, MN.
$650,000 Middlebury College, Middlebury, VT.
$900,000 Mount Holyoke College, S. Hadley, MA.
$1,200,000 Nebraska Wesleyan University, Lincoln, NE.
$600,000 Oakland University, Rochester, MI.
$600,000 Oberlin College, Oberlin, OH.
$800,000 Occidental College, Los Angeles, CA.
$650,000 Ohio Wesleyan University, Delaware, OH.
$750,000 Point Loma Nazarene College, San Diego, CA.
$900,000 Pomona College, Claremont, CA.
$700,000 Reed College, Portland, OREG.
$1,300,000 St. Olaf College, Northfield, MN.
$1,600,000 Smith College, Northhampton, MA.
$800,000 Spelman College, Atlanta, GA.
$1,000,000 St. John's College, Annapolis, MD.
$600,000 St. Mary's University, San Antonio, TX.
$1,200,000 Swarthmore College, Swarthmore, PA.
$600,000 Tuskegee University, Tuskegee, AL.
$750,000 University of TX, San Antonio, TX.
$1,600,000 Villanova University, Villanova, PA.
$600,000 Washington and Jefferson College, Washington, PA.
$1,500,000 Wellesley College, Wellesley, MA.
$750,000 Wesleyan University, Middletown, CT.
$150,000 Audubon Institute
$175,000 California Museum of Science and Industry
$100,000 Academy of Natural Sciences, Philadelphia, PA. Produce teaching resource kits and curriculum materials to enable middle school science teachers to introduce object-oriented, inquiry-based instruction into their classrooms. Kits will contain natural history specimens from Academy's exhibit collection. Accompanying curriculum guides will provide lesson plans and suggested activities to promote inquiry and discussion. Up to 400 teachers will be trained, and 40,000 students, grades 5-8, will be reached in greater Philadelphia area. Teachers will receive pedagogic orientation and training in use of kits. Real specimens will be used to stimulate learning in such topics as animal behavior, life cycles, and relationships between animals and their habitats, drawing on Academy's expertise in aquatic ecology research. Lessons will be designed to encourage all students to participate, including those who do not thrive in traditional classroom settings.
$500,000 Amherst College, Amherst, MA. Attract and retain students in sciences, including women and minority students underrepresented in scientific fields, to include such components as academic-year laboratory research experiences, science dormitory for student researchers, travel to scientific meetings, symposia to present research, and enhanced mentoring and advising.
$250,000 Arizona Museum of Science and Technology, Phoenix, AZ. Create Desert Web, a five-year interactive science outreach program for minority and disadvantaged children, including those studying English as second language. Teacher workshops will cover integration of hands-on experiments and projects into 1st- through 3rd-grade curriculum in targeted school districts of Phoenix area. Desert Web will include in-service class time of Museum staff members. Program will use desert-related sciences to encourage students to explore, question, and investigate world around them. Participating teachers will receive 16 hours of initial instruction and 2 hours of subsequent workshops. By infusing interactive exhibitry and experimentation into school curricula, Desert Web will attempt to breach linguistic and cultural barriers affecting segments of Arizona population.

Directors, Officers, Trustees:

Bearn, Alexander G., M.D., Trustee
Choppin, Purnell W., M.D., Officer
Copley, Helen K., Trustee
Cowan, W. Maxwell, M.D., Officer
Gay, Frank William, Trustee
Gilliam, James H., Jr., Trustee
Gray, Hanna Holborn, Trustee
Hughes, Howard R. (d), Donor
Leonard, Joan S., Officer
Lummis, William R., Trustee
Perpich, Joseph G., M.D., Officer

Shapiro, Irving S., Trustee
Strauss, Jon C., Officer
Thorn, George W., M.D., Trustee
Wolfe, C. F., Officer
Wolfensohn, James D., Trustee

Life Sciences Research Foundation

115 W. University Pkwy.
Baltimore, MD 21210
(410) 467-2597

Application address:
c/o Lewis Thomas Laboratories
Washington Rd.
Princeton University
Princeton, NJ 08544
(609) 258-3551
EIN: 521231801
Source Date: 5/96

To Whom:
Postdoctoral research fellowships to graduates of medical schools and graduate schools in biological sciences.

For What:
Research, fellowships.

Financial info:
Assets: $629,000.
Giving: $1,229,100 for 40 grants to individuals (high: $35,000; low: $10,000).

Application info:
Applications accepted. Application form required (3 copies). Deadline is Oct. 3 and supporting letters must be received by Nov. 2. Final notification is in Mar.

Directors, Officers, Trustees:
Baltimore, David, Advisor
Berg, Paul, Advisor
Bloch, Konrad, Advisor
Blotsein, David, Advisor
Brown, Donald D., Director, Officer
Brown, Michael S., Advisor
Cuatrecasas, Pedro, Advisor
Darnell, James E., Jr., Advisor
Davie, Joseph M., Advisor
Englar, Patricia, Officer
Frederickson, Donald, Advisor
Nathans, Daniel, Director
Redden, Roger, Officer
Smith, Hamilton O., Advisor
Snyder, Solomon H., Director
Thomas, Lewis, M.D., Advisor
Watson, James, Advisor

PHH Foundation, Inc.

c/o Pilar Page, VP
11333 McCormick Rd.
Hunt Valley, MD 21031
(301) 771-2733
EIN: 526040911
Source Date: 4/96

Geographic Restrictions:
Limited to the Baltimore, MD, area.

Restrictions:
No grants for governmental or political organizations, endowments, conferences, research, or individuals.

To Whom:
Health Care (65% of funding): neighborhood health and human services, public information programs designed to improve specific health and nutrition services, **nationally established health care organizations for support of local projects in research**, training, and treatment, national [U.S.] health, human services, and youth organizations, hospitals, local youth and health and human services organizations for safety, recreation, family planning, drug abuse, and disaster relief.

Education (15% of funding): higher education, elementary and secondary educational institutions, state and local fundraising groups, economic education groups.

Arts and Culture (10% of funding): cultural arts, youth programs, visual and performing arts, libraries, museums, cultural center, arts funds and councils, public broadcasting, and community activities.

Civic Improvement (5% of funding): health and civic environment, national organizations in public policy research, community improvement, environment and ecology, justice and law organizations, local community improvement organizations, transportation, housing, law and order, fire prevention, study groups to resolve social problems.

Religion activities and support for special sports or patriotic events.

For What:
Operating budgets, continuing support, annual campaigns, seed money, emergency funds, building funds, equipment, land acquisition, employee matching gifts, scholarship funds.

Financial info:
Assets: $97,600.
Giving: $524,900 for 45 grants (high: $100,000; low: $500).

Application info:
Applications accepted. Submit letter. No deadline. Board meets in June, Sept., Dec., and Mar. Publishes application guidelines.

Directors, Officers, Trustees:
Arbaugh, Eugene A., Officer
Kridler, Terry E., Officer
Kunisch, Robert D., Officer
Page, Pilar M., Officer
Wright, S. H., Officer

Massachusetts

John W. Alden Trust

c/o State St. Bank & Trust Company
Attn: Deborah A. Robbins, VP
P.O. Box 351
Boston, MA 02101
(617) 482-5328
EIN: 222719727
Source Date: 9/95

Geographic Restrictions:
Primarily in eastern MA.

Restrictions:
No grants to individuals.

To Whom:
Children who are blind, retarded, disabled, or who are either mentally or physically ill, **medical and scientific research** for the prevention or cure of diseases and disabilities particularly affecting children, **hospitals**, education, therapy for children.

For What:
Research, seed money, special projects.

Financial info:
Assets: $7,012,500.
Giving: $273,600 for 20 grants (high: $25,000; low: $2,500).

Application info:
Applications accepted. Submit letter (3 copies). Deadline is Jan. 15, Apr. 15, July 15, and Oct. 15. Board meets in Feb., May, Aug., and Nov. Publishes application guidelines.

Directors, Officers, Trustees:
Alden, Priscilla (d), Donor
State Street Bank & Trust Company, Trustee
Tyler, William B., Trustee

Grass Foundation

c/o Mary G. Grass, Secretary
77 Reservoir Rd.
Quincy, MA 02170
(617) 843-0219
EIN: 046049529
Source Date: 12/95

Geographic Restrictions:
Limited to North America with emphasis on the U.S.

To Whom:
Research and education in biology, physiology, neurobiology, and neurophysiology and allied fields of science and medicine, fellowships for summer study at a marine biological laboratory, higher education.

For What:
Fellowships, **research**, lectureships.

Financial info:
Assets: $5,684,300.
Giving: $393,100 for 10 grants (high: $350,000; low: $500) and $327,400 for 10 grants to individuals (high: $100,000; low: $3,000).

Application info:
Applications accepted. Submit letter. Deadline is Dec. 1 for Fellowships in Neurophysiology and Nov. 1 for Robert Morris Fellowship. Board meets in Feb. and July. Publishes application guidelines.

Directors, Officers, Trustees:
Acheson, George H., M.D., Trustee
Barry, Daniel T., M.D., Trustee
Cannon Manufacturing Company, Donor
DeLorenzo, Robert J., M.D., Trustee
Goldring, Sidney R., M.D., Trustee
Grafstein, Bernice, Officer
Grass, Albert M. (d), Donor
Grass, Ellen R., Donor, Officer, Trustee
Grass, Henry J., M.D., Trustee
Grass, Mary G., Officer, Trustee
Grass Instrument Company, Donor
Hoy, Ronald R., Trustee
Lindsley, Donald B., Trustee
Miledi, Ricardo, M.D., Trustee
Woodward, Richmond B., Officer, Trustee
Wurtz, Robert H., Trustee
Zottoli, Steven J., Ph.D., Trustee

Harcourt General Charitable Foundation, Inc.

(Formerly General Cinema Corporation Charitable Foundation, Inc.)
c/o Kay M. Kilpatrick, Contributions Admin.
27 Boylston St.
Chestnut Hill, MA 02167-1700
(617) 232-8200
EIN: 223026002
Source Date: 2/97

Geographic Restrictions:
Limited to the greater Boston, MA, area.

Restrictions:
No grants to individuals, political or religious purposes.

To Whom:
Medical research in AIDS, cancer, diabetes, and heart disease, children and youth, arts, education, homeless, minorities, social services.

For What:
Building funds, seed money, capital campaigns, special projects, annual campaigns, matching funds, general purposes.

Financial info:
Assets: $24,591,100 (from 1994 990PF).
Giving: $3,500,000 for 5 grants (high: $500,000; low: $350).

Application info:
Applications accepted. Submit letter. Deadline is Jan. 2, Apr. 1, July 1, and Oct. 1. Board meets in Jan., Apr., July and Oct.

Directors, Officers, Trustees:
Cook, John R., Director
Harcourt General, Inc., Donor
Knez, Brian J., Director
Smith, Richard A., Director, Officer
Smith, Robert A., Director
Tarr, Robert J., Jr., Director

Charles H. Hood Foundation

c/o Raymond Considine, Exec. Dir.
95 Berkeley St., Suite 201
Boston, MA 02116
(617) 695-9439
EIN: 046036790
Source Date: 12/95

Geographic Restrictions:
Limited to New England area of U.S.

Restrictions:
No grants for nutrition, public health, mental health, education, social or general welfare, individuals, building or endowment funds, operating budgets, general support, publications, scholarships, fellowships, fundraising campaigns, or matching gifts.

To Whom:
Biomedical or clinical research into the health problems of children, junior faculty studying childhood diseases.

For What:
Research.

Financial info:
Assets: $36,203,100.
Giving: $1,413,300 for 20 grants (high: $350,000; low: $15,000).

Application info:
Applications accepted. Application form required (10 copies). Deadline is Apr. and Oct. Publishes application guidelines.

Directors, Officers, Trustees:
Boutwell, Jeffrey, Committee
Considine, Raymond, Exec.Director
Hood, Charles H. (d), Donor
Hood, Charles H., II, Member, Officer
Parker, John O., Committee
Sanders, Henry M., Committee

Charles A. King Trust

c/o Fleet Bank
Attn: Kerry Herlihy Sullivan, Dir., Grantmaking
75 State St.
Mail Stop: MA BO F07B
Boston, MA 02109-1810
(617) 346-2493
EIN: 046012742
Source Date: 12/94

Geographic Restrictions:
Limited to MA.

Restrictions:
No grants to individuals.

To Whom:
Medical and surgical research projects.

For What:
Research, fellowships.

Financial info:
Assets: $11,850,500.
Giving: $340,700 for 15 grants (high: $30,000; low: $10,000).

Application info:
Applications accepted. Application form required (17 copies). Deadline is Oct. 1 for projects to start on or after Feb 1 of following year. Board meets in Jan.

Directors, Officers, Trustees:
Dane, Edward N., Trustee
Fleet Bank, Massachusetts, Trustee
King, Charles A. (d), Donor
Lovell, Richard H., Trustee

Lederman Family Foundation

P.O. Box 426
Marblehead, MA 01945
(617) 631-8603
EIN: 046605802
Source Date: 12/95

Geographic Restrictions:
Primarily in U.S. and Israel.

To Whom:
Jewish welfare, higher and other education, science and technology, **medical research**.

For What:
Scholarship funds, seed money, special projects, conferences and seminars, lectureships, **research**.

Financial info:
Assets: $346,900.
Giving: $3,900 for 3 grants.

Application info:
Applications accepted. Submit letter. Deadline is Oct. 1.

Directors, Officers, Trustees:
Lederman, David M., Donor, Trustee
Lederman, Jeanine E., Trustee
Lederman, Jonathan S., Trustee
Lederman, Natalie F., Trustee

June Rockwell Levy Foundation, Inc.

136 Ridgeway Rd.
Weston, MA 02193
EIN: 046074284
Source Date: 12/95

Geographic Restrictions:
Primarily in RI.

Restrictions:
No grants for individuals or religious purposes.

To Whom:
Hospitals, disabled, **medical research**, cultural programs, higher and secondary education, youth.

For What:
Building funds, continuing support, equipment, capital campaigns, **research**, general purposes, scholarship funds, seed money.

Financial info:
Assets: $21,114,000.
Giving: $984,600 for 95 grants (high: $50,000; low: $1,000).

Application info:
Applications accepted. Submit letter. No deadline. Board meets in Feb., Apr., June, Aug., Oct. and Dec.

Recent Grants:

$25,000	Lincoln School, Providence, RI. Professional development of faculty and staff and endow the June Rockwell Levy Professional Development Fund.

Directors, Officers, Trustees:
Edwards, James K., Trustee
Helm, George T., Trustee
Levy, Austin T. (d), Donor
Loring, Jonathan B., Officer, Trustee
Menard, Raymond N., Trustee
Noonan, James W., Officer, Trustee
Osgood, Edward H., Trustee
Smith, Nancy, Officer
Thompson, Winifred H., Trustee
White, James M., Jr., Trustee

E. F. Merkert Foundation

c/o Merkert Enterprises
500 Turnpike St.
Canton, MA 02021
(617) 828-4800
EIN: 046111832
Source Date: 12/95

Geographic Restrictions:
Primarily in MA.

Restrictions:
No grants to individuals.

To Whom:
Higher and other education, voluntarism, social services, **medical research**, hospitals.

For What:
Endowment funds, **research**.

Financial info:
Assets: $1,116,400.
Giving: $93,400 for 40 grants (high: $25,000; low: $500).

Application info:
Applications accepted. Submit letter. No deadline.

Directors, Officers, Trustees:
Merkert, Eugene F., Donor, Trustee
Merkert Enterprises, Inc., Donor

Peabody Foundation, Inc.

c/o Sherburne, Powers, & Needham
1 Beacon St.
Boston, MA 02108
EIN: 042104767
Source Date: 9/95

Geographic Restrictions:
Limited to MA, with emphasis on the Boston, MA, area.

Restrictions:
No grants to individuals.

To Whom:
Medical research, rehabilitation, education, child welfare, treatment relating to disabled children.

For What:
Research.

Financial info:
Assets: $13,922,100.
Giving: $599,300 for 20 grants (high: $100,000; low: $1,000).

Application info:
Applications accepted. Submit letter. Deadline is Feb. 1.

Directors, Officers, Trustees:
Barr, Harry C., Trustee
Brown, Dorothy A., Trustee
Cave, Edwin F., Mrs., Trustee
Damon, John L., Mrs., Trustee
Harvey, Kenneth L., Trustee
Haydock, Francis B., Mrs., Officer, Trustee
Hewitt, John H., Trustee
Hurlbut, Sally D., Trustee
Jessiman, Andrew G., M.D., Trustee
Nicholson, Norman C., Jr., Officer, Trustee
Paine, Stephen D., Mrs., Trustee
Stevens, Sylvia L., Trustee
Thorndike, W. Nicholas, Mrs., Trustee
Tripp, William V., III, Officer, Trustee

Harold Whitworth Pierce Charitable Trust

c/o Nichols & Pratt
Attn: Elizabeth D. Nichols, Grant Admin.
50 Congress St.
Boston, MA 02109
(617) 523-6800
EIN: 046019896
Source Date: 12/95

Geographic Restrictions:
Primarily in Boston, MA, area.

Restrictions:
No grants to individuals.

To Whom:
Hospitals, **medical research**, higher, secondary, and other education, youth, museums, cultural programs, family planning, open space, historic preservation, environmental conservation.

For What:
Capital campaigns, scholarship funds, seed money, **research**.

Financial info:
Assets: $16,214,800.
Giving: $651,000 for 35 grants (high: $150,000; low: $1,500).

Application info:
Applications accepted. Submit proposal. Deadline is May 1 and Nov. 1. Board meets in May and Nov. Publishes application guidelines.

Directors, Officers, Trustees:
Nichols, James R., Trustee
Pierce, Harold Whitworth (d), Donor
Pratt, Harold I., Trustee

Pittsfield Anti-Tuberculosis Association

46 Alfred Dr.
Pittsfield, MA 01201
EIN: 042104839
Source Date: 12/95

Geographic Restrictions:
Primarily in NY and MA.

To Whom:
Tuberculosis research, education, and seminars.

For What:
General purposes, conferences and seminars, **research.**

Financial info:
Assets: $1,923,000.
Giving: $60,300 for 5 grants (high: $25,000; low: $1,000).

Application info:
Applications accepted. Submit letter. No deadline.

Radionucleides in Nephrology Foundation for Medical Research & Education

95 Puddle Wharf
Marshfield, MA 02050
EIN: 042738844
Source Date: 4/96

Geographic Restrictions:
Primarily in MA and UT.

Restrictions:
No grants to individuals.

To Whom:
Renal and cardiovascular medical research.

For What:
Research, seed money.

Financial info:
Assets: $1,680,500.
Giving: $25,000 for grants.

Application info:
Applications accepted. Submit letter. No deadline. Board meets in Jan. and June.

Directors, Officers, Trustees:
Hollenberg, Norman K., M.D., Director
Pletka, Peter, M.D., Director
Rennie, I. Drummond, M.D., Director

Thoracic Foundation

c/o Taylor, Ganson & Perrin
160 Federal St.
Boston, MA 02110

Application address:
135 Francis St.
Boston, MA 02215
(617) 738-7810
EIN: 042226641
Source Date: 12/95

Geographic Restrictions:
Primarily in MA.

To Whom:
Medical research, hospitals providing service to thoracic cases.

For What:
Research, publications, conferences and seminars.

Financial info:
Assets: $3,360,200.
Giving: $100,300 for 5 grants.

Application info:
Applications accepted. Submit letter. No deadline.

Directors, Officers, Trustees:
Cook, Bradley R., Trustee
Mikelson, Thomas, Rev., Trustee
Overholt, Richard H., M.D. (d), Donor
Stone, Galen, Trustee

Edwin S. Webster Foundation

c/o Grants Management Associates, Inc.
Attn: Phillip Hall
230 Congress St., 3rd Flr.
Boston, MA 02110
(617) 426-7172
EIN: 046000647
Source Date: 12/95

Geographic Restrictions:
Primarily in the Northeastern U.S., with emphasis on MA, NH, and NY.

Restrictions:
No grants to individuals, seed money, emergency funds, deficit financing, publications, or conferences.

To Whom:
Cultural programs, hospitals, **medical research**, higher and secondary education, youth, community funds, alcohol and drug abuse, handicapped, minorities.

For What:
Operating budgets, continuing support, annual campaigns, building funds, equipment, land acquisition, capital campaigns, endowment funds, matching funds, scholarship funds, professorships, internships, fellowships, special projects, **research**.

Financial info:
Assets: $27,379,400.
Giving: $1,262,000 for 55 grants (high: $75,000; low: $2,500).

Application info:
Applications accepted. Submit proposal. Deadline is Mar. and Sept. Board meets in June and Dec. Publishes application guidelines.

Directors, Officers, Trustees:
Harris, Henry Upham, Jr., Trustee
Harris, Henry U., III, Trustee
Harte, Richard, Jr., Officer, Trustee
Hiam, Edwin W., Trustee
Webster, Edwin S. (d), Donor

Michigan

James & Lynelle Holden Fund

802 E. Big River
Troy, MI 48083-1404
EIN: 386052154
Source Date: 10/95

Geographic Restrictions:
Primarily in Detroit, MI.

Restrictions:
No grants to individuals or endowments.

To Whom:
Medical research, medical and higher education, hospitals, youth, child welfare, minorities, seniors, cultural programs, at risk youth.

For What:
Annual campaigns, general purposes, building funds, equipment, **research**, scholarship funds, fellowships, matching funds, continuing support, operating budgets.

Financial info:
Assets: $7,382,500.
Giving: $895,500 for 30 grants (high: $300,000; low: $2,500).

Application info:
Applications accepted. Submit letter or proposal. No deadline. Board meets in Jan., Apr., July and Oct.

Directors, Officers, Trustees:
Dahling, Louis F., Officer, Trustee
Holden, James S. (d), Donor
Holden, Lynelle A. (d), Donor
Kaufman, Arthur, Officer, Trustee
Wilson, Herbert J., Officer, Trustee

Kresge Foundation

c/o John Marshall, III, Pres.
3215 W. Big Beaver Rd.
P.O. Box 3151
Troy, MI 48007-3151
(810) 643-9630
Source Date: 12/96
EIN: 381359217

Geographic Restrictions:
U.S. and international giving.

Restrictions:
No grants for elementary or secondary schools, individuals, operating or special project budgets, furnishings, conferences, seminars, church building projects, endowments, student aid, scholarships, fellowships, research, debt retirement, completed projects, or general purposes.

To Whom:
Challenge grants in U.S. for higher education, health care and long-term care, social services, assist colleges and universities, teaching hospitals, **medical schools and independent research institutions to obtain scientific equipment**, science and the environment, children, youth, family services, animal welfare, seniors, recreation, leadership development, arts, humanities, public affairs.

Education (24% of funding), Arts and Humanities (19% of funding), Human Services (27% of funding), Health and Long-term Care (14% of funding), Public Affairs (1% of funding), Science and Environment (5% of funding).

For What:
Construction and/or renovation of facilities [building], purchase of major capital equipment or an integrated system, purchase of real estate.

Financial info:
Assets: $1,470,803,400 (from 1994 990PF).
Giving: $72,848,300 for 145 grants (high: $1,500,000; low: $40,000).

Application info:
Applications accepted. Application form required. Deadline is Jan. 15, Feb. 15, May 15, July 15, Aug. 15, and Nov. 15 Board meets in May, June, Sept., Nov., Dec., and Mar. Publishes annual report and application guidelines.

Recent Grants:

$350,000	The Scripps Research Institute, San Diego, CA. Construction of laboratory facility for chemistry and biology Programs.

$1,000,000	Whitehead Institute for Biomedical Research, Cambridge, MA. Purchase of property and construction of addition for laboratories and meeting areas.
$400,000	West Virginia Wesleyan College, Buckhannon, WV. Construction of Campus Dining Center.
$500,000	Wittenberg University, Springfield, OH. Construction of outdoor athletic facilities.
$350,000	Visiting Nurse Health System, Atlanta, GA. Purchase of property and construction of inpatient hospice facility.
$750,000	Yale-New Haven Hospital, New Haven, CT. Construction and renovation of replacement patient rooms and support areas.
$400,000	The Washington Ballet, Washington, DC. Purchase and renovation of facilities and construction of wing to house studio and rehearsal space.
$150,000	William A. Farnsworth Library and Art Museum, Rockland, ME. Phase I renovation and expansion of galleries, auditorium, and library.

Directors, Officers, Trustees:

Conway, Jill K., Trustee
Kresge, Bruce A., M.D., Officer, Trustee
Kresge, Sebastian S. (d), Donor
Langdon, George D., Jr., Trustee
Larson, Robert C., Trustee
Marshall, John E., III, Officer, Trustee
Page, David K., Trustee
Smith, Margaret T., Officer, Trustee
Storey, Robert D., Trustee
Taylor, Alfred H., Jr., Trustee

Elsa U. Pardee Foundation

c/o James A. Kendall, Secretary
P.O. Box 1866
Midland, MI 48641-1866
(517) 832-3691
EIN: 386065799
Source Date: 12/94

Restrictions:
No grants to individuals, building funding, equipment (except when used in a specific project), fellowships, or fundraising campaigns.

To Whom:
Cure and control of cancer. Grants to hospitals, higher education, and institutes in U.S. for **cancer medical research and control**.

For What:
Research.

Financial info:
Assets: $71,314,300.
Giving: $3,216,800 for 50 grants (high: $200,000; low: $5,000).

Application info:
Applications accepted. Application form required (original and 7 copies). No deadline. Board meets 3 times a year. Publishes annual report with application guidelines.

Recent Grants:

$2,000	Chesaning Cultural Society/Chesaning Showboat, Symphony concert.
$1,000	Juneteenth Festival Committee, Juneteenth Festival.
$3,832	City of Saginaw Police Department, begin Mounted Patrol Unit.
$1,000	Saginaw County Chamber of Commerce Foundation, Racial Harmony Forum.
$2,500	Guardianship Services of Saginaw County, computer equipment.
$2,500	Luther Manor, building renovations.
$1,000	Field Neurological Institute, program support.
$1,000	Delta College Broadcasting, Right Now, a teen-produced television series.
$500	Michigan Lutheran Seminary, drug and alcohol prevention program.

Directors, Officers, Trustees:

Parish, Barbara J., Officer
Parish, Preston S., Donor, Officer
Roschek, Kathy A., Officer

Milton M. Ratner Foundation

c/o C. R. McDonald, VP-Secretary
17515 W. Nine Mile, Suite 875
Southfield, MI 48075
(810) 424-9373
EIN: 386160330
Source Date: 8/95

Geographic Restrictions:
Primarily in MI and GA.

Restrictions:
No grants to individuals.

To Whom:
Higher and other education, cultural programs, urban affairs, hospice, blind, youth, Jewish giving and welfare, housing, recreation, child welfare, hospitals, **medical research**.

For What:
Building funds, equipment, publications, **research**, scholarship funds, special projects, general purposes.

Financial info:
Assets: $7,139,300.
Giving: $299,100 for 60 grants (high: $40,000; low: $300).

Application info:
Applications accepted. Submit proposal. Deadline is Sept. 1. Board meets in Oct.

Recent Grants:

$10,000	Temple Beth El, Dalton, GA.
$5,000	Shepherd Spinal Center, Calhoun, GA.
$3,000	Northwest Georgia Boy Scouts, Atlanta, GA.
$1,000	Southern Fdn for Education & Medical Research, Calhoun, GA.
$2,000	St. John Health Corp., Calhoun, GA.
$10,000	Calhoun High School Media Center Foundation, Calhoun, GA.
$1,000	Habitat For Humanity Inc., Americus, GA.

Directors, Officers, Trustees:
Corley, Mary Jo Ratner, Officer, Trustee
Langford, J. Beverly, Officer, Trustee
McDonald, Charles R., Officer, Trustee
NBD Bank, Agent
Ratner, Milton M. (d), Donor

May Mitchell Royal Foundation

c/o Comerica Bank-Midland
201 McDonald St.
Midland, MI 48640

Application address:
2266 Kings Lake Blvd.
Naples, FL 33962
(813) 774-0420
EIN: 382387140
Source Date: 9/95

Geographic Restrictions:
Primarily in MI, FL, and HI.

To Whom:
Hospitals, **eye research and treatment**, health associations, **heart and cancer research**, nursing, hospice.

For What:
Equipment, scholarship funds, **research**.

Financial info:
Assets: $2,335,200.
Giving: $101,000 for 15 grants (high: $20,000; low: $500).

Application info:
Applications accepted. Submit letter. Deadline is May 31.

Directors, Officers, Trustees:
Comerica Bank-Midland, Trustee
Gillespie, Tyrone W., Committee
Hartley, Richard O., Committee
Lishman, Ruth C., Committee
Royal Trust, May Mitchell, Donor

Minnesota

Edwin H. Eddy Family Foundation

c/o Norwest Bank Duluth
Capital Mgmt. Trust Dept.
230 W. Superior St.
P.O. Box 488
Duluth, MN 55801-0488
(218) 723-2773
Source Date: 6/94

Geographic Restrictions:
Limited to the Duluth, MN, area. Scholarship priorities: first priority for Duluth, MN, area residents at the University of Minnesota, Duluth; second priority for area residents at other institutions; and third priority for non-residents at the University of Minnesota, Duluth.

Restrictions:
No grants for capital improvements or salaries.

To Whom:
Research educational work treatment and rehabilitation in the field of communicative disorders and related fields in neuro-pathology. Scholarships for students studying in the field of communication disorders.

For What:
Student aid, conferences and seminars, continuing support, individuals, internships, lectureships, matching funds, professorships, **research**, **scholarship** funds, technical assistance.

Financial info:
Assets: $2,713,300.
Giving: $69,000 for 5 grants (high: $25,000; low: $3,000) and $49,500 for 35 grants to individuals (high: $3,000; low: $1,000).

Application info:
Applications accepted. Submit proposal (8 copies). No deadline. Application form required for scholarships. Deadline is Mar. 31 for scholarships. Board meets June 1 for scholarships. Publishes application guidelines.

Directors, Officers, Trustees:
Eddy, Edwin H., Jr. (d), Donor
Edwards, Rodney J., Trustee
Norwest Bank Minnesota, N.A., Trustee
Spencer, Eben S., Trustee

Helen Lang Charitable Trust

c/o First Trust Company
Attn: Jeffrey T. Peterson, Trust Off.
P.O. Box 64704
St. Paul, MN 55164-0704
(612) 291-5128
Source Date: 8/94

Geographic Restrictions:
Primarily in MN.

Restrictions:
No grants to individuals.

To Whom:
Secondary and other education, youth, conservation, hospitals, theater, broadcasting, **medical research.**

For What:
Research, general purposes.

Financial info:
Assets: $1,219,900.
Giving: $118,500 for 5 grants (high: $40,000; low: $2,500).

Application info:
Applications accepted. Submit proposal. No deadline.

Directors, Officers, Trustees:
First Trust, N.A., Trustee
Lang, A. Scheffer, Trustee
Lang, Helen (d), Donor

McKnight Endowment Fund for Neuroscience

TCF Tower, Suite 600
121 S. Eighth St.
Minneapolis, MN 55402
(612) 333-4220
EIN: 411563321
Source Date: 12/95

Geographic Restrictions:
Limited to U.S. citizens or permanent residents.

To Whom:
Neuroscience research as it pertains to memory and to a clearer understanding of diseases affecting memory and its biological substrates.

McKnight Senior Investigator Awards: investigative programs of outstanding quality involving established neuroscientists and their associations.

McKnight Investigator Awards: support innovative research by gifted midcareer neuroscientists.

McKnight Scholars Awards: M.D. and/or Ph.D. applicants who have completed formal postdoctoral training, have demonstrated meritorious research in areas pertinent to the areas of interest of the endowment fund and are in the early stages of establishing their own independent laboratory and research career.

For What:
Individuals, **research**.

Financial info:
Assets: $2,800.
Giving: $1,680,000 for 40 grants to individuals (high: $50,000; low: $35,000).

Application info:
Applications accepted. Applications for the McKnight Scholar Awards available in Sept. of each year. Deadline is Jan. 2. Notification of award in May. Applications for the McKnight Investigator Award and Senior Investigator Awards solicited by invitation only following an extensive nominating process.

Directors, Officers, Trustees:
Barondes, Samuel H., M.D., Director, Officer
Boynton, Cynthia Binger, Director
Fischbach, Gerald D., M.D., Director
Goodman, Corey S., Director
Graybiel, Ann M., Director, Officer
Kandel, Eric, M.D., Director
McKnight Foundation, The, Donor
O'Keefe, Michael, Director, Officer
Stevens, Charles F., M.D., Director
Weisel, Torsten N., M.D., Director

Alice M. O'Brien Foundation

c/o Alvina W. O'Brien, Secretary
480 Grand Hill
St. Paul, MN 55102
Source Date: 12/93

Geographic Restrictions:
Primarily in MN.

Restrictions:
No grants to individuals, endowments, scholarships, fellowships, or matching gifts.

To Whom:
Secondary and higher education, **medical** education and **research**, social services, cultural programs, historic preservation, drug and alcohol abuse.

For What:
Operating budgets, annual campaigns, seed money, building funds, equipment, **research**.

Financial info:
Assets: $3,123,900.
Giving: $211,500 for 30 grants (high: $40,000; low: $500).

Application info:
Applications accepted. Submit proposal. No deadline. Board meets in Sept.

Directors, Officers, Trustees:
O'Brien, Alice M. (d), Donor
O'Brien, Eleanor M., Director
O'Brien, Terrance G., Director
O'Brien, Thomond R., Director, Officer
Wilcox, Dick, Director

I. A. O'Shaughnessy Foundation, Inc.

c/o Gertrude C. Mathews, Secretary
W-1271 First Nat'l Bank Bldg.
St. Paul, MN 55101
Source Date: 12/93

Geographic Restrictions:
Limited to the U.S., with emphasis on MN, IL, KS, and TX.

Restrictions:
No grants for religious missions, individual parishes, or individuals.

To Whom:
Cultural programs, secondary and higher education, social services, **medical research**, Catholic giving.

For What:
Annual campaigns, building funds, equipment, endowment funds, **research**, general purposes, continuing support.

Financial info:
Assets: $55,084,900.
Giving: $2,869,500 for 90 grants (high: $200,000; low: $3,000).

Application info:
Applications accepted. Submit letter. No deadline. Grants usually initiated by the directors. Board meets in June and Nov.

Directors, Officers, Trustees:
Globe Oil and Refining Companies, Donor
Lario Oil and Gas Company, Donor
Lyman, Charles E., Director
O'Shaughnessy, Donald E., Director
O'Shaughnessy, Eileen A., Director
O'Shaughnessy, I. A. (d), Donor
O'Shaughnessy, John F. (d), Donor
O'Shaughnessy, John F., Director
O'Shaughnessy, Lawrence M., Director

Peerless Chain Foundation

1416 E. Sanborn St.
P.O. Box 349
Winina, MN 55987
EIN: 410944373
Source Date: 3/96

Geographic Restrictions:
Limited to the Winona, MN, area.

To Whom:
Medical research, cancer, higher education.

For What:
Scholarship funds, **research**, general purposes.

Financial info:
Assets: $18,000.
Giving: $10,000 for 1 grant.

Application info:
Applications accepted. Submit letter. No deadline.

Recent Grants:
$10,000 Mayo Foundation, Rochester, MN.

Directors, Officers, Trustees:
Frankard, James M., Director, Officer
Jeresek, James J., Director, Officer
Lind, Sheila I., Director, Officer

Unity Avenue Foundation

c/o Sherburne & Coughlin, Ltd.
Attn. Philip S. Sherburne, Assist. Treas.
510 Thresher Sq. East
708 S. 3rd St.
Minneapolis, MN 55415
(612) 338-4345
Source Date: 5/94

Geographic Restrictions:
Limited to U.S. non-profits serving North America.

Restrictions:
No grants to individuals.

To Whom:
Public policy, Native Americans, libraries, higher education, **medical research**, environment, race relations, wildlife, women.

For What:
General purposes, endowment funds, **research**.

Financial info:
Assets: $1,248,000.
Giving: $52,500 for 10 grants (high: $10,000; low: $2,500).

Application info:
Applications accepted. Application form required (10 copies). Deadline is June 10. Board meets in Aug. Publishes application guidelines.

Directors, Officers, Trustees:
Cowles, Charles Fuller, Officer
Cowles, Constance M., Director
Cowles, Jane Sage, Officer
Cowles, John, III, Director
Cowles, John, Jr., Director
Cowles, Page Knudsen, Director
Cowles, Sage Fuller, Director
Flores, Sage, Director
Stephens, Ann Maria, Officer

Mississippi

Vicksburg Hospital Medical Foundation

c/o W. K. Purks, M.D., Pres.
P.O. Box 1578
Vicksburg, MS 39180-1578
(601) 636-5514
EIN: 646025312
Source Date: 12/94

Geographic Restrictions:
Primarily in MS and GA.

Restrictions:
No grants to individuals.

To Whom:
Medical education, nursing, **medical research.**

For What:
Scholarship funds, endowment funds.

Financial info:
Assets: $9,064,000.
Giving: $505,000 for 5 grants (high: $250,000; low: $5,000).

Application info:
Applications accepted. Submit letter. No deadline. Board meets quarterly.

Directors, Officers, Trustees:
Andrews, H. D., Trustee
Gage, H. N., Jr., Trustee
Knox, I. C., Jr., Officer, Trustee
Purks, W. K., M.D., Officer, Trustee
Watson, P. B., Officer, Trustee

Missouri

Harry Edison Foundation

501 N. Broadway
St. Louis, MO 63102
(314) 331-6540
EIN: 436027017
Source Date: 12/93

Geographic Restrictions:
Primarily in St. Louis, MO.

Restrictions:
No grants to individuals.

To Whom:
Higher and medical education, Jewish welfare, youth, social services, cultural programs, hospitals, family planning, **medical research**.

For What:
Professorships, **research**, building funds, scholarship funds, annual campaigns.

Financial info:
Assets: $36,016,500.
Giving: $2,285,900 for 75 grants (high: $1,000,000; low: $100).

Application info:
Applications accepted. Submit letter. No deadline.

Directors, Officers, Trustees:
Edison, Bernard, Director, Officer
Edison, Harry (d), Donor
Kohn, Henry, Director
Newman, Eric P., Director, Officer

J. M. Forrest Charitable Trust

c/o NationsBank
P.O. Box 419038
Kansas City, MO 64183
Source Date: 12/94

Geographic Restrictions:
Primarily in Kansas City, MO, area.

To Whom:
Social services, **medical research**.

For What:
Research, general purposes.

Financial info:
Giving: $47,100 for 2 grants (high: $40,100; low: $7,000).

Application info:
Applications accepted. Submit letter. No deadline.

Directors, Officers, Trustees:
NationsBank, Trustee

Lettie B. McIlvain Frederic Fund

c/o NationsBank
14 W. Tenth St.
Kansas City, MO 64105
(816) 234-7481
Source Date: 12/94

Geographic Restrictions:
Primarily in Kansas City, MO, and Lawrence, KS.

To Whom:
Medical research on strokes.

For What:
Research.

Financial info:
Giving: $58,600 for 5 grants (high: $20,000; low: $10,000).

Application info:
Applications accepted. Submit proposal. No deadline.

Directors, Officers, Trustees:
NationsBank, Trustee

Allen P. & Josephine B. Green Foundation

P.O. Box 523
Mexico, MO 65265
(314) 581-5568
Source Date: 12/95

Geographic Restrictions:
Primarily in Mexico, MO, area. Limited to continental U.S.

Restrictions:
No grants to individuals, scholarships, fellowships, or operating funds.

To Whom:
Medical research (27% of funding), youth (10% of funding), hospitals (4% of funding), religion (4% of funding), health (6% of funding), relief and social services (19% of funding), museums and historic preservation (8% of funding), education (22% of funding), and environment and conservation.

For What:
Seed money, emergency funds, building funds, equipment, endowment funds, scholarship funds, special projects, conferences and seminars, matching funds, capital campaigns, fellowships, renovation projects.

Financial info:
Assets: $6,030,000.
Giving: $275,600 for 40 grants (high: $35,000; low: $1,000).

Application info:
Applications accepted. Submit letter. Deadline is Apr. 1 or Oct. 1. Board meets in May and Nov. Publishes annual report with application guidelines.

Recent Grants:

$1,000	Arrow Rock Lyceum Theatre, Arrow Rock, MO. Continued support of the Theatre.
$6,000	ABLE Learning Center, Jefferson City, MO. Adult literacy education.
$10,000	Community R-VI School District, Laddonia, MO. Computer equipment and software for junior high.
$10,000	Community R-VI School District, Laddonia, MO. Funds for softball/baseball fields.
$1,600	Wareaw Middle School, Wareaw, MO. Books for middle schoolers.
$10,000	Whitfield School, St. Louis, MO. 1996 Coalition Summer Student Academy & Teacher Institute.
$26,000	Williams Family Support Center, Mexico, MO. Parent Training Room in new Head Start facility
$10,000	Asthma & Allergy Foundation of America, St. Louis Chapter, Olivette, MO. Comprehensive asthma-management program.
$5,000	Montreat Conference Center, Montreat, NC. Scholarships for conferences at Montreat.
$10,000	Audrain County Nutrition Site Council, Mexico, MO. Expansion of Senior Center.
$2,000	Audrain County Crisis Intervention Services, Mexico, MO. Training materials for crisis center.
$500	Cedar Creek Therapeutic Riding Center, Columbia, MO. Scholarships.
$6,000	Crider Center for Mental Health, Wentzville, MO. Capital campaign for community mental health center.
$5,000	Family Resource Center, St. Louis, MO. Services to fight child abuse.
$20,000	Independence Center, St. Louis, MO. Community Support Services team.
$6,000	Mexico Area Family YMCA, Mexico, MO. Fitness equipment and computer.
$6,000	Saline County Cooperative Workshops, Inc., Sedalia, MO. Start-up costs for commercial herb garden.
$10,000	Springfield Family Y, Springfield, MO. Scholarships for Prime Time students.
$25,000	Boy Scouts of America, Great Rivers Council, Columbia, MO. Camp Thunderbird & Hahn Scout Reservation capital campaign.
$5,000	Camp Penuel, Luke Killarney, Ironton, MO. Nature program and scholarships.
$6,000	Cathedral Mission Society, St. Louis, MO. Funds for day care center.
$2,000	Top of the Ozarks Resource Conservation & Development, Inc. Houston, MO. Books and shelves for the Library.
$2,600	Scattering Fork Outdoor Center, Mexico, MO. Native American Tepee Project.
$12,600	University of Missouri, St. Louis, MO. Support of Engelmann Mathematics & Science Institute.
$10,000	Webster University, St. Louis, MO. Funds to update technology to educate nursing students.

$5,000	The Wellness Community of Greater St. Louis, St. Louis, MO. Support for cancer victims.
$10,000	Audrain County Historical Society, Mexico, MO. Expansion of facilities.
$10,000	St. Louis Children's Hospital, St. Louis, MO. Children's Cancer Fund.
$6,000	CHILDHAVEN, St. Louis, MO. Scholarship for Elementary Age Behavioral Services Program.
$5,000	Handi-Shop, Inc., Mexico, MO. Additional building, lot and enclosing of dock.
$10,000	Hospice of Jefferson City & Mid-MO Jefferson City, MO. Heating and cooling system for in-bed patient unit.
$10,000	Paralyzed Veterans of America, Gateway Chapter, St. Louis, MO. Support for programs and projects in St. Louis.
$8,000	Audrain County 4-H Foundation, Mexico, MO. Improvements to buildings and grounds at 4-H Center.
$3,000	Girls Incorporated of St. Louis, St. Louis, MO. Friendly PEERsuasion program.
$2,500	Youth In Need, Inc., St. Charles, MO. Transitional living program for homeless youth

Directors, Officers, Trustees:

Bond, A. D., III, Director, Officer
Bond, Christopher S., Director
Collins, Robert R., Director
Green, Allen P. (d), Donor
Green, Josephine B. (d), Donor
Marks, Martha S., Director
McHenry, James F., Director
McIntosh, Robert E., Director
Staley, Walter G., Director, Officer
White, Nancy, Director
Willson, George C., III, Director, Officer
Wood, Robert A., Director

Hoechst Marion Roussel Foundation

(Formerly Marion Merrell Dow Foundation)
c/o Comm. Affairs Dept., KG2-M0838
P.O. Box 9627
Kansas City, MO 6413
EIN: 431503440
Source Date: 12/96

Geographic Restrictions:
Primarily in Kansas City, MO.

Restrictions:
No grants to individuals.

To Whom:
Medical research, elementary and secondary education with emphasis on math and science, economic education to promote the free enterprise system, medical care for the disadvantaged, community development, scientific research and training through partnerships and collaborative efforts with higher education.

Financial info:
Assets: $16,238,100 (from 1994 990PF).
Giving: $4,372,500 for 5 grants (high: $2,000,000; low: $35,000).

Application info:
Applications accepted. Submit letter (2 page limit). No deadline.

Directors, Officers, Trustees:

Connolly, Edward M., Officer, Trustee
Crampton, Ann C., Officer, Trustee
Hoechst Marion Roussel, Inc., Donor
Ladell, Peter W., Trustee
Lehr, Carolyne S., Officer
Mitchum, James P., Trustee

Edward Mallinckrodt, Jr. Foundation

c/o A. G. Edwards & Sons, Inc.
Attn: Oliver M. Langenberg, Pres.
1 N. Jefferson
St. Louis, MO 63103
(314) 955-3136
EIN: 436030295
Source Date: 12/96

Restrictions:
No grants to individuals directly.

To Whom:
Biomedical research.

For What:
Research grants to medical universities.

Financial info:
Assets: $22,786,400 (from 1993 990PF).
Giving: $1,085,000 for 20 grants (high: $75,000; low: $10,000).

Application info:
Applications accepted. Submit letter. No deadline. Board meets in Feb. or Mar., June, and Sept.

Directors, Officers, Trustees:

Allen, Charles C., Jr., Director, Officer
Cori, Carl T., Director, Officer
Deuel, Thomas F., M.D., Director, Officer
Dodge, Philip R., M.D., Director, Officer
Langenberg, Oliver M., Director, Officer
Mallinckrodt, Edward, Jr. (d), Donor

James S. McDonnell Foundation

c/o John T. Bruer, Pres.
287 N. Lindbergh, Suite 202
St. Louis, MO 63141
(314) 721-1532
Internet: http://www.jsmf.org
EIN: 436030988
Source Date: 12/95

Geographic Restrictions:
Limited to U.S.

Restrictions:
No grants to individuals, political purposes, sectarian religious groups, endowments, capital campaigns, annual appeals, ongoing operating expenses, equipment, building funding, renovations.

To Whom:
Research to Improve the Quality of Life: research in the biological and behavioral sciences, projects that integrate biological and behavioral approaches in the study of higher brain function, applications of biological and behavioral research to improve diagnostic, therapeutic, or preventive interventions, research to improve the treatment and diagnosis of cancer and AIDS.

Research and Innovation in Education: research in the cognitive, behavioral, and social sciences to improve curricula, teaching, learning, and teacher training, implementation of cognitive, behavioral and social research in classrooms, particularly interventions intended to meet the educational needs of diverse student populations, innovative or experimental programs to improve educational opportunities in St. Louis area.

Research to Improve Global Understanding: activities related to current program interested in quality of life and education, which require international collaboration and address the needs of developing countries.

Foundation initiated programs include: McDonnell-Pew Program in Cognitive Neuroscience, Cognitive Studies for Educational Practice, and Molecular Medicine in Cancer Research.

For What:
Special projects, **research**, conferences and seminars.

Financial info:
Assets: $318,983,600.
Giving: $12,394,600 for 50 grants (high: $1,000,000; low: $500).

Application info:
Applications accepted. Submit letter of inquiry. No deadline. Publishes annual report with application guidelines on computer disk.

Recent Grants:

$440,000	Washington University
$1,000,000	Washington University School of Medicine
$76,503	Northwestern University
$162,782	Ontario Institute for Studies in Education
$236,920	Ontario Institute for Studies in Education
$75,337	St. Louis Public Schools
$115,000	St. Louis Science Center
$195,972	St. Louis Science Center
$35,145	St. Louis Science Center-Transferred from Public School St. Louis
$111,336	University of California, Berkeley

$237,127	Vanderbilt University
$29,700	Columbia University, Teacher's College
$29,700	Florida State University
$29,700	Northwestern University
$11,500	Council on Foundations
$100,000	Davis and Elkins College
$20,000	Gilman School
$50,000	Missouri Botanical Garden
$50,000	Municipal Theatre Association
$12,500	Planned Parenthood of the St. Louis Region
$1,000	The Foundation Center
$10,000	Cooperating School Districts
$12,500	Vassar College
$59,336	Carnegie Mellon University
$59,797	Columbia University
$60,000	Duke University
$90,000	Harvard Medical School
$90,000	Harvard University
$60,000	Massachusetts General Hospital
$412,649	Massachusetts Institute of Technology
$334,170	University of Arizona

Directors, Officers, Trustees:
Bruer, John T., Officer
McDonnell, James S. (d), Donor
McDonnell, James S., III, Donor, Director, Officer
McDonnell, John F., Donor, Director, Officer
Witunski, Michael, Director

Messing Family Charitable Foundation

c/o Wilma Messing
30 Westwood Country Club Grounds
St. Louis, MO 63131
(314) 432-8898
EIN: 436034863
Source Date: 12/95

Geographic Restrictions:
Primarily in St. Louis, MO.

To Whom:
Hospitals, **medical research**, education, Jewish giving.

For What:
Research, student aid.

Financial info:
Assets: $2,703,500.
Giving: $121,400 for 85 grants (high: $25,000; low: $50).

Application info:
Applications accepted. Submit letter. No deadline.

Directors, Officers, Trustees:
Goodman, Harold S., Trustee
Hefty, Noel M., Trustee
Hefty, Terrance, Trustee
Messing, Roswell, Jr., Donor
Messing, Roswell, Jr., Mrs., Donor
Messing, Roswell, III, Trustee
Messing, Wilma E., Trustee
Naschke, Arlene M., Trustee

Paul Patton Charitable Trust

c/o NationsBank
P.O. Box 419038, Trust Dept.
Kansas City, MO 64183
(816) 691-7481
EIN: 446009254
Source Date: 12/93

Geographic Restrictions:
Primarily in Kansas City, MO, area.

To Whom:
Pediatric medical research and education.

For What:
Research.

Financial info:
Assets: $3,256,700.
Giving: $95,000 for 5 grants.

Application info:
Applications accepted. Submit letter (3 page limit). No deadline.

Directors, Officers, Trustees:
Evans, William L., Jr., Trustee
McCarter, C. Ted, Trustee
NationsBank, Trustee

J. B. Reynolds Foundation

c/o Walter E. Bixby, Treasurer
3520 Broadway
P.O. Box 419139
Kansas City, MO 64141
(816) 753-7000
EIN: 446014359
Source Date: 12/96

Geographic Restrictions:
Primarily in a 150-mile radius of Kansas City, MO.

Restrictions:
No grants to individuals.

To Whom:
Medical research, social services, youth, civic affairs, cultural programs.

For What:
Annual campaigns, seed money, emergency funds, building funds, equipment, land acquisition, **research**, publications, conferences and seminars, continuing support.

Financial info:
Assets: $13,019,200 (from 1995 990PF).
Giving: $600,800 for 120 grants (high: $30,000; low: $100).

Application info:
Applications accepted. Submit letter. No deadline. Board meets in Apr. and Dec.

Directors, Officers, Trustees:
- Bixby, Joseph Reynolds, Officer
- Bixby, Walter E., Officer
- Bixby, Walter Edwin, Sr. (d), Donor
- Finn, Richard L., Officer
- Hudsop, Nancy, Officer
- Reynolds, Pearl G. (d), Donor

Victor E. Speas Foundation

c/o NationsBank
14 W. Tenth St., Trust Dept.
Kansas City, MO 64183
(816) 691-7481
EIN: 446008340
Source Date: 12/94

Geographic Restrictions:
Limited to Jackson, Clay, Platte, and Cass counties in MO.

Restrictions:
No grants for endowments. No loans or scholarships except to medical students at the University of Missouri at Kansas City.

To Whom:
Medically-related higher education, loans for medical students at University of Missouri at Kansas City, preventive health care, AIDS, hospice, drug and alcohol abuse, mental health, women, voluntarism, **medical research,** health care needs of seniors, youth, disabled, hospitals, rehabilitation, child welfare, cancer, heart disease, mental health, safety, women.

For What:
Seed money, emergency funds, equipment, **research,** special projects, renovation projects, capital campaigns, matching funds, operating budgets, student loans.

Financial info:
Assets: $25,229,700.
Giving: $1,214,900 for 60 grants (high: $100,000; low: $2,000).

Application info:
Applications accepted. Submit letter (3 page limit). No deadline. Board meets bimonthly.

Directors, Officers, Trustees:
- NationsBank, Trustee
- Speas, Effie E. (d), Donor
- Speas, Victor E. (d), Donor
- Speas Company, Donor

Norman J. Stupp Foundation

c/o Commerce Bank
8000 Forsyth, Suite 1305
St. Louis, MO 63105
(314) 746-8577
EIN: 436027433
Source Date: 6/94

Geographic Restrictions:
Primarily in St. Louis, MO.

Restrictions:
No grants to individuals.

To Whom:
Hospitals, **medical research**, youth, social services, public affairs, science and technology, higher, engineering, and other education.

For What:
Capital campaigns, endowment funds, operating budgets, **research**, scholarship funds, special projects.

Financial info:
Assets: $12,223,900.
Giving: $600,000 for 65 grants (high: $75,000; low: $500).

Application info:
Applications accepted. Submit proposal. Deadline is Apr. 1 and Oct. 1. Board meets in May and Nov.

Directors, Officers, Trustees:
Commerce Bank of St. Louis, N.A., Trustee
Stupp, Norman J. (d), Donor

Nevada

Lincy Foundation

c/o James D. Aljian, Pres.
4835 Kozal Ln.
Las Vegas, NV 89109
(702) 737-8060
EIN:954238697
Source Date: 9/95

Geographic Restrictions:
Primarily in CA.

Restrictions:
No grants to individuals.

To Whom:
Armenian giving, international relief, seniors, hospitals, **medical research**, arts.

Financial info:
Assets: $68,284,000.
Giving: $11,747,400 for 150 grants (high: $2,000,000; low: $1,000).

Application info:
Applications accepted. Submit letter. No deadline.

Directors, Officers, Trustees:
Aljian, James D., Officer
Kerkorian, Kirk, Officer
Mandekic, Anthony, Officer
Sharp, Walter M., Officer
Yemenidjian, Alex, Officer

E. L. Wiegand Foundation

c/o Kristen A. Avansino, Exec. Dir.
Wiegand Ctr.
165 W. Liberty St.
Reno, NV 89501
(702) 333-0310
EIN: 942839372
Source Date: 10/96

Geographic Restrictions:
Public Affairs grants primarily in CA, Washington, DC, and New York, NY, NV; Education primarily in NV, CA, OREG, ID, UT, WA, and AZ; Health and Medical Research: NV, CA, OR, ID, UT, and AZ; Civic and Community Affairs: NV and CA (north of Los Angeles County); Arts and Cultural Affairs: NV and CA (north of Los Angeles County).

Restrictions:
No grants for organizations receiving significant support from public tax funds, organizations with beneficiaries of their own choosing, federal, state, or local government agencies or institutions, individuals, endowments, fundraising campaigns, operating expenses, emergency funding, political groups, publications, films, or media presentations, religious institutions for building construction, institutions that have in existence for less than 5 years, and institutions served by the United Way.

To Whom:
Educational institutions in areas of science, business, fine arts, law, and medicine, **health and medical research in areas of heart, eye, cancer surgery, treatment and research with priority given to programs that benefit children**, civic and community affairs, public affairs, arts and cultural affairs.

For What:
Equipment, special projects.

Financial info:
Assets: $80,568,300.
Giving: $3,962,100 for 115 grants (high: $350,000; low: $50).

Application info:
Applications accepted. Submit inquiry letter. Application form required for full proposal. No deadline. Board meet in Feb., June, and Oct. Publishes application guidelines.

Recent Grants:

$219,729	George Washington University Medical Center, Dept. of Emergency Medicine, Washington, DC. Wiegand Health Professional Center in the Czech Republic.

Directors, Officers, Trustees:
Avansino, Kristin A., Officer
Avansino, Raymond C., Jr., Officer, Trustee
Carrico, James T., Officer
Fahrenkopf, Frank J., Jr., Trustee
Fruehauf, Harvey C., Jr., Trustee
Gabelli, Mario J., Trustee
Hildahl, Joanne C., Officer
Melarkey, Michael J., Officer
Wiegand, Ann K. (d), Donor
Wiegand, Edwin L. (d), Donor

New Jersey

Brunetti Foundation

1655 U. S. Hwy. 9
Old Bridge, NJ 08857
(908) 727-3300
EIN: 237346205
Source Date: 12/95

Geographic Restrictions:
Primarily in NJ, NY, and FL.

Restrictions:
No grants to individuals.

To Whom:
Higher and other education, **medical research**, child welfare, hospitals, Catholic giving.

For What:
Research, endowment funds, scholarship funds.

Financial info:
Assets: $3,455,500.
Giving: $163,600 for 130 grants (high: $25,000; low: $100).

Application info:
Applications accepted. Submit letter. No deadline.

Directors, Officers, Trustees:
Aldercrest Development Corp., Donor
Brunetti, Anna G., Director
Brunetti, John J., Donor, Director, Officer
Brunetti, John J., Jr., Officer

Charles Edison Fund

c/o Paul Christiansen, Pres.
101 S. Harrison St.
East Orange, NJ 07018
(201) 675-9000
EIN: 221514861
Source Date: 12/95

Geographic Restrictions:
Primarily in NY-NJ metropolitan area.

Restrictions:
No grants to individuals, building or endowment funding, scholarships, fellowships, or matching gifts.

To Whom:
Historic preservation, with emphasis on the homes of Thomas Alva Edison, and science education, **medical research**.

For What:
Operating budgets, continuing support, seed money, special projects, **research**, equipment.

Financial info:
Assets: $31,370,100.
Giving: $718,900 for 70 grants (high: $100,000; low: $50).

Application info:
Applications accepted. Submit letter or proposal. Deadline is 3 weeks prior to board meetings. Board meets in Mar., June, Sept., and Dec.

Directors, Officers, Trustees:
Allman, Edward L., Trustee
Arnn, Nancy M., Trustee
Christiansen, Paul J., Officer, Trustee
Edison, Charles (d), Donor
Ench, Alberta, Officer
Henderson, William M., Trustee
Howe, James E., Trustee
Keegan, John P., Officer
Murray, Robert E., Trustee
Schullinger, John N., M.D., Trustee
Smoot, J. Thomas, Jr., Trustee

Johnson & Johnson Family of Companies Contribution Fund

c/o Helen Hughes, Mgr., Corp. Contributions
1 Johnson & Johnson Plaza
New Brunswick, NJ 08933
(908) 524-3697
EIN: 226062811
Source Date: 12/95

Geographic Restrictions:
Primarily in U.S. and Puerto Rico where the corporation has a presence.

Restrictions:
No grants to individuals, capital or endowment funding, travel, or political activities.

To Whom:
Health with special emphasis given to research, prevention, and improved access and quality **of health**

care for the medically underserved (especially mothers and children), hospitals, higher education and minority higher education, elementary and secondary education for new ways of teaching math and pre-school education, employment and training which provide at-risk people with job skills, enhancement of the family and family values projects which enrich or protect the integrity of the family, community and cultural activities which strengthen family relationships, projects that seek to eliminate problems that disrupt family life (drug/alcohol abuse prevention).

Civic (11% of funding), **Health and Medical Research (17% of funding),** Education (12% of funding), Culture/Arts (13% of funding).

For What:
Employee matching gifts only.

Financial info:
Assets: $252,100.
Giving: $3,718,300 for 370 grants (high: $800,000; low: $500).

Application info:
Applications accepted. Submit preliminary letter. No deadline. Board meets in Mar., June, Sept., and Dec. Publishes annual report and application guidelines.

Recent Grants:

$100,000 European Network of Health Promoting Schools. Finance the development of training courses for public school teachers involved in educating students about preventive health including regular exercise, nutrition and other healthy behaviors as part of an integrated curriculum. The countries involved include the Czech Republic, Hungary, Poland and the Slovak Republic.

$45,000 Paranaque (Philippines) Community Hospital. Expand and modernize the hospital's nursery and pediatric rooms. Established in 1978, the 75-bed facility now assists significantly more medically underserved children.

$25,000 The President's Committee on Employment of People with Disabilities. Help sponsor a new Educational Training Center in Washington, DC. The center is the first of its kind and will be the focal point for national and international educational training meetings for individuals with disabilities.
Pediatric Burns Center Established in South Africa. The success of an existing Johnson & Johnson Burns Center at Baragwanath Hospital in Soweto, South Africa, has led to the development of a pediatric wing for children suffering from severe burn injuries. The original center, established with seed money from the Corporation in 1990, is multiracial and serves all of South Africa. Both centers focus on training, preventive measures and treatment. Combined support from Johnson & Johnson and its South African affiliates totals some $1.1 million.

$50,000 Bucks County Historical Society/Mercer Museum, Doylestown, PA. "Healing Arts" exhibit. The exhibit consists of medical objects related to the development of the medical arts in the 19th and 20th centuries and has a unique focus on health care topics.

$64,000 Yale University. Research and development of a School Health Module, which is intended to pave the way for better early childhood health care education for America's preschool and elementary school students.

Directors, Officers, Trustees:
Alstrup, J. Andrea, Trustee
Barker, Frank H., Trustee
Bzdak, Michael J., Officer
Cooper, Aldrage B., Trustee
Dearstyne, William D., Trustee
Edelson, Ruth C., Trustee
Fine, Roger S., Officer, Trustee
Gelbman, Ronald G., Trustee
Gussin, Robert Z., Trustee
Hartnett, Edward J., Trustee
Heisen, JoAnn H., Trustee
Johnson and Johnson, Donor
Larson, Peter N., Trustee
Logan, Wendy B., Trustee
Mays, Alfred T., Trustee
Mullen, John R., Trustee
Nielsen, Willard D., Trustee
Weeden, Curtis G., Officer, Trustee

Robert Wood Johnson Foundation

c/o Edward H. Robbins, Proposal Mgr.
P.O. Box 2316
Princeton, NJ 08543-2316
(609) 452-8701
Internet: http://www.rwjf.org
EIN: 223048720
Source Date: 12/96

Geographic Restrictions:
Limited to the U.S.

Restrictions:
No grants for basic biomedical research, individuals, operating expenses, deficit financing, endowment or capital funds, construction, renovation, equipment, conferences or symposia, publications or media projects, research on unapproved drug therapies or devices, or international programs and institutions.

To Whom:
Access: assure that Americans of all ages have access to basic health care, explore options for expanded coverage for the uninsured and underinsured, develop and evaluate new payment incentives to promote primary care services, stimulate the U.S. debate on restructuring health care financing, influence the supply and distribution of generalist physicians and other primary care providers, address the underrepresentation of minorities in health care professions, strengthen primary care infrastructure and the public health safety net, increase understanding of the contribution of race, socioeconomic status, and culture in health and health care, work with communities to identify and address their health problems, help providers become more responsive to needs of diverse patient populations.

Drug and Alcohol Abuse: encourage service demonstration models that connect substance abuse services to organizations that reach significant populations of individuals, such as juvenile justice system, education system, business community, religion community, and neighborhood centers, models that connect substance abuse services with larger health care system, understand the causes of substance abuse and its prevention and treatment, including identification, evaluation, and dissemination of promising new approaches that are appropriate for persons with varied environmental and risk factors, comprehensive community-wide communications projects and efforts to change societal norms regarding the use of substances, improve the effectiveness of substance abuse services, the organization, delivery, and financing, policy research, promote changes in community and social environments that will reduce substance abuse.

Chronic Health Conditions: development and testing of exemplary models for reorganization and delivery of needed services to those with chronic health conditions, research projects and policy analysis, promote better clinical practice in chronic care, alter the focus of medical practice to include the effective management of services for people with chronic illness, communications projects that illuminate the complexity of the problem.

Cost Containment: policy analysis, **health services research and demonstration projects that explore the feasibility of new cost control strategies**, evaluate the impact of different cost control strategies on costs, access and quality, as well as on different sectors of the economy, educate the public about the tradeoffs inherent in different cost control strategies, bring together the major actors in health policy to promote better understanding of the long-term problems facing the health care system and the need for more systemic approach to controlling health care expenditures.

For What:
Seed money, **research**, special projects, fellowships, program-related investments.

Financial info:
Assets: $5,257,995,500 (from 1995 990PF).
Giving: $255,193,500 for 945 grants.

Application info:
Applications accepted. Submit letter of inquiry (4 page limit). No deadline. Board meets quarterly. Publishes newsletter and application guidelines.

Recent Grants:

$1,600,000	Memorial Hospital, Pawtucket, RI. For the Volunteer Physician Technical Resource Program.
$2,500,000	University of California, CA. For improving access to care by restructuring provider payments.
$50,000	Children's Hospital Foundation of Austin, TX. For planning for the privatization of a school-based health services program.
$450,000	The Greater Kansas City Community Foundation, Kansas City, MO. For a campaign to mobilize the community to address the needs of children.
$200,000	Marshall Heights Community Development Organization, Washington, DC. For planning a primary care delivery network.
$349,199	National Academy of Sciences Institute of Medicine, Washington, DC. For a study of children, health insurance and access to care.
$100,000	Public Health Foundation Enterprises, City of Industry, CA. For wellness care at work sites in Central Los Angeles.

$250,000 The Urban Institute, Washington, DC. For assessing the new federalism in New Jersey.

$220,679 Greater Cleveland Hospital Association. Linking Supply to Demand: A Long-Range Nursing Workforce Project.

$1,500,000 American Medical Association, Chicago, IL. For a program to train physicians in end-of-life care.

$773,644 George Washington University, Washington, DC. For assessing the implementation of health-related provisions of the Welfare Reform Act.

$188,804 the Alliance for Health Reform, Washington, DC. For issue briefings on managed care and vulnerable populations for Washington-based policymakers and the media.

$489,307 Family Voices, Algodones, NM. For resources for families with special-needs children.

$197,045 Group Health Cooperative of Puget Sound, Seattle, WA. For planning for a program of chronic disease management in organized health systems.

$180,000 University of Maryland Center on Aging, College Park. MD. For focus groups and surveys for RWJF Cash and Counseling Demonstration and Evaluation Program.

$498,640 Medical Pathfinders, Anchorage, AK. For development of a computerized patient support network for people with chronic illnesses.

$203,018 National Conference of State Legislatures, Denver. CO. For education for state policymakers on workers' compensation health reform issues.

$113,280 National Hospice Organization, Arlington, VA. For a project to train residents in end-of-life care.

$355,703 National Multiple Sclerosis Society, New York. NY. For a syndicated radio program on chronic health conditions.

$184,998 New Jersey Institute of Technology Foundation, Newark, NJ. For a manual to assist parents of children with physical disabilities in creating a supportive home environment.

$100,000 University of North Carolina at Chapel Hill School of Nursing, NC. For a project to update a nursing text on death and dying.

$379,954 University of Southern Mississippi Institute for Disability Studies, Hattiesburg, MS. For improving systems of care for chronically ill Mississippians.

$110,068 University of Virginia Health Sciences Center, Charlottesville, VA. For a national survey of hospice volunteers and staff.

$810,223 University of Minnesota School of Public Health, Minneapolis, MN. For evaluation of RWJF's Reducing Underage Drinking Through Community and State Coalitions.

$482,219 American Bar Association Fund for Justice and Education, Washington, DC. For development of unified family courts to assist families with substance abuse problems.

$138,404 Boston University School of Public Health, MA. For coordinating community coalition participation in Home Box Office outreach activities.

$2,200,000 University of California, Los Angeles, CA, Center for Health Sciences. For a household survey on substance abuse and mental health care.

$95,050 The National Center on Addiction and Substance Abuse at Columbia University, New York, NY. For a survey of Californians' understanding of Proposition 215: Medical Use of Marijuana.

$451,185 National Foundation for the Centers for Disease Control and Prevention, Atlanta, GA. For research on racial and gender differences in teen smoking.

$96,991 Treatment Research Institute, Philadelphia. PA. For research on the effects on employers of covering substance abuse services.

$853,446 East Bay Community Recovery Project, Oakland, CA. Fighting Back: Community Initiatives to Reduce Demand for Illegal Drugs and Alcohol.

$500,000 American Cancer Society, Georgia Division, Atlanta, GA. SmokeLess States: Statewide Tobacco Prevention and Control Initiatives.

$899,375 The Carter Center, Atlanta, GA. For developing community responses to youth firearm violence.

$237,533 Aspira of Puerto Rico, San Juan. Emergency assistance for the victims of Hurricane Hortense in Puerto Rico.

$200,000 Association of Academic Health Centers, Washington, DC. For a study of the organizational structures of academic health centers.

$230,000 Harvard Law School, Cambridge, MA. For research to develop policy models aimed at assuring that children grow up in nurturing homes.
$351,228 Institute for the Arts of Democracy, Brattleboro, VT. For expansion of a news service on civic engagement.
$425,000 National Academy of Sciences & Institute of Medicine. For a study of injuries in the US and the response of public and private agencies.
$450,000 National Academy of Sciences & Institute of Medicine. For a research study on health and behavior.
$499,944 The New York Academy of Medicine, New York, NY. For defining and measuring community benefit in managed health care.
$440,011 University of Pennsylvania, The Annenberg School for Communication, Philadelphia, PA. For improving educational television opportunities for children.
$350,000 The United Way of Central Jersey, Milltown, NJ. Support for the 1996-97 campaign.
$1,100,000 New Jersey Health Initiatives, awards to six sites.
$50,000 Assessment of sexuality research opportunities Social Science Research Council, New York, NY
$287,642 Design and implement a system for monitoring quality of care and beneficiary and provider satisfaction Commonwealth of Puerto Rico, Puerto Rico Health Insurance Administration, San Juan, PR
$594,385 Improving Service Systems for People with Disabilities, Stavros Center for Independent Living, Inc. Amherst, MA
$100,000 Partners in Caregiving. The Dementia Services Program, Central Adult Daycare Services, Inc. Warwick, RI
$50,000 Using graphic displays of medication history to improve psychiatric care. State of Vermont, Department of Mental Health, Waterbury, VT
$572,827 Expansion of model needle exchange program. City of New Haven, Department of Health, New Haven, CT
$495,206 Managed care model for high-risk families, The Center for Mental Health, Inc. Washington, DC
$977,728 Improving the Quality of Hospital Care. Public Hospital Institute, San Mateo, CA
$149,829 Healthy Nations:Reducing Substance Abuse Among Native Americans. Confederated Tribes of the Colville Reservation, Nespelem, WA
$968,895 SmokeLess States Program - Implementation. Alaska Native Health Board, Anchorage, AK
$150,000 Healthy Nations:Reducing Substance Abuse Among Native Americans. White Mountain Apache Tribe of the Fort Apache Indian Reservation, Whiterriver, AZ

Directors, Officers, Trustees:

Andrews, Edward C., Jr., M.D., Trustee
Burke, James E., Trustee
Campbell, Robert E., Trustee
Clare, David R., Trustee
de Tornay, Rheba, Trustee
Foster, Lawrence G., Trustee
Gilliam, John, Officer
Goodwin, Peter, Officer
Griego, Linda, Officer, Trustee
Hearn, Ruby P., Officer
Heldrich, John J., Trustee
Horan, John J., Trustee
Jellinek, Paul S., Officer
Johnson, Robert Wood (d), Donor
Karel, Frank, III, Officer
Kaufman, Nancy J., Officer
Kean, Thomas H., Trustee
Knickman, James R., Officer
Matthews, Edward E., Trustee
Owen, Jack W., Trustee
Raines, Franklin D., Trustee
Reynolds, Richard C., M.D., Officer
Rosenberg, Norman, M.D., Trustee
Sandy, Lewis G., Officer
Schroeder, Steven A., M.D., Officer, Trustee
Steele, John H., Trustee
Wentz, Sidney F., Officer, Trustee
Wood, J. Warren, III, Officer

Fannie E. Rippel Foundation

c/o Nancy L. Ryan, Secretary
180 Mt. Airy Rd., Suite 200
Basking Ridge, NJ 07920-2021
(908) 766-0404
Internet: http://fdncenter.org/grantmaker/rippel/index.html
EIN: 221559427
Source Date: 4/96

Geographic Restrictions:
Limited to U.S. organizations, with emphasis on NJ, New York, NY, the northeast U.S. and the Middle Atlantic Seaboard.

Restrictions:
No grants to individuals, general purposes, operating funds, continuing support, annual campaigns, deficit financing, scholarships, fellowships, endowment or building funding, or matching gifts.

To Whom:
Aid, assist, found, equip, and provide for the relief and care of aged women [seniors], build and equip hospitals, treatment of and/or **research concerning heart disease and cancer**, through higher education, **medical research**, and hospitals.

For What:
Equipment, **research**, renovation projects, special projects.

Financial info:
Assets: $69,780,700.
Giving: $2,016,000 for 15 grants (high: $500,000; low: $25,000).

Application info:
Applications accepted. Submit letter. No deadline. Publishes annual report with application guidelines.

Recent Grants:

$139,000 **Arizona State University, Tempe, AZ. For the University's Cancer Research Institute to pay for the costs of collecting and recollecting marine animal specimens which may contain anticancer agents.**

$500,000 The Cancer Institute of New Jersey, an operating division of the New Brunswick Affiliated Hospitals, New Brunswick, New Jersey. Toward the cost of the Patient Education Area on the first floor of the Institute's new research and patient care facility.

$150,000 **Children's Memorial Medical Center, Chicago, IL. Toward the cost of establishing Transgenic and Targeted Mutagenesis Facilities at the Medical Center's Children's Memorial Institute for Education Research.**

$150,000 **DOROT, Inc., New York, NY. Toward the cost of personnel for the program staff and the medical consultants' fees for ElderStanding, a study to test the effectiveness of volunteers as agents of intervention in the prevention of falls among the homebound elderly.**

$200,000 Duke University Medical Center, Durham, NC. Toward the cost of completing a laboratory suite within Duke's new Medical Science Research Building for the establishment of the "Fannie E. Rippel Foundation Laboratories in Transplant Biology."

$150,000 Fox Chase Cancer Center, Philadelphia, PA. Toward the cost of establishing a Biotechnology Core Facility, including the purchase of state-of-the-art instrumentation for use therein.

$100,000 Good Samaritan Hospital Regional Medical Center, Suffern, NY. Toward the cost of purchasing an Information System and three pieces of state-of-the-art equipment for the Medical Center's newly established Radiation Therapy Center.

$150,000 Jersey City Medical Center, Jersey City, NJ. Toward the cost of purchasing a Management Information System Network, including installation of necessary equipment at the Medical Center's newly renovated Family Health Center.

$25,000 Jersey Shore Medical Center, Inc., Neptune, NJ. Toward the cost of completing an OB/GYN suite as part of the $23 million expansion of the Medical Center's Emergency Department/Trauma Center area.

$150,000 **Memorial Sloan-Kettering Cancer Center, New York, NY. Toward the cost of conducting a research study entitled "Addressing Ethical Dilemmas in Cancer Care: A Model Program for Cancer Centers."**

$100,000	New York University Medical Center, New York, NY. Toward the cost of purchasing new laboratory equipment to be used in a cancer research study of Tumor Rejection Antigens in the Department of Cell Biology at the University's Kaplan Cancer Center.
$150,000	University of Rochester Medical Center, Rochester, NY. To pay for planning activities and reimburse for future expenditures to complete a two-year Rural Health Network Quality Measurement and Management Project.
$52,000	State of New Jersey Commission on Cancer Research, Trenton, NJ. Toward the cost of developing a New Jersey Interactive Cancer Registry Network, including the cost of necessary personnel to operate the interactive network system and the purchase of an optical scanner.

Directors, Officers, Trustees:

Bensley, Bruce N., Trustee
Brinton, S. Jervis, Jr., Officer, Trustee
Hockenjos, G. Frederick, Trustee
Kidde, John L., Trustee
Limpert, Eleanor O., Officer
Luther, Janet E., Officer
Probert, Edward W., Officer, Trustee
Rippel, Julius S. (d), Donor
Ryan, Nancy L., Officer

New York

Marjorie C. Adams Charitable Trust

c/o Chase Manhattan Bank
Attn: Gail P. Fitch, Trust Off.
270 Park Ave., 21st Flr.
New York, NY 10017-2070
(212) 270-9066
EIN: 136897539
Source Date: 12/94

Restrictions:
No grants to individuals.

To Whom:
Research, education, care or treatment of **deafness or blindness**.

Financial info:
Giving: $149,000 for 15 grants (high: $20,000; low: $1,000).

Application info:
Applications accepted. Submit letter. Deadline is June 30.

Directors, Officers, Trustees:
Chase Manhattan Bank, N.A., Trustee

Aitken Brain Trauma Foundation, Inc.

c/o Peter C. Quinn, Exec. Dir.
523 East 72nd St., 8th Flr.
New York, NY 10021
(212) 772-0608
Source Date: 12/94

Restrictions:
No grants to individuals, capital or endowment funding, operating expenses, or deficit financing. No funding for research relating to head injury prevention or post-injury rehabilitation. Limited to applications from institutions in the U.S.

To Whom:
Pilot medical research related to the pathophysiology and therapy of brain injury in the early post-traumatic period, facilitating communication among scientists, clinicians, and victims of head injury, their families and friends to ensure the rapid and ready exchange of information.

For What:
Conferences and seminars, fellowships.

Financial info:
Giving: $174,800 for 5 grants (high: $50,000; low: $25,000).

Application info:
Applications accepted. Submit letter or proposal (2-3 page limit). Deadline is Dec. 15 for full proposal. Publishes application guidelines.

Directors, Officers, Trustees:
Atkin Trust, Annie-Laurie, Donor
Becker, Donald P., M.D., Med.Adv.Board
Betts, Henry B., M.D., Director
Blair, William McCormick, Jr., Mrs., Director
Fishman, Robert A., M.D., Med.Adv.Board
Ghajar, Jamshid B. G., M.D., Med.Adv.Board
Gurley, George Morris, Director, Officer
Hariri, Robert J., M.D., Med.Adv.Board
Isham, Ala Auersperg, Director, Officer
Isham, Ralph Heyward, Director, Officer
Jeffries, Yasmin Aga Khan, Director, Officer
Narayan, Raj K., M.D., Med.Adv.Board
Patterson, Russel, M.D., Med.Adv.Board
Patterson, Russel H., Jr.,M.D., Director
Plum, Fred, M.D., Med.Adv.Board
Spivack, Marilyn Price, Director
von Auersperg, Alexander, Director, Officer

Rita Allen Foundation, Inc.

c/o Milton Cassel
550 Park Ave.
New York, NY 10021
EIN: 136116429
Source Date: 12/95

Restrictions:
No grants to individuals (except university research scientists), building funds, or operating expenses.

To Whom:
Medical research, with emphasis on cancer, multiple sclerosis, cerebral palsy, and euphoric and analgesics related to terminally ill, limited giving for welfare and religion.

Financial info:
Assets: $15,718,800.
Giving: $550,100 for 40 grants (high: $15,000; low: $100).

Application info:
Applications accepted. Submit letter. Deadline is Jan. 15. Board meets annually.

Directors, Officers, Trustees:
Cassel, Milton E., Director, Officer
Cassel Rita Allen, Donor
Gates, Moore, Jr., Director, Officer
Hitch, Harry M., Director

Allyn Foundation, Inc.

c/o Margaret O'Connell, Exec. Dir.
P.O. Box 22
Skaneateles, NY 13152
EIN: 156017723
Source Date: 3/97

Geographic Restrictions:
Limited to Skaneateles and Onondaga and Cayuga counties, NY, area.

Restrictions:
No grants for religious programs, individuals, or endowments.

To Whom:
Higher, medical, and other education, youth, social services, **medical research**, hospitals, child welfare, community development.

For What:
Building funds, equipment, fellowships, renovation projects, **research**, scholarship funds.

Financial info:
Assets: $7,122,200 (from 1995 990PF).
Giving: $300,000 for 30 grants (high: $100,000; low: $1,000).

Application info:
Applications accepted. Application form required. Board meets 3 times per year.

Directors, Officers, Trustees:
Allyn, Dawn N., Director
Allyn, Eric, Director
Allyn, Janet J., Director
Allyn, Lew F., Director, Officer
Allyn, William F., Director, Officer
Allyn, William G., Director, Officer
Allyn, William N. (d), Donor
Falcone, Tasha, Director
Infanger, Marie, Director, Officer
O'Connell, Margaret M., Director
Soderberg, Elsa A., Director
Soderberg, Peter, Director
Soderberg, Robert C., Director
Townsend, Wilbur L., Director

ASDA Foundation

c/o First Spring Corp.
499 Park Ave., 26th Flr.
New York, NY 10022
(212) 688-4010
EIN: 521319624
Source Date: 12/94

To Whom:
Higher education, **medical research**, AIDS, Jewish museums.

For What:
General purposes, **research**.

Financial info:
Assets: $7,975,400.
Giving: $969,300 for grants.

Application info:
Applications accepted. Submit letter. No deadline.

Directors, Officers, Trustees:
Conley, Jeanne, Director
de Gunzburg, Alain, Director
de Gunzburg, Charles, Director
de Gunzburg, Jean, Director
Goldman, Guido, Director, Officer
Musen, Kenneth N., Director
Penn, Kevin, Officer
Rodriguez, Lynne, Officer
Sauerteig, B. Lance, Director, Officer

Baird Foundation

c/o Catherine Schweitzer, Mgr.
P.O. Box 1210, Ellicott Station
Buffalo, NY 14205
(716) 883-2429
EIN: 166023080
Source Date: 12/94

Geographic Restrictions:
Primarily in Erie County, NY.

Restrictions:
No grants to individuals.

To Whom:
Higher education, disadvantaged, religion, arts, historic preservation, hospitals, **medical research**, social services, drug and alcohol abuse, community funds, museums, environment, youth.

For What:
Research, matching funds, general purposes, capital campaigns.

Financial info:
Giving: $414,800 for 120 grants (high: $200,000; low: $100).

Application info:
Applications accepted. Submit letter. No deadline. Board meets quarterly with notification in 3 months.

Directors, Officers, Trustees:
Baird, Cameron (d), Donor
Baird, Flora M. (d), Donor
Baird, Frank B., Jr. (d), Donor
Baird, William C. (d), Donor
Cryer, Arthur W., Trustee
Gruber, Carl E., Officer
Irwin, Robert J. A., Trustee
Irwin, William Baird, Trustee
Wiesmore, Molly, Officer

Elmer & Mamdouha Bobst Foundation, Inc.

c/o The Elmer Holmes Bobst Library
New York Univ.
70 Washington Sq. South, Rm. 1209
New York, NY 10012
EIN: 132616114
Source Date: 12/95

To Whom:
Health, cancer and **cancer research, medical research**, hospitals, higher education, animal welfare, cultural programs, Catholic giving, youth, U.S. and international Islamic organizations.

Financial info:
Assets: $38,565,800.
Giving: $1,782,100 for 35 grants (high: $500,000; low: $100).

Application info:
Applications accepted. Submit letter. No deadline.

Directors, Officers, Trustees:
as-Sayid, Farouk, Director
Bobst, Elmer H. (d), Donor
Bobst, Mamdouha S., Director, Officer
Kabbani, Raja, Director
Mahon, Arthur J., Officer
Rockefeller, Mary, Director
Rose, Milton C., Director

Bristol-Myers Squibb Foundation, Inc.

c/o Manager
345 Park Ave.
New York, NY 10154
(212) 546-4331
Source Date: 3/97

Geographic Restrictions:
Limited to areas of company operations: Clairol, Inc., Stamford, CT and New York, NY; Zimmer, Inc., Warsaw, IN; Biochem, Syracuse, NY; Bristol-Myers Products and Clairol, Inc., Stamford, CT; Conva Tec, Skillman, NJ; Linvatec, Largo, FL; Matrix Essentials Inc., Solon, OH; Mead Johnson Nutritional Group, Evansville, IN; Westwood-Squibb Pharmaceuticals, Buffalo, NY; Wallingford, CT; New Brunswick and Princeton, NJ.

Restrictions:
No grants for political, fraternal, social or veterans organizations, religious or sectarian organizations not engaged in a significant project benefiting the entire community, specific public broadcast programs or films, individuals, endowments, courtesy advertising. Through its matching gift program, it contributes to both public and private institutions of higher learning and to accredited independent secondary schools.

To Whom:
Unrestricted Biomedical Medical Research and Health: cancer, cardiovascular, infectious disease, neuroscience, nutrition, orthopedic, and pain research, empower women to make informed decisions regarding their health care by educating them about prevention, detection and treatment, hospitals and health care organizations in communities where we conduct business, and research, evaluation, and resolution of issues important to public policy regarding the health care industry.

Education: private higher education, wider opportunities for women and minorities, math, science and health education and the shortage of qualified teachers in these subjects.

Civic and Community Services: strengthen economic and community development, provide equal opportunity and job training for socially or economically disadvantaged groups, improve the operation of our system of law and justice, environmental issues, institutions engaged in public policy research to help advance better understanding of the free enterprise system, well-rounded development of young people, support of seniors, and disabled.

Cultural Activities: nationally recognized performing arts centers and major natural history, science and art museums.

For What:
General purposes, employee matching gifts.

Financial info:
Giving: $12,617,700 for 1,480 grants (high: $2,000,000; low: $500).

Application info:
Applications accepted. Submit proposal. Deadline is Oct. 1. Publishes application guidelines.

Directors, Officers, Trustees:
Bristol-Myers Squibb Company, Donor
Damonti, John, President

Henrietta B. & Frederick H. Bugher Foundation

c/o Davis, Polk & Wardwell
Attn: D. Nelson Adams, Trustee
450 Lexington Ave.
New York, NY 10017
(212) 450-4000
Source Date: 12/94

Restrictions:
No grants to individuals.

To Whom:
Cardiovascular research.

For What:
Research.

Financial info:
Giving: $1,404,400 for 10 grants (high: $500,000; low: $5,000)

Application info:
Applications accepted. Submit letter. No deadline.

Directors, Officers, Trustees:
Adams, D. Nelson, Trustee
Adams, Daniel N., Jr., Trustee
Bugher, Frederick McLean (d), Donor
Crestar Bank, N.A., Trustee
Robinson, Robert A., Trustee
Ward, Gayliss, Trustee

Frances L. & Edwin L. Cummings Memorial Fund

c/o Elizabeth Costas, Admin. Dir.
501 Fifth Ave., Suite 708
New York, NY 10017-6103
(212) 286-1778
EIN: 136814491
Source Date: 7/95

Geographic Restrictions:
Primarily in the New York City, NY, area, including northern NJ and southern Westchester.

Restrictions:
No grants for the cultural arts, alcoholism or drug prevention, individuals, capital building campaigns, general operating expenses, annual fund raising campaigns, conferences, day care programs, environmental programs,

camping programs, documentaries, films, and videos, moving expenses, private elementary and secondary schools, public opinion polls, surveys, and research studies, public policy or advocacy groups, scholarship programs, or well-endowed institutions.

To Whom:
Social welfare: child abuse, homeless, juvenile delinquency, teenage pregnancy, parenting education, youth employment and job training.

Education: public education, minority groups, the disadvantaged, and the physically and\or mentally disabled.

Health Care: institutions serving economically and socially disadvantaged populations.

Medical research: AIDS and cancer.

For What:
Research, consulting services, endowment funds, professorships, seed money, special projects.

Financial info:
Assets: $31,639,600.
Giving: $1,206,500 for 50 grants (high: $100,000; low: $8,500).

Application info:
Applications accepted. Submit letter (7 page limit, 3 copies; 4 copies of attachments). Deadline is Apr. 1 or Oct. 1. Board meets in June and Dec. with notification 10 days after board meeting. Publishes biennial report with application guidelines.

Recent Grants:

$20,000	Access Development Fund, New York, NY. Salaries for staff involved in opening three newly renovated residences in the South Bronx for homeless mentally disabled and "housing needy" single adults.
$37,500	Boys & Girls Clubs of Mt. Vernon, NY. Provide salary, benefits and training support for a full-time program director.
$30,000	Community Agencies Corp. of NJ, Newark, NJ. "Community Partners for Youth", a consortium of Newark-based youth and family agencies which is piloting a family-centered, case management program for youth.
$25,000	The Big Sisters, Inc., New York, NY. Creation of the Bank Street Center for Family Support.
$25,000	Beth Israel Medical Center, Manhattan, NY. NICU Early Intervention Project, which will work with drug-exposed infants and their mothers or caregivers.
$20,000	Institutes of Religion and Health, New York, NY. Expand counseling services to adolescents and children from low and moderate income families.

James H. Cummings Foundation, Inc.

c/o William J. McFarland, Exec. Dir.
1807 Elmwood Ave., Rm. 112
Buffalo, NY 14207-2334
(716) 874-0040
EIN: 160864200
Source Date: 12/95

Geographic Restrictions:
Limited to Buffalo, NY, Hendersonville, NC, and Toronto, Ontario, Canada.

Restrictions:
No grants for national health organizations, individuals, endowments, operating expenses, deficit financing, scholarships, or fellowships.

To Whom:
Advancing medical science, research, and education (85% of funding); services to underprivileged boys and girls (12% of funding); assist seniors and infirm persons (3% of funding).

For What:
Building funds, seed money, equipment, land acquisition, matching funds, consulting services, **research.**

Financial info:
Assets: $19,007,100 (from 1994 990PF).
Giving: $832,100 for 20 grants (high: $100,000; low: $250).

Application info:
Applications accepted. Submit letter (2 page limit, 7 copies). Deadline is Feb. 15, May 15, Aug. 15, and Nov. 15. Board meets quarterly, usually in Mar., June, Sept., and Dec. Publishes annual report with application guidelines.

Recent Grants:

$50,000	Blue Ridge Community Health Services, NC
$10,000	Boys & Girls Clubs of Buffalo, NY
$39,145	Buffalo General Hospital
$50,000	Hospice Buffalo
$30,000	Western New York Public Broadcasting Association
$25,000	SPCA

Directors, Officers, Trustees:
Alford, Kenneth M., M.D., Director, Officer
Cummings, James H. (d), Donor
Gisel, William G., Director, Officer
Irwin, Robert J. A., Director, Officer
Naughton, John, M.D., Director
Scheu, Robert S., Director
Walsh, John N., Jr., Director

Samuel & Rae Eckman Charitable Foundation

c/o Bayer, Marks & Upham
Attn: Stephen F. Selig, Pres.
805 Third Ave., 20th Flr.
New York, NY 10022
(212) 702-5700
EIN: 237051411
Source Date: 12/95

Geographic Restrictions:
Primarily in New York, NY.

To Whom:
Medical research in cancer and allied diseases, homes for seniors, education of indigent or at risk youth, AIDS.

For What:
Continuing support, general purposes, operating budgets, **research**.

Financial info:
Assets: $2,013,500.
Giving: $137,400 for 20 grants (high: $15,000; low: $1,000).

Application info:
Applications accepted. Submit proposal. No deadline. Board meets quarterly. Publishes application guidelines.

Directors, Officers, Trustees:
Briloff, Abraham J., Director, Officer
Eckman, Rae (d), Donor
Eckman, Samuel (d), Donor
Harris, Theodore, Director
Norden, William B., Director
Selig, Stephen F., Director, Officer

Eppley Foundation for Research, Inc.

c/o Huyler C. Held, Secretary
245 Park Ave.
New York, NY 10167-0034
(212) 371-1660
EIN: 136058048
Source Date: 12/95

Restrictions:
No grants for social sciences, computer sciences, or educational programs.

To Whom:
Post-doctoral research in the physical and biological sciences.

For What:
Research.

Financial info:
Assets: $2,569,700.
Giving: $90,700 for 10 grants (high: $25,000; low: $2,000).

Application info:
Applications accepted. Applicant must be affiliated with recognized institution. Application form required. Deadline is Feb. 1, May 1, Aug. 1, and Nov. 1 with notification in 3 months.

Recent Grants:

$17,891	The Pennsylvania State University "Rheological and Mechanical Properties of Precursors to Synthetic Bone".
$28,255	The University of Chicago "Anatomical Diversity- and functional Convergence in Metazoan Fluid Transport Systems".
$20,000	American Museum of Natural History "Paleontological Expedition to the Gobi Desert"

$12,500	Purdue University "A Study of Possible Superconducting Phenomena in Oxygen Deficient Lanthanum Nickelates and in Copper Iridium Thiospinels".
$18,000	Mount Sinai School of Medicine "Alternative Vaccine Approach for Pseudomonas aeruginosa".
$9,200	The University of Akron "Pollination Ecology of Himalayan-Pedicularis"
$6,922	The University of Chicago "Expedition to Morocco: Preliminary Report and Proposal for Partial Development Support".
$25,000	The New York Botanical Garden "The Guide To The Vascular Plants Of Central French Guiana".
$15,000	University of California, Davis "Evaluation of Native Populations of Entomopathogenic Nematodes and Their Potential for Their Implementation in Biological Control Programs".

Directors, Officers, Trustees:
Eppley, Marion (d), Donor
Held, Huyler C., Director, Officer
Seldes, Timothy, Director
Winant, Joan O'Meara, Director
Winant, Rivington R., Director, Officer

Eugene & Estelle Ferkauf Foundation

67 Allenwood Rd.
Great Neck, NY 11023-2213
(516) 773-3269
EIN: 132621094
Source Date: 12/95

Geographic Restrictions:
Limited to NY.

Restrictions:
No grants to individuals.

To Whom:
Higher education, fine arts, hospitals, museums, music, theater, **medical research**.

For What:
Research, building funds, continuing support.

Financial info:
Assets: $4,531,500.
Giving: $227,300 for 35 grants (high: $50,000; low: $200).

Application info:
Applications accepted. Submit letter in Jan., July, and Dec.

Directors, Officers, Trustees:
Bronstein, Lenore, Trustee
Bronstein, Robert, Trustee
Dicke, Richard M., Trustee
Dor, Barbara, Trustee
Dor, Benny, Trustee
Ferkauf, Estelle, Donor, Trustee
Ferkauf, Eugene, Donor, Trustee
Shapira, Amy, Trustee
Shapira, Israel, Trustee

Gebbie Foundation, Inc.

c/o John D. Hamilton, Pres.
308 Hotel Jamestown Office Bldg.
P.O. Box 1277
Jamestown, NY 14702-1277
(716) 487-1062
E-mail: gebfnd@servtech.com
Internet: http://www.gebbie.org/
Source Date: 9/95

Geographic Restrictions:
Primarily in Jamestown/Chautauqua County and in neighboring areas of western NY; In other areas, if they fall within our guidelines.

Restrictions:
No grants for sectarian or religious organizations, higher education, (except to institutions what were recipients of lifetime contributions of the donor), individuals, annual campaigns, operating support, or endowments.

To Whom:
Libraries, hospitals, youth, education, historic preservation, health, cultural programs, social services, **medical research related to metabolic diseases of the bone and in detection of deafness in children and their education.**

For What:
Seed money, building funds, equipment, matching funds, general purposes, loans, scholarship funds, continuing support, capital campaigns.

Financial info:
Assets: $56,853,400.
Giving: $2,623,400 for 65 grants (high: $500,000; low: $1,000).

Application info:
Applications accepted. Submit letter of inquiry. Deadline is Apr. 1, Aug. 1, and Dec. 1. Board meets in Mar., July, and Nov. with notification in 1 to 4 months. Publishes annual report with application guidelines.

Recent Grants:

$40,500	Chautauqua Institution. Annual support School of Music, program support,Chautauqua Fund, Bellinger art award.
$175,000	Civic Center Development Corporation, Inc. Toward the Paragon Cable project at the Field & Wright Building. Income to support Civic Center.
$6,000	Das Puppenspiel Puppet Theatre, Inc.Toward purchase of computer/printer equipment.
$10,200	Fenton Historical Society. Renovation of space for education/based room.
$14,000	Fredonia Chamber Players. To establish a county resident professional orchestra.
$90,000	Fund for the Arts in Chautauqua County, Inc. Toward annual campaign.
$5,000	Berry College. Annual grant to Gebbie-Bellinger Scholarship fund.
$25,000	Berry College. Toward renovations of Blackstone Hall.
$28,856	Chautauqua-Cattaraugus Library System. Renewal of book plan/subscriptions to School Library Journal.
$6,000	Chautauqua Region Community Foundation. Scholarship fund for minority students in Chautauqua County.
$5,000	Chautauqua Region Community Foundation. Toward seminar for education scholarships "Expo 95".
$38,500	Chautauqua Striders,Inc. Continued support for Lighted Schoolhouse project.
$5,000	Clymer-French Creek Free Library. Toward improvements to the building.
$100,000	Fredonia College Foundation-SUNY. To update and enhance the college library.
$20,000	Independent College Fund of New York. Annual grant for NYS private colleges.
$750,000	Jamestown Community College. Toward capital construction/renovations.
$115,000	Jamestown Community College. To continue programs at Jamestown Community Schools.
$62,500	James Prendergast Free Library. For district heating installation/electronic controls.
$12,000	Jamestown Public Schools. A memorial to Justice Robert Jackson at Love School.
$16,025	Jamestown Area School & Business Alliance. To expand services to 7th & 8th grades/6-districts.
$2,000	Language Development Program of WNY. Biggwood play on fire engine.
$5,000	Literacy Volunteers of Chautauqua County. Toward continuation of Family Literacy Program.
$1,000	The Nichols School. Annual contribution for Bellinger Laboratory.
$1,000	Wheaton College. Annual grant to Alumnae Fund.
$20,000	Brooks Memorial Hospital. Toward purchase of six new defibrillators.
$1,000	Corry Memorial Hospital Annual Grant - Unrestricted.
$15,000	Lake Shore Hospital. Toward purchase of an arthroscopic video system.
$15,000	Lutheran Social Services. To upgrade and expand computer system.
$30,850	The Resource Center (TRC). To purchase diagnostic equipment for audiological services.
$401	W.C.A. Hospital. Annual grant for Snack Bar Equipment.
$1,000	Westfield Memorial Hospital. Annual grant - unrestricted.
$21,500	Jamestown Audubon Society. Matching grant toward youth nature education.
$10,000	Chautauqua Area Habitat for Humanity. Toward building costs of five houses over the next five years.
$2,750	Chautauqua County Health Department Michael Carrara - Teen Pregnancy Prevention.
$45,000	Chautauqua Region Community Foundation. For Research & Planning for Human Services.
$50,000	C.O.D.E. Matching grant for neighborhood development program.
$40,000	Effective Parenting Information for Children. Toward implementing EPIC Parenting Programs.
$15,000	Foster Grandparent Program. To increase the number of foster grandparents in the area.

$13,500	Girl Scout Council, Chautauqua Area. For a water system.
$3,800	Jamestown Community College. Toward the PEACE program for divorcing parents.
$25,000	Joint Neighborhood Project. Matching grant for operations.
$66,000	Young Women's Christian Association (YWCA). Toward operating expenses for Family Violence/Sexual assault network program for 1995.
$48,000	Young Women's Christian Association (YWCA). Toward operations for TEAM Project.
$184,158	Young Women's Christian Association (YWCA). SB6 Grant/Expansion of "TLC" Program & 3 1/2 Year Grant.
$15,000	Young Women's Christian Association (YWCA). Dow Park Playground.
$2,000	Chautauqua County Sheriff's Department. To implement "Are You Okay" program for senior citizens.
$10,000	Leadership Chautauqua (Fredonia College Foundation).Toward development of local leadership network.
$310,000	United Way of Southern Chautauqua County. Toward annual campaign.
$33,600	United Way of Southern Chautauqua County. Repairs on the TEW Mansion roof.
$6,000	First Presbyterian Church of Jamestown. Annual grant - unrestricted.

Directors, Officers, Trustees:
Bellinger, Geraldine G. (d), Donor
Eisenhardt, Dianne L., Officer
Franks, Myron B., Director, Officer
Gebbie, Marion B. (d), Donor
Hall, Charles T., Director, Officer
Halsted, Robert E., Member
Hamilton, John D., Director, Officer
Henderson, Rhoe B., III, Director
Johnson, Kay, Member
Ney, Lillian V., Director
Parker, Bertram B., Director
Parker, Geraldine, Director
Rappole, Albertus W., Member
Sandberg, Paul W., Director

Patrick A. Gerschel Foundation

c/o Patrick A. Gerschel, Pres.
720 Fifth Ave., 10th Flr.
New York, NY 10019-4173
(212) 399-4288
EIN: 133317180
Source Date: 12/94

Geographic Restrictions:
Primarily in NY.

To Whom:
Asian cultural programs, arts, **medical research**, museums, intercultural relations, community development, higher and secondary education.

For What:
Individuals, **research**.

Financial info:
Assets: $5,886,500.
Giving: $345,000 for 35 grants (high: $125,000; low: $200).

Application info:
Applications accepted. Submit letter. No deadline.

Directors, Officers, Trustees:
Gerschel, Patrick A., Officer
Richter, Charles H., Officer

Greenwall Foundation

c/o William C. Stubing, Pres.
2 Park Ave., 24th Flr.
New York, NY 10016
(212) 679-7266
EIN: 136082277
Source Date: 12/95

Geographic Restrictions:
Primarily in New York, NY, for arts and humanities; U.S. for **medical research** and education.

Restrictions:
No grants for state or religious schools, individuals, building or endowment funding, operating expenses, annual campaigns, deficit financing, publications, conferences, or arts in education.

To Whom:
Medicine: **Basic medical research and clinical investigation, especially in bone tumors, insulin depen-**

dent diabetes mellitus and geriatrics. Interested in the moral dilemmas of medical decision making.

Education: Assist minority and disadvantaged youth, in elementary and secondary schools, science and math education with an emphasis on bringing minorities and women into these areas of study.

Arts and Humanities: visual, performing and literary arts, libraries, museums.

For What:
Continuing support, seed money, emergency funds, equipment, professorships, **research**, special projects.

Financial info:
Assets: $73,992,800.
Giving: $2,621,000 for 100 grants (high: $100,000; low: $2,000).

Application info:
Applications accepted. Submit letter by Feb. 1 and Aug. 1. Board meets in spring and fall. Publishes annual report with application guidelines.

Recent Grants:

$10,000	Aaron Davis Hall (Friends of the Davis Center, Inc.), New York, NY. To support the Fund for New Works component of New Faces/New Voices/New Visions.
$2,500	Accra Shepp (New York Foundation for the Arts), New York, NY. To support creation of the photographer's artist's book, "Atlas."
$10,000	The Acting Company, New York, NY. To support commissioning and development of a new play by Lynn Nottage.
$10,000	Alvin Ailey American Dance Theatre, New York, NY. To support choreographic commissioning fees for a new work by Shapiro & Smith
$20,000	American Museum of the Moving Image, Astoria, NY. To commission a sculpture by Gregory Barsamian for the Museum's permanent core exhibition, "Behind the Screen".
$5,000	Amiel Malale Dance (Circum Arts Foundation, Inc.), New York, NY. To support development of a new work.
$5,000	The Architectural Hague of New York, New York, NY. To support the Young Architects Forum in 1995.
$7,500	The Architectural League of New York, New York, NY. Renewed support for the Young Architects Forum in 1996.
$5,000	Arden Party, New York, NY. To support the workshop and production of "Victor, or The Children Take Over."
$3,000	The Asian American Writers' Workshop, New York, NY. Renewed support for the Poetry Caravan Series in 1994/95.
$7,500	Bang on a Can, New York, NY. To support the 1995 and 1996 Bang on a Can festivals at Lincoln Center.
$4,000	Bill Young & Dancers (Hundred Grand Dance Foundation, Inc.), New York, NY. To support development of a new work, "Kindling."
$5,000	Bronx Council on the Arts, Bronx, NY. Renewed support for the Longwood Arts Project in 1994/95.
$30,000	Brooklyn Academy of Music, Inc., Brooklyn, NY. To support BAM'S Visual Arts Initiative.
$5,000	Buglisi/Foreman Dance (Circum Arts Foundation, Inc.), New York, NY. To support the company and creation of "Bare to the Wall" in 1995/96.
$5,000	The Builders Association (The Performance Zone, Inc.), New York, NY. To support a new multimedia theatrical production of"Faust."
$5,000	Celebrate Brooklyn (Fund for the Borough of Brooklyn, Inc.), Brooklyn, NY. To support a week-long dance residency during the 1995 festival.
$3,000	Chinatown History Museum, New York, NY. To support development of Jason Kao Hwang's opera, "Immigrant of the Womb."
$10,000	Circum Arts Foundation, Inc., New York, NY. To support fees for New York-based choreographers in the 1995 season of "Dance! The Circum Arts/Miller Theater Series.
$4,000	City Lore, New York, NY. To support the City Lore Festival of Film and Video in 1995.
$5,000	City Lore, New York, NY. Renewed support for the City Lore Festival of Film and Video in 1996.
$5,000	Vineyard Theatre, New York, NY. Renewed support for the Lab production program.
$10,000	Whitney Museum of Amencan Art, New York, NY. To support installations by New York artist Nari Ward in the 1995 Biennial.
$5,000	WPA Theatre, New York, NY. To support development of a new musical theatre work by Jason Robert Brown.

$7,500 The Writer's Voice (Young Men's Christian Association), New York, NY. To support First Books and the Capricorn Awards in 1994 and 1995

$30,000 American Museum of Natural History, New York, NY. To support three core teacher training programs at the Museum.

$15,000 Boys' Club of New York, New York, NY. To support the Teacher Training Institute at Camp Cromwell Summer School.

$25,000 Brooklyn Botanic Garden, Brooklyn, NY. Renewed support for teacher training in "Project Green Reach" in 1994/95.

$22,887 Brooklyn College of The City University of New York (Brooklyn College Foundation), Brooklyn, NY. To support the "Athena Math and Science Project" at the Center for Educational Change

$24,415 The City College of The City University of New York (Research Foundation of CUNY), New York, NY. To support the "Middle School Mathematics Teacher Preparation Program for Mid-Career Changers".

$98,307 The City College of The City University of New York (Research Foundation of CUNY), New York, NY. To implement a second cycle of the "Middle School Mathematics Teacher Preparation Program for Mid-Career Changers" (two-year grant).

$34,000 Columbia University, New York, NY. To support the "Summer Research Program for Secondary School Science Teachers" at the College of Physicians & Surgeons.

$50,000 Donors' Education Collaborative (Community Funds, Inc.), New York, NY. To support "Constituency Building for School Reform."

$35,000 Fund for New York City Public Education, New York, NY. To support dissemination of the videotapes, "Approaching the Vision of the NCTM Standards," development and dissemination of accompanying print materials, teacher networking and professional development in New York City, and a formative evaluation.

$35,000 Lehman College / New York City Mathematics Project (Research Foundation of CUNY), Bronx, NY. To support the Bronx Mathematics/Science/Technology Collaborative.

$30,000 National Action Council for Minorities in Engineering (NACME), New York, NY. Renewed support for the professional development seminars in the "TechForce Partnership for Scientific Learning."

$4,200 The New York Academy of Sciences, New York, NY. To support preparation, circulation, and maintenance of a directory and online data base for New York City teachers, "Professional Development Opportunities in Science Teaching"

$32,000 The New York Academy of Sciences, New York, NY. To support "Opportunities in Science Education: A Comprehensive Inventory of Resources, Programs, and Reform Efforts in New York City."

$25,000 New York Association for New Americans, New York, NY. To support implementation of a second cycle of "Teacher Training for Soviet Emigres."

$40,000 New York Botanical Garden, Bronx, NY. To support a new position, Manager for Teacher Enhancement Programs.

$15,000 New York Hall of Science, Corona, NY. To support the "In-Service Professional Development Program for Beginning Teachers".

$101,050 New York Hall of Science, Corona, NY. Renewed support for an expanded "In-Service Professional Development Program for Beginning Teachers".

$21,180 Queens College of The City University of New York (Research Foundation of CUNY), Flushing, NY. To support a new initiative, "Preservice and Inservice Professional Development in Mathematics for the Elementary Grades"

$35,000 American College of Obstetricians and Gynecologists, Washington, DC. Operating support for the National Advisory Board on Ethics in Reproduction.

$69,230 **Baystate Medical Center, Springfield, MA. Research support: "Termination of Dialysis: The Decision to Die and the Quality of Dying"**

$163,380 Choice in Dying, New York, NY. Project support: "Integrating Education About Care of the Dying Into Existing Medical School Programs".

$50,000	Choice in Dying, New York, NY. Project support: Evaluation Component of "Integrating Education About Care of the Dying Into Existing Medical School Programs"
$8,330	**The Cleveland Clinic Foundation, Cleveland, OH. Research support: "Androgyny, Empathy, and Ethical Decision-Making Among Physicians".**
$101,405	Dartmouth College / Institute for the Study of Applied & Professional Ethics, Hanover, NH. Project support: "Dreams and Dilemmas: The Practice of Family-Centered Neonatal care."
$22,500	**Duke University Medical Center, Durham, NC. Research support: "How Do Expert Physicians Communicate with Their Patients About Advance Directives?"**

Directors, Officers, Trustees:
Billings, Chester, Jr., Director
Bugliarello, George, Director
Cahill, George F., Jr., M.D., Director, Officer
Cassel, Christine K., M.D., Director
Donahue, Donald J., Director
Greenwall, Anna A. (d), Donor
Greenwall, Frank K. (d), Donor
Hamburg, Beatrix A., M.D., Director
Kresky, Edward M., Director
MacGrath, Andrew A., Director
MacGrath, Francis F., Director
MacGrath, Susan A.T., Director
Menges, Carl B., Director
Perpich, Joseph G., M.D., Director
Rosenblatt, Roger, Director
Salzer, Richard L., Director, Officer
Salzer, Richard L., Jr., M.D., Director
Stamas, Stephen, Director, Officer
Stubing, William Charles, Director, Officer
Vaun, William S., M.D., Director, Officer

Lila Gruber Research Foundation

301 Baltustrol Cir.
North Hills, NY 11576
(516) 365-2248
EIN: 116035223
Source Date: 12/95

Geographic Restrictions:
Primarily in NY.

To Whom:
Jewish religion, Jewish welfare, Jewish education, **medical research**, social services.

For What:
Research, general purposes.

Financial info:
Assets: $1,908,700.
Giving: $92,200 for 50 grants (high: $30,000; low: $50).

Application info:
Applications accepted. Submit letter. Deadline is Nov. 15.

Directors, Officers, Trustees:
Gruber, Barry, Donor
Gruber, Daryl, Donor
Gruber, Murray P., Donor, Trustee

Hearst Foundations

c/o Robert M. Frehse, Jr., Exec. Dir.
888 Seventh Ave., 45th Flr.
New York, NY 10106-0057
(212) 586-5404

Address for applicants from west of the Mississippi River:
c/o Thomas Eastham, Western Dir.
90 New Montgomery St., Suite 1212
San Francisco, CA 94105
(415) 543-0400
Source Date: 3/97

Geographic Restrictions:
Limited to the U.S. and its possessions. Organizations serving larger geographical areas are favored over those of a neighborhood or narrow community nature.

Restrictions:
No grants for political purposes, individuals or fundraising events.

To Whom:
Education: undergraduate higher education through establishment of endowed scholarships at private liberal arts colleges, endowed scholarship support for professional study in teaching, medicine, nursing, engineering, math, science, and the health care professions at the undergraduate and graduate levels, private elementary and secondary education with outstanding academic programs and demonstrated track records of outreach to economically disadvantaged students.

Health: improve and increase care, facilitate wellness, prevention and rehabilitation, hospitals, increase access for underserved urban and rural populations, areas of interest include perinatology and pediatrics, cancer, stroke, aging, women's health issues, and **medical research.**

Social Services: technical assistance, management training, and leadership development designed to help nonprofit agencies deliver services more efficiently and effectively.

Cultural Programs: increase access and educational opportunities for diverse populations and underserved communities, endow arts education and/or community outreach programs through major cultural programs.

For What:
Endowment funds, **research**, scholarship funds, matching funds, general purposes, special projects, operating budgets.

Financial info:
Giving: $21,360,000 for 230 grants (high: $250,000; low: $10,000).

Application info:
Applications accepted. Submit letter. No deadline. Board meets in Mar., June, Sept., and Dec. Publishes application guidelines.

Recent Grants:

	American Music Theatre of San Jose, CA. Program support.
$35,000	Western States Arts Federation, Santa Fe, NM. Technical assistance.
$35,000	Bay State Skills Corp., Boston, MA. "Communities and Schools for Career Success"
$30,000	Youth Service American, Washington, DC. Fund for Social Entrepreneurs.
$25,000	St. Vincent Senior Citizens Nutrition Program, Los Angeles, CA.
$50,000	American Health Foundation, New York, NY. Know Your Body Comprehensive School Health Promotion Program in Harlem.

Directors, Officers, Trustees:
Bennack, Frank A., Jr., Director, Officer
Boudjakdji, Millicent H., Director, Officer
Conomikes, John G., Director, Officer
Cuomo, Ralph J., Officer
Deems, Richard E., Director, Officer
Eastham, Thomas, Officer
Frehse, Robert M., Jr., Director, Officer
Ganzi, Victor F., Officer
Hearst, George R., Jr., Director, Officer
Hearst, John R., Jr., Director, Officer
Hearst, Randolph A., Director, Officer
Hearst, William Randolph, Donor
Hearst, William Randolph, III, Director
Kingsbury-Smith, J., Director, Officer
Lipton, Harvey L., Director, Officer
Massi, Frank, Director, Officer
Maurer, Gilbert C., Director, Officer
Petersen, Raymond J., Director, Officer

Irma T. Hirschl Trust for Charitable Purposes

c/o Chase Manhattan Bank
600 Fifth Ave.
New York, NY 10020
(212) 957-1654
EIN: 136356381
Source Date: 10/95

Geographic Restrictions:
Primarily in New York, NY.

Restrictions:
No grants to individuals.

To Whom:
Medical schools for medical research projects, medical scholarships, social services, health.

For What:
Research, scholarship funds.

Financial info:
Assets: $42,089,000.
Giving: $1,860,000 for 80 grants (high: $100,000; low: $10,000).

Application info:
Applications accepted. All applications must be submitted by designated medical schools. Application form required. Deadline is Oct. 15.

Directors, Officers, Trustees:
Chase Manhattan Bank, N.A., Trustee
Hirschl, Irma T. (d), Donor
Lang, Robert Todd, Trustee

International Paper Company Foundation

c/o Sandra C. Wilson, VP
2 Manhattanville Rd.
Purchase, NY 10577-2196
(914) 397-1503
EIN: 136155080
Source Date: 12/94

Geographic Restrictions:
Primarily in communities where there are company plants and mills: AL, AR, LA, ME, MS, NY, OR, SC, TN, and TX.

Restrictions:
No grants for athletic organizations, religious groups, individuals, endowments, capital expenses of cultural, civic, or educational institutions, veterans or labor groups.

To Whom:
Arts and culture: zoos, libraries, theater companies, museums, visual and performing arts, arts-in-education.

Civic and Community: literacy, youth, seniors, environmental conservation, and volunteerism.

Health and Welfare: cancer, **research on children's diseases**, counter drug abuse, outreach programs for health, welfare, and youth organizations.

Education: higher education, minority education: preschool, elementary, secondary, adult, and higher education in the science and engineering fields; Precollege education: public elementary and secondary education for computer literacy, writing and reading, critical thinking, at-risk students.

Economic Education: basic economic principles in elementary and secondary education.

Environmental programs: conservation and preservation of natural resources.

For What:
Seed money, special projects, annual campaigns, **research,** publications, matching funds, employee matching gifts, continuing support, fellowships, operating budgets, program related investments.

Financial info:
Giving: $2,697,000 for 650 grants (high: $100,000; low: $100).

Application info:
Applications accepted. Address requests from organizations in company communities to the local company mill or plant manager. Application form required. Deadline is Mar. 1. Publishes annual report and application guidelines.

Recent Grants:
- Atlanta School District, Atlanta, TX
- Beaufort County School District, Beaufort, SC
- Binghamton City School District, Binghamton, NY
- Camden Fairview Public Schools, Camden, AR
- Crown Point Central School District, Crown Point, NY
- Dallas County School System, Selma, AL
- DeSoto Parish School Board, Mansfield, LA
- Dollarway Public School, Pine Bluff, AR
- Emerson School District #66, Emerson, AR
- Erie City Schools, Erie, PA
- Gill-Montague Regional School District, Turners Falls, MA
- Gurdon Public Schools, Gurdon, AR
- Hadley-Luzerne Central School, Lake Lazerne, NY
- Hamilton City School District, Hamilton, 0H
- Harmony Grove Public Schools, Camden, AR
- Jay School Department, Jay, ME
- Kaukauna School District, Kaukauna, WI
- Keystone Central School District, Lock leaven, PA
- Mobile County Public School System, Mobile, AL
- Morehouse Parish School Board, Bastrop, LA
- Moriah Central School District, Port Henry, NY
- Moss Point Municipal Separate School District, Moss Point, MS
- Natchez Special Municipal Separate School District, Natchez, MS
- Pascagoula Municipal Separate School District, Pascagoula, MS
- Pine Bluff School District #3, Pine Bluff, AR
- Rapides Parish School, Alexandria, LA
- Reedsport School District, Reedsport, OREG
- School District of Georgetown County, Georgetown, SC
- Selma City Schools, Selma, AL
- Taylor Public Schools, Taylor, AR
- Texarkana Independent School District, Texarkana, TX
- Ukiah Unified School District, Ukiah, CA
- Vicksburg Warren School District, Vicksburg, MS
- Watson Chapel Schools, Pine Bluff, AR
- Mississippi Children's Home Society, Jackson, MS
- Mobile Bay Area Partnership for Youth, Inc., Mobile, AL
- Mobile County Health Department, Mobile, AL
- New Directions of Southwest Louisiana, Oberlin, LA
- North Country Life Flight, Inc., Saranac Lake, NY
- Pennsylvania Association for the Blind, Erie, PA
- Project Sanctuary, Inc., Ukiah, CA

Red River Regional Council on Alcoholism, Texorkana, TX
Saratoga County Task Force on Child Abuse and Neglect, Saratoga Springs, NY
Sexual Assault Victims Emergency Services, Inc., Farmington, ME
Task Force for Housing, Inc., Lock Haven, PA
United Cerebral Palsy of Mobile, Inc., Mobile, AL
Visiting Nurse Hospice of Pioneer Valley, Inc., Springfield, MA
Volunteers of America of North Louisiana, Shreveport, LA
Welcome House of Northern Kentucky, Inc., Covington, KY
Western Maine Community Action, Inc., East Wilton, ME

Directors, Officers, Trustees:
Berardi, Carol, Officer
Freda, Patricia, Officer
Georges, John A., Director
International Paper Company, Donor
Melican, James P., Jr., Director
State Street Bank & Trust Company, Trustee
Suwyn, Mark A., Director
Wallace, Arthur, Officer
Wilson, Sandra C., Officer

Marion Esser Kaufmann Foundation

c/o Weber & Cardillo
Attn: Allen Weber, Treasurer
2525 Palmer Ave.
New Rochelle, NY 10801
(914) 636-8400
EIN: 133339941
Source Date: 12/95

Restrictions:
No grants to individuals.

To Whom:
Higher education, **medical research in the fields of Sudden Infant Death Syndrome and Alzheimer's disease.**

For What:
Research, scholarship funds.

Financial info:
Assets: $8,694,900.
Giving: $446,000 for 10 grants (high: $100,000; low: $10,000).

Application info:
Applications accepted. Submit letter. No deadline.

Directors, Officers, Trustees:
Bissinger, Frederick L., Trustee
Esser, Richard, Trustee
Kaufmann, Marion Esser (d), Donor

Kekst Family Foundation

784 Park Ave.
New York, NY 10021
EIN: 133382250
Source Date: 12/95

Geographic Restrictions:
Primarily in NY.

Restrictions:
No grants to individuals.

To Whom:
Jewish giving and welfare, theological education, education, **medical research** to combat medical and genetic diseases and afflictions which affect Jewish infants and children.

For What:
Research, scholarship funds.

Financial info:
Assets: $3,329,900.
Giving: $1,176,000 for 15 grants (high: $500,000; low: $5,000).

Application info:
Applications accepted. Submit proposal. No deadline.

Directors, Officers, Trustees:
Kekst, Carol, Officer
Kekst, Gershon, Donor, Officer

Calvin Klein Foundation

c/o Nathan Berkman & Company
29 Broadway, Rm. 2800
New York, NY 10006-3103
EIN: 133094765
Source Date: 6/95

Geographic Restrictions:
Primarily in NY.

Restrictions:
No grants to individuals.

To Whom:
Medical research, hospitals, health associations, **AIDS research**, Jewish giving, dance, museums, literacy, performing arts.

Financial info:
Assets: $547,000.
Giving: $350,800 for 65 grants (high: $25,000; low: $200).

Application info:
Applications accepted. Submit letter. No deadline.

Directors, Officers, Trustees:
DiPaola, Robert, Trustee
Kabay, John K., Trustee
Klein Industries, Calvin, Inc., Donor

Esther A. & Joseph Klingenstein Fund, Inc.

c/o John Klingenstein, Pres.
787 Seventh Ave., 6th Flr.
New York, NY 10019-6016
(212) 492-6181
EIN: 136028788
Source Date: 9/95

Geographic Restrictions:
Limited to U.S.

Restrictions:
No grants to individuals or building or endowment funding.

To Whom:
Major interest: Neuroscience research bearing on epilepsy; independent secondary education.

Minor Programs: separation of church and state and the preservation of religion liberty, use of animals in biomedical research for the advancement of medicine.

Grants also made to organizations concerned with family planning and teenage pregnancy, minority affairs, and public policy.

For What:
Research, special projects, publications, conferences and seminars, fellowships, operating budgets, seed money, general purposes, continuing support.

Financial info:
Assets: $97,136,900.
Giving: $4,932,600 for 130 grants (high: $500,000; low: $1,000).

Application info:
Applications accepted. Submit letter or proposal. No deadline. Board meets 4 or 5 times a year. Publishes informational brochure.

Directors, Officers, Trustees:
Fields, Kenneth H., Director
Klingenstein, Frederick A., Director, Officer
Klingenstein, John, Director, Officer
Klingenstein, Patricia D., Director
Klingenstein, Sharon L., Director
List, Claire, Officer

Larsen Fund, Inc.

c/o Patricia S. Palmer, Grants Admin.
575 Madison Ave., Suite 1006
New York, NY 10022
Source Date: 12/95

Geographic Restrictions:
Primarily in New York, NY, area, Minneapolis, MN, area, and CT.

Restrictions:
No grants to individuals.

To Whom:
Higher, secondary, and **medical education**, educational research, youth, family services, **hospitals**, libraries, law and justice, intercultural relations, conservation, arts, wildlife, family planning, urban affairs, population studies, museums, theater.

For What:
Fellowships, professorships, **research**, internships, land acquisition, lectureships, scholarship funds, special projects.

Financial info:
Giving: $458,000 for 60 grants (high: $50,000; low: $500).

Application info:
Applications accepted. Submit letter. Deadline is Apr. 1 and Oct. 15. Board meets in June and Dec.

Directors, Officers, Trustees:
Larsen, Christopher, Director, Officer
Larsen, Jonathan Z., Director, Officer
Larsen, Robert R., Director, Officer
Larsen, Roy E. (d), Donor
Simonson, Larsen Anne, Director, Officer

Lucius N. Littauer Foundation, Inc.

Pamela Brumberg, Pgm. Off.
60 East 42nd St., Suite 2910
New York, NY 10165
(212) 697-2677
EIN: 131688027
Source Date: 12/96

Geographic Restrictions:
Primarily in NY for medical ethics and environmental projects.

Restrictions:
No grants to individuals, capital projects or operating funds.

To Whom:
Funds for scholars engaged in research in Jewish studies, Judaic Book Funds on campuses [higher education] throughout the U.S., **medical research with an emphasis on medical ethics**, and the environment.

For What:
Research, publications, conferences and seminars, endowment funds, matching funds, lectureships, special projects.

Financial info:
Assets: $27,453,800.
Giving: $1,488,200 for 150 grants (high: $250,000; low: $250).

Application info:
Applications accepted. Submit brief proposal. No deadline. Board meets annually. Publishes application guidelines.

Recent Grants:

$10,000	American Friends of Beth Hatefutsoth. Exhibition Catalogue: "Blue and White in Color: The 100th Anniversary of the First Zionist Congress."
$3,000	The Beate Klarsfeld Foundation, Children's Memorial Book Project.
$5,000	Conference on Jewish Social Studies. Publication support.
$15,000	The HealthCare Chaplancy, Inc. Jewish Chaplain program.
$25,000	National Foundation for Jewish Culture. Doctoral dissertation fellowship program.
$5,000	YIVO Institute for Jewish Research. Publication support.
$25,000	University of Michigan. Endowment: The Irving M. Hermelin Curator of Judaica.

Directors, Officers, Trustees:
Berlin, Charles, Director
Bilski, Berthold, Director
Brumberg, Pamela Ween, Director
Frost, William Lee, Director, Officer
Harris, George, Director, Officer
Littauer, Lucius N. (d), Donor
Lowett, Henry A., Director, Officer
Solomon, Peter J., Director

Richard Lounsbery Foundation, Inc.

c/o Benjamin F. Borden, VP
159A East 61st St.
New York, NY 10021
(212) 319-7033
EIN: 136081860
Source Date: 12/94

Geographic Restrictions:
U.S. giving.

Restrictions:
No grants to individuals, capital or endowment funding, conferences or seminars.

To Whom:
Biomedical **research**, improvement of the teaching and learning of science and mathematics in secondary and elementary education, human rights.

For What:
Seed money, **research**.

Financial info:
Assets: $18,245,400.
Giving: $1,184,700 for 80 grants (high: $150,000; low: $100).

Application info:
Applications accepted but not encouraged. Submit letter. No deadline. Board meets the last Wednesday of Jan., Apr., July, and Oct.

Directors, Officers, Trustees:
Borden, Benjamin F., Director, Officer
Lounsbery Foundation Trust, Richard, Inc., Donor
McGill, William J., M.D., Director
McHenry, Bruce, Director
Mendelsohn, John, Director
Seitz, Frederick, M.D.

Leon Lowenstein Foundation, Inc.

126 East 56th St., 28th Flr.
New York, NY 10022
(212) 319-0670
EIN: 136015951
Source Date: 12/95

Geographic Restrictions:
Primarily in the New York, NY, area.

To Whom:
Medical research, elementary, secondary, business, and higher education, hospitals, libraries, youth, Jewish giving.

For What:
General purposes, **research**, seed money, special projects.

Financial info:
Assets: $101,086,000.
Giving: $1,428,400 for 110 grants (high: $500,000; low: $100).

Application info:
Applications accepted. Submit letter. No deadline.

Directors, Officers, Trustees:
Bendheim, John, Jr., Director
Bendheim, John M., Director, Officer
Bendheim, Robert, Director, Officer
Lowenstein, Leon (d), Donor
Rapoport, Bernard R., Director, Officer
Thoman, Lynn B., Director
Van Gorder, John F., Director

Robert Mapplethorpe Foundation, Inc.

c/o Anise Richey, Fdn. Mgr.
120 Wooster St., 4th Flr.
New York, NY 10012
(212) 941-4760
EIN: 133480472
Source Date: 5/95

Geographic Restrictions:
Limited to U.S. organizations.

To Whom:
Medical research to advance the cure and treatment of AIDS and HIV infection, photography as an art form by assisting museums or higher education, creation or expansion of photography department, publishing quality books and materials.

For What:
Research, publications, special projects, equipment.

Financial info:
Assets: $575,100.
Giving: $650,400 for 20 grants (high: $300,000; low: $100).

Application info:
Applications accepted. Submit letter (3 page limit). No deadline. Publishes application guidelines.

Recent Grants:

$725,000	**New England Deaconess Hospital, Boston, MA. Robert Mapplethorpe Laboratory for AIDS Research.**
$1,050,000	**American Foundation for AIDS Research, New York, NY. General support for research grants.**
$1,000,000	Beth Israel Hospital, New York, NY. Robert Mapplethorpe Aids Treatment Facility.

$178,000	**St. Vincent's Hospital and Medical Center, New York, NY. Funding research of the SPECT scanning project.**

Directors, Officers, Trustees:
Davis, Lynn, Director, Officer
Kennedy, Mame, Officer
Levas, Dimitri, Director, Officer
Lipsky, Burton, Director, Officer
Mapplethorpe, Robert (d), Donor
Stout, Michael Ward, Director, Officer

G. Harold & Leila Y. Mathers Charitable Foundation

103 S. Bedford Rd., Suite 101
Mount Kisco, NY 10549-3440
(914) 242-0465
EIN: 237441901
Source Date: 12/95

Restrictions:
No grants to individuals.

To Whom:
Medical research.

For What:
Research, general purposes.

Financial info:
Assets: $132,920,300.
Giving: $10,021,800 for 70 grants (high: $400,000; low: $5,000).

Application info:
Applications accepted. Submit letter, with 1 copy of research proposal. No deadline.

Directors, Officers, Trustees:
Fizer, Don, Director, Officer
Handelman, Donald E., Director, Officer
Handelman, Joseph W., Director, Officer
Handelman, William R., Director, Officer
Hay, John, Director, Officer
Young, John R., Director

John L. McHugh Foundation, Inc.

c/o Stanley B. Rich, Secretary
60 East 42nd St.
New York, NY 10165
(212) 490-0139
Source Date: 3/97

Geographic Restrictions:
Primarily in New York, NY.

To Whom:
Medical research, performing arts, social services.

For What:
Research, special projects, scholarship funds, general purposes, exchange programs.

Financial info:
Giving: $45,000 for 35 grants (high: $3,000; low: $200).

Application info:
Applications accepted. Submit letter. No deadline.

Recent Grants:

$1,000	The Actors' Fund of America, New York, NY. Unrestricted.
$250	Alliance of Guardian Angels, Inc., Brooklyn, NY. Safety patrol, community service.
$1,500	**American Foundation for AIDS Research, New York, NY.**
$200	The Animal Medical Center, New York, NY. Unrestricted.
$300	B'Nai Brith Hillel, Burlington, VT. Unrestricted.
$500	The Boys Choir of Harlem, Inc., New York, NY. Unrestricted.
$100	Bridgeport Hospital Foundation, Inc., Bridgeport, CT. Childrens' Holiday Gift.
$3,000	Channel 13-WNET, New York, NY. Unrestricted.
$1,000	Channel 21-WLIW, Plainview, NY. Unrestricted.
$100	Channel 49, Hartford, CT. Unrestricted.
$500	Children's Dream Foundation, Rye Brook, NY. Children's cancer center.
$100	The Connecticut Hospice, Inc., Branford, CT. Care of terminally ill patients.

Directors, Officers, Trustees:
Barton, Trumbull, Officer, Trustee
Harwood, Sally R., Officer, Trustee
Hollerith, Charles, Officer, Trustee
McHugh, John L. (d), Donor
Rich, Stanley B., Officer, Trustee

Metropolitan Life Foundation

c/o Sibyl Jacobson, Pres.
1 Madison Ave.
New York, NY 10010-3690
(212) 578-6272
EIN: 132878224
Source Date: 12/96

Restrictions:
No grants for private foundations, religious, fraternal, athletic, political, social, or veterans' organizations, organizations receiving support from United Way, local chapters of national organizations, disease-specific organizations, labor groups, organizations whose activities are mainly international, organizations primarily engaged in patient care or direct treatment, drug treatment centers and community health clinics, hospital capital fund campaigns, elementary or secondary schools, individuals, endowments, courtesy advertising or festival participation.

To Whom:
Health (21% of funding): health education of the public to promote better health maintenance and illness prevention, training and recruitment of minorities in medical and health care fields, **basic research conducted at distinguished institutions**, safety promotion, **research**, and education, improved efficiency of health care delivery.

Education (26% of funding): higher education, developing opportunities for minorities, education in insurance, actuarial science, business, and economics, improving the quality of basic elementary and secondary education.

Culture (12% of funding): national [U.S.] art centers, major museums that perform a specialized function or serve as a repository in the field of art, humanities, or science, public media, traveling exhibits, performance or tours that bring cultural opportunities to audiences across the country, provide access to the written, performing, and visual arts, train and develop young talent, art in education, improve the management and fiscal capabilities of arts organizations.

Civic and Public Policy (11% of funding): socially or economically disadvantaged, social services, youth, improve the legal system, family services, economic and public policy research, environment.

United Ways (14% of funding).

For What:
Operating budgets, continuing support, employee matching gifts, **research**, program-related investments, general purposes, publications, special projects, equipment, matching funds, scholarship funds, employee-related scholarships, seed money.

Financial info:
Assets: $108,039,000 (from 1995 990PF).
Giving: $14,700,000 for 500 grants (high: $250,000; low: $1,000).

Application info:
Applications accepted. Submit letter. No deadline. Publishes report of contributions with application guidelines.

Recent Grants:

$1,000	AIDS Committee of Ottawa, Canada
$1,500	Alliance for Quality Education
$1,000	Alabama Council on Economic Education, AL
$10,000	American Enterprise Institute
$1,000	Atlanta Arts Alliance, GA
$2,000	Baltimore Aquarium, MD
$20,000	New York Public Library
$1,000	Art Institute of Chicago, IL
$5,000	Jobs for Youth
$2,300	Northeast Dupage Special Recreation Association
$25,000	Citizens Crime Commission of NY

Directors, Officers, Trustees:
Creedon, John J., Director
Crimmins, Robert J., Officer
Friedewald, William T., M.D., Director
Jacobson, Sibyl C., Director, Officer
Metropolitan Life Insurance Company, Donor
Moynahan, John D., Jr., Director
Rein, Catherine A., Director
Reusing, Vincent P., Director
Typermass, Arthur G., Director, Officer

Milstein Family Foundation, Inc.

c/o Seymour Milstein, Chairman
1271 Ave. of the Americas, Suite 4200
New York, NY 10020
(212) 708-0800
Source Date: 12/94

Geographic Restrictions:
Primarily in NY.

To Whom:
Medical research, hospitals, Jewish giving, historic preservation.

For What:
Research.

Financial info:
Giving: $6,377,200 for 90 grants (high: $3,500,000; low: $500).

Application info:
Applications accepted. Submit letter. No deadline.

Directors, Officers, Trustees:
Builtland Partners, Donor
Flanzer, Gloria M., Donor, Director
Habif, David V., Officer
Lederman, Constance M., Director
Meyer, Roslyn M., Director
Milstein, Edward L., Director
Milstein, Howard P., Director
Milstein, Irma P., Director
Milstein, Paul, Donor, Officer
Milstein, Philip L., Officer
Milstein, Seymour, Donor, Director, Officer
Milstein, Vivian, Director
Zalaznick, Barbara M., Director

Murray Foundation for Eye Research, Inc.

(Formerly John P. Murray, Jr. Foundation, Inc.)
c/o Pegg & Pegg
370 Lexington Ave., Rm. 1007
New York, NY 10017-6503
(212) 532-4287
Source Date: 12/94

To Whom:
Eye medical research, blind.

For What:
General purposes, **research**.

Financial info:
Giving: $285,900 for 10 grants (high: $100,000; low: $2,000).

Application info:
Applications accepted. Submit letter. No deadline.

Directors, Officers, Trustees:
Hosea, Elizabeth, Director
Kelsey, Ellen, Director
Murray, James M., Director, Officer
Murray, John P., Donor, Director, Officer
Murray, John P., III, Director, Officer
Murray, Mary T., Director, Officer
Murray, Matthew T., Director
Murray, Robert S., Director
Murray, W. Stephen, Director, Officer

Oncologic Foundation of Buffalo, Inc.

South 5361 Fairgrounds Rd.
Hamburg, NY 14075-3008
(716) 648-3132
Source Date: 12/94

Geographic Restrictions:
Primarily in Buffalo, NY.

Restrictions:
Applicant must be researcher employed by research institute or university.

To Whom:
Medical research in photodynamic therapy, cancer.

For What:
Research, endowment funds.

Financial info:
Giving: $204,600 for 5 grants individuals (high: $100,000; low: $10,000).

Application info:
Applications accepted. Submit proposal. No deadline.

Directors, Officers, Trustees:
Buerk, John A., Officer
Dougherty, Thomas J., Donor, Officer
Quadro Logic Technologies, Inc., Donor
Riechert, Raymond, Officer
Weishaupt, Kenneth R., Officer

Parapsychology Foundation, Inc.

228 East 71st St.
New York, NY 10021
(212) 628-1550
EIN: 131677742
Source Date: 12/95

Geographic Restrictions:
U.S. and international giving.

Restrictions:
No grants for travel, graduate or undergraduate studies, endowments, or operating expenses.

To Whom:
Students wishing to pursue the academic study of the science of parapsychology. Scientists, universities, laboratories conducting research in telepathy, precognition, psychokinesis, clairvoyance and related phenomena.

For What:
Research, individuals.

Financial info:
Assets: $1,682,200.
Giving: $12,000 for 5 grants (high: $3,000; low: $1,000) and $26,700 for 10 grants to individuals (high: $5,000; low: $500).

Application info:
Applications accepted. Application form required (2 copies) following preliminary letter. Deadline is July 15 with notification Aug. 1. Publishes application guidelines.

Directors, Officers, Trustees:
Angoff, Allan, Trustee
Coly, Eileen, Officer, Trustee
Coly, Lisette, Officer, Trustee
Coly, Robert R., Officer, Trustee
Martin, William, Trustee
Miller, Sandra R., Trustee
Powers, Stephen E., Trustee

Ramapo Trust

c/o Danylle Rudin, Pgm. Off.
126 East 56th St.
New York, NY 10022-3668
(212) 308-7355
Source Date: 12/94

Geographic Restrictions:
Primarily in New York, NY, and NJ areas.

Restrictions:
No grants to individuals, capital or building funding, operating expenses, continuing support, annual campaigns, media or the arts, or deficit financing.

To Whom:
Gerontological and geriatric research and innovative services [seniors], health, higher education, Alzheimer's disease, and intergenerational programs.

For What:
Seed money, matching funds, special projects, research, conferences and seminars, emergency funds, internships.

Financial info:
Giving: $4,724,400 for 65 grants (high: $1,000,000; low: $200).

Application info:
Applications accepted. Application form required. No deadline. Board meets monthly. Publishes application guidelines.

Directors, Officers, Trustees:
Field, Arthur Norman, Trustee
Hart, Karen Schwartz, Trustee
Montebello Trust, Donor
Schreier, Andrew M., Trustee
Schreier, William S., Trustee
Schwartz, Henry L. (d), Donor
Schwartz, Stephen L., Trustee
Shaffer, Rebecca, Trustee
Van Clief, Mary Ann, Trustee

Billy Rose Foundation, Inc.

805 Third Ave., 22nd Flr.
New York, NY 10022
EIN: 136165466
Source Date: 12/95

Geographic Restrictions:
Primarily in New York, NY.

Restrictions:
No grants to individuals.

To Whom:
Museums, performing and fine arts, theater, higher education, **medical research**.

For What:
Research, special projects.

Financial info:
Assets: $10,204,300.
Giving: $887,500 for 85 grants (high: $100,000; low: $1,000).

Application info:
Applications accepted. Submit letter. No deadline. Board meets in June.

Directors, Officers, Trustees:
Cantor, Arthur, Director, Officer
Cherry, James R., Director, Officer
Mangino, Terri C., Officer
Rose, Billy (d), Donor
Walsh, Edward T., Jr., Officer
Wohlstetter, Charles, Officer

Charles & Mildred Schnurmacher Foundation, Inc.

1114 First Ave.
New York, NY 10021
(212) 838-7766
Source Date: 12/94

Geographic Restrictions:
Primarily in New York, NY, area.

Restrictions:
No grants to individuals.

To Whom:
Medical research, AIDS, Jewish giving, higher education, hospitals.

For What:
Continuing support, endowment funds, equipment, **research**, scholarship funds, seed money.

Financial info:
Giving: $616,000 for 50 grants (high: $75,000; low: $500).

Application info:
Applications accepted. Submit letter. No deadline. Board meets monthly.

Directors, Officers, Trustees:
Plotkin, Fred, Officer
Schnurmacher, Adolph, Officer
Schnurmacher, Charles M. (d), Donor
Weinstein, Ira J., Officer

Alexandrine & Alexander L. Sinsheimer Fund

c/o Chase Manhattan Bank
Attn: Gail P. Fitch, Trust Off.
270 Park Ave., 21st Flr.
New York, NY 10017-2070
(212) 270-9066
Source Date: 12/94

Geographic Restrictions:
Limited to the New York, NY, area.

To Whom:
Medical research.

For What:
Research.

Financial info:
Giving: $377,500 for 10 grants (high: $50,000; low: $20,000).

Application info:
Applications accepted. Application form required. Deadline is Feb. 15.

Directors, Officers, Trustees:
Chase Manhattan Bank, N.A., Trustee
Sinsheimer, Alexander L. (d), Donor
Sinsheimer, Alexandrine (d), Donor

Dr. Louis Sklarow Memorial Fund

c/o Key Trust Company
35 State St.
Albany, NY 12207
EIN: 166201243
Source Date: 5/95

Restrictions:
No grants for travel or faculty salaries.

To Whom:
Biomedical research into the causes and cures of disabling or fatal diseases for which there has been no known solution.

Emphasis on heart diseases, cancer, stroke, and neuromuscular disorders.

For What:
Research.

Financial info:
Assets: $1,496,900.
Giving: $118,400 for 4 grants.

Application info:
Applications accepted. Submit proposal. Deadline is Dec. 20 with notification in 2 months.

Recent Grants:

$30,000	Albert Einstein College of Medicine. Research.
$28,386	Yeshiva University, New York, NY. Research.
$30,000	University of Minnesota Medical School, MN. Research.
$30,000	University of Pennsylvania, School of Medicine, PA. Research.

Directors, Officers, Trustees:
Bank of New York, The, Trustee
Hoffman, Joseph, Trustee

Joseph F. Stein Foundation, Inc.

30 Glenn St.
White Plains, NY 10603
EIN: 136097095
Source Date: 12/95

Geographic Restrictions:
Primarily in NY and FL.

Restrictions:
No grants to individuals or matching gifts.

To Whom:
Jewish welfare and giving, higher and secondary education, **medical research**.

For What:
General purposes, equipment, **research**.

Financial info:
Assets: $15,725,200.
Giving: $539,900 for 200 grants (high: $500,000; low: $50).

Application info:
Applications accepted. Submit letter. No deadline. Board meets monthly.

Directors, Officers, Trustees:
Stein, Allen A., Esq. (d), Donor
Stein, Elaine S., Director, Officer
Stein, Joseph F. (d), Donor
Stein, Melvin M. (d), Director, Officer
Stein, Roger H., Director, Officer
Stein, Stuart M., Director, Officer

Miles Hodsdon Vernon Fund, Inc.

c/o Dennis M. Fitzgerald, VP
49 Beekman Ave.
P.O. Box 701
North Tarrytown, NY 10591
(914) 631-4226
EIN: 136076836
Source Date: 12/95

Geographic Restrictions:
Primarily in NY.

Restrictions:
No grants to individuals.

To Whom:
Medical research, primarily on encephalitis and other brain disorders, youth, aged [seniors], and education.

For What:
Scholarship funds, **research**.

Financial info:
Assets: $7,252,900.
Giving: $319,000 for 45 grants (high: $50,000; low: $500).

Application info:
Applications accepted. Submit proposal. No deadline. Publishes application guidelines.

Directors, Officers, Trustees:
Fitzgerald, Dennis M., Director, Officer
Hodsdon, Louise (d), Donor
Kinney, Martha Hodsdon (d), Donor
Thomson, Eleanor C., Director
Thomson, Robert C., Jr., Director, Officer
Vernon, Miles Hodsdon (d), Donor
Whalen, Gertrude, Director

John L. Weinberg Foundation

c/o Goldman, Sachs & Company
Attn: John L. Weingberg, Trustee
85 Broad St. 22nd Flr.
New York, NY 10004
EIN: 136028813
Source Date: 4/96

Geographic Restrictions:
Primarily in New York, NY, and Greenwich, CT.

Restrictions:
No grants to individuals.

To Whom:
Hospitals, **medical research**, secondary and higher education, and Jewish welfare.

For What:
Annual campaigns, operating budgets, professorships, program-related investments, renovation projects, **research**.

Financial info:
Assets: $25,253,500.
Giving: $721,000 for 120 grants (high: $200,000; low: $50).

Application info:
Applications accepted. Submit letter. No deadline.

Directors, Officers, Trustees:
Altschul, Arthur G., Trustee
Weinberg, Jean H., Trustee
Weinberg, John L., Donor, Trustee
Weinberg, John S., Trustee
Weinberg, Sue Ann, Trustee

Ralph R. Wilkins Foundation, Inc.

c/o John Kimmich, Pres.
P.O. Box 628
Cortland, NY 13045
(607) 756-7548
EIN: 161188525
Source Date: 9/95

Geographic Restrictions:
Primarily in Cortland County and central NY.

Restrictions:
No grants to individuals.

To Whom:
Community funds, social services, recreation, Protestant religion, Catholic welfare, **medical research**.

For What:
Building funds, scholarship funds, **research**, general purposes.

Financial info:
Assets: $1,737,900.
Giving: $50,300 for 35 grants (high: $10,000; low: $100).

Application info:
Applications accepted. Application form required. No deadline. Board meets 6 times a year. Publishes application guidelines.

Directors, Officers, Trustees:
Albro, Harley M., Director, Officer
Camp, David, Director
Kimmich, John, Director, Officer
Porter, Patricia K., Director, Officer
Van Sant, Grant, Director
Wilkins, Carrie (d), Donor
Wilkins, Ralph (d), Donor

Stony Wold-Herbert Fund, Inc.

c/o Cheryl S. Friedman, Exec. Dir.
136 East 57th St., Rm. 1705
New York, NY 10022
(212) 753-6565
EIN: 132784124
Source Date: 12/95

Geographic Restrictions:
Primarily in New York, NY, area.

Restrictions:
No grants for capital or endowment funding, operating expenses, annual campaigns, seed money, emergency funds, or matching gifts.

To Whom:
Clinical and basic research in the field of tuberculosis, pulmonary disease, allied chest diseases, and to related fundamental problems, basic disciplines of physiology, chemistry, pathology which relate to respiratory diseases, Community Services grants to hospitals to train health care workers or counseling and therapy to groups of individuals afflicted with various respiratory ailments.

For What:
Continuing support, deficit financing, fellowships, special projects, research, conferences and seminars, student aid.

Financial info:
Assets: $5,861,100.
Giving: $220,000 for 15 grants and $61,400 for 40 grants to individuals.

Application info:
Applications accepted. Application form required (8 copies). Deadline is Oct. 15 and application guidelines.

North Carolina

Burroughs Wellcome Fund

c/o Martha G. Peck, Exec. Dir.
4709 Creekstone Dr., Suite 100
Durham, NC 27703
(919) 991-5100
Internet: http://www.webpress.net/bwfund/
EIN: 237225395
Source Date: 12/96

Geographic Restrictions:
Limited to the U.S. and Canada.

Restrictions:
No grants to building or endowment funding, equipment, operating funds, conferences, individuals, or publications.

To Whom:
Research in the basic medical sciences within the U.S. (81% of funding for biomedical research); George Herbert Hitchings Award for Innovative Methods in Drug Design and Discovery: a competitive annual award, $350,000 paid over five years; Toxicology Scholar Award of $350,000, paid over five years; Developing Investigator Award in Immunopharmacology of Allergic Diseases of $350,000 paid over 5 years; Molecular Parasitology Award of $350,000 paid over five years; Clinical Oncology ($30,000/year); Pharmacy ($5,000/year); Virology ($30,000/year).

Fellowships area: clinical epilepsy, infectious diseases, life sciences, obstetrics and Gynecology, and sexually transmitted diseases; Wellcome Visiting Professorships in the Basic Medical Sciences, administered by the Federation of American Societies for Experimental Biology; Wellcome Visiting Professorships in Microbiological Sciences administered by the American Society of Microbiology; Wellcome Research Travel Grants to Britain/Ireland; competitive awards for postdoctoral research fellowships administered by national medical, pharmacy, and life sciences organizations;

New Investigator Award in the Basic Pharmacological Sciences; Experimental Therapeutics Award of $350,000, paid over five years. **Scholars Awards of $350,000 paid over 5 years for emerging fields of research in special need of funds and recognition.**

For What:
Scholarship funds, **research**, professorships, fellowships, lectureships.

Financial info:
Assets: $197,499,500 (from 1994 990PF).
Giving: $13,892,200 for 235 grants (high: $500,000; low: $500).

Application info:
Applications accepted. Submit brief proposal (2 copies). Deadlines vary. Board meets bimonthly, beginning in Feb. Publishes annual report and application guidelines and deadlines.

Recent Grants:

$1,387,475	Career Awards in the Biomedical Sciences
$1,006,089	Hitchings-Elion Fellowships
$91,309	Hitchings-Elion Trust Fellowships
$324,000	**Life Sciences Research Foundation Fellowships**
$195,788	**Wellcome Research Travel Grants**
$27,240	History of Medicine Travel Grants
$4,000	Wellcome Trust Travel Grants
$715,000	**Scholar Awards in Molecular Parasitology**
$600,000	**New Investigator Awards in Molecular Parasitology**
$100,000	**New Initiatives in Malaria Research Awards**
$60,000	**Scholar Awards in Molecular Pathogenic Mycology**
$25,000	**New Investigator Awards in Molecular Pathogenic Mycology**
$31,800	Infectious Diseases Society of America Fellowships
$94,500	**Infectious Diseases Society of America New Investigator Awards in Virology**
$162,500	**New Investigator Awards in the Basic Pharmacological Sciences**
$774,375	**Scholar Awards in Toxicology**
$837,500	**Scholar Awards in Experimental Therapeutics**
$80,000	Fellowships American Association of OB/GYN Foundation Fellowships
$47,093	American Social Health Association Fellowships in Sexually Transmitted Diseases
$485,865	Student Science Enrichment Program Awards
$160,280	Wellcome Visiting Professorships in the Basic Medical Sciences
$26,662	Wellcome Visiting Professorships in the Microbiological Sciences
$33,000	Royal Society of Medicine Foundation Visiting Professorships
$4,500,000	BWF 40th Anniversary One-Time Awards Education/Training
$100,000	**Malaria Genome Sequencing Project**
$587,391	**Medical Research/Education**
$270,845	Science Education

$367,000	Communications
$223,500	Hitchings Awards for Innovative Methods in Drug Design
$210,000	Scholar Awards in Immunopharmacology
$350,000	Harvard Medical School.
$350,000	Stanford University School of Medicine, CA.
$350,000	Johns Hopkins University School of Medicine.
$350,000	University of California-Irvine, CA.
$350,000	Washington University School of Medicine.
$350,000	Brown University.
$350,000	University of MI Medical School.

Directors, Officers, Trustees:
Avery, Mary Ellen, M.D., Director
Bond, Enriqueta C., Director
Burroughs-Wellcome Company, Donor
Corman, Stephen D., Director, Officer
Elion, Gertrude B., Director
Friesen, Henry G., M.D., Director
Katz, Samuel L., M.D., Director
Kipnis, David M., M.D., Director
Krenitsky, Thomas A., Director
Nathans, Daniel, M.D., Director
Pagano, Joseph S., M.D., Director
Peck, Martha G., Officer
Tracy, Philip R., Director
Whitten, Jerry L., Director

Seby B. Jones Family Foundation

c/o Roger F. Eller, Trustee
P.O. Box 19067
Raleigh, NC 27619
(919) 829-2161
EIN: 581543120
Source Date: 6/94

Geographic Restrictions:
Primarily in NC.

To Whom:
Higher education, social services, hospitals, **medical research.**

For What:
Building funds, **research**, general purposes.

Financial info:
Assets: $1,376,100.
Giving: $227,800 for 20 grants (high: $100,000; low: $50).

Application info:
Applications accepted. Submit letter. No deadline.

Directors, Officers, Trustees:
Eller, Roger F., Trustee
Jones, Seby B., Donor

Nickel Producers Environmental Research Association, Inc.

c/o Lawrence N. Curcio, Exec. Dir.
100 Capitola Dr., Suite 104
Durham, NC 27713
(919) 544-8500
EIN: 133070077
Source Date: 12/96

Geographic Restrictions:
Primarily in the U.S., Europe, Canada, Australia, and Japan.

To Whom:
Research investigations, studies, and surveys **relating to occupational health and safety** aspects of the nickel producing industries and related environmental issues.

For What:
Fellowships, **research.**

Financial info:
Assets: $1,060,800 (from 1993 990PF).
Giving: $700,000 for grants (high: $100,000; low: $5,000) and $189,100 for 5 grants to individuals (high: $100,000; low: $3,000).

Application info:
Applications accepted. Submit proposal. No deadline.

Directors, Officers, Trustees:
Curcio, Lawrence N., Officer
Matt, Seilo, Officer
Swennen, Bert, Officer
Warner, J. Stuart, Officer
Williams, C. J. D., Officer

Surtman Foundation

2326 Ferncliff Rd.
Charlotte, NC 28211
(704) 366-2282
EIN: 566056565
Source Date: 7/94

Geographic Restrictions:
Primarily in Charlotte and Mecklenburg County, NC. U.S. giving for **research**.

Restrictions:
No grants to individuals.

To Whom:
Medical research, family planning, child abuse, education, social services, Episcopal religion, community funds.

For What:
Annual campaigns, continuing support, emergency funds, endowment funds, **research**, scholarship funds.

Financial info:
Assets: $661,800.
Giving: $351,500 for 20 grants (high: $300,000; low: $500).

Application info:
Applications accepted. Submit proposal. No deadline.

Directors, Officers, Trustees:
Chanter, Irene S., Trustee
Surtman, J. R., Donor
Surtman, Marguerite P., Trustee
Van Allen, William K., Trustee

Ohio

Akron Community Foundation

c/o Jody Bacon, Exec. Dir.
159 S. Main St., Suite 830
Akron, OH 44308-1318
(330) 376-8522
EIN: 341087615
Source Date: 3/95

Geographic Restrictions:
Limited to Summit County, OH.

Restrictions:
No grants to individuals, religious purposes, endowments, scholarships, or fellowships.

To Whom:
Culture/Humanities: performing arts, music, theater, dance, humanities, art museums, historic preservation, museums, libraries, media, language/literature, journalism.

Education: elementary, secondary, and higher education, vocational education, adult/continuing education, enrichment and literacy.

Health and Social Services: promotion of wellness, **medical research**, care, treatment and education as well as public health programs, drug and alcohol abuse, mental health, child care, seniors, volunteerism, family services, children's homes, hunger and food banks, emergency relief.

Civic Affairs: business and employment, community development, fire departments, voter groups, community planning, consumer interests, crime and law enforcement, crime prevention, environment and energy programs, equal rights, recreation, zoos, parks, athletic organizations, camps, boys and girls clubs, neighborhood associations, urban development.

For What:
Matching funds, **research**, special projects, scholarship funds, seed money.

Financial info:
Giving: $1,348,700 for 340 grants (high: $50,000; low: $50).

Application info:
Applications accepted. Submit proposal (20 copies) with cover sheet. Deadline is Apr. 1 for Culture/Humanities, July 1 for Education, Oct. 1 for Health and Human Services, and Jan. 2 for Civic Affairs. Board meets quarterly. Publishes annual report and application guidelines.

Recent Grants:

$10,000	Abstinence-The Better Choice Inc. Responsible Social Values Program
$29,000	Access Inc. Emergency shelter for homeless women and children
$5,000	Akron Blind Center and Workshop Inc. Low Vision Clinic
$10,000	Akron Zoological Park Picnic area for disabled
$5,000	Akron-Urban Minority Alcoholism Drug Abuse.
$15,000	Archbishop Hoban High School. Handicap accessible elevator

Robert F. Frankel Endowment Fund of University Hospitals of Cleveland

c/o Carol A. Frankel, Trustee
3290 Kersdale Rd.
Cleveland, OH 44124
Source Date: 12/96

Geographic Restrictions:
Primarily in OH.

To Whom:
Medical research with emphasis on geriatric medicine, musical arts, American theater.

Financial info:
Giving: $110,900 for grants (high: $15,000; low: $1,500).

Application info:
Applications accepted. Submit letter. No deadline.

Directors, Officers, Trustees:
Frankel, Carol A., Trustee

Heed Ophthalmic Foundation

c/o F. A. Gutman, M.D.
Cleveland Clinic Foundation
9500 Euclid Ave.
Cleveland, OH 44195-5024
(216) 445-8145
EIN: 366012426
Source Date: 7/93

Geographic Restrictions:
Limited to U.S. citizens.

To Whom:
Fellowships for graduates of medical schools accredited by the AMA to further their education if the field of diseases of the eye and eye surgery or to do research in ophthalmology.

For What:
Fellowships.

Financial info:
Giving: $225,600 for 45 grants to individuals.

Application info:
Applications accepted. Application form required. Deadline is Dec. 31. Board meets in Aug. and Nov.

Directors, Officers, Trustees:
Fine, Stuart, M.D., Trustee
First National Bank of Chicago, Trustee
Gutman, Froncie A., M.D., Officer, Trustee
Heed, Thomas D. (d), Donor
Heed, Thomas D., Mrs. (d), Donor
Jampol, Lee, M.D., Trustee
Kramer, Steve, M.D., Trustee
Society of Heed Fellows, Donor
Straatsman, Bradley, M.D., Officer, Trustee

Mark P. Herschede Foundation

1144 Edwards Rd.
Cincinnati, OH 45208
(513) 321-3161
EIN: 316030571
Source Date: 12/95

Geographic Restrictions:
Primarily in Cincinnati, OH.

Restrictions:
No grants to individuals.

To Whom:
Cultural programs, education, **medical research**, community funds, zoos, performing arts, museums.

For What:
Annual campaigns, **research**.

Financial info:
Assets: $741,900.
Giving: $46,900 for 25 grants (high: $20,000; low: $50).

Application info:
Applications accepted. Application form required. No deadline. Board meets quarterly.

Directors, Officers, Trustees:
Herschede, Joan R., Trustee
Huffman, Deborah L., Trustee
Marriott, Robert S., Trustee

Michelson Foundation Charitable Trust

705 Merriman Rd.
Akron, OH 44303
EIN: 346616858
Source Date: 12/94

Geographic Restrictions:
Primarily in Akron, OH, area.

Restrictions:
No grants to individuals.

To Whom:
Religion, community funds, child development, community development, **medical research**, hospitals, historic preservation, museums.

For What:
Endowment funds, continuing support, **research**.

Financial info:
Giving: $59,800 for 55 grants (high: $10,000; low: $100).

Application info:
Applications accepted. Submit letter. No deadline.

Directors, Officers, Trustees:
Michelson, Albert S. (d), Donor
Michelson, Richard A., Sr., Donor, Officer
Michelson, Richard A., Jr., Trustee

Peerless Foundation

1821 Summit Rd., Suite 020
Cincinnati, OH 45237
(513) 821-5992
EIN: 310741546
Source Date: 12/95

To Whom:
Medical research at higher education institutions and hospitals.

For What:
Equipment, **research.**

Financial info:
Giving: $25,200 for 5 grants (high: $15,000; low: $200).

Application info:
Applications accepted. Submit letter. No deadline.

Directors, Officers, Trustees:
Froikin, Roger, Officer
Lindner, Carl H., Donor
Peerless, Louis, Officer
Peerless, Sidney A., M.D., Donor, Officer
Schwartz, Howard, Officer

Elisabeth Severance Prentiss Foundation

c/o National City Bank
Attn: Richard W. Mack, Secretary
P.O. Box 5756
Cleveland, OH 44101
(216) 575-2760
EIN: 34651243
Source Date: 12/95

Geographic Restrictions:
Primarily in the Cleveland, OH, area.

Restrictions:
No grants for national fundraising organizations and foundations, individuals, or scholarships.

To Whom:
Medical and surgical research, acquisition, advancement and dissemination of knowledge of medicine and surgery, and of means of maintaining health, promote public health, hospitals and health institutions, improve methods of hospital management and administration, programs to make hospital and medical care available to all, especially to low-income populations, AIDS.

For What:
Research, operating budgets, continuing support, seed money, building funds, equipment, endowment funds, special projects, renovation projects.

Financial info:
Assets: $73,065,700.
Giving: $2,661,900 for 20 grants (high: $500,000; low: $4,000).

Application info:
Applications accepted. Submit proposal. Deadline is May 15 and Nov. 15. Board meets in June and Dec. Publishes annual report with application guidelines.

Recent Grants:

$1,050,629	St. Luke's Hospital Association
$12,000	Hitchcock Center for Women, Inc. Purchase of Saint Mary Seminary building to assist chemically dependent women.
$25,000	Case Western Reserve University School of Medicine, University Hospitals of Cleveland. Research program in schizophrenia.
$20,000	American Red Cross Greater Cleveland Chapter. New building.
$20,000	Heather Hill, Inc. Construct, furnish and equip Corinne Dolan Alzheimer Center at Heather Hill.
$4,000	North Coast Health Ministry. Cover medical professional liability insurance for physicians, nurses and other clinic volunteers.

Directors, Officers, Trustees:
Alexander, Quentin, Manager, Officer
Bolwell, Harry J., Manager
DeLancey, William J., Manager
Mack, Richard W., Manager, Officer
Miller, Kate W., Donor
Miller, Luther L., Donor
National City Bank, Trustee
Prentiss, Elisabeth Severance (d), Donor
Robertson, William R., Manager

Mack Snyder Rau Foundation

3200 National City Ctr.
1900 E. Ninth St.
Cleveland, OH 44114-3485
(216) 861-7528
EIN: 341489556
Source Date: 12/93

To Whom:
Medical research, hospice, higher education.

For What:
Research.

Financial info:
Giving: $80,000 for 2 grants (high: $50,000; low: $30,000).

Application info:
Applications accepted. Submit letter. No deadline.

Directors, Officers, Trustees:
Rau, Alice W, Officer, Trustee
Rau, David A., Trustee
Rau, Norma Dean, Trustee
Rau Charitable Head Trust, Mark Snyder, Donor
Vogt, Peter W., Trustee
Weil, Edward, Officer, Trustee

Reinberger Foundation

c/o Robert N. Reinberger, Trustee
27600 Chagrin Blvd.
Lyndhurst, OH 44122
(216) 292-2790
EIN: 346574879
Source Date: 12/93

Geographic Restrictions:
Primarily in the Cleveland and Columbus, OH, areas.

Restrictions:
No grants to individuals, seed money, emergency funds, land acquisition, demonstration projects, or conferences.

To Whom:
Arts, social services, Protestant religion, higher education, **medical research.**

For What:
Operating budgets, continuing support, annual campaigns, building funds, equipment, endowment funds, matching funds, scholarship funds, **research**, publications, special projects, deficit financing, capital campaigns.

Financial info:
Giving: $2,674,900 for 60 grants (high: $150,000; low: $1,500).

Application info:
Applications accepted. Submit proposal. No deadline. Board meets in Mar., June, Sept., and Dec. Publishes application guidelines.

Recent Grants:

$210,129	Otterbein College, Westerville, OH. Reinberger Electronic Design Studio, to upgrade the lighting systems in Cowan Hall and Riley Auditorium and purchase musical instruments.
$122,565	Capital University, Columbus, OH. Link classrooms and faculty studios in the Conservatory of Music to the main campus library and the internet.

Directors, Officers, Trustees:
Dyer, Sara R., Trustee
Hooser, Karen R., Trustee
Oman, Richard H., Trustee
Reinberger, Clarence Thompson (d), Donor
Reinberger, Louise Fischer (d), Donor
Reinberger, Robert N., Trustee, Committee
Reinberger, William C., Trustee, Committee
Society National Bank, Trustee

Oklahoma

Samuel Roberts Noble Foundation, Inc.

c/o Michael A. Cawley, Pres.
P.O. Box 2180
Ardmore, OK 73402-2180
(405) 223-5810
EIN: 730606209
Source Date: 10/96

Geographic Restrictions:
Primarily in the Southwest U.S., with emphasis on OK.

Restrictions:
No grants to individuals.

To Whom:
Basic biomedical research and plant biology research, agricultural research, consultation, and demonstration.

Capital funds for higher education, health research and delivery systems.

For What:
Research, employee-related scholarships, seed money, building funds, equipment, endowment funds, matching funds, employee matching gifts.

Financial info:
Assets: $556,925,900.
Giving: $11,960,600 for 115 grants (high: $2,500,000; low: $500) and $109,500 for 45 grants to individuals (high: $3,000; low: $1,500).

Application info:
Applications accepted. Submit letter of inquiry. Deadline is Dec. 1, Mar. 1, June 1, and Sept. 1. Board meets in Jan., Apr., July, and Oct. Publishes application guidelines.

Directors, Officers, Trustees:
Aldridge, Elizabeth A., Officer
Brown, Ann Noble, Trustee
Brown, David R., Trustee
Cawley, Michael A., Officer, Trustee
Dubose, Vivian N., Trustee
Goddard, William R., Trustee
Noble, Edward E., Trustee
Noble, Lloyd (d), Donor
Noble, Mary Jane, Trustee
Noble, Rusty, Trustee
Pulliam, Larry, Officer
Snodgrass, John F., Trustee

Presbyterian Health Foundation

c/o Jean G. Gumerson, Pres.
711 Stanton L. Young Blvd., Suite 604
Oklahoma City, OK 73104
EIN: 730709836
Source Date: 12/96

Geographic Restrictions:
Primarily in OK with emphasis on Oklahoma City area.

Restrictions:
No grants for individuals or operating funds.

To Whom:
Medical education, **medical research**, community health related organizations.

Financial info:
Assets: $131,047,000 (from 1995 990PF).
Giving: $5,700,000 for 50 grants (high: $1,000,000; low: $150).

Application info:
Applications accepted. Submit letter. No deadline. Board meets quarterly.

Recent Grants:

$425,500 University Of Oklahoma Health Sciences Center. Recruitment support for nationally renowned Dermatologist, Lynn Drake, M.D., to serve as Chairman of the Department of Dermatology.

$500,000 University Of Oklahoma Health Sciences Center. Support to further develop the Department of Psychiatry and Behavioral Sciences.

$75,000 University Of Oklahoma College Of Allied Health. Support of the Oklahoma Assistive Technology Center.

$38,400 University Of Oklahoma College Of Medicine. Presbyterian Health Foundation/Harris Student Scholarship Program.

$982,240 University Of Oklahoma College Of Medicine. Support of resident program for the academic year.

$180,000 University Of Oklahoma College of Medicine. Bridge funding support for the Department of Pediatrics.

$24,913 University Of Oklahoma College Of Medicine Department of Anatomical Sciences. Research study: An in vitro model system for nerve regeneration studies.

$18,203 University Of Oklahoma College Of Medicine Department of Anatomical Sciences. Research study: Neurochemicai Spinal Circuitry and Uterine Innervation

$25,000 University Of Oklahoma College Of Medicine Department of Biochemistry and Molecular Biology. Matching support for the Distinguished Lecturer Series and Graduate Course titled - ADVANCES IN HUMAN MOLECULAR GENETICS.

$38,333 University Of Oklahoma College Of Medicine Department of Hematology/Oncology. Research study: Characterization of Lysosomal Enzyme Phosphotransferase.

$4,250 University Of Oklahoma College Of Medicine Department of Medicine. Matching support to upgrade the Department of Medicine's cardiovascular disease simulator known as Harvey.

$7,380 University Of Oklahoma College Of Medicine Department of Microbiology and Immunology. Research study: Experimental Infection, Iron and Pathogenesis of Bordetella bronchiseptica.

$45,000 University Of Oklahoma College Of Medicine Department of Ophthalmology. Research study: Second Messengers in the Retina.

$43,850 University Of Oklahoma College Of Medicine Department of Ophthalmology. Research study: Role of Tyrosine Phosphorylation in Mammalian Retina.

$50,794 University Of Oklahoma College Of Medicine Department of Microbiology and Immunology. Research study: Identification and characterization of endothelial-derived toxic factors.

$44,650 University Of Oklahoma College Of Medicine Department of Microbiology and Immunology. Research study: Monocyte specific chemoattractant from human PMN.

$25,000 University Of Oklahoma College Of Medicine Department of Microbiology and Immunology. Research study: A New Potential Virulence Factor on the Surface of Faecalis.

$50,000 University Of Oklahoma College Of Medicine Department of Pediatrics. Support for the Oklahoma Fetal and Infant Mortality Analysis Program.

$65,000 University Of Oklahoma College Of Medicine Department of Pediatrics. Research study: Cryptosporidial genes invoked in membrane alteration.

$3,442 University Of Oklahoma College Of Medicine Department of Radiological Sciences. Research study: Heat and Radiation - Induced Changes in the Nuclear Matrix.

$98,240 University Of Oklahoma College Of Medicine Department of Surgery - OU Breast Health Institute. Support to establish a Genetic Counseling Program for Hereditary Breast Cancer.

$25,000 University Of Oklahoma College Of Nursing. Stipend support for the Nurse Practitioner Program

$10,942 University Of Oklahoma College Of Pharmacy Department of Medicinal Chemistry and Pharmaceutics. Research study Effects of Transcutaneous Electrical Nerve Stimulation (TENS) on Dorsal Horn Cell Activity during Pharmacological Challenge in Cats.

$24,400 University Of Oklahoma College Of Pharmacy Department of Medicinal Chemistry and Pharmaceutics. Research study: Design and Synthesis of Mechanism-based Peptide Inhibitors of cAPK

$25,000 University Of Oklahoma College Of Pharmacy Department of Medicinal Chemistry and Pharmaceutics. Research study Design, synthesis and biological evaluation of novel nicotinic acetylcholine receptor agonists

$24,550 University Of Oklahoma College Of Pharmacy Department of Obstetrics and Gynecology. Research study: Passive Fetal Antibody Transfer After Maternal Vaccination.

$24,318 University Of Oklahoma College Of Public Health Department of Health Administration & Policy. Support of the Oklahoma Public Health Leadership Institute

$24,972 University Of Oklahoma College Of Public Health Oklahoma Center on Aging. Research study Health,

	Ethnicity and Aging in Rural Oklahoma - An Investigation of Elders In and Near Oklahoma's All Black Towns
$25,000	University Of Oklahoma College Of Public Health Department of Health Promotion Sciences. Research study Public Health Methods to Increase Physical Activity Rates in a Minority Population
$25,000	Bacone College. Support of the Fitness/Wellness Program in the new Student Life Center.
$147,925	Dean McGee Eye Institute. Support of the renovation of the J.E. and L.E. Mabee Animal Research Laboratory and the Microsurgical Research and Training Suite.
$350,000	Indian Nations Presbytery, Presbyterian Church USA and The Episcopal Diocese of Oklahoma. Support of the joint Clinical Pastoral Education Program for the year beginning June 1, 1996.
$25,000	Langston University. Support of the University's Scholarship Program in Physical Therapy.
$5,000	Leadership Oklahoma. Health and Medical Services Day.
$5,000	Leadership Oklahoma City. Health and Medical Services Day.
$10,000	Murray State College Foundation. Support of the"LINK" Program.
$5,000	Oklahoma Alliance for Public Policy Research. Support of a feasibility study and plan development for a multi-purpose medical research, health care and educational/training center.
$10,000	Oklahoma City Public Schools Foundation.Excellence in Education Annual Campaign.
$10,000	Oklahoma City-County Health Department. Support of the Weed and Seed Program.
$15,000	Oklahoma School of Science & Mathematics Foundation. Support of a consultant to the OSSM Foundation.
$200,000	Oklahoma State University Foundation. Support of laser applications in medical research projects at the Oklahoma State University Center for Laser Research.
$8,000	Planned Parenthood. Matching support of the Planned Parenthood of Central Oklahoma's Technology Project.
$10,000	Presbyterian Health Foundation Nursing Scholarship Program. Support of the nursing scholarship program for 1996.
$50,000	Samuel Roberts Noble Foundation. Support for an Oklahoma historical preservation project.
$35,000	University of Central Oklahoma Foundation. Support for computers, software and videos to enhance the Department of Nursing's programs and upgrade of technological skills for graduates.
$25,000	United Way. Capital Campaign.
$50,000	Variety Health Center. Support of a new maternal and child health care clinic.
$50,000	University Of Oklahoma Foundation. Senior Vice President and Provost and Vice President for Health Affairs and Associate Provost at the OU Health Sciences Center.
$170,000	University Of Oklahoma Foundation. Presbyterian Health Foundation Chair in Experimental Pathology (Human Genetics Program).

Directors, Officers, Trustees:

Anderson, Michael D., Officer, Trustee
Barnes, William F., M.D., Trustee
Beard, William M., Officer, Trustee
Carl, R. Barton, M.D., Trustee
Dotter, Richard G., M.D., Trustee
Edwards, Carl, Trustee
Ellis, Nancy Payne, Trustee
Ellis, Robert S., M.D., Trustee
Gumerson, Jean G., Officer, Trustee
Kizer, Melissa, Officer
McGrath, Dennis, Officer
Parke, David W., II, M.D., Trustee
Smith, J. V., Trustee
Tate, Harry B., M.D., Trustee
Tolbert, James, Trustee
Vannatta, Jerry, Trustee
Williams, G. Rainey, M.D., Trustee
Young, Stanton L., Officer, Trustee
Zahn, Fred II., Officer, Trustee

Oregon

Collins Medical Trust

c/o Nancy Helseth, Admin.
1618 S.W. First Ave., Suite 300
Portland, OR 97201
(503) 227-1219
EIN: 936021895
Source Date: 9/95

Geographic Restrictions:
Limited to OR.

Restrictions:
No grants to individuals, annual operating funds, or deficit financing.

To Whom:
Aid, further, promote, develop, encourage and sponsor research, experiment and work in the cause, cure and treatment of human disease or in any field of medical research and to aid further and promote medical education.

For What:
Equipment, **research**, scholarship funds, fellowships, special projects, lectureships.

Financial info:
Assets: $2,167,400.
Giving: $197,700 for 10 grants (high: $50,000; low: $5,000).

Application info:
Applications accepted. Submit letter. Deadline is Jan. 1, May 1, and Sept. 1. Board meets in Jan., May, and Sept. Publishes application guidelines.

Directors, Officers, Trustees:
Bishop, Timothy R., Officer
Collins, Maribeth W., Trustee
Collins, Truman W. (d), Donor
Collins, Truman W., Jr., Trustee
Helseth, Nancy L., Officer
Paquet, Joseph F., M.D., Trustee
Patterson, James R., M.D., Trustee

Louisiana-Pacific Foundation

c/o Michael J. Tull, VP, Human Resources
111 S.W. Fifth Ave.
Portland, OR97204
(503) 221-0800
EIN: 237268660
Source Date: 12/95

Geographic Restrictions:
Primarily in areas of company operations.

To Whom:
Primary purpose is to grant scholarships to dependents of company employees. Higher education, social services, community funds, health, youth, performing arts, arts, museums, **medical research**, disabled.

For What:
Annual campaigns, capital campaigns, continuing support, general purposes, employee-related scholarships, emergency funds.

Financial info:
Giving: $1,522,700 for 140 grants (high: $150,000; low: $100).

Application info:
Applications accepted. Application form required for scholarships. Submit letter. No deadline. Board meets quarterly.

Directors, Officers, Trustees:
Davis, Anita M., Trustee
Hebert, William, Officer
Kayser, Don, Officer
Kirchoff, Anton C., Officer
Louisiana-Pacific Corp., Donor
Maffei, Gary R., Trustee
Selis, Pamela A., Officer, Trustee
Simpson, Lee, Officer

Northwest Osteopathic Medical Foundation

c/o David N. Rianda, Exec. Dir.
Suite 780, Tiffany Ctr.
1410 S.W. Morrison St.
Portland, OR 97205
(503) 222-7161
Source Date: 12/94

Geographic Restrictions:
Limited to Pacific Northwest area of U.S including OR, WA, ID, MT, and AK.

To Whom:
Osteopathic medicine, medical education, wellness and prevention, seniors, hospice, **health research,** social services, medical equipment, public education, family services, youth, health education.

Financial info:
Giving: $160,800 for 55 grants (high: $10,000; low: $50).

Application info:
Applications accepted. Submit letter. Deadline is Mar. 1, June 1, Sept. 1, Dec. 1. Publishes application guidelines.

Recent Grants:

$2,000	Catholic Community Services of Portland. Drug intervention/prevention program.
$500	Children's Farm Home, Corvallis. Wheelchair ramp construction.
$500	Children's Home Society, Vancouver, WA. Program support for deaf children and their families.
$1,266	Christie School. Medical equipment.
$1,000	Coalition of Community Health Clinics. Prescription medications for low income population.
$2,500	Comprehensive Options for Drug Abusers. Early intervention and prevention program.
$2,000	Crisis Intervention Services, Medford. Family Focus program, parents' support services.
$500	Douglas County AIDS Council/Ruby House. AIDS hospice outreach program.

Directors, Officers, Trustees:
Cook, James L., Officer
Foltz, Lawrence E., Officer
Minniti, Blair, Officer
Oliverio, Maureen J., Officer

Pennsylvania

Alcoa Foundation

c/o F. Worth Hobbs, Pres.
425 Sixth Ave., Rm. 3029
Pittsburgh, PA 15219-1850
(412) 553-2348
EIN: 251128857
Source Date: 12/96

Geographic Restrictions:
Primarily in areas of company operations: Davenport, IA, Knoxville, TN, Massena, NY, Pittsburgh, PA, Evansville, IN, Cleveland, OH, and Rockdale, TX.

Restrictions:
No grants for sectarian religious organizations, political purposes, individuals, endowments, tickets, souvenir programs, advertising, golf outings, trips, tours, or student exchange programs, deficit financing, documentaries and videos, hospital capital funds.

To Whom:
Education:(45% of funding) higher education, pre-college (early childhood, elementary and secondary), math and science, minorities, literacy.

Health and Welfare: (29% of funding) hospitals, medical centers, **research**, sick, disabled, needy, drug and alcohol abuse, battered women, abused children, seniors, homeless.

Cultural: (10% of funding) performing arts, historical preservation, music, theater, dance, literature, crafts, traditional customs.

Civic and Community: (11% of funding) hunger, new housing for low-income people, land conservation.

Youth: (4% of funding) advance education, economic education, dropout prevention, develop character and provide fitness opportunities, youth at-risk.

For What:
Annual campaigns, building funds, conferences and seminars, continuing support, emergency funds, employee matching gifts, equipment fellowships, matching funds, operating budgets, **research**, scholarship funds, seed money, employee-related scholarships, capital campaigns, general purposes, renovation projects, special projects.

Financial info:
Assets: $306,405,300.
Giving: $12,846,500 for 2,275 grants (high: $300,000; low: $100).

Application info:
Applications accepted. Submit proposal. No deadline. Board meets monthly. Publishes annual report with application guidelines.

Recent Grants:
- Apollo Memorial Library. Apollo, PA. Children's Corner parent and child reading area
- Appalachian Ballet Company. Knoxville, TN.
- Arc Services, Inc. Albemarle, NC. Stanly County community outreach efforts to establish 150 child licensed day care center
- Arizona State University. Tempe, AZ. College of Fine Arts Scholarships
- The Ark, Inc. Evansville, IN.
- Arkansas Arts Center Foundation. Little Rock, AR. Community outreach programs
- Arkansas Association for Hearing Impaired Children. Little Rock, AR. Parent/child weekend learning seminar
- Arkansas Community Foundation, Inc. Little Rock, AR. Arkansas Governor's Commission on People with Disabilities
- Arkansas Community Foundation, Inc. Little Rock, AR. SILO Undergraduate Research Fellowship program
- Arnold Volunteer Fire Department. Arnold, PA.
- Arsenal Family and Children's Center. Pittsburgh, PA. Clairton center, equipment; Lawrenceville center, creative play yard
- Art Association of Richmond. Richmond, IN. Educational programs
- Arthritis Foundation. Evansville, IN.
- Artists Raising the Consciousness of Humanity, Inc. Pittsburgh, PA. CityKids Training/Employment program
- Arts Council of Albemarle-Stanly County Chamber of Commerce. Albemarle, NC. Community Arts Association, Stanly County Arts Guild, Stanly County Chorale, and Uwharrie Players
- Arts Council of Northern Beaufort County. Beaufort, SC. "Connections" program
- Arts Council of Southwestern Indiana, Inc.. Evansville, IN.
- Arts and Education Council of Greater St. Louis. St. Louis, MO.
- Associacao Obra do Berco. Sao Paulo, Brazil. Management training pilot program for 14 to 17 year old teens
- Associated Colleges of the St. Lawrence Valley. Potsdam, NY. Bebe Miller Dance Company three-week residency
- Associated Marine Institute, Inc.. Juno Beach, FL. Computer lab and software
- Association of Governing Boards of Universities and Colleges. Washington, DC.

The Association for Guidance, Aid, Placement and Empathy. Nashville, TN. Partial cost of foster care for one child.
Association of Science-Technology Centers. Washington, DC. National Science Teachers Association conference.
Atlantic Legal Foundation, Inc. Harrisburg, PA.
Augustana College. Rock Island, IL. Scholarships
Avonmore Borough. Avonmore, PA. Avonmore Public Library, computer
Badin, Town of Badin, NC. New fire engine
Baldwin-Wallace College. Berea, OH.
Beaufort Chamber Orchestra. Beaufort, SC.
Beaufort County Government. Beaufort, SC. Sea Island Science Fair
Beaufort County Public Education Foundation. Beaufort, SC. Mini-Grants for Teachers program
Beautiful Blount, Inc.. Maryville, TN.
Bellefaire. Shaker Heights, OH.
Bellflower Center for Prevention of Child Abuse. Cleveland, OH.
Benton Middle School. Benton, AR. Arkansas Water Education Team project
Bethany Home. Moline, IL. Parents Too Soon program
Bethlehem Haven. Pittsburgh, PA.
Big Brothers & Big Sisters Association (Knoxville). Maryville, TN. Blount County branch office
Big Brothers & Sisters of Greater Pittsburgh, Inc.. Pittsburgh, PA. At-Risk program
Big Brothers/Big Sisters of Beaufort County. Beaufort, SC. Reading materials
Big Brothers/Big Sisters (Quad Cities). Davenport, IA.
Big Brothers/Big Sisters of Tiftarea. Tifton, GA.
Bijou Theatre Center. Knoxville, TN. Educational outreach programs
Bill Wilkerson Hearing & Speech Center. Nashville, TN.
Birmingham-Southern College. Birmingham, AL. Environmental Resource Center
CONTACT Pittsburgh, Inc. Pittsburgh, PA. Education and training program for Crisis Line, KidsLine PhonePals and Reassurance Calling for Senior Adults volunteers
Cornell University. Ithaca, NY. Efficacy Seminars in Diversity program
Cornell University. Ithaca, NY. Women's program office, Introduction to Engineering
Cornwall Iron Furnace Associates, Inc. Cornwall, PA. Site preservation and student educational programs
Cornwall-Lebanon School District. Lebanon, PA. Tech-Prep Joint Partnership program

Directors, Officers, Trustees:
Aluminum Company of America, Donor
Bridenbaugh, Peter R., Director
Buechel, Kathleen W., Officer
Burgan, Kathleen R., Officer
Diederich, John L., Director
Edwards, Ernest J., Director
Fischer, Richard L., Director
Hobbs, F. Worth, Director, Officer
Hoffman, Ronald R., Director
Kelson, Richard B., Director
Mellon Bank, N.A., Trustee

AMETEK Foundation, Inc.

c/o Robert W. Yannarell, Assist. Secretary
Station Sq. 4
Paoli, PA 19301
(215) 647-2121
EIN: 136095939
Source Date: 12/94

Geographic Restrictions:
Limited to organizations located in the vicinities of plant operations.

Restrictions:
No grants to individuals or matching gifts.

To Whom:
Community funds, hospitals, **medical research**, **cancer research**, higher, elementary, and minority education, arts, social services, Jewish giving.

For What:
Annual campaigns, building funds, **research**, employee-related scholarships, scholarship funds, technical assistance, general purposes, exchange programs, equipment, endowment funds.

Financial info:
Giving: $663,800 for 100 grants (high: $75,000; low: $500).

Application info:
Applications accepted. Submit letter. Deadline is Feb. 28 and Sept. 30. Board meets in Apr. and Nov.

Directors, Officers, Trustees:
AMETEK, Inc., Donor
Blankley, Walter, Director, Officer
Cole, Lewis, Director
Friedlaender, Helmut N., Director
Varet, Elizabeth R., Director
Yannarell, Robert W., Director, Officer

AO North America, Inc.

P.O. Box 308
Devon, PA 19333
(610) 251-9007
EIN: 232701788
Source Date: 6/96

To Whom:
Medical orthopaedic research.

For What:
Research.

Financial info:
Assets: $660,200.
Giving: $107,300 for 5 grants (high: $35,000; low: $5,000).

Application info:
Applications accepted. Application form required. No deadline.

Directors, Officers, Trustees:
AO/ASIF Foundation, Donor
Bone, Larry, Officer
Gerry, James E., Officer
Trafton, Peter, Officer

Boiron Research Foundation, Inc.

6 Campus Blvd., Bldg. A.
Newton Square, PA 19073
EIN: 521268329
Source Date: 12/93

Geographic Restrictions:
Limited to U.S.

To Whom:
Homeopathic medical research and auto-hemic therapy.

For What:
Individuals.

Financial info:
Giving: $108,900 for 5 grants to individuals and $39,100 for foundation administered programs.

Application info:
Applications accepted. Submit proposal. Deadline is Sept. 30.

Directors, Officers, Trustees:
Boiron, Christian, Officer
Boiron, Jean, Officer
Boiron, Inc., Donor
Montfort, Thierry, Officer

Charles Talbot Campbell Foundation

c/o National City Bank
300 Fourth Ave.
Pittsburgh, PA 15278
EIN: 251287221
Source Date: 1/96

Geographic Restrictions:
Primarily in western PA.

Restrictions:
No grants for community funds, United Way, or individuals.

To Whom:
Hospitals, **ophthalmological medical research**, disabled, music.

For What:
Continuing support, general purposes, operating budgets, **research**.

Financial info:
Assets: $4,147,500.
Giving: $200,000 for 10 grants (high: $50,000; low: $5,000).

Application info:
Applications accepted. Submit letter. No deadline.

Directors, Officers, Trustees:
Campbell, Charles Talbot (d), Donor
National City Bank, Trustee

Foundation for Basic Cutaneous Research

210 W. Rittenhouse Sq., Suite 3302
Philadelphia, PA 19103
EIN: 232439001
Source Date: 7/95

To Whom:
Dermatology medical research.

For What:
Research.

Financial info:
Assets: $1,710,700.
Giving: $234,100 for 20 grants (high: $75,000; low: $100) and $10,300 for 5 grants to individuals (high: $4,000; low: $500).

Application info:
Applications accepted. Submit proposal. No deadline.

Directors, Officers, Trustees:
- Ajinomoto U.S.A., Inc., Donor
- Clairol-Gelb Foundation, Donor
- Hoechst Company, Donor
- Johnson & Johnson Baby Products, Donor
- Kligman, Lorraine H., M.D., Officer
- Lever Brothers Company, Donor
- Ortho Pharmaceutical, Donor
- Upjohn Company, The, Donor

Josiah W. & Bessie H. Kline Foundation Inc.

c/o Harry R. Bughman, Secretary
42 Kline Village
Harrisburg, PA 17104
(717) 232-0266
EIN: 236245783
Source Date: 12/95

Geographic Restrictions:
Primarily in south central PA.

Restrictions:
No grants to individuals, endowments, operating expenses, or religious programs.

To Whom:
Aid blind or incapacitated persons or disabled children in need of financial assistance; private higher education and to hospitals; and **scientific or medical research** to be performed by scientific professionals or by colleges, universities, or research institutions.

For What:
General purposes, continuing support, annual campaigns, emergency funds, building funds, equipment, scholarship funds, matching funds, renovation projects, capital campaigns, land acquisition, lectureships, **research**.

Financial info:
Assets: $22,292,800.
Giving: $792,000 for 45 grants (high: $200,000; low: $500).

Application info:
Applications accepted. Submit proposal. No deadline. Board meets in Mar. and Nov. Publishes application guidelines.

Recent Grants:

$200,000	Susquehanna University, Selingsgrove, PA. Capital campaign and construct new business and communications building.
$200,000	Wilson College, Chambersburg, PA. Implement information-technology plan.

Directors, Officers, Trustees:
- Boswell, William D., Director
- Bughman, Harry R., Director, Officer
- Burdge, Jeffrey J., Director
- Jordan, Richard E., Director, Officer
- King, William J., Director, Officer
- Kline, Bessie H. (d), Donor
- Kline, Josiah W. (d), Donor
- Marley, James A., Director
- Nation, Robert F., Director, Officer
- Ross, Samuel D., Director
- Smith, David A., Director
- Tuten, John C., Director

Millstein Charitable Foundation

Cherry Creek Commons, P.O. Box K
Youngwood, PA 15697-0347
EIN: 256064981
Source Date: 9/96

Geographic Restrictions:
Primarily in western PA.

To Whom:
Jewish welfare and giving, education, **medical research**, community funds, homeless, hospice, hospitals, humanities.

For What:
Annual campaigns, building funds, capital campaigns, emergency funds, **research**, special projects.

Financial info:
Assets: $6,316,200.
Giving: $186,600 for 120 grants (high: $75,000; low: $50).

Application info:
Applications accepted. Submit letter. No deadline. Board meets annually.

Directors, Officers, Trustees:
Millstein, David J., Officer, Trustee
Millstein, Jack H., Jr., Trustee

Mudge Foundation

c/o PNC Bank
Trust Div. 970
1 Oliver Plaza
Pittsburgh, PA 15265
(412) 762-3866
EIN: 256023150
Source Date: 12/95

Geographic Restrictions:
Primarily in TX, ME, and PA.

Restrictions:
No grants to individuals.

To Whom:
Natural resource and science projects, **medical research**, environment, higher education, public policy, museums.

For What:
General purposes, **research**.

Financial info:
Assets: $3,074,400.
Giving: $107,500 for 5 grants (high: $25,000; low: $1,000).

Application info:
Applications accepted. Submit letter. No deadline.

Directors, Officers, Trustees:
PNC Bank, Trustee

National Organization for Hearing Research

1325 Morris Dr., Suite 201
Wayne, PA 19087
(610) 664-3260
EIN: 232528578
Source Date: 12/93

Geographic Restrictions:
U.S. and international giving.

To Whom:
Biomedical research for prevention, cause, and cure of hearing loss and deafness.

For What:
Individuals, **research**, seed money.

Financial info:
Giving: $310,700 for 20 grants (high: $100,000; low: $5,000).

Application info:
Applications accepted. Submit letter. No deadline.

Oberkotter Foundation

c/o George H. Nofer, J.D., Co-Trustee & Exec. Dir.
1600 Market St., 34th Flr.
Philadelphia, PA 19103
(215) 751-2601
EIN: 232686151
Source Date: 2/97

To Whom:
Research and treatment of diabetes, research, education, and treatment **of hearing impairment**. In the area of hearing impairment, grants to teaching institutions are limited to those involved solely in the auditory/oral approach.

Financial info:
Giving: $2,663,600 for 10 grants (high: $900,000; low: $10,000).

Application info:
Applications accepted. Submit letter. No deadline. Do not publish guidelines or annual reports.

Directors, Officers, Trustees:
Moog, Jean Sachar, Director
Nofer, George H., Director, Trustee
Oberkotter, Mildred L., Trustee
Oberkotter, Paul, Trustee

Dorothy Rider Pool Health Care Trust

(Formerly Rider-Pool Foundation)
c/o Edward F. Meehan, Exec. Dir.
1050 Cedar Crest Blvd., Suite 202
Allentown, PA 18103
(610) 770-9346
EIN: 236207356
Source Date: 12/95

Geographic Restrictions:
Primarily in Lehigh Valley, PA, area.

Restrictions:
No grants to individuals, political of fraternal organizations, operating or capital funds, sectarian institutions, hospitals, fundraising events, United Way member agencies, or publications.

To Whom:
Development of Regional Leadership in Health Affairs: programs for hospital board members to enhance their ability to provide leadership to the community on such issues as ethics in the beginning and end of life, health policy conferences, regional symposia.

Educational Program Development: programs that would lead to the provision of primary care services (pediatrics, family medicine, and general internal medicine) for the region, foster community nursing and the role of nurses in primary care service delivery, regional health professions education consortia to cooperatively develop mechanisms for meeting the demand for primary care health professionals.

Improved Health Status of the Citizens of the Region: development of managed care systems for low-income and uninsured people, improvement in health care services for children, particularly when these services can be integrated with other human and social services, facilitation of improved dental health, childhood immunization, infant mortality, and incidence of low birth weight, improved health status for minorities, the poor, and the disenfranchised.

Health Services Research.

For What:
General purposes, building funds, emergency funds, endowment funds, fellowships, renovation projects, research, special projects.

Financial info:
Giving: $3,224,700 for 30 grants (high: $50,000; low: $500).

Application info:
Applications accepted. Submit letter of intent. Deadline is Oct. 1 and May 1. Board meets in Mar. and Oct. Publishes annual report and application guidelines.

Recent Grants:

$225,000	Chairman of Surgery Discretionary Fund. To enable the Chair of the Department of Surgery to pursue educational and other initiatives which will advance the mission of Lehigh Valley Hospital.
$9,900	Conference on Health Care Reform. To enable Lehigh Valley Hospital board members and other community leaders to consider the ethical implications of health care reform.
$6,400	Council on Foundations. To continue support of a national organization that provides leadership and service in the field of organized philanthropy.
$68,400	Child Health Initiative Planning. Do support a nine-month planning process to develop the potential for a series of initiatives that would measurably improve child health in Lehigh County.

$32,400 Family Practice Residency. To support six months of salaries, consulting fees, etc., to aid the development of a family practice residency program at Lehigh Valley Hospital.

$30,000 Pool Trust Good Health Library. To maintain, expand, and keep current community health and education information at the Allentown Public Library.

$36,000 Allentown EMS Automated Defibrillation. To expand and enhance Allentown EMS response by underwriting the expense of six Automated External Defibrillation units, which enables non-paramedic firefighters to administer the life-saving defibrillation procedure.

$70,000 Delivery of Behavioral Health Services in the Lehigh Valley. To study how to reconfigure public and private mental health funding and services in Lehigh and Northampton Counties and to guarantee appropriate care for those patients unable to be placed in community or alternative settings. Reallocated re sources would be redirected toward the Lehigh Valley mental health services system.

$478,292 Coalition for a Smoke-Free Valley, Phase III. To continue support of a comprehensive approach to tobacco control in the Lehigh Valley, focusing on tobacco-use prevention, adult cessation, and enhancing smoking restrictions in public places over the next five-year period. Interventions to reach the measurable objectives related to each of these goals will be based upon the results of the 1995 Time II comprehensive research on local smoking prevalence and attitudes.

$1,725,000 Medical Education in a Community Model of Care. To guide medical educational program development at Lehigh Valley Hospital through seven initiatives: (1) Become a national model of community-based medical education, (2) Facilitate collaborative educational relationships with community-based partners, (3) Support creative and innovative teaching and educational research, (4) Expand the role, scope, and significance of research in medical education, (5) Incorporate evolving information technology into medical education, (6) Redesign the office of education and develop integrated systems to support the strategic initiatives for education, and (7) Develop, stable and innovative funding for medical education.

$180,000 Baseline and Preliminary Analysis for Measurable Health Status Improvement in the Lehigh Valley. To conduct a baseline analysis for measurable health status improvement in the Lehigh Valley.

$120,000 Northeast Pennsylvania Lions Eye Bank, Inc. To support and train staff to significantly increase the number of corneas available for transplant through the "In-Situ" process - removing only the cornea rather than the whole eye from donors.

$193,500 Burn Prevention Foundation Partnership Marketing Enhancement. To increase the foundation's ability to provide customer valued and supported professional and community burn care and prevention programs in eastern Pennsylvania and western New Jersey

$49,815 Cities in Schools of the Lehigh Valley, Inc. To plan a comprehensive and collaborative adolescent health initiative with Lehigh Valley Hospital and other health and human services providers in Allentown.

Directors, Officers, Trustees:

Cheston, S. Brooke, Trustee
Holt, Leon C., Jr., Trustee
Levitt, Lawrence P., M.D., Trustee
McCarthy, Carol M., Trustee
Meehan, Edward F., Trustee
PNC Bank, Trustee
Rider-Pool, Dorothy (d), Donor
Stemmler, Edward J., M.D., Trustee

Rockwell International Corporation Trust

c/o William R. Fitz, Dir., Contributions & Comm. Rel.
625 Liberty Ave.
Pittsburgh, PA 15222-3123
(412) 565-5803
EIN: 251072431
Source Date: 9/96

Geographic Restrictions:
Primarily in areas of company operations, including Australia, Canada, France, Germany, Japan, and the United Kingdom, except for selected U.S. organizations and universities which are sources of recruits.

Restrictions:
No grants to individuals, hospital building campaigns, or endowments.

To Whom:
Priority is engineering/math/science education in elementary, secondary, and higher education.

Education (54% of funding): higher education, economic education, minorities, educating future science and engineering faculty, improve the quality of elementary and secondary education, teacher preparation programs for retired engineers interested in second careers as educators.

Community Funds (17% of funding).

Health and Human Services (13% of funding): hospitals, medical centers, **medical research**, health services, youth, rehabilitation, mental health, mentally and physically disabled, disadvantaged, seniors, disaster relief services.

Civic and Community (9% of funding): community improvement/development agencies, job training, retraining, and placement services, conservation, environment and ecology, public policy research.

Culture and the Arts (7% of funding): museums, public broadcasting, symphony orchestras, libraries, cultural and performing arts, theaters for the performing arts.

For What:
Operating budgets, building funds, employee matching gifts, scholarship funds, fellowships, professorships.

Financial info:
Assets: $13,587,300.
Giving: $9,145,100 for 1,320 grants (high: $500,000; low: $1,000).

Application info:
Applications accepted. Submit proposal. No deadline. Board meets monthly. Publishes annual report and application guidelines.

Recent Grants:

$500,000	New American Schools Development Corp., Cudahy, CA. Develop "break the mold" school.
$250,000	United Negro College Fund. "Ladders of Hope" program to prepare Los Angeles, CA minority youth to attend college.
$400,000	Society of Automotive Engineers. Develop "A World in Motion" program.
$155,000	American Red Cross

Roth Foundation

3993 Huntingdon Plaza, Suite 310
Huntingdon Valley, PA 19006
(215) 947-3750
EIN: 236271428
Source Date: 10/94

Geographic Restrictions:
Primarily in PA.

To Whom:
Nursing education, **medical research**.

For What:
Student aid, **research**.

Financial info:
Giving: $50,400 for 5 grants.

Application info:
Applications accepted. Submit letter. No deadline. Applicants must have completed one year in a school of nursing. Scholarship awards are made directly to nursing institution on recipient's behalf.

Directors, Officers, Trustees:
Rosenberger, Henry, Trustee
Roth, Abraham (d), Donor
Roth, Edythe M., Donor, Trustee
Roth, Roland P., Trustee
Schwartz, Linda, Trustee

W. W. Smith Charitable Trust

c/o Frances R. Pemberton, Trust Admin.
10 S. Bryn Mawr Ave.
Bryn Mawr, PA 19010
(610) 525-9667
EIN: 236648841
Source Date: 6/96

Geographic Restrictions:
Primarily in the Delaware Valley, including Philadelphia, PA and its 5 neighboring counties. Grants to hospitals (for indigent care) and financial aid programs by invitation only.

Restrictions:
No grants to individuals, deficit financing, endowments.

To Whom:
Financial aid programs for undergraduate students at accredited higher education institutions (28% of funding), hospitals programs for free medical care of the poor and needy (11% of funding), **basic medical research programs dealing with cancer, AIDS, and heart disease** (39% of funding), and programs providing shelter, food, and clothing for children and seniors (21% of funding).

For What:
Scholarship funds, **research**, operating budgets, seed money, emergency funds, building funds, equipment, land acquisition, special projects, publications, matching funds, general purposes, continuing support, renovation projects, capital funds.

Financial info:
Assets: $120,934,100.
Giving: $4,617,500 for 110 grants (high: $150,000; low: $5,000).

Application info:
Applications accepted. Applications forms for medical research grants (4 copies) due June 15 for cancer and AIDS, and Sept. 15 for heart research; for financial aid programs, May 1; no deadline for food clothing and shelter programs. Board meets in Mar., Sept., June, and Dec. Notification is within 30 days. Publishes biennial report with application guidelines.

Recent Grants:

$22,000	Eastern College, St. Davids, PA. Financial aid.
$22,000	Moore College of Art and Design, Philadelphia, PA. Scholarships.
$29,000	University of the Arts, Philadelphia, PA. Scholarships.
$165,000	**Coriell Institute for Medical Research. "200 k-D Receptor Tyrosine Kinase in Tumor Cells."**

Directors, Officers, Trustees:
CoreStates Bank, N.A., Trustee
Smith, Mary L., Trustee
Smith, William Wikoff (d), Donor

Margaret Dorrance Strawbridge Foundation of Pennsylvania II, Inc.

125 Strafford Ave.
Bldg. 3, Suite 108
Wayne, PA 19087-3367
(610) 688-9261
EIN: 232371943
Source Date: 12/95

Geographic Restrictions:
Primarily in the eastern U.S., with emphasis on PA and FL.

Restrictions:
No grants to individuals, capital or endowment funding, scholarships, or fellowships.

To Whom:
Higher and secondary education, hospitals, **medical research**, environment.

For What:
Operating budgets, continuing support, **research**, annual campaigns.

Financial info:
Giving: $289,700 for 65 grants (high: $25,000; low: $100).

Application info:
Applications accepted. Submit letter. No deadline.

Directors, Officers, Trustees:
Strawbridge Foundation, Margaret Dorrance, Donor
Wister, Diana S., Director, Officer

USX Foundation, Inc.

(Formerly United States Steel Foundation, Inc.)
c/o James L. Hamilton, III, Gen. Mgr.
600 Grant St., Rm. 2640
Pittsburgh, PA 15219-4776
(412) 433-5237
EIN: 136093185
Source Date: 11/95

Geographic Restrictions:
Primarily in areas of company operations, including Bucks County and Pittsburgh, PA, Birmingham, AL, Gary, IN, and northeastern MN, and activities of a national nature.

Restrictions:
No grants for religious organizations for religious purposes, individuals, conferences, seminars, travel, publications, or films.

To Whom:
National and Community social services, **medical and health (research and training**, planning, prevention and treatment), public affairs (international, U.S., and regional), cultural affairs (symphony, opera, performing arts, art and cultural centers, councils, and societies), scientific affairs, Aid to Education.

For What:
General purposes, operating budgets, continuing support, annual campaigns, seed money, emergency funds, building funds, equipment, land acquisition, endowment funds, special projects, **research**, employee matching gifts, capital campaigns, renovation projects.

Financial info:
Assets: $6,184,600.
Giving: $4,800,000 for 370 grants (high: $200,000; low: $500).

Application info:
Applications accepted. Submit letter (2 pages limit). Deadline is Jan. 15 for Public/Cultural/Scientific Affairs; Apr. 15 for Education; July 15 for Social Services and Health. Board meets in Apr., June, and Oct. Publishes biennial report with application guidelines.

Recent Grants:
- Montana College of Mineral Science & Technology, Butte, MT, equipment for engineering labs.
- Alaska Council on Economic Education Anchorage, AK
- American Spectator Educational Foundation, Arlington, VA
- Cities In Schools, Southwestern Pennsylvania, Pittsburgh, PA
- ARC House, Pittsburgh, PA, acquisition of an additional facilit.
- Controlled Environment Horticulture, Sewickley, PA, facilities improvements
- Bluffton Family Recreation, Bluffton, OH, new community center
- Gleaners Community Food Bank, Detroit, MI, facilities expansion

Directors, Officers, Trustees:
Dauphin Deposit Bank & Trust Company, Trustee

Wyss Foundation

1690 Russell Rd.
P.O. Box 1766
Paoli, PA 19301-1262
(610) 647-9700
EIN: 232627904
Source Date: 12/95

Geographic Restrictions:
Primarily in Flagstaff, AZ.

To Whom:
Orthopedic medical research, environment, conservation, women, wildlife.

Financial info:
Assets: $5,957,900.
Giving: $1,356,300 for 50 grants (high: $50,000; low: $100).

Application info:
Applications accepted. Submit letter. No deadline.

Directors, Officers, Trustees:
Douse, Robert S., Trustee
Wyss, Hansjoerg, Donor, Trustee

Rhode Island

Lalor Foundation

c/o Lalor Burdick, Secretary
P.O. Box 2493
Providence, RI 02906-0493
(401) 272-1973
EIN: 516000153
Source Date: 12/96

Geographic Restrictions:
International and U.S. giving.

Restrictions:
No grants to individuals, operating expenses, capital or endowment funding, continuing support, annual campaigns, seed money, emergency funds, deficit financing, matching gifts.

To Whom:
Postdoctoral research applicable to mammalian reproductive physiology and biochemistry for yielding improved methods of contraception, termination of pregnancy and/or sterilization.

For What:
Fellowships, **research.**

Financial info:
Assets: $9,530,100 (from 1995 990PF).
Giving: $314,500 for 25 grants (high: $30,000; low: $5,000).

Application info:
Applications accepted. Application form required. Deadline is Jan. 15 with notification by Mar. 15. Publishes application guidelines.

Directors, Officers, Trustees:
Braun, Andrew G., Trustee
Burdick, Lalor, Officer, Trustee
Chandler, Carol, Trustee
Lalor, Willard A. (d), Donor
Patterson, Cynthia B., Officer, Trustee
Zeckhauser, Sally H., Officer, Trustee

Edwin Phillips Trust

c/o Fleet Trust Company, Trust Dept.
P.O. Box 14777
East Providence, RI 02914
EIN: 046025549
Source Date: 12/94

Geographic Restrictions:
Primarily in Plymouth County, MA.

Restrictions:
No grants to individuals.

To Whom:
Research and services for physically or mentally disabled children, hospitals, blind.

For What:
Continuing support, equipment, **research,** special projects.

Financial info:
Giving: $322,400 for 35 grants (high: $75,000; low: $500).

Application info:
Applications accepted. Submit proposal. No deadline.

Directors, Officers, Trustees:
Galvin, Robert E., Trustee
Hall, Richard A., Trustee
Phillips, Edwin, Donor
Rogerson, Francis C., Jr., Trustee
Tingley, Janice C., Trustee
Trocki, Margaret C., Trustee

Fred M. Roddy Foundation, Inc.

c/o The R.I. Hospital Trust Nat'l Bank
Attn: Deirdre W. S. Martin, Asst. VP
1 Hospital Trust Plaza
Providence, RI 02903
(401) 278-8752
EIN: 056037528
Source Date: 12/92

Geographic Restrictions:
Primarily in RI and MA.

To Whom:
Medical research and organizations providing medical services to the community, higher education, hospitals.

Financial info:
Giving: $497,400 for 25 grants (high: $100,000; low: $3,000).

Application info:
Applications accepted. Application form required. No deadline. Board meets quarterly.

Directors, Officers, Trustees:
Buckless, Shawn P., Trustee
Kintzel, Lee, Trustee
McIntyre, John W., Trustee
Roddy, Fred M. (d), Donor

South Carolina

Fullerton Foundation, Inc.

c/o W. E. Cavell, Exec. Dir.
P.O. Box 2208
Gaffney, SC 29342-2208
(803) 489-6678
EIN: 570847444
Source Date: 11/93

Geographic Restrictions:
Primarily in NC and SC.

Restrictions:
No grants to individuals, endowments, deficit financing, or operating funds.

To Whom:
Hospitals, health, **medical research**, higher education.

For What:
Equipment, scholarship funds, special projects, matching funds, seed money.

Financial info:
Giving: $1,469,900 for 35 grants (high: $200,000; low: $1,000).

Application info:
Applications accepted. Submit brief proposal. Deadline is Apr. 1 and Aug. 1. Board meets twice yearly. Publishes application guidelines.

Directors, Officers, Trustees:
Beattie, Catherine Hamrick, Director
Cavell, Walter E., Officer
Fullerton, Alma H. (d), Donor
Hamrick, Charles F., Director
Hamrick, Charles F., II, Director
Hamrick, John M., Director, Officer
Hamrick, Lyman W., Director
Hamrick, Wylie L., Director, Officer
Valentine, Volina Cline, Director, Officer

Tennessee

Robert H. & Monica M. Cole Foundation

c/o Home Federal Bank, Trust Dept.
Attn: J. Robert Page, VP
P.O. Box 1230
Knoxville, TN 37901
EIN: 626137973
Source Date: 9/94

Geographic Restrictions:
Limited to eastern TN, including Knoxville, and southeast KY.

To Whom:
Medical research on Parkinson's disease, cultural programs, civic affairs.

For What:
Operating budgets, **research**.

Financial info:
Giving: $190,500 for 45 grants (high: $50,000; low: $1,000).

Application info:
Applications accepted. Submit letter. Deadline is Oct. 1. Board meets in Oct.

Recent Grants:

$15,000	Cole Neuroscience Foundation
$40,000	University of Tennessee

Directors, Officers, Trustees:
Cole, Monica M., Trustee
Davis, William W., Sr., Trustee
Home Federal Bank, Trustee

Joe C. Davis Foundation

c/o Bond Davis DeLoache, Trustee
908 Audubon Rd.
Nashville, TN 37204
(615) 297-1030
EIN: 626125481
Source Date: 9/94

Geographic Restrictions:
Primarily in the Nashville, TN, area.

To Whom:
Early childhood and elementary education, health, **medical research**, cancer, alcohol and drug abuse, and general charitable giving.

For What:
Matching funds, **research**, seed money, special projects, student loans.

Financial info:
Giving: $2,236,700 for 65 grants (high: $1,000,000; low: $250).

Application info:
Applications accepted. Submit letter (2 page limit). Deadline is July 1. Board meets in Sept. Publishes application guidelines.

Recent Grants:

$100,000	Dede Wallace Center, Nashville, TN. Annual campaign for mental health center.

Directors, Officers, Trustees:
Davis, Joe C. (d), Donor
DeLoache, Bond Davis, Trustee
DeLoache, William R., M.D., Trustee
DeLoache, William R., Jr., Trustee

Justin & Valere Potter Foundation

c/o NationsBank of TN, Trust Dept.
Attn: Cherie Scannel, Trust Off.
1 NationsBank Plaza
Nashville, TN 37219-1697
(615) 749-3336
EIN: 626033081
Source Date: 12/93

Geographic Restrictions:
Primarily in Nashville, TN.

Restrictions:
No grants to individuals.

To Whom:
Higher and medical education, cultural programs, social services, **medical research.**

For What:
Scholarship funds, operating budgets, special projects, **research.**

Financial info:
Giving: $1,490,000 for 30 grants (high: $300,000; low: $5,000).

Application info:
Applications accepted. Submit letter. No deadline.

Directors, Officers, Trustees:
Menefee, Albert L., Jr., Committee
NationsBank, Trustee,
Potter, Justin (d), Donor
Potter, Valere Blair (d), Donor
Wilson, Justin P., Committee

Thompson Charitable Foundation

c/o Monica Luke, Admin. Mgr.
4823 Old Kingston Pike
P.O. Box 10516
Knoxville, TN 37939-0516
(423) 588-0491
EIN: 581754763
Source Date: 6/94

Geographic Restrictions:
Limited to Knox, Anderson, Scott, and Blount counties, TN; Bell, Clay, Laurel and Leslie counties, KY; and Buchanan and Tazewell counties, VA.

Restrictions:
No grants for deficit financing or endowments.

To Whom:
Cancer research, higher education, music, hospitals, housing.

For What:
General purposes.

Financial info:
Giving: $2,968,900 for 35 grants (high: $1,000,000; low: $1,500).

Application info:
Applications accepted. Submit letter (2 page limit). Deadline is Mar. 31, June 30, Sept. 30, and Dec. 31. Board meets quarterly. Publishes application guidelines.

Directors, Officers, Trustees:
Ensor, Carl, Jr., Director
Thompson, B. R., Sr. (d), Donor
Thompson, B. Ray, Jr., Director
Thompson, Jesse J., Director
Wolfe, Merle D., Director, Officer
Young, Lindsay, Director

Texas

Abercrombie Foundation

c/o D. Merril Cummings, Gen. Mgr.
5005 Riverway, Suite 500
Houston, TX 77056
(713) 627-2500
EIN: 760229183
Source Date: 12/94

Geographic Restrictions:
Primarily in Houston, TX.

Restrictions:
No grants to individuals.

To Whom:
Higher, medical, and secondary education, preserve natural resources and beautify the environment in rural and urban areas, medical services, information, and assistance, **medical research to alleviate current health problems**, children in physical or emotional distress.

For What:
Building funds, operating budgets, **research**.

Financial info:
Giving: $596,200 for 15 grants (high: $150,000; low: $2,500).

Application info:
Applications accepted. Submit proposal. Deadline is May 15 and Nov. 15.

Directors, Officers, Trustees:
Abercrombie, Josephine E., Donor, Officer, Trustee
Bowen, Freda, Trustee
Cummings, D. Merril, Officer

Ellen Knox Beck-MKB Foundation

c/o NationsBank
Attn: Scott A. Wagoner, VP
P.O. Box 831515
Dallas, TX 75283

EIN: 756233396
Source Date: 5/94

Geographic Restrictions:
Limited to Coleman County, TX.

To Whom:
Education and **medical research to health problems of lungs, bronchial tubes, kidneys, blood, teeth, and cancer.**

For What:
Student aid.

Financial info:
Assets: $622,500.
Giving: $53,800 for grants to individuals.

Application info:
Applications accepted. Submit proposal. Deadline is Apr. 1.

Directors, Officers, Trustees:
Knox, Chris O., Trustee
Knox, E. Beck, Trustee
Knox, Jack L., Trustee
NationsBank, Trustee

Bosque Foundation

2911 Turtle Creek Blvd., Suite 900
Dallas, TX 75219
(972) 559-0088
EIN: 756380232
Source Date: 12/95

Geographic Restrictions:
Primarily in TX.

Restrictions:
No grants to individuals.

To Whom:
Higher education, **medical research**, social services, youth, literacy.

For What:
Capital campaigns, building funds, **research**.

Financial info:
Assets: $4,570,700.
Giving: $792,700 for 20 grants (high: $250,000; low: $1,000).

Application info:
Applications accepted. Submit letter (1 page limit). No deadline.

Directors, Officers, Trustees:
Beecherl, John T., Trustee
Beecherl, Julia T., Donor, Trustee
Beecherl, Louis A., Jr., Donor, Trustee
Beecherl, Louis A., III, Trustee
Beecherl, William C., Trustee
Davis, Julianna B., Trustee
Dillard, Mary B., Trustee

Cain Foundation

(Formerly The Effie & Wofford Cain Foundation)
c/o Harvey L. Walker, Exec. Dir.
4131 Spicewood Springs Rd., Suite A-1
Austin, TX 78759
(512) 346-7490
EIN: 756030774
Source Date: 10/94

Geographic Restrictions:
Limited to TX.

Restrictions:
No grants to individuals.

To Whom:
Higher, medical, and secondary education, community development, civic affairs, child development, arts, cultural programs, museums, fine arts, performing arts, religion, handicapped, disadvantaged, health, hospitals, **medical research**.

For What:
Building funds, endowment funds, seed money, operating budgets, **research**, scholarship funds, annual campaigns, continuing support, fellowships, internships, capital campaigns, professorships.

Financial info:
Giving: $2,586,000 for 90 grants (high: $300,000; low: $1,000).

Application info:
Applications accepted. Submit 1 page letter. Deadline is Aug. 31. Board meets in Oct.

Directors, Officers, Trustees:
Cain, Effie Marie, Donor
Cain, James B., Director, Officer
Cain, John C., Director
Cain, R. Wofford (d), Donor
Denius, F. Wofford, Director
Denius, Franklin W., Director, Officer
McGill, Chamaine D., Director
Walker, Harvey L., Officer

Cimarron Foundation

c/o Texas Commerce Bank
Attn: Terry Crenshaw, VP
P.O. Drawer 140
El Paso, TX 79980
(915) 546-6515
EIN: 742489868
Source Date: 12/95

Geographic Restrictions:
Primarily in El Paso, TX.

Restrictions:
No grants to individuals.

To Whom:
Medical research, social services, child development and welfare, disabled, disadvantaged, education, **cancer research**.

For What:
Research, general purposes, building funds, capital campaigns, operating budgets.

Financial info:
Assets: $3,668,100.
Giving: $185,900 for 60 grants (high: $25,000; low: $50).

Application info:
Applications accepted. Submit letter. No deadline.

Directors, Officers, Trustees:
Hunt, Gayle G., Officer, Trustee
Hunt, Jack L., Trustee
Hunt, Woody L., Donor, Officer, Trustee
Texas Commerce Bank, Trustee

Lizanell & Colbert Coldwell Foundation

c/o Texas Commerce Bank
Attn: Terry Crenshaw, Trust Off.
P.O. Drawer 140
El Paso, TX 79980-0001
(915) 546-6515
EIN: 742576133
Source Date: 3/96

Geographic Restrictions:
Limited to TX, with emphasis on El Paso.

Restrictions:
No grants to individuals.

To Whom:
Advancement of medical science and to aid in educational and research activities to include, but not limited to, research for the prevention and cure of heart disease, defects and cancer.

For What:
Equipment, **research.**

Financial info:
Assets: $4,026,000.
Giving: $163,500 for 10 grants (high: $30,000; low: $1,000).

Application info:
Applications accepted. Submit letter. Deadline is Apr. 30.

Directors, Officers, Trustees:
Coldwell, Lizanell (d), Donor
Collins, William E., Trustee
Nickey, Laurance, M.D., Trustee
Texas Commerce Bank-El Paso, Administrator

Denton A. Cooley Foundation

6624 Fannin, No. 2700
Houston, TX 77030
(713) 799-2700
EIN: 746053213
Source Date: 11/95

Geographic Restrictions:
Primarily in Houston, TX, area.

Restrictions:
No grants to individuals, scholarships, fellowships, publications, or conferences.

To Whom:
Medical education and **research**, health.

For What:
Operating budgets, building funds, endowment funds, special projects, **research.**

Financial info:
Assets: $1,435,600.
Giving: $154,400 for 90 grants (high: $20,000; low: $50).

Application info:
Applications accepted. Submit proposal. No deadline. Board meets quarterly.

Directors, Officers, Trustees:
Berardo, James, Officer
Cooley, Denton A., M.D., Donor, Officer, Trustee
Cooley, Louise T., Donor, Officer, Trustee
Gerrie, Katherine, Officer

John S. Dunn Research Foundation

c/o Lloyd J. Gregory, Jr., M.D.
Exec. VP & Medical Adv.
3355 W. Alabama, Suite 720
Houston, TX 77098-1718
(713) 626-0368
EIN: 741933660
Source Date: 12/95

Geographic Restrictions:
Limited to TX.

Restrictions:
No grants to individuals.

To Whom:
Health and medical-related organizations, hospitals, **cancer and other medical research.**

For What:
Endowment funds, matching funds.

Financial info:
Assets: $93,823,100.
Giving: $4,064,400 for 25 grants (high: $1,000,000; low: $5,000).

Application info:
Applications accepted. Submit letter of inquiry. No deadline. Board meets monthly. Publishes application guidelines.

Directors, Officers, Trustees:
- Dunn, John S., Sr. (d), Donor
- Dunn, John S., Jr., Officer, Trustee
- Dunn, Milby Dow, Officer, Trustee
- Gipe, Dagmar Dunn Pickens, Officer, Trustee
- Gregory, Lloyd J., Jr., M.D., Officer, Trustee
- Howard, Jerome L., Officer, Trustee
- Kennedy, Murry D., Officer, Trustee

R. W. Fair Foundation

c/o Wilton H. Fair, Pres.
P.O. Box 689
Tyler, TX 75710
(903) 592-3811
EIN: 756015270
Source Date: 12/95

Geographic Restrictions:
Primarily in the southwest area of U.S., with emphasis on TX.

Restrictions:
No grants to individuals or operating funds.

To Whom:
Protestant religion, secondary, legal, and higher education, civic affairs, hospitals, **cancer and heart disease research**, youth, social services, libraries, museums, cultural programs.

For What:
Seed money, building funds, equipment, general purposes, endowment funds, research, special projects, scholarship funds, matching funds.

Financial info:
Assets: $13,151,900.
Giving: $1,092,400 for 115 grants (high: $100,000; low: $50).

Application info:
Applications accepted. Application form required. Deadline is Mar. 1, June 1, Sept. 1, and Dec. 1. Board meets in Mar., June, Sept., and Dec.

Directors, Officers, Trustees:
- Bright, Sam, Director, Officer
- Fair, James W., Director, Officer
- Fair, Mattie Allen (d), Donor
- Fair, R. W. (d), Donor
- Fair, Wilton H., Director, Officer
- Goodwin, Nat F., Director, Officer
- Knight, Will A., Director
- Palmore, B. B., Director
- Ray, Richard L., Director

William Stamps Farish Fund

10000 Memorial Dr., Suite 920
Houston, TX 77024
EIN: 746043019
Source Date: 6/94

Geographic Restrictions:
Primarily in Houston, TX.

Restrictions:
No grants to individuals, annual campaigns, deficit financing, operating funds, exchange programs, or consulting services.

To Whom:
Higher and secondary education, hospitals, museums, family services, **medical research**, social services.

For What:
Research, general purposes.

Financial info:
Giving: $4,696,000 for 100 grants (high: $400,000; low: $2,500).

Application info:
Applications accepted. Submit proposal. Deadline is Mar. 1. Board meets annually.

Directors, Officers, Trustees:
- Chadwick, Laura Farish, Trustee
- Corbett, Cornelia G., Trustee
- Farish, Libbie Rice (d), Donor
- Farish, W. S., Officer, Trustee
- Gerry, Martha Farish, Officer, Trustee
- Rotan, Caroline P., Officer
- Ward, Terry W., Officer

Feldman Foundation

c/o Robert L. Feldman, Trustee
P. O. Box 1046
Dallas, TX 75221
(972) 689-4337
EIN: 756011578
Source Date: 2/97

Geographic Restrictions:
U.S. giving with emphasis on TX and NY based organizations benefitting the State of Israel.

Restrictions:
No grants to individuals.

To Whom:
Jewish welfare, cultural programs, **medical research**, hospitals, higher education, and social services which are usually under Jewish auspices.

For What:
Research, building funds, general purposes, scholarship funds, special projects.

Financial info:
Assets: $24,223,800 (from 1995 990PF).
Giving: $1,401,200 for 35 grants (high: $400,000; low: $1,000).

Application info:
Applications accepted. Submit proposal. No deadline. Board meets in spring and fall.

Recent Grants:

$50,000	New Israel Fund
$35,000	American Friends of Melitz
$2,500	American Associations, Ben-Gurion, University of the Negev
$5,000	The Southern Poverty Law Center
$3,000	American Friends of the Israel Philharmonic Orchestra
$4,000	American Friends of the Hebrew University

Directors, Officers, Trustees:
Commercial Metals Company, Donor
Feldman, Daniel E., Trustee
Feldman, Moses, Trustee
Feldman, Robert L., Trustee

FINA Foundation

(Formerly American Petrofina Foundation)
c/o Cullen M. Godfrey, Dir.
P.O. Box 2159
Dallas, TX 75221
(972) 750-2400
EIN: 237391423
Source Date: 12/95

Geographic Restrictions:
Primarily in TX and in areas where we have a significant concentration of employees. National [U.S.] giving for education, energy, environment, and public policy issues.

Restrictions:
No grants to individuals.

To Whom:
Health, hospitals, **cancer and other medical research**, community funds, civic affairs, fine and performing arts, museums, cultural programs, higher and other education, family and social services, environment.

For What:
Employee matching gifts, annual campaigns, continuing support.

Financial info:
Assets: $4,688,500.
Giving: $330,000 for 75 grants (high: $100,000; low: $50).

Application info:
Applications accepted. Submit proposal. No deadline. Application form required for employee matching gifts. Board meets annually. Periodically publishes annual report with application guidelines.

Directors, Officers, Trustees:
Cullers, Jeanne E., Director, Officer
FINA Oil & Chemical Company, Donor
Godfrey, Cullen M., Director, Officer
Haddock, Ronald W., Director, Officer
Lartigue, Henry J., Director, Officer

Ray C. Fish Foundation

2001 Kirby Dr., Suite 1005
Houston, TX 77019
(713) 522-0741
EIN: 746043047
Source Date: 1/97

Geographic Restrictions:
Primarily in TX, with emphasis on Houston.

Restrictions:
No grants to individuals.

To Whom:
Higher education, hospitals, **medical research**, youth, social services, cultural programs, performing arts.

For What:
General purposes, operating budgets.

Financial info:
Giving: $1,123,700 for 135 grants (high: $60,000; low: $500).

Application info:
Applications accepted. Submit letter to request guidelines. No deadline.

Directors, Officers, Trustees:
Cruikshank, Robert J., Officer
Daniel, Barbara F., Officer
Daniel, Christopher J., Officer
Daniel, James L., Jr., Officer
Fish, Mirtha G. (d), Donor
Fish, Raymond Clinton (d), Donor
Hooton, Paula, Officer

Gulf Coast Medical Foundation

c/o Dee McElroy, Exec. VP
P.O. Box 30
Wharton, TX 77488
(409) 532-0904
EIN: 741285242
Source Date: 12/95

Geographic Restrictions:
Primarily in Wharton, Matagorda, Jackson, Colorado, Fort Bend, and Brazoria counties, TX.

Restrictions:
No grants to individuals.

To Whom:
Medical education and research, mental health.

For What:
Capital campaigns, operating budgets, building funds, continuing support, matching funds, endowment funds, special projects.

Financial info:
Assets: $14,251,400.
Giving: $696,000 for 40 grants (high: $50,000; low: $400).

Application info:
Applications accepted. Application form required. No deadline.

Directors, Officers, Trustees:
Caraway, R. B., M.D., Trustee
Davis, Charles, Officer
Drees, Charles F., Trustee
Hill, Kent, Officer, Trustee
Huebner, Bert, Trustee
McElroy, Dee, Officer
Moore, Irving, Officer
Moore, Jack, Director, Officer

George & Mary Josephine Hamman Foundation

c/o A. Alan Fritsche, Admin.
910 Travis St., Suite 1990
Houston, TX 77002-5816
(713) 658-8345
EIN: 746061447
Source Date: 4/96

Geographic Restrictions:
Limited to TX, with emphasis on the Houston area.

Restrictions:
No grants for post-graduate education, individuals (except for scholarships to high schools seniors in the immediate Houston area), deficit financing, maintenance of buildings, or endowments.

To Whom:
Hospitals, **medical treatment and research**, religion, higher and other education, cultural programs, social services, and youth.

For What:
Annual campaigns, building funds, equipment, **research**, scholarship funds, continuing support, matching funds, student aid.

Financial info:
Giving: $560,900 for 125 grants (high: $100,000; low: $1,000) and $275,800 for 110 grants to individuals (high: $2,500; low: $1,000).

Application info:
Applications accepted. Submit letter. No deadline. Application form required for scholarships. Deadline is Feb. 28 for scholarships. Board meets monthly.

Directors, Officers, Trustees:
Hamman, George (d), Donor
Hamman, Henry R., Director, Officer
Hamman, Mary Josephine (d), Donor
Milby, Charles D., Director, Officer
Milby, Charles D., Jr., Director
Shepherd, Anne H., Director

Donald D. Hammill Foundation

c/o Catherine Cox, Secretary
8700 Shoal Creek Blvd.
Austin, TX 78758-6897
(512) 451-0784
EIN: 742499947
Source Date: 9/96

Geographic Restrictions:
Primarily in Austin and Travis County, TX for Personal Crises, Organizational, and Individual Improvements grants. Research Scholarships (open to individuals in all geographic areas), Research, and Symposia grants open to U.S. organizations.

To Whom:
Personal Crises Grants: organizations to satisfy some critical need in a patient's life: homeless, hunger, illness, food, home electricity, prosthetic devices or special equipment.

Organizational Grants.

Individual Improvement Grants: support the preparation of professionals to work with individuals who are disabled or disadvantaged.

Research Scholarships: assist doctoral students to complete their dissertation.

Research Grants: support study into the nature of conditions that cause disabilities and related problems and methods for their remediation or prevention.

Symposia Grants: must be related to individuals who are financially disadvantaged or disabled.

For What:
Conferences and seminars, emergency funds, individuals, **research**, seed money, special projects.

Financial info:
Assets: $3,074,000.
Giving: $73,000 for 20 grants (high: $10,000; low: $400) and $26,000 for 10 grants to individuals (high: $5,000; low: $1,000).

Application info:
Applications accepted. Submit proposal. Deadline is Dec. 15. Board meets in Feb.

Recent Grants:
Lynchburg College, VA. Scholarship assistance to graduate students in special education.
Ronald McDonald House, Austin, TX.
Family Eldercare, Austin, TX.
Salvation Army, Austin, TX.
AIDS Services, Austin, TX.
ARC of Texas, Austin, TX.
Texas Runaway Hotline, Austin, TX.
Capital Area Food Bank, Austin, TX.

Hillcrest Foundation

c/o NationsBank, Trust Div.
Attn: Daniel J. Kelly, VP
P.O. Box 830241
Dallas, TX 75283-0241
(972) 508-1965
EIN: 756007565
Source Date: 5/95

Geographic Restrictions:
Limited to TX, with emphasis on Dallas.

Restrictions:
No grants to individuals, endowments, operating funds, scholarships, or fellowships.

To Whom:
Higher, secondary, adult, vocational, business, and other education, nursing, cancer, health, hospitals, **medical research**, dentistry, social services, youth, child welfare, drug abuse, homeless, housing, hunger, seniors, handicapped, and rehabilitation.

For What:
Building funds, equipment, land acquisition, seed money, **research**, matching funds, continuing support, special projects, general purposes, renovation projects.

Financial info:
Assets: $135,621,500.
Giving: $7,746,100 for 140 grants (high: $200,000; low: $1,000).

Application info:
Applications accepted. Submit proposal. Deadline is Nov. 30, Mar. 31, and Aug. 31. Board meets in Jan., May, and Oct. Publishes application guidelines.

Recent Grants:

$42,000	Bishop Dunne High School, Dallas. Purchase bus for school use to replace old vehicle.
$25,000	Dallas CAN! Academy, Dallas. Learning program, education for low income single parents.
$20,000	El Centro College, Dallas County Community College District. Nurse technician and allied health education programs

$30,000	Grace Academy of Dallas. Purchase computers for labs and classrooms.
$25,000	Jarvis Christian College, Hawkins. Academic instruction, computer supplies, upward bound program.
$66,000	Schreiner College, Kerrville. Renovate campus buildings; upgrade energy management system.
$30,000	All Saints Health System, Fort Worth. Construction costs, new neonatal intensive care unit.
$15,000	Alzheimer's Association of Dallas. Caregiver program, assist families with Alzheimer's patients.
$50,000	Camp Sweeney, Southwestern Diabetic Foundation, Gainesville. Renovate and enlarge camping facilities.
$35,000	Gladney Fund for Gladney Center, Fort Worth. Repair and improve dormitories, residence for birth mothers.
$20.000	Lions Sight and Tissue Foundation, Dallas. Eye exams and eyeglasses, eye clinic for poor children. Dallas County.
$50,000	Texas Scottish Rite Hospital for Children, Dallas. Construct Child Development Center for learning disabilities
$20,000	Boys & Girls Clubs of Greater Dallas. Programs for gang prevention and early intervention.
$100,000	Child Care Group, Dallas. Expand services, Child Development Centers, East & South Dallas.
$40,500	Dallas Habitat for Humanity. Construct new homes for low income families, Pleasant Grove area.
$20,000	Dallas youth Services Corps. Support programs to provide training and skills, work for young people.
$25,000	Texas Baptist Home for Children. Waxahachie. Renovate gym, activity center, for abused and troubled youth.
$30,000	Union Gospel Mission, Dallas. Renovate facility for homeless men, vocational training center.

Directors, Officers, Trustees:

Byrd, D. Harold, Jr., Trustee
Caruth, Mabel P., Trustee
Caruth, W. W., Sr., Mrs. (d), Donor
NationsBank of Texas, Trustee
Shuford, Harry A., Trustee
Storey, Chas P., Trustee

Kimberly-Clark Foundation, Inc.

c/o Colleen B. Berman, VP
P.O. Box 619100
Dallas, TX 75261-9100
(972) 830-1200
EIN: 396044304
Source Date: 12/95

Geographic Restrictions:
Primarily in areas of company operations: Avent, Inc., Tucson, AZ; K-C Aviation, Inc., Neenah, WI; Coosa Pines, AL; Conway and Maumelle, AR; Fullerton, CA [southern]; New Milford and Shelton, CT; La Grange, GA; Lee and Westfield, MA; Munising, MI; Corinth, MS; Omaha, NE; Hendersonville and Lexington, NC; Spotswood and Montvale, NJ; Islip and Ancram, NY; Jenks, OK; Beech Island, SC; Loudon, TN; Paris and Dallas, TX; Ogden, UT; Appleton and Milwaukee, WI, Bahrain, Canada, China, Colombia, Costa Rica, El Salvador, France, Germany, Honduras, India, Indonesia, Korea, Malaysia, Mexico, Netherlands, Panama, Peru, Philippines, Saudi Arabia, Singapore, South Africa, Thailand, United Kingdon, Argentina, Australia, Venezuela.

Restrictions:
No grants for preschool, elementary, or secondary education, state-supported institutions, denominational religious organizations, sports or athletics, or individuals.

To Whom:
Social Welfare, Medicine, and Health: youth, family services, social services.

Hospitals and Health: **Cancer research**, hospitals.

Education: minorities for higher education, private education, science and mathematics education.

For What:
Annual campaigns, building funds, continuing support, equipment, land acquisition, operating budgets, seed money, scholarship funds, general purposes, capital campaigns, program-related investments.

Financial info:
Assets: $3,064,600.
Giving: $4,742,300 for 145 grants (high: $400,000; low: $100).

Application info:
Applications accepted. Submit proposal. No deadline. Publishes annual report.

Recent Grants:
- Family Gateway, Dallas, TX
- Rawhide Boys Ranch, New London, WI
- University of TX Cancer Center/M.D. Anderson Hospital and Tumor Institute, Houston, TX

Atlanta International School, Atlanta, GA
McLennan Community College Fdn., Waco, TX
North Texas Public Broadcasting, Dallas, TX
Irving Symphony, Irving, TX
National Safety Council, Chicago, IL

Directors, Officers, Trustees:
Barry, Tina S., Officer
Berman, Colleen B., Officer
Crook, Donald M., Officer
Everbach, O. George, Director
Gamron, W. Anthony, Director, Officer
Kimberly-Clark Corp., Donor
Sanders, Wayne R., Director

Robert J. Kleberg, Jr. & Helen C. Kleberg Foundation

700 N. St. Mary's St., Suite 1200
San Antonio, TX 78205
(210) 271-3691
EIN: 746044810
Source Date: 12/95

Geographic Restrictions:
Limited to U.S. Community organizations limited to TX.

Restrictions:
No grants to individuals, endowments, deficit financing, or ongoing operating expenses.

To Whom:
Medical research (66% of funding), veterinary science, wildlife, and animal sciences (18% of funding), community services (1% of funding), education (4% of funding), health services (6% of funding), arts and humanities (5% of funding).

For What:
Building funds, equipment, **research**, conferences and seminars, matching funds, renovation projects.

Financial info:
Assets: $152,905,000.
Giving: $2,627,900 for 30 grants (high: $200,000; low: $2,000).

Application info:
Applications accepted. Submit proposal. No deadline. Board meets in June and Dec. Publishes annual report with application guidelines.

Recent Grants:

$7,500	Alamo Area Boy Scouts, San Antonio, TX. Hispanic recruitment and barrio outreach project.
$6,000,435	Baylor College of Medicine, Houston, TX. Human genetics and neurobiology research.
$40,000	Kleberg County Sheriff's Department, Kingsville, TX. Drug abuse education and prevention in schools.
$5,000	San Antonio Performing Arts Association, San Antonio, TX. Youth concerts sponsorship.
$683,106	Spohn-Kleberg Memorial Hospital, Kingsville, TX. Ambulance and radiology equipment.
$6,327,369	University of Texas System Cancer Center, Houston, TX. Provide support for innovative cancer research.

Directors, Officers, Trustees:
Alexander, Caroline R., Director
Alexander, Helen C., Director, Officer
Alexander, Henrietta K., Director
Alexander, John D., Jr., Director, Officer
Carter, John B.,Jr., Director
Groves, Helen K., Director, Officer
Kleberg, Helen C. (d), Donor
Kleberg, Robert J., Jr. (d), Donor
Matz, Dorothy A., Director
Sherrill, H. Virgil, Director

Marcia & Otto Koehler Foundation

c/o NationsBank
Attn: Greg Muenster, VP
P.O. Box 121
San Antonio, TX 78291-0121
(210) 270-5313
EIN: 742131195
Source Date: 12/95

Geographic Restrictions:
Primarily in Bexar County, TX.

Restrictions:
No grants to individuals.

To Whom:
Medical research and medical care facilities, fine and performing arts, youth, education, recreation, health.

For What:
Operating budgets, renovation projects, building funds, **research.**

Financial info:
Assets: $8,015,000.
Giving: $333,400 for 40 grants (high: $25,000; low: $1,000).

Application info:
Applications accepted. Application form required. Deadline is June 1.

Recent Grants:

$25,000	San Antonio Children's Museum. Because of Mrs. Koehler's interest in the performing arts, a grant was awarded to build a theater for children in the downtown facility. It will provide children a hands-on opportunity to learn all facets of the theater from performances to behind the scenes activities. Outside groups will utilize the Koehler Theater to provide theatrical programs for the children.
$5,000	Southwest Craft Center. The Center offers a Saturday Morning Discovery Program which introduces children to various creative projects and venues. The grant helped provide opportunities like painting, weaving and sculpture for children to discover their talents and appreciate arts and crafts in a structured environment.
$10,000	Academy of Creative Education
$15,147	Alamo Public Television - KLRN
$1,000	Alcoholic Rehabilitation Center
$1,000	Any Baby Can, Inc.
$10,000	Arts! San Antonio
$2,500	Assistance League of San Antonio
$3,000	Advance, Inc.
$4,000	Bexar County Master Gardeners
$1,000	Carver Community Center
$25,000	Centro Alameda
$3,000	Children's Fine Arts Series
$1,000	Christian Senior Services
$2,500	Class Acts
$2,500	Communities In Schools
$5,000	Family Services Association
$17,250	Fellowship of Christian Athletes
$8,750	Funding Information Center
$2,500	German Heritage Park
$2,500	Guide Dog Foundation
$1,500	Hospice San Antonio
$25,000	Incarnate Word College
$2,000	Junior Achievement
$20,000	Las Casas Empire Theatre
$21,500	McNay Art Museum
$10,000	Mission Road Development Center
$6,000	Palmer Drug Abuse Program
$2,500	Presa Community Center
$1,000	San Antonio Art League
$5,500	San Antonio Botanical Center
$10,000	San Antonio Education Fund
$1,500	San Antonio Little Theatre
$2,500	San Antonio Opera Company
$5,000	St. Mary's University
$10,000	Texas Public Radio (KPAC)
$10,000	Welcome Lodge of San Antonio
$1,500	Winston School of San Antonio
$5,000	Youth Alternatives
$5,000	Youth Orchestra of San Antonio

Directors, Officers, Trustees:
Koehler, Marcia (d), Donor
NationsBank, Trustee

McGovern Fund for the Behavioral Sciences

(Formerly Texas Allergy Research Foundation)
6969 Brompton St.
Houston, TX 77025
(713) 661-1444
EIN: 742086867
Source Date: 11/94

Geographic Restrictions:
Primarily in the southwest U.S. and TX, with emphasis on Houston.

To Whom:
Education, training, **research, and treatment, relating to alcohol and drug addiction, family dynamics, and behavioral sciences.**

For What:
Research, building funds, conferences and seminars, continuing support, emergency funds, endowment funds, general purposes, lectureships, matching funds, professorships, publications, scholarship funds.

Financial info:
Giving: $3,067,900 for 275 grants (high: $2,000,000; low: $100).

Application info:
Applications accepted. Submit letter. No deadline. Grants primarily initiated by the foundation except for requests in the area of alcohol or drug abuse. Board meets in Nov.

Directors, Officers, Trustees:
Collette, Gay, Director, Officer
McGovern, John P., M.D., Director, Officer
McGovern, Kathrine G., Director, Officer
McGovern Foundation, John P., Donor

Robert E. & Evelyn McKee Foundation

c/o Louis B. McKee, Pres.
P.O. Box 220599
6006 N. Mesa St., Suite 906
El Paso, TX 79913-2599
(915) 581-4025
EIN: 746036675
Source Date: 12/95

Geographic Restrictions:
Primarily in Austin, Dallas, El Paso, Galveston, San Antonio, and Houston, TX, Henderson, CO, Albuquerque, Las Cruces, and Santa Fe, NM.

Restrictions:
No grants for religious organizations, except local Episcopal churches, individuals, endowments, or deficit financing.

To Whom:
Civic, Cultural and Religion (8% of funding), Education and Scholarships (10% of funding), Hospitals (5% of funding), **Medical and Medical Research (21% of funding),** Welfare, Rehabilitation, and Mental Health (39% of funding), United Way (11% of funding), and Youth (6% of funding).

For What:
Operating budgets, continuing support, annual campaigns, seed money, emergency funds, building funds, equipment, scholarship funds, **research.**

Financial info:
Assets: $6,664,200.
Giving: $301,000 for 95 grants (high: $50,000; low: $100).

Application info:
Applications accepted. Submit proposal. Deadline is Dec. 10. Board meets in Jan. with notification after Feb. 1. Publishes annual report with application guidelines.

Recent Grants:

$1,000	Adults & Youth United Development Association - El Paso, TX
$3,200	Alzheimer's Association - El Paso Chapter - TX
$2,000	American Foundation for the Blind - Dallas, TX
$2,000	American Red Cross - El Paso, TX
$1,000	Assistance League of El Paso, TX
$5,000	The Bridges School - El Paso, TX
$5,150	Candlelighters of the El Paso Area - TX
$3,000	Camp Courageous & Camp Bravo - El Paso, TX
$5,000	Child Crisis Center of El Paso, TX
$2,000	El Paso Alliance for the Mentally Ill - TX
$5,000	El Paso Rehabilitation Center - TX
$5,000	El Paso Shelter for Battered Women - TX
$1,000	Employment Opportunity Services - El Paso, TX
$1,500	The Family Place - Dallas, TX
$1,000	Help Resources Group - El Paso, TX
$1,500	Hope Cottage Adoption Center - Dallas, TX
$7,500	The Hospice Center, Inc. - Santa Fe, NM
$7,500	Hospice of El Paso - TX
$1,500	Juliette Fowler Homes - Dallas, TX
$3,000	La Mariposa Hospice at Providence - El Paso, TX
$3,000	Latch Key Centers Unlimited, Inc. - El Paso, TX
$3,000	Melrose Senior Center - NM
$3,000	National Center for Employment of the Disabled - El Paso, TX
$6,000	New Mexico Boys Ranch & Girls Ranch - Albuquerque
$1,000	Special Olympics Texas - El Paso
$2,000	Therapeutic Horsemanship of El Paso - TX
$7,500	Visiting Nurse Association - El Paso, TX
$7,500	VNS-Health Services, Inc. - Santa Fe, NM
$1,000	West Texas Council on Alcoholism and Drug Abuse - El Paso, TX
$1,000	Young Life of El Paso - TX
$1,000	Nell Gardner Pilot Home, Inc.
$1,000	The Rescue Mission
$2,000	Herald Post "Operation Noel"
$1,000	El Paso Times "Oldsters Fund"
$1,000	Ballet El Paso - TX
$1,500	Center for Christian Leadership - Dallas, TX
$3,000	Crime Stoppers of El Paso, Inc. - TX
$1,000	El Paso County Historical Society-Password Journal - TX
$1,000	El Paso Symphony Orchestra - TX
$2,000	El Paso Zoological Society - TX
$3,500	Humane Society of El Paso - TX

$1,000 International Dance Theatre - El Paso, TX
$2,000 KCOS 13 - El Paso, TX
$2,000 KRWG-TV - Las Cruces, NM
$1,500 St. Clementis Episcopal Church - El Paso, TX
$1,500 St. Francis on the Hill Episcopal Church - El Paso, TX
$1,500 St. Markis Day School - El Paso, TX
$3,000 Viva El Paso - TX
$1,000 New Mexico State University - Las Cruces, NM
$1,000 University of New Mexico - Albuquerque, NM

Vangee L. Moore Memorial Foundation

Rte. 4, Box 88
Richmond, TX 77469
(713) 342-7150
Source Date: 12/94

Geographic Restrictions:
Primarily in New York, NY.

Restrictions:
Physicians or Ph.D.'s must be members of the teaching or research faculties of publicly supported medical schools or research hospitals.

To Whom:
Medical research scientists with five or fewer years active experience.

For What:
Research, fellowships.

Financial info:
Giving: $63,900 for 5 grants (high: $50,000; low: $1,000).

Application info:
Applications accepted. Submit proposal from Sept. to Mar. Deadline is Mar. 31 with notification by May 15.

Directors, Officers, Trustees:
Graham, Sherrie, Trustee
Hirschfeld, Bruce, Trustee
HOR Energy Company, Donor
Imparato, Joseph A., Donor, Director, Trustee
McConnell, Robert W., Committee
Merrill, Joseph M., Committee
Ryan, Christa M., Donor
Ryan, John J., Donor

Morrison Trust

c/o Frost National Bank
Attn: William L. Clyborne, Jr., Admin.
P.O. Box 2950
San Antonio, TX 78296-2950
(210) 220-4449
EIN: 746013340
Source Date: 9/95

Geographic Restrictions:
Primarily in TX, CA, and NM.

Restrictions:
No grants to individuals.

To Whom:
Medical research, medical education, **development of new methods of treatment in the fields of nutrition, blood chemistry, and radionics and electricity.**

For What:
Research.

Financial info:
Assets: $2,529,900.
Giving: $101,700 for 5 grants (high: $50,000; low: $10,000).

Application info:
Applications accepted. Submit proposal. Deadline is July 1.

Directors, Officers, Trustees:
Frost National Bank, Trustee

Harry S. Moss Heart Trust

c/o NationsBank
Attn: Connie A. Rogers, VP
P.O. Box 830241
Dallas, TX 75283-0241
(972) 508-1936
EIN: 756147501
Source Date: 9/95

Geographic Restrictions:
Limited to TX, with emphasis on Dallas County.

To Whom:
Heart disease research.

For What:
Research, building funds, deficit financing, equipment.

Financial info:
Assets: $29,626,500.
Giving: $1,475,000 for 5 grants (high: $850,000; low: $25,000).

Application info:
Applications accepted. Submit proposal. No deadline.

Kathryn Murfee Endowment

2200 Post Oak Blvd., Suite 320
Houston, TX 77056
(713) 622-5855
EIN: 760007237
Source Date: 8/95

Geographic Restrictions:
Primarily in the Houston, TX, area.

Restrictions:
No grants to individuals.

To Whom:
Medical research, higher education, Protestant and other religion, arts.

For What:
General purposes, **research.**

Financial info:
Assets: $3,496,600.
Giving: $125,000 for 10 grants (high: $50,000; low: $2,500).

Application info:
Applications accepted. Application form required. No deadline.

Directors, Officers, Trustees:
Japhet, Dan R., Trustee
Nabb, June R., Trustee
Walzel, James V., Trustee

Florence Oeding Estate Trust

c/o Paul Huser
506 Simpson St.
P.O. Box 324
Schulenburg, TX 78956
(409) 743-3750
EIN: 746247707
Source Date: 12/95

Geographic Restrictions:
Primarily in TX.

To Whom:
Prevent, treat, or **research heart diseases, infantile paralysis, cancer, and tuberculosis,** health associations, **medical research.**

Financial info:
Assets: $238,400.
Giving: $6,500 for 5 grants (high: $5,000; low: $200).

Application info:
Applications accepted. Submit proposal. Deadline is Oct. 1.

Directors, Officers, Trustees:
Huser, Paul, Officer

Pearle Vision Foundation, Inc.

c/o Trina L. Parasiliti, Admin.
P.O. Box 227175
Dallas, TX 75222
(972) 277-5993
EIN: 752173714
Source Date: 2/97

Geographic Restrictions:
Limited to the U.S.

To Whom:
Vision-oriented giving, examinations and eye surgery for needy individuals, **ophthalmology research**, education programs, museums, parks and media programs that improve the quality of life for the visually impaired.

For What:
Special projects.

Financial info:
Assets: $526,200 (from 1995 990PF).
Giving: $310,000 for 45 grants (high: $25,000; low: $1,500) and $55,000 for 25 grants to individuals (high: $5,000; low: $200).

Application info:
Applications accepted. Application form required. Deadline is Dec. 15 and June 15. Board meets in Jan. and July. Publishes application guidelines.

Recent Grants:

$4,000	Broward Community Foundation, Hollywood, FL. Fund needy students with eye exams and eyeglasses.
$20,000	New Eyes for the Needy, Short Hills, NJ. Provide needy individuals nationwide with eyeglasses.
$15,655	Retina Foundation of the Southwest, Dallas, TX. Purchase equipment for a vision-related research project.
$4,000	VISION Foundation, Watertown, MA. Provide low vision aids and services to the elderly.
$5,000	University of Rochester, Rochester, NY. Support a vision-related research project.

Directors, Officers, Trustees:
Benning, James D., O.D., Director
Davis, Alan D., M.D., Director
McAninch, Barbara, Director, Officer
Parasiliti, Trina, Officer
Pearle, Inc., Donor
Pearle, Stanley C., O.D., Director
Shaw, Ian, Officer
Smith, Jeff, O.D., Director, Officer

Sid W. Richardson Foundation

c/o Valleau Wilkie, Jr., Exec. Dir.
309 Main St.
Fort Worth, TX 76102
(817) 336-0494
EIN: 756015828
Source Date: 12/96

Geographic Restrictions:
Limited to TX, with emphasis on Fort Worth.

Restrictions:
No grants for religious organizations, individuals, scholarships or fellowships.

To Whom:
Education: secondary economic education, ESL, literacy, minorities, museums, religion broadcasting, parental involvement, libraries, geography education, educational broadcasting, at-risk students, public policy research, higher education, disabled.

Human Service: seniors, community funds, career development and job placement, youth, shelter, day care, hunger, urban development, juvenile offenders, zoos, historical preservation, wildlife, low-income families, family planning, environment, blind, housing.

Health: **mdical research**, blind, hospitals.

Arts: theater, museums, ballet, opera, symphony, multicultural arts.

For What:
Operating budgets, seed money, building funds, equipment, land acquisition, endowment funds, **research,** publications, conferences and seminars, matching funds, special projects, renovation projects, continuing support, general purposes.

Financial info:
Assets: $240,941,300 (from 1995 annual report).
Giving: $8,264,100 for 80 grants (high: $500,000; low: $1,000).

Application info:
Applications accepted. Application form required. Deadline is Mar. 1, June 1, and Sept. 1. Board meets in the spring, summer and fall. Publishes annual report with application guidelines.

Recent Grants:

$7,500	Fort Worth Clean City, Inc., Fort Worth, TX. This grant provided support for the Youth Education Program in the Fort Worth ISD during 1995-96.

$402,500 Fort Worth Country Day School, Fort Worth, TX. Two grants supported faculty participation in workshops and conferences within the state of Texas and the Faculty Bonus Trust.

$2,200 Fort Worth Independent School District, Fort Worth, TX. These funds supported field trips for students et William James Middle School.

$10,000 Fort Worth Metropolitan Industrial Development, Inc., Fort Worth, TX. This grant provided support for educational programs and conventions.

$25,000 Fort Worth Museum of Science and History, Fort Worth, TX. These funds provided support for the museum's education program for 1995-96.

$250,000 Fort Worth Public Library, Fort Worth, TX. This grant provided assistance in the renovation of the Central Public Library.

$40,000 Game Conservation International, San Antonio, TX. This grant provided support for the Junior Wildlife Art program.

$25,000 The Billy Graham Evangelistic Association, Minneapolis, MN. These funds will support the radio ministry within the state of Texas during 1996.

$75,000 Jarvis Christian College, Hawkins, TX. This grant provided continued support for the Institute for Innovative Pedagogy.

$70,000 Lutheran Welfare Society of Texas, Austin, TX. This grant provided support for a model program developed by the Allied Communities of Tarrant in association with the Lutheran Welfare Society for increasing parental involvement and student attendance and achievement in the Fort Worth ISD. These funds provided support for further expansion, consulting services, and training for the project.

$4,000 National Hispanic Institute, Maxwell, TX. Funds provided support for the Collegiate Leadership Network program for college students which was held at UT El Paso.

$120,000 Adolescent Pregnancy Prevention, Inc., Fort Worth, TX. These funds provided support for the development and implementation of a pri mary pregnancy prevention project which is modeled after Dr. Michael Carrera's program in Harlem.

$25,000 Alliance for Children, Inc., Arlington, TX. Alliance for Children unites the efforts of public agencies and the community to lessen the emotional trauma to child abuse victims. This grant provided general support for the program.

$5,000 American National Red Cross, Tarrant County Chapter, Fort Worth, TX. These funds assisted in meeting the expenses involved in the violent spring storms in North Texas.

$5,000 Aransas County Council On Aging, Rockport, TX. This grant provided general support for the program.

$4,000 Aransas County United Fund, Inc., Rockport, TX. Funds provided support for the 1996 Campaign.

$2,500 Blue Raider Athletic Association, Fort Worth, TX. This grant provided support for the improvement of athlete fields.

$25,000 Border, City Of, Border, TX. Funds provided support for the purchase of a fire truck designed to battle fires on rough terrain.

$35,000 Boy Scouts of America, Longhorn Council, Fort Worth, TX. This grant provided support for Urban Emphasis, an outreach program for children in disadvantaged neighborhoods.

$5,000 Citizens Crime Commission of Tarrant County, Fort Worth, TX. This grant assisted with the AmeriCorps Youth Mime Commission program whose mission is to empower youth to develop leadership and interpersonal skills, and to provide training in conflict resolution and violence prevention.

$1,000 Airlifeline of Texas' Inc., Houston, TX. AirLifeLine is a volunteer organization which provides emergency air transportation of blood, organs, and medical supplies. This grant provided general support for the program

$250,000 All Saints Health Foundation, Fort Worth, TX. This grant provided assistance for the renovation and expansion of All Saints' Heart Center, Obstetrics & Gynecological Center, Carter Rehabilitation and Fitness Center, and the Radiology Unit.

$40,000 American Heart Association, Fort Worth, TX. These funds provided support for the 1995-96 education programs.

$75,000 Baylor College of Medicine, Houston, TX. This grant will support the Cullen Eye Institute research program entitled, "Studies in Ocular Bacterial and Fungal Infections," during 1996-97.

$557,000 Fort Worth Education and Research Foundation for Pain Management, Fort Worth, TX. Two grants provided general support for the multidisciplinary pain program and support for a pain management research project to be carried on jointly by the Center for Pain Management and the University of Texas Southwestern Medical School.

$75,000 Harlingen Community Emergency Care Foundation, Inc., Harlingen, TX. This grant provided support for Valley Air Care, an air ambulance service in the Rio Grande Valley.

$5,000 Living Bank International, Houston, TX. Funds provided support for the education program of the Living Bank, an organ and tissue donor registry.

$12,000 Texas Society To Prevent Blindness, Fort Worth, TX. These funds supported the Glaucoma Alert Program.

$25,000 Conference of Southwest Foundations, Inc., Corpus Christi, TX. This grant provided assistance with relocation expenses.

$750,000 Downtown Fort Worth Initiatives, Inc., Fort Worth, TX. These funds will assist in the construction of housing in a blighted area near downtown Fort Worth.

$30,000 Executive Service Corps of Fort Worth, Inc., Fort Worth, TX. ESC is an organization of retired executives who provide low-cost management consulting services to nonprofit organizations. This grant provided continued support for its programs.

$100,000 First Texas Council of Camp Fire, Inc., Fort Worth, TX. This grant provided continued support for the Family Child Care Center during 1996.

$20,000 Fort Worth Challenge, Inc., Fort Worth, TX. Challenge, Inc. is an advocacy organization formed to help reduce substance abuse and its harmful effects in Tarrant County by developing and implementing comprehensive, coordinated plans with existing agencies. This grant provided general support for the program.

$10,000 Fort Worth Teen Court, Inc., Fort Worth, TX. Teen Court brings juvenile offenders to this special court to be judged by their peers in cases of minor offense. Funds provided general support for the program.

$200,000 Friends of Children, Inc., Fort Worth, TX. This grant provided support for the construction of a new Ronald McDonald House.

$40,000 Habitat for Humanity International, Inc., Fort Worth, TX. These funds provided assistance for the purchase of a facility which will serve as the base of operations for the Fort Worth Area Habitat for Humanity.

$5,000 Taping for the Blind, Houston, TX. Taping for the Blind furnishes reading and radio services for the blind and physically handicapped. This grant provided general support for the program.

$10,000 Tarrant Council On Alcoholism and Drug Abuse, Fort Worth, TX. This grant provided general support for the program.

$35,000 Tarrant County Association for the Blind, Fort Worth, TX. Funds provided support for general operating expenses

$50,000 Texas, State Of, Austin, TX. This grant provided assistance to the Capitol Fund State Preservation Board for the Capitol Historical Furnishings Project.

$25,000 Trinity Cathedral Church, Fort Worth, TX. These funds assisted in the establishment of the Trinity Youth Center in the Woodhaven area of Fort Worth.

$2,000 Union Gospel Mission, Fort Worth, TX. This grant provided general support for the program.

$25,000 United Community Centers, Inc., Fort Worth, TX. These funds provided support for ACT III, a program for at-risk young people in the Diamond Hill and Southeast areas of Fort Worth.

$60,000 United Way of Metropolitan Tarrant County, Fort Worth, TX. This grant provided support for the 1995 United Way campaign, specifically the Community Initiatives Fund.

$75,000 What About Remembering Me, Inc., Fort Worth, TX. This grant provided general support for the WARM

	Place, a grief support center for children.
$1,000	Wildlife Conservation Fund of America, Columbus, OH. These funds provided general support for the conservation program in Texas.
$5,000	Woman's Club of Fort Worth, Fort Worth, TX. This grant provided general support for the Woman's Club Historical Preservation Trust.
$5,000	Northside Inter Church Agency, Fort Worth, TX. NICA provides assistance to low-income families in the Northside area. These funds provided support for the* emergency financial relief and counseling services.
$7,500	Planned Parenthood of North Texas, Inc., Fort Worth, TX. This grant provided assistance in upgrading the security system.
$10,000	SEARCH Association, Inc., Fort Worth, TX. Two grants provided general support for the community program and the emergency assistance program for young people.

Directors, Officers, Trustees:

Bass, Lee M., Director, Officer
Bass, Nancy Lee, Director, Officer
Bass, Perry R., Donor, Director, Officer
Bass, Sid R., Director, Officer
Chappell, M. E, Director, Officer
Richardson, Sid W. (d), Donor
Rosacker, Jo Helen, Officer
Wilkie, Valleau, Jr., Officer

San Antonio Area Foundation

c/o William M. Kromer, Grant Dir.
P.O. Box 120366
110 Broadway, Suite 230
San Antonio, TX 78212-9566
(210) 225-2243
Internet: http://www.qvision.com/SAF/
EIN: 746065414
Source Date: 12/96

Geographic Restrictions:
Limited to TX, with emphasis on the Bexar County and San Antonio area.

Restrictions:
No grants for political or religious programs, individuals, endowments, annual funds, deficit financing, ongoing research, publications, conferences and seminars, building funds, or salaries.

To Whom:
Arts/Culture, Community/Social Services, Education, Environment, Animal Services, and Health Care/**Medical research**.

For What:
Operating budgets, continuing support, annual campaigns, seed money, emergency funds, equipment, land acquisition, matching funds, scholarship funds, special projects, **research**, student aid, general purposes, lectureships, professorships, renovation projects.

Financial info:
Giving: $3,120,000 for 660 grants (high: $250,000; low: $50).

Application info:
Applications accepted. Submit letter of intent with background information form by Jan. 15. Full proposal due Apr. 1. Board meets in May. Publishes annual report and application guidelines.

Recent Grants:

$10,500	Witte Museum. "What About AIDS?" exhibit.
$6,000	Delta San Antonio. Animal Ambassadors program for nursing home residents.
$3,000	Leukemia Society of America. Minority Bone Marrow Donor Drive.
$10,000	San Antonio Museum of Art. Summer Internship Program for local minority students.
$5,000	St. Ann School. Expansion and updating of computer lab and software.
$10,000	Jewish Community Center. Expansion of Friendship and Cultural Exchange program for elementary school students of different backgrounds.
$22,000	University of Texas Health Science Center, San Antonio, TX. Establishment of Retina Reading Center for research on diabetes among Mexican-Americans.
$15,000	Warm Springs Rehabilitation Foundation. Rehabilitation program for victims of violence.

SBC Foundation

(Formerly Southwestern Bell Foundation)
175 E. Houston, Suite 200
San Antonio, TX 78205
(210) 351-2215
EIN: 431353948
Source Date: 12/96

Geographic Restrictions:
Primarily in KS, MO, TX, AR, and OK.

Restrictions:
No grants for political activities, religious organizations, fraternal veterans' or labor groups, individuals, operating funds for hospitals, capital funds, operating funds for United Way-supported organizations, advertising, local school systems or school-system foundations, disease specific organizations, or ticket/dinner purchases.

To Whom:
Education: strengthen the teaching profession, restructure schools, redesign teacher education and recognize outstanding teachers, address adult literacy, higher education, build both enrollment and quality of education, educational associations aimed at development of quality economic education, retrain the economically displaced, seniors and disadvantaged.

Health and Social Services: United Way, **applied research**, education and innovative programs in preventive health care, particularly as applied to youth and seniors, assist disabled, blind, deaf or speech impaired, children's needs, particularly those which deal with issues related to working parents.

Cultural and Arts Outreach: performing arts in major metropolitan areas, particularly those with outreach potential and which are enjoyed by a broad spectrum of the public, performing arts and cultural programs that promise to enlarge public interest and support for cultural presentation, performing arts programs that provide professional training at various levels.

Community Economic Development: economic development, broaden opportunities for growth and enhance the economic stability of communities.

For What:
Conferences and seminars, employee matching gifts, lectureships, matching funds, **research**, seed money, special projects, technical assistance.

Financial info:
Assets: $105,965,400 (from 1995 990PF).
Giving: $21,300,000 for 2,360 grants (high: $500,000; low: $100) and $1,028,100 for 6,375 employee matching gifts.

Application info:
Applications accepted. Submit letter. No deadline. Publishes annual report and application guidelines.

Recent Grants:

$20,000	American Association of Colleges for Teacher Education, Washington, DC
$40,500	Oklahoma State University Fdn., Stillwater, OK
$12,000	YWCA, Topeka, KS
$10,000	American Bar Association, Chicago, IL
$10,000	Alexander Graham Bell Association for the Deaf, Inc., Washington, DC
$13,500	Arkansas Opera Theatre, Little, AR
$10,000	Valley Zoological Endowment, Brownsville, TX

Directors, Officers, Trustees:
Adams, James R., Director
Alexander, Larry J., Officer
Blatherwick, Gerald D., Officer
Caldwell, Royce S., Director
DeRiemer, Charles O., Director
Ellis, James D., Director
Foster, Charles E., Director
Pope, Robert G., Director
Rainbolt, Harold E., Officer
Southwestern Bell Corp., Donor
Wohlert, Roger W., Officer

Bob Smith, M.D. Foundation

(Formerly Bordeaux Foundation)
c/o Jean K. Smith, Grants Admin.
3811 Turtle Creek Center, Suite 2150
Dallas, TX 75219
(972) 521-3461
EIN: 510137245
Source Date: 9/94

Geographic Restrictions:
Primarily in Dallas, TX.

Restrictions:
No grants to individuals.

To Whom:
Higher, medical, and other education, museums, health associations, **medical research.**

For What:
General purposes, building funds, operating budgets, scholarship funds.

Financial info:
Giving: $1,251,600 for 40 grants (high: $300,000; low: $300).

Application info:
Applications accepted. Submit letter. No deadline.

Directors, Officers, Trustees:
Kelley, Marty S., Director
Nicoud, George A., Jr., Director, Officer
Smith, C. R., M.D., Director, Officer
Smith, Jean K., Director, Officer
Smith, Patty A., Director, Officer
Smith, Scott R., Director
Wallace, Sally S., Director
Welfelt, Suzanne S., Director

Southwest Digestive Diseases Foundation

c/o Clara L. Campbell, Pres.
5242 Park Ln.
Dallas, TX 75220
EIN: 237086925
Source Date: 12/95

Geographic Restrictions:
Primarily in Dallas, TX.

To Whom:
Research in the field of gastroenterology, research directed toward finding cures for peptic ulcers, pancreatitis, liver disease, and other gastric related disorders.

Financial info:
Assets: $678,900.
Giving: $1,100 for 4 grants.

Application info:
Applications accepted. Submit letter. No deadline.

Recent Grants:

$550	The Brady Center, Dallas, TX.
$350	The Salvation Army, Dallas, TX.
$100	Discalced Carmelite Nuns, Dallas, TX.
$100	Texas Scottish Rite Hospital, Dallas, TX.

Directors, Officers, Trustees:
Campbell, Claire P., Donor, Officer
Campbell, Clara L., Officer
Campbell, Hugh P., Jr., Officer

W. B. & Ellen Gordon Stuart Trust

c/o Bank One
Attn: Rick Piersall, Trust Div.
P.O. Box 2050
Fort Worth, TX 76113
(817) 884-4442
EIN: 756014224
Source Date: 6/95

Geographic Restrictions:
Primarily in TX.

To Whom:
Treatment or research of heart disease, cancer, and infant paralysis.

For What:
Equipment, general purposes, operating budgets.

Financial info:
Assets: $3,180,400.
Giving: $157,500 for 20 grants (high: $15,000; low: $50).

Application info:
Applications accepted. Submit proposal. Deadline is Sept. 30.

Directors, Officers, Trustees:
Bank One, Texas, Trustee

Roy & Christine Sturgis Charitable & Educational Trust

c/o NationsBank
Attn: Daniel J. Kelly, VP
P.O. Box 830241
Dallas, TX 75283-0241
EIN: 756331832
Source Date: 12/95

Geographic Restrictions:
Primarily in AR (67%) and TX (33%).

Restrictions:
No grants to political organizations, individuals, scholarships, or seminars.

To Whom:
Education, health, arts, libraries, **medical research**, hospitals, science and technology, social services, disadvantaged.

For What:
Building funds, capital campaigns, endowment funds, general purposes, matching funds, operating budgets, **research**, special projects.

Financial info:
Assets: $52,169,000.
Giving: $2,602,000 for 45 grants (high: $400,000; low: $1,500).

Application info:
Applications accepted. Application form required (2 copies). Deadline is Dec. 31. Board meets in Apr. with notification by May 15. Publishes application guidelines.

Recent Grants:

$100,000	Arkansas State University.Jonesboro. The grant is initial payment on a $1,000,000 commitment for an endowment for the Sturgis Scholars. The program makes awards to top students from Arkansas high schools for scholarships based on high academic achievement, citizenship and financial need.
$30,000	Daughters of Charity Services, Dumas. This primary care clinic provides health care services for low-income women and children in the southeastern area of the state. The grant was used to purchase medical equipment to improve medical services, health education and medical care.
$50,000	Arkansas Easter Seal Society, Little Rock
$20,000	Arkansas Handicapped Athletic Assoc., Hot Springs
$60,000	Boys and Girls Clubs, Benton
$60,000	Boys and Girls Clubs, El Dorado
$60,000	Boys Club, Little Rock
$10,000	The Cathedral School, Little Rock
$100,000	Central High School, Little Rock ISD
$35,000	Foodbank of North Central Arkansas, Norfork
$20,000	Humane Society of Pulaski County, Little Rock
$20,000	Lions World Services for the Blind, Little Rock
$50,000	Lyon College, Batesville
$25,000	Mt. St. Mary Academy, Little Rock
$20,000	Our Lady of Holy Souls School, Little Rock
$10,000	Perryville School District, Perryville
$50,000	Positive Attitude Reaches Kids, Little Rock
$25,000	Salvation Army, Mountain Home
$20,000	Southeast Arkansas Regional Library, Lake Village
$50,000	Southern Arkansas University, Magnolia
$575,000	University of Arkansas, Fayetteville
$20,000	Urban Family Outreach, Little Rock
$200,000	Wildwood Park for the Performing Arts, Little Rock
$50,000	Youth Home, Little Rock
$75,000	YWCA - Bess Chisum Stephens, Little Rock
$20,000	Maple Avenue Economic Development Corp. This agency concentrates on solving problems through economic resources in central Dallas. The funds were used to construct an on-site child care center for parents who participate in programs of family literacy instruction, parenting, child development and employment training.
$60,000	Zale Lipshy University Hospital. Grant funds will purchase new Accuray Neurotron equipment for accurate and safe treatment of cancer and brain tumors. It will advance medical treatment in oncology and neurosurgery at this hospital and the University of Texas Southwestern Medical Center.
$13,000	Alameda Heights Community Outreach Center
$20,000	All Saints Health System
$5,000	Boy Scouts of America - Longhorn Council
$20,000	CONTACT 214
$30,000	Dallas Museum of Art
$25,000	Dallas Symphony
$30,000	Family Gateway
$20,000	Girls Incorporated of Metropolitan Dallas
$50,000	Greenhill School
$25,000	Habitat for Humanity
$40,000	M. D. Anderson Cancer Center
$15,000	Merriman Park Elementary School
$60,000	Performing Arts Fort Worth
$50,000	Southern Methodist University
$50,000	Texas Scottish Rite Hospital
$50,000	University of Texas Southwestern Medical School
$30,000	Ursuline Academy of Dallas
$30,000	Vogel Alcove Child Care Center
$200,000	YMCA of Metropolitan Dallas
$24,000	Young Audiences of Greater Dallas

Directors, Officers, Trustees:
NationsBank, Trustee
Sturgis, Christine (d), Donor

T. L. L. Temple Foundation

c/o Tami Musick, Asst. Grants Admin.
109 Temple Blvd.
Lufkin, TX 75901
(409) 639-5197
EIN: 756037406
Source Date: 11/96

Geographic Restrictions:
Primarily in deep East TX in 23 counties: Anderson, Angelina, Bowie, Cass, Cherokee, Hardin, Harris, Houston, Jasper, Jefferson, Liberty, Nacogdoches, Newton, Orange, Panola, Polk, Rusk, Sabine, San Augustine, San Jacinto, Shelby, Trinity, and Tyler.

Restrictions:
No grants for private foundations, religious organizations for religious purposes, individuals, continuing support, annual campaigns, deficit financing, or endowments.

To Whom:
Education: enhance the vitality and professional commitment of faculty, improve facilities and equipment, advance library development, stimulate curricular reform, financial aid through scholarships.

Health: biomedical health care organizations, social, educational, and environmental entities which contribute to the health of individuals, **construction of facilities and purchase of equipment to advance treatment efforts and research**, stimulate expansion of health care delivery, encourage preventive care, develop public understanding of factors affecting community and individual health.

Community and Social Services: rehabilitation, community development, crime prevention, disabled, seniors, mental health, drug and alcohol abuse, disadvantaged, minorities.

Cultural Arts and Humanities: build and preserve the collections of museums, enhance the volumes and manuscripts of libraries, document, preserve, and interpret cultural heritages.

For What:
Emergency funds, building funds, equipment, matching funds, scholarship funds, special projects, **research**, general purposes.

Financial info:
Assets: $259,581,600 (from 1995 990PF).
Giving: $12,696,500 for 110 grants (high: $1,000,000; low: $500).

Application info:
Applications accepted. Application form required. No deadline. Board meets monthly.

Directors, Officers, Trustees:
Burke, Ward R., Trustee
Leach, Phillip M., Officer, Trustee
Munz, Georgie T. (d), Donor
Temple, Arthur, Officer, Trustee
Temple, Arthur, III, Trustee
Temple, Katherine S. (d, Donor
Webber, W. Temple, Jr., Trustee
Zeagler, M. F., Director, Trustee

Texas Commerce Bank Foundation of Texas Commerce Bank-Houston, Inc.

c/o Texas Commerce Bank-Houston
Attn: Susan Robertson, Comm. Rel.
P.O. Box 2558
Houston, TX 77252-8050
(713) 236-4004
EIN: 746036696
Source Date: 12/95

Geographic Restrictions:
Limited to the Houston, TX, area.

Restrictions:
No grants to individuals.

To Whom:
Community funds and development, cultural programs, libraries, museums, performing arts, higher, secondary, and elementary education, **health, cancer, medical research**, social services, minorities, child welfare, homeless, civic affairs, urban affairs, race relations, housing, conservation, drug abuse.

For What:
Annual campaigns, building funds, continuing support, employee matching gifts, **research**, capital campaigns, in-kind gifts, endowment funds, renovation projects, equipment.

Financial info:
Assets: $281,000.
Giving: $1,283,900 for 270 grants.

Application info:
Applications accepted. Submit letter. Deadline is the 15th of each month. Board meets monthly.

Vale-Asche Foundation

2001 Kirby Dr., Suite 1010
Houston, TX 77019
(713) 520-7334
EIN: 516015320
Source Date: 11/95

Geographic Restrictions:
Primarily in Houston, TX.

Restrictions:
No grants to individuals, endowments, or on-going operating expenses.

To Whom:
Medical research, health, child welfare, seniors, disabled, AIDS, drug abuse, minorities, hunger, rehabilitation, secondary education, cultural programs, homeless.

For What:
Equipment, **research**, special projects.

Financial info:
Assets: $7,865,900.
Giving: $320,500 for 20 grants (high: $40,000; low: $1,500).

Application info:
Applications accepted. Submit proposal. Deadline is Aug. 15. Board meets annually. Publishes application guidelines.

Directors, Officers, Trustees:
Ackerman, Asche, Trustee
Asche, Fred B. (d), Donor
Blummer, William E., Officer, Trustee
Murray, Bettyann Asche, Officer, Trustee
Russell, Vale Asche, Mrs., Officer, Trustee
Vale, Ruby (d), Donor

E. Paul & Helen Buck Waggoner Foundation, Inc.

c/o Gene W. Willingham, Dir.
P.O. Box 2130
Vernon, TX 76385-2130
(817) 552-2521
EIN: 751243683
Source Date: 4/96

Geographic Restrictions:
Primarily in TX.

To Whom:
Higher and secondary education, agricultural research, **medical research**, youth.

For What:
Building funds, scholarship funds, **research**.

Financial info:
Giving: $307,800 for 10 grants (high: $250,000; low: $1,000).

Application info:
Applications accepted. Submit proposal. No deadline.

Directors, Officers, Trustees:
Biggs, Electra Waggoner, Officer
Waggoner, E. Paul (d), Donor
Waggoner, Helen Buck (d), Donor
Willingham, Gene W., Officer
Willingham, Helen Biggs, Officer
Winston, Charles F., Director
Winston, Electra Biggs, Director

Neva & Wesley West Foundation

P.O. Box 7
Houston, TX 77001
(713) 520-0400
EIN: 746039393
Source Date: 4/97

Geographic Restrictions:
Limited to TX.

Restrictions:
No grants to individuals.

To Whom:
Higher and other education, literacy, museums, fine arts, music, dance, homeless, hospitals, **medical research**, health.

For What:
General purposes, building funds, equipment, research, operating budgets.

Financial info:
Assets: $18,990,100.
Giving: $1,215,000 for 25 grants (high: $250,000; low: $10,000).

Application info:
Applications accepted. Submit letter or proposal. Deadline is Dec. 1. Board meets in Dec. Publishes annual report which is available after May 15.

Recent Grants:

$250,000	Houston Grand Opera
$200,000	Texas A & M University, The Institute of Biosciences and Technology
$10,000	Texas Public Policy Foundation
$75,000	Child Development Center of the Houston-Galveston Psychoanalytic Institute
$75,000	Alley Theatre
$50,000	Baylor College of Medicine

Directors, Officers, Trustees:
Stedman, Betty Ann West, Trustee
Stedman, Stuart West, Trustee
West, Neva Watkins, Donor, Trustee

Wills Foundation

c/o Alice E. Pratt, Pres.
P.O. Box 27534
Houston, TX 77227-7534
(713) 965-9043
EIN: 746078200
Source Date: 7/95

Geographic Restrictions:
U.S. giving.

To Whom:
Research relevant to Huntington's Disease.

For What:
Research, fellowships.

Financial info:
Giving: $339,200 for grants.

Application info:
Applications accepted. Submit letter, proposal, and curriculum vitae (original and 5 copies). Deadline is Sept. 1 and Mar. 1. Board meets in Jan. and July. Publishes application guidelines.

Directors, Officers, Trustees:
Dillingham, Charles, Director, Officer
Heldenfels, John O., Director
Murray, Michael J., M.D., Director
Pratt, Alice Evans, Director, Officer
Pratt, Fletcher S. (d), Donor
Pratt, Fletcher S., Mrs., Donor
Pratt, Peter E., Director, Officer
Seifert, St. Clare Pratt, Director, Officer

Lola Wright Foundation, Inc.

c/o Patrick H. O'Donnell, Jr., Pres.
P.O. Box 1138
Georgetown, TX 78627-1138
(512) 255-5353
EIN: 746054717
Source Date: 2/97

Geographic Restrictions:
Limited to 50 mile radius of Austin, TX, area.

Restrictions:
No grants to individuals or operating funds.

To Whom:
Social services, drug and alcohol abuse, minorities, family services and planning, aged [seniors], youth, legal services, community funds, health, hospitals, rehabilitation, **AIDS research, heart disease research**, handicapped, arts and culture, fine and performing arts, early childhood, adult, higher and other education, media and communications, environment.

For What:
Matching funds, building funds, equipment, endowment funds, continuing support, renovation projects, special projects.

Financial info:
Assets: $11,339,400.
Giving: $791,600 for 70 grants (high: $25,000; low: $1,500).

Application info:
Applications accepted. Submit proposal (9 copies). Deadline is Feb. 28 or Aug. 31. Board meets in May and Nov. Publishes application guidelines.

Directors, Officer, Trustees:

Flowers, Wilford, Director, Officer
Guererro, Linda, Director
Hilgers, Paul, Director
Meyers, James, Director
O'Donnell, Patrick H., Jr., Director, Officer
Rylander, Carole, Director
Todd, Vivian E., Director, Officer
Wright, Johnie E. (d), Donor

Utah

Dialysis Research Foundation

c/o Janeane Hovey, Assist. Admin.
5575 South 500 East
Ogden, UT 84405
(801) 479-0351
EIN: 942819009
Source Date: 12/96

Geographic Restrictions:
Primarily in UT.

To Whom:
Dialysis related programs, **including research**, treatment centers, and qualified patients.

For What:
Research.

Financial info:
Giving: $49,500 for 30 grants (high: $25,000; low: $100).

Application info:
Applications accepted. Submit proposal. No deadline. Will review projects for future budget years.

Directors, Officers, Trustees:
- Brockman, Ruth, Trustee
- Galvez, Fred, Trustee
- Harris, Leo N., Trustee
- Hovey, Jancane, Trustee
- Jones, Mary Jo, Trustee
- Lindsay, Mark, Officer, Trustee
- Orme, H. J., Officer, Trustee
- Robinson, Phil, Trustee
- Scnekjian, Harry, M.D., Trustee
- Trimble, Dave, Officer, Trustee

Willard L. Eccles Charitable Foundation

c/o Ray, Quinney & Nebeker
Attn: Clark P. Giles, Secretary
P.O. Box 45385
Salt Lake City, UT 84145-0385
(801) 532-1500
EIN: 942759395
Source Date: 3/94

Geographic Restrictions:
Primarily in UT, with emphasis in the Ogden, UT, area.

Restrictions:
No grants to individuals, land acquisition, building purposes, or to endow medical education positions.

To Whom:
Hospitals to acquire medical equipment for research and for rendering health care services, medical education and research.

For What:
Equipment, **research.**

Financial info:
Giving: $1,264,200 for 65 grants (high: $125,000; low: $1,000).

Application info:
Applications accepted. Submit proposal (6 copies). Deadline is one month preceding board meetings. Board meets in Mar., June, and Oct. Publishes application guidelines.

Directors, Officers, Trustees:
- Coit, Barbara E., Committee
- Coit, William E., M.D., Committee
- Coit, William H., Committee
- Denkers, Stephen E., Committee
- Denkers, Stephen G., Committee
- Denkers, Susan E., Committee
- Eccles, Ruth P., Officer
- First Security Bank of Utah, N.A., Trustee
- Giles, Clark P., Officer
- Hatch, Robert A., Trustee

George S. & Dolores Dore Eccles Foundation

c/o Lisa Eccles, Exec. Asst.
Deseret Bldg.
79 S. Main St., 12th Flr.
Salt Lake City, UT 84111
(801) 350-5336
EIN: 876118245
Source Date: 12/95

Geographic Restrictions:
Primarily in the Intermountain area, particularly UT. Limited to U.S. organizations.

Restrictions:
No grants to individuals, operating costs, political activities, conferences, seminars or research, or endowments.

To Whom:
Performing and visual arts, higher education, youth, **medical research**, social services, banking, finance and related disciplines.

For What:
Annual campaigns, building funds, capital campaigns, equipment, general purposes, matching funds, professorships, program-related investments, scholarship funds.

Financial info:
Assets: $389,985,700.
Giving: $14,276,100 for 185 grants (high: $1,000,000; low: $1,000).

Application info:
Applications accepted. Application form required (2 copies). No deadline. Board meets in spring, summer, fall, and winter. Publishes annual report with application guidelines.

Recent Grants:

$250,000	University of Utah, Salt Lake City, UT, Department of Internal Medicine. Establish George S. Eccles Professorship in Clinical Medicine. House Ear Institute, Los Angeles, CA. Remodel Eccles Temporal Bone Laboratory.
$175,000	National Society to Prevent Blindness, Salt Lake City, UT. Free eye screening programs in Utah.
$15,000	Ogden Surgical Society, Ogden, UT, George S. and Dolores Dore Eccles Annual Lecture.
$5,000	United Cerebral Palsy of Utah, Salt Lake City, UT. Rehabilitation Assistive Technology Program, which provides low-income individuals with equipment or devices needed to improve their lives.
$17,500	United States Ski Education Foundation, Park City, UT. Academic and Tuition Assistance Program, which provides tuition grants to United States Ski Team athletes.

Directors, Officers, Trustees:
Eccles, Delores Dore, Director
Eccles, George S. (d), Donor
Eccles, Spencer F., Director, Officer
Gardner, David Pierpont, Director, Officer
Graham, Robert M., Officer
Watson, Alonzo W., Jr., Director, Officer

Marriner S. Eccles Foundation

c/o Erma E. Hogan, Mgr.
701 Deseret Bldg.
79 S. Main St.
Salt Lake City, UT 84111
(801) 322-0116
EIN: 237185855
Source Date: 12/96

Geographic Restrictions:
Limited to UT. No grants outside the U.S.

Restrictions:
No grants to individuals or capital expenditures for construction of buildings.

To Whom:
Higher education, health, hospitals, **medical research**, arts, cultural programs, performing arts, fine arts, museums, family and social services, rehabilitation, seniors, drug and alcohol abuse, welfare, youth, women, homeless.

For What:
Equipment, operating budgets, general purposes, scholarship funds, research, matching funds.

Financial info:
Assets: $26,646,800.
Giving: $1,006,100 for 65 grants (high: $100,000; low: $2,000).

Application info:
Applications accepted. Submit proposal (7 copies). No deadline. Board meets when necessary. No set dates. Publishes application guidelines.

Directors, Officers, Trustees:
Eccles, C. Hope, Advisor
Eccles, Spencer F., Director, Officer
First Security Bank of Utah, N.A., Trustee
Hogan, Erma E., Mgr.
Steele, Harold J., Director, Officer
Steele, James M., Director, Officer
Tucker, Elmer D., Director
Watson, Alonzo W., Jr., Director, Officer

Ben B. & Iris M. Margolis Charitable Foundation for Medical Research

c/o First Security Bank of Utah
Attn: Julie Webster, Sr. Operations Asst.
P.O. Box 30007
Salt Lake City, UT 84130-0007
(801) 246-5361
EIN: 876180864
Source Date: 3/96

Geographic Restrictions:
Limited to UT.

Restrictions:
No grants to individuals, scholarships, fellowships, or endowments.

To Whom:
Medical research relating to causes, diagnosis, treatment, prevention, or control of physical or mental disease, AIDS, hospitals.

For What:
Research.

Financial info:
Assets: $6,264,600.
Giving: $60,000 for 10 grants (high: $15,000; low: $5,000).

Application info:
Applications accepted. Submit proposal. No deadline. Board meets quarterly.

Directors, Officers, Trustees:
First Security Bank of Utah, N.A., Trustee
Margolis, Ben B. (d), Donor
Margolis, Iris M. (d), Donor

Margaret E. Oser Foundation

c/o Carl Mitchell, Pres.
7070 Pinebrook Rd.
Park City, UT 84098
(801) 649-0337

California Address:
2081 Business Center, Suite 110
Irvine, CA 92715
EIN: 330210168
Source Date: 12/96

Geographic Restrictions:
Primarily in southern CA.

Restrictions:
No grants to individuals.

To Whom:
Elementary and secondary education, performing arts, hospitals, **medical research**, domestic violence, youth, civic affairs, Protestant religion, homeless, seniors, women.

For What:
Emergency funds, equipment, scholarship funds, seed money, special projects.

Financial info:
Assets: $8,000,000.
Giving: $346,400 for 25 grants (high: $50,000; low: $2,000).

Application info:
Applications accepted. Submit proposal. Deadline is July 1 and Dec. 1. Board meets in July and Dec.

Recent Grants:

$25,000	UCI Arboretum, Irvine, CA
$5,000	Art Institute of S. CA, Laguna Beach, CA
$25,000	City of Hope, Los Angeles, CA
$2,000	Orange County Rescue Mission, Santa Ana, CA
$3,000	Orange County Christian School, Anaheim, CA
$33,000	Harvey Mudd College Scholarship Fund, Claremont, CA

Directors, Officers, Trustees:
Doyle, Edith M., Officer
Mitchell, Carl, Officer
Oser, Margaret E. (d), Donor

Thrasher Research Fund

c/o Robert M. Briem, Assoc. Dir.
50 E. North Temple St., 7th Flr.
Salt Lake City, UT 84150
(801) 240-4753
EIN: 876179851
Source Date: 12/94

Geographic Restrictions:
U.S. and international giving.

Restrictions:
No grants for studies in the areas of abortions or reproductive physiology, contraceptive technology, research in the area of sexually transmitted disease, projects involving the use of therapeutically aborted human fetal tissue, conferences, workshops, symposia, general operations, construction or renovation of buildings or facilities, scholarships, or purchase of equipment.

To Whom:
U.S. and international child health research.

Scientific Fund: child health research in major nutritional deficiencies with emphasis on the micronutrients iodine, vitamin A, and iron, measurement of nutritional status, and promotion of breast feeding, infectious diseases with emphasis on enteric infections, acute respiratory infections, relationships between nutrition and infection, and oral nutritional management of acute diarrhea.

Innovative Fund: improve the health and well-being of mothers and children, child health concerns such as clean water and sanitation, immunization practices, nutrition, maternal and child health, and tobacco use.

For What:
Research.

Financial info:
Giving: $1,883,300 for 25 grants (high: $150,000; low: $25,000).

Application info:
Applications accepted. Submit proposal (3-4 pages, 8 copies). No deadline. Board meets in Apr. and Oct. Publishes annual report with application guidelines.

Directors, Officers, Trustees:
Brown, Victor L., Committe
Clyde, Aileen H., Committee
Edgley, Richard C., Bishop, Committee, Officer
Ferguson, Isaac C., Committee
Huber, Clayton S., Committee
McMullin, Keith B., Committee
Rogers, Sandra, Committee
Samuelson, Cecil O., Jr., M.D., Committee
Thrasher, E. W., Committee, Donor, Officer
Wood, Mary Ann Q., Committee

Virginia

Dalis Foundation

c/o Goodman & Company
P.O. Box 3247
Norfolk, VA 23514
EIN: 546046229
Source Date: 5/95

Geographic Restrictions:
Primarily in Norfolk VA.

To Whom:
Hospitals, **medical research**, international health, libraries, AIDS.

Financial info:
Assets: $5,712,200.
Giving: $261,100 for 10 grants.

Application info:
Applications accepted. Submit letter. No deadline.

Directors, Officers, Trustees:
Dalis, M. Dan (d), Donor
Martone, Joan Dalis, Officer
Norment, Sandra W., Officer

Mabel H. Flory Charitable Trust

c/o First Virginia Bank
Attn: Charles J. Connor, Jr., Trust Off.
6400 Arlington Blvd.
Falls Church, VA 22046-2336
(703) 241-3260
EIN: 546207168
Source Date: 6/96

Geographic Restrictions:
Primarily in VA and Washington, DC.

To Whom:
Medical research to develop or discover new cures and methods of treatment for arthritis, aphasia, hearing and sight problems of children.

For What:
Research.

Financial info:
Assets: $712,500.
Giving: $34,200 for grants.

Application info:
Applications accepted. Submit letter. Deadline is Aug. 31.

Recent Grants:

$2,000	RP Foundation Fighting Blindness
$8,054.	National Children's Eye Care
$8,054	University of Virginia. Research into vision
$8,054	Georgetown University Hospital

Directors, Officers, Trustees:
First Virginia Bank, Trustee

Thomas F. & Kate Miller Jeffress Memorial Trust

c/o NationsBank, Trust Div.
Attn: J. Samuel Gillespie, Jr., Advisor
P.O. Box 26606
Richmond, VA 23261-6903
(804) 788-2964
EIN: 546094925
Source Date: 6/96

Geographic Restrictions:
Primarily in VA.

Restrictions:
No grants for clinical research or individuals.

To Whom:
Higher education for **research in medical**, chemical and other scientific activities.

For What:
Research.

Financial info:
Assets: $25,609,700.
Giving: $794,300 for 10 grants (high: $250,000; low: $200).

Application info:
Applications accepted. Submit proposal (15 page limit, original and five copies). Deadline is Mar. 1 and Sept. 1. Board meets in May and Nov. Publishes application guidelines.

Directors, Officers, Trustees:

Belcher, Dennis I., Committee
Brandt, Richard B., Committee
Broman, George E., M.D., Committee
Gillespie, J. Samuel, Jr., Advisor
Gresham, T. Cary, Committee
Jeffress, Robert M. (d), Donor
Middleditch, Leigh B., Jr., Committee
NationsBank of Virginia, N.A., Trustee

Lind Lawrence Foundation

c/o L. P. Martin & Company
4132 Innslake Dr.
Glen Allen, VA 23060-3307
EIN: 237310359
Source Date: 9/94

Geographic Restrictions:
Primarily in Richmond, VA, and Los Angeles, CA [southern].

To Whom:
Neurosurgery research.

For What:
Operating budgets, research, building funds, capital campaigns.

Financial info:
Giving: $232,400 for 10 grants (high: $100,000; low: $1,000).

Application info:
Applications accepted. Submit letter. Deadline is July 31.

Directors, Officers, Trustees:

Bernhardt, Fred J., Jr., Trustee
Lawrence, Lind (d), Donor
Martin, Lee P., Jr., Trustee

Little River Foundation

Whitewood Farm
The Plains, VA 22171
(703) 253-5540
EIN: 237218919
Source Date: 11/95

Geographic Restrictions:
Primarily in Mid-Atlantic area of U.S.

To Whom:
Hospitals, **medical research**, AIDS, drug abuse, higher, secondary, early childhood, legal, and other education, literacy, international studies in Africa, environmental conservation, agriculture, animal welfare, legal services, Christian religion, community funds.

For What:
Building funds, conferences and seminars, endowment funds, operating budgets, **research**.

Financial info:
Assets: $311,300.
Giving: $611,500 for 70 grants (high: $50,000; low: $300).

Application info:
Applications accepted. Submit letter. No deadline. Board meets in Sept.-Oct.

Directors, Officers, Trustees:

Horkau, G. A., Jr., Officer
Ohrstrom, George L., Officer
Ohrstrom, Ricard R., Officer
Ohrstrom Foundation, Donor

Edward W. & Betty Knight Scripps Foundation

Eagle Hill Farm HCR 1, Box 38
Charlottesville, VA 22901
(804) 973-3345
EIN: 541426826
Source Date: 4/96

To Whom:
Historic preservation, education, **medical research.**

Financial info:
Assets: $1,305,000.
Giving: $760,900 for 3 grants.

Application info:
Applications accepted. Submit letter. No deadline. Board meets in May or June.

Recent Grants:

$25,000	The Santa Fe Opera, Santa Fe, NM. Opera apprentice program.
$443,356	International Red Cross, Geneva Switzerland.
$292,583	University of Virginia, Charlottesville, VA.

Directors, Officers, Trustees:
Scripps, Betty Knight, Donor, Director, Officer
Scripps, Edward W., Director, Officer
Scripps League Newspapers, Inc., The, Donor

Universal Leaf Foundation

c/o Nancy G. Powell, Mgr., Corp. Relations
P.O. Box 25099
Richmond, VA 23260
(804) 359-9311
EIN: 510162337
Source Date: 6/96

Geographic Restrictions:
Primarily in VA communities in which the company has a physical presence.

To Whom:
Higher and business education, community funds, museums, youth, health, **medical research**, the environment and animal welfare, civic affairs, public policy, the homeless, and the arts.

For What:
Annual campaigns, building funds, capital campaigns, emergency funds, employee matching gifts, operating budgets, renovation projects, research, technical assistance, internships, professorships, seed money.

Financial info:
Assets: $11,473,500.
Giving: $397,500 for 135 grants (high: $40,000; low: $100).

Application info:
Applications accepted. Submit letter of inquiry. No deadline.

Directors, Officers, Trustees:
Chandler, Wallace L., Director, Officer
Dozier, O. Kemp, Officer
Harrell, Harry H., Director
Lowden, Francis V., III, Officer
Powell, Nancy C., Officer
Towers, T. R., Director, Officer
Universal Leaf Tobacco Company, Inc., Donor
White, J. M., Director

Washington

Paul G. Allen Foundation for Medical Research

1111 Third Ave., Suite 3400
Seattle, WA 98101-3299
EIN: 943082530
Source Date: 12/95

Restrictions:
No grants to individuals.

To Whom:
Medical research and education, **cancer research**.

For What:
Research.

Financial info:
Assets: $4,300.
Giving: $216,000 for grants.

Application info:
Applications accepted. Submit proposal. No deadline.

Directors, Officers, Trustees:
Allen, Paul G., Officer
Kolde, Bert, Officer

Norman Archibald Charitable Foundation

First Interstate Bank of Washington
c/o Trust Department
Stuart Prestrud, Secretary
P.O. Box 21927
Seattle, WA 98111
(206) 292-3451
EIN: 911098014
Source Date: 9/95

Geographic Restrictions:
Primarily in the Puget Sound region of WA (comprising the area from the Cascades to the Olympics and from Whatcom and San Juan Counties on the north to Thurston on the south).

Restrictions:
No grants for ongoing operation budgets, government entities, individuals, deficit financing, endowments, or scholarships.

To Whom:
Youth and child development, **AIDS and other medical research**, higher education, libraries, museums, the arts, seniors, handicapped, housing, animal welfare, and conservation.

Seniors and disabled (34% of funding), youth (21% of funding), cultural programs (16% of funding), science and museums (9% of funding), conservation (5% of funding), schools and education (5% of funding), hospitals and medicine (4% of funding).

For What:
General purposes, seed money, building funds, equipment, land acquisition, conferences and seminars, program-related investments, publications, renovation projects, **research**, special projects.

Financial info:
Assets: $8,257,800.
Giving: $268,800 for 105 grants (high: $15,000; low: $1,000).

Application info:
Applications accepted. Submit letter or brief proposal (3 copies). No deadline. Board meets bimonthly from Sept. to May. Publishes application guidelines.

Directors, Officers, Trustees:
Alkire, Durwood, Bd.Gov.
Archibald, Norman (d), Donor
First Interstate Bank of Washington, Trustee
Mullin, J. Shan, Bd.Gov., Officer
Prestrud, Stuart H., Bd.Gov.

Benaroya Foundation

1001 4th Ave Plaza, Suite 4700
Seattle, WA 98154
EIN: 911280516
Source Date: 11/95

Geographic Restrictions:
Primarily in Seattle, WA.

To Whom:
Health, **medical research for diabetes**, medical education, museums.

For What:
Equipment.

Financial info:
Assets: $14,138,000.
Giving: $1,756,500 for 10 grants (high: $400,000; low: $5,000).

Application info:
Applications accepted. Submit proposal. No deadline.

Directors, Officers, Trustees:
Benaroya, Alan G., Director
Benaroya, Donna R., Officer
Benaroya, Jack A., Donor, Officer
Benaroya, Larry R., Donor, Officer
Benaroya, Rebecca B., Director
Benaroya, Sherry-Lee, Director

Robert G. Hemingway Foundation

c/o U. S. Bank, Washington
P.O.Box 720
Seattle, WA 98111
EIN: 876176774
Source Date: 4/9

Geographic Restrictions:
Primarily in ID and WA.

Restrictions:
No grants to individuals.

To Whom:
Higher education, **medical research**, legal services.

For What:
Scholarship funds, **research**, general purposes.

Financial info:
Giving: $283,700 for 10 grants (high: $50,000; low: $1,000).

Application info:
Applications accepted. Submit letter before Mar. 1.

Directors, Officers, Trustees:
Hemingway, Susan, Director
Seafirst Bank, Trustee

Florence B. Kilworth Charitable Foundation

c/o Key Trust Company
Attn: Kathy Schwer, Admin. Asst.
P.O. Box 11500, MS WA31-01-0310
Tacoma, WA 98411-5052
(206) 305-7206
EIN: 916221495
Source Date: 12/94

Geographic Restrictions:
Primarily in the Tacoma and Pierce counties, WA.

Restrictions:
No grants to individuals.

To Whom:
Hospitals, **medical research** and education, education, recreation, arts, Christian religion, missionary programs.

For What:
Annual campaigns, building funds, capital campaigns, operating budgets, **research**, scholarship funds, special projects.

Financial info:
Giving: $179,300 for 60 grants (high: $10,000; low: $500).

Application info:
Applications accepted. Application form required (original and 1 copy). Deadline is Nov. 1. Board meets quarterly.

Directors, Officers, Trustees:
Key Trust Company of the Northwest, Trustee
Morris, Florence, Trustee

Norcliffe Foundation

c/o Mary Ellen Hughes, Pres.
999 Third Ave., Suite 1006
Seattle, WA 98104
(206) 682-4820
EIN: 916029352
Source Date: 12/96

Geographic Restrictions:
Primarily in the Puget Sound Region in and around Seattle, WA.

Restrictions:
No grants to individuals, deficit financing, scholarships, or fellowships.

To Whom:
Health associations, **health research**, early childhood, higher and secondary education, social services, civic affairs, religion, historic preservation, cultural programs, arts, Catholic giving, homeless, disabled, wildlife, hospice, child welfare, youth, seniors, environment (animals, land, water, air, plants).

For What:
Operating budgets, capital campaigns, continuing support, annual campaigns, seed money, emergency funds, building funds, equipment, land acquisition, **research**, special projects, conferences and seminars, general purposes, renovation projects, scholarship funds, endowment funds, fellowships.

Financial info:
Assets: $35,622,700 (from 1995 990PF).
Giving: $2,748,700 for 245 grants (high: $800,000; low: $50).

Application info:
Applications accepted. Submit letter proposal. No deadline. Board meets as required with notification in 3 to 6 months. Publishes application guidelines.

Directors, Officers, Trustees:
Hefferline, Arline, Officer
Hughes, Mary Ellen, Officer
Pigott, Charles M., Trustee
Pigott, Dana, Trustee
Pigott, James C., Trustee
Pohl, Susan W., Trustee
Scheumann, Theiline P., Trustee
Wyckoff, Ann Pigott, Officer, Trustee

Pemco Foundation

c/o Stan McNaughton, Secretary-Treasurer
325 Eastlake Ave. East
Seattle, WA 98109
(206) 628-7900
EIN: 916072723
Source Date: 6/96

Geographic Restrictions:
Limited to WA residents for scholarships.
Organizational support primarily in Seattle, WA.

To Whom:
Heavy emphasis on funding programs that provide basic or rehabilitative education to those who are in need. Disadvantaged children and youth, social services, hospitals, **medical research**.

For What:
Research, student aid, scholarship funds.

Financial info:
Giving: $994,400 for 170 grants (high: $35,000; low: $50) and $148,400 for 305 grants to individuals (high: $1,500; low: $100).

Application info:
Applications accepted. Submit letter or brief proposal. No deadline.

Directors, Officers, Trustees:
Evergreenbank, Donor
Kurack, Sandra, Officer, Trustee
McNaughton, Stanley O., Officer, Trustee
Merlino, Astrid I., Officer, Trustee
Pemco Corp., Donor
Washington School Employees Credit Union, Donor

Poncin Scholarship Fund

c/o SeaFirst Bank
Attn: Mollie Determan, Trust Off.
P.O. Box 24565
Seattle, WA 98124-0565
(206) 242-8325
EIN: 916069573
Source Date: 12/95

Geographic Restrictions:
Limited to WA.

Restrictions:
No grants for operating expenses, continuing support, annual campaigns, seed money, emergency funds, deficit financing, buildings or endowments, scholarships, fellowships, matching gifts, special projects, publications, or conferences.

To Whom:
Medical research.

For What:
Research, individuals.

Financial info:
Assets: $4,836,100.
Giving: $241,900 for 20 grants to individuals (high: $15,000; low: $5,000).

Application info:
Applications accepted. Application form required. Application must be approved by head of applicant's institution. Requests are reviewed in May. Trust officers committee meets weekly with notification in 2 weeks. Publishes application guidelines.

Directors, Officers, Trustees:
Poncin, Cora May (d), Donor
Seafirst Bank, Trustee

Titcomb Foundation

c/o James R. Hanson, Secretary
Tacoma Financial Ctr., Suite 1500
P.O. Box 1278
Tacoma, WA 98401
(206) 272-8336
EIN: 916020513
Source Date: 12/95

Geographic Restrictions:
Primarily in WA.

Restrictions:
No grants to individuals.

To Whom:
Hunger: support of food banks and emergency food providers, support for requests that seek long-term solutions to the hunger problem.

Education: improving the quality of education, both public and private, through curricula development, teacher trainings and development.

Women and Girls: enhance self-sufficiency and self-esteem of disadvantaged women and girls through job counseling, training, and education, eliminate domestic violence and sexual abuse.

Medicine: **assist centers of medical and biomedical research** and support health care providers treating predominately disadvantaged.

For What:
General purposes, operating budgets.

Financial info:
Assets: $1,682,100.
Giving: $35,500 for 25 grants (high: $5,000; low: $500).

Application info:
Applications accepted. Submit letter (1 page). No deadline. Board meets in Sept. or Oct. to make funding decisions. Publishes application guidelines.

Directors, Officers, Trustees:
Behringer, Linda R., Officer
Hanson, James R., Officer
Titcomb, David R., Director, Officers
Titcomb, Diane C., Director
Titcomb, John W., Director
Titcomb, John W., Jr., Director
Titcomb, Stephen T., Director

West Virginia

Greater Kanawha Valley Foundation

c/o Betsy VonBlond, Exec. Dir.
1426 Kanawha Blvd., East
Charleston, WV 25301
(304) 346-3620
EIN: 556024430
Source Date: 12/94

Geographic Restrictions:
Limited to the Greater Kanawha Valley, WV, area, except scholarships which are limited to residents of WV.

Restrictions:
No grants for annual campaigns, deficit financing, or general endowments.

To Whom:
Higher and other education, social services, child welfare, family services, women, housing, health, **research on AIDS, heart disease, cancer**, fine and performing arts, ecology and the environment, recreation, community development.

College scholarships (25% of funding), arts (23% of funding), social services (14% of funding), recreation (9% of funding), health (4% of funding).

For What:
Operating budgets, continuing support, seed money, building funds, equipment, student aid, special projects, **research**, publications, conferences and seminars, technical assistance, annual campaigns, capital campaigns, general purposes, student loans.

Financial info:
Giving: $1,232,200 for 275 grants (high: $10,000; low: $500) and $384,800 for 275 grants to individuals (high: $10,000; low: $500).

Application info:
Applications accepted. Submit proposal (2 page limit). Deadline is Feb. 17, May 25, Aug. 24, and Nov. 9. Board meets in Mar., June, Sept., and Dec. Publishes annual report with application guidelines.

Recent Grants:

$3,000	Action Youth Care, Step by Step Program. Production of A Place Like Alice.
$748	Boone County Schools. Ashford-Rumble Elementary School-Poetry Alive!.
$25,000	WPBY-TV. Replacement of broadcasting equipment.
$500	Barbour County Reading Council. Born To Read Program.
$1,000	Belle Elementary School. Electronic Bookshelf.
$974	WomenCare. TV/VCR to initiate a home childbirth education program.
$2,500	Charleston District Outreach Ministries, Inc. Avesta Drive and Coal Branch Heights Community Centers.
$3,000	Childhood Language Disorders Center, Inc.. Computer system and Talking Touch software.

Directors, Officers, Trustees:
Arbogast, Paul, Trustee
Bank One, N.A., Trustee
Capito, Charles L., Jr., Trustee
Carter, Elsie P., Trustee
City National Bank, Trustee
Faber, Deborah A., Trustee
Huntington National Bank, Trustee
Loeb, Charles W., Officer
McElwee, Charles R., Officer, Trustee
Murphy, Sandra M., Trustee
One Valley Bank, N.A., Trustee
Rugeley, Gina, Trustee
Sinclair, K. Richard C., Officer, Trustee
Southworth, Louis S., II, Trustee
United National Bank, Trustee
VonBlond, Betsy B., Officer
Wetzel, Thomas C., Trustee

Huntington Clinical Foundation, Inc.

P.O. Box 5527
Huntington, WV 25703
EIN: 310979390
Source Date: 12/95

Geographic Restrictions:
Limited to Huntington, WV.

Restrictions:
No grants to individuals.

To Whom:
Medical research, medical and hospital care of med-

ically indigent, pre-medical education, dental education, post-dental education.

For What:
Research, general purposes.

Financial info:
Assets: $177,900.
Giving: $75,400 for 10 grants (high: $5,000; low: $500).

Application info:
Applications accepted. Application form required. No deadline. Board meets quarterly.

Directors, Officers, Trustees:
- Bailes, James R., Director
- Childers, John P., Director
- Fry, Carroll E., Director, Officer
- Heiner, Earl W., Jr., Director
- Jenkins, John E., Jr., Director
- John, Winfield C., M.D., Director
- Justice, Carroll, Director
- McGinnis, Kermit E., Director
- Morgan, James H., Jr., Director, Officer
- Neal, W. L., Director
- Norton, L. Frank, Director
- Poindexter, J. B., Jr., Director
- Scott, Thomas F., Director
- Switzer, Rufus, Donor
- Thompson, Richard, Director
- Vanston, Gerald E., Director, Officer

Huntington Foundation, Inc.

c/o Alyene Arthur, Exec. Secretary
208 Chafin Bldg.
517 Ninth St.
P.O. Box 2548
Huntington, WV 25726-2548
(304) 522-0611
EIN: 550370129
Source Date: 12/95

Geographic Restrictions:
Primarily in Huntington, WV, area.

Restrictions:
No grants to individuals or operating expenses.

To Whom:
Medical education and research, cultural programs, recreation, seniors, health, youth.

For What:
Equipment, general purposes, land acquisition.

Financial info:
Assets: $6,917,700.
Giving: $203,300 for 10 grants (high: $100,000; low: $2,500).

Application info:
Applications accepted. Application form required (6 copies). No deadline. Board meets in Jan., Apr., July, and Oct. Publishes application guidelines.

Directors, Officers, Trustees:
- Arthur, Alyene, Officer
- Hanshaw, Frank E., Jr., Director
- John, Winfield C., M.D., Director
- McGinnis, Kermit E., Director, Officer
- McKown, C. H., Director, Officer
- Underwood, Cecil H., Director, Officer

Wisconsin

A. Ward Ford Memorial Institute, Inc.

c/o Sandra S. Robarge, Admin.
813 Second St.
Wausau, WI 54403
(715) 845-9282
EIN: 370983948
Source Date: 6/96

Geographic Restrictions:
Primarily in WI and UT.

To Whom:
Scientific health care projects, **cardiology research using laser equipment**.

For What:
Research, consulting services.

Financial info:
Assets: $1,509,100.
Giving: $74,700 for 5 grants.

Application info:
Applications accepted. Application form required (original and 5 copies). Deadline is Apr. 30. Board meets in June and Sept.

Recent Grants:

$2,000	American Society For Laser Medicine And Surgery, Inc., Wausau, WI. William B. Mark Memorial Award to worthy recipient at ASLMS Annual Meeting.
$22,000	Foundation For Laser Subsurface Imaging Development, San Diego, CA. Empirical Study of Radioactive Transport in Soft Tissue to Quantify Laser Radiation Depth.
$10,707	Marathon County Chapter Of The American Red Cross, Wausau, WI. Funding for Continuation of Hypertension Screening Program.
$20,000	Michigan State University, East Lansing, MI. Efficacy and Reliability of the Use of Transdermal Laser Illumination for Lowering Serum Cholesterol.
$20,000	University Of Miami, Coral Gables, FL. Laser Light Scattering of Porcine intestinal Submucosa as a Vascular Substitute.

Directors, Officers, Trustees:

Drake, Ellet H., Officer, Trustee
Lundberg, James T., Trustee
Mark, Caroline S., Officer, Trustee
Morehead, Richard, Trustee
Owen, William R., M.D., Trustee
Robarge, Sandra S., Officer
Tuchscherer, Konrad T., Officer, Trustee

Helen Bader Foundation, Inc.

c/o Daniel J. Bader, Pres.
777 E. Wisconsin Ave., Suite 3275
Milwaukee, WI 53202
(414) 244-6464
E-mail: info@bader.org
EIN: 391710914
Source Date: 8/96

Geographic Restrictions:
Primarily in Milwaukee, WI, area.

Restrictions:
No grants to individuals, deficit financing, fundraising, or operating expenses.

To Whom:
Alzheimer's Disease and dementia: community-based programs and services, education and training, environmental designs for dementia, and **medical and scientific research**.

Israel: utilize the inherent education potential of its new immigrants in the workplace.

Milwaukee Jewish education and philanthropy: improve the current educational format to ensure a positive learning environment for both students and education professionals.

Education reform: educationally sound public policy, creative school/system development, effective leadership development.

For What:
Scholarship funds, general purposes, capital campaigns, special projects, **research**, conferences and seminars, seed money, technical assistance.

Financial info:
Giving: $7,500,400 for 215 grants (high: $200,000; low: $500).

Application info:
Applications accepted. Application form required.

Deadline is May 7 and Oct. 22. Board meets in Feb. and Aug. Publishes annual report with application guidelines.

Recent Grants:

$119,000	Milwaukee County Department On Aging
$75,000	National Association of Area Agencies on Aging, Inc., Washington, DC.
$66,700	Medical College of Wisconsin, Inc.
$40,000	Family Service Association of Manitowoc County, Inc., Manitowoc, WI.
$30,000	Milwaukee Jewish Home
$29,000	Meriter Retirement Services, Inc., Madison, WI.
$9,000	Bay Area Agency on Aging, Inc., Green Bay, WI.
$5,000	AgeAdvantage, Inc., Madison, WI.
$5,000	United Lutheran Program for the Aging, Inc.
$15,000	Bethany Lutheran Homes, Inc., LaCrosse, WI.
$15,000	Curative Workshop of Green Bay, Inc., WI.
$15,000	Northwoods Hospital Association, Inc., Phelps, WI.
$119,000	National Association of Counties Research Foundation, Washington, DC.
$80,000	Catholic Social Services of the Archdiocese of Milwaukee, Inc., WI.
$49,000	Marquette University, WI Geriatric Education Center
$26,000	The Gerontological Society of America, Washington, DC.
$6,000	Wisconsin Coalition for Advocacy, Inc.
$5,000	Coalition of Wisconsin Aging Groups, Inc.
$60,000	Rush-Presbyterian-St. Luke's Medical Center, Chicago, IL.
$37,000	The Monroe Clinic Foundation for Medical Research and Education, Inc., Monroe, WI.
$6,000	Retired Senior Volunteer Program of Waukesha, WI.
$30,000	Community Baptist Church of Greater Milwaukee, WI.
$25,000	Milwaukee Innercity Congregations Allied for Hope, Inc.,
$5,000	Greater Milwaukee Education, Inc.
$230,000	Public Policy Forum, Inc.
$180,000	United Community Center, Inc.
$60,000	Milwaukee Public Schools
$45,000	School District of Brown Deer, Brown Deer, WI.
$40,000	Holy Redeemer Church of God in Christ, Inc.
$25,000	Council for Basic Education, Washington, DC.
$20,000	School Sisters of Notre DAme, Milwauee Province, Inc.
$14,500	Urban Day School, Inc.
$11,000	Riveredge Nature Center, Inc., Newburg, WI.
$9,000	Blessed Tinity Catholic School
$7,250	Milwaukee Center for School Change, Inc.
$5,000	Alpha Kappa Alpha Educational Advancement Foundation Inc.
$103,300	Carroll College, Inc., Waukesha, WI.
$65,000	Crusade to Save Our Children, Inc.
$60,000	State of Wisconsin, Dept. of Public Instruction
$40,000	Multicultural Alliance, Ross, CA.
$15,000	Rethinking Schools Limited
$120,000	Planning Council for Health and Human Services, Inc.
$100,000	National Center for Neighborhood Enterprise, Washington, DC.
$80,000	Family House Inc.
$40,000	Planning Council for Health and Human Services, Inc. Transportation Planning Project. Collaborative planning project designed to improve paratransit services for elderly and disabled in Milwaukee County.
$25,000	National Alliance of Black School Educators, Inc. Positive Change. Conference to assess current status of African American children in Milwaukee Public Schools and develops future action plan.
$200,000	Public Policy Forum, Inc. School-to-Work (STW). Examine impact of STW on district staff employers, school staff classroom practice and students.
$35,000	Family Service of Milwaukee. Family Empowerment. Help parents become better parents producing results in terms of more caring families and less child abuse and neglect.
$75,000	Chabad's Children of Chernobyl. Evacuation from Chernobyl. New York, New York Chabad's Children of Chernobyl helps evacuate children to Israel from areas affected by nuclear reactor explosion in former Soviet Union.
$25,000	The American Pardes Foundation, Inc. Milwaukee Jewish Continuity Fund Jerusalem, Israel The Milwaukee Jewish Continuity Fund, program to encourage college graduates, community leaders and teachers from Milwaukee to study at Pardes.

Directors, Officers, Trustees:
Bader, Daniel J., Director, Officer
Bader, David M., Director, Officer
Bader, Linda C., Director
Bader, Michelle Henkin, Director
DeVey, Richard W., Director
Klitsner, Marvin E., Director
McGaffey, Jere D., Director, Officer

Harnischfeger Industries Foundation, Inc.

c/o Dave Brukardt
P.O. Box 554
Milwaukee, WI 53201
EIN: 391659070
Source Date: 2/97

Geographic Restrictions:
Bulk of contributions made in and around Milwaukee, WI.

Restrictions:
No grants to individuals, endowments, research, scholarships, fellowships, or matching gifts.

To Whom:
Health and Welfare: hospitals, **medical research**, social services engaged in treatment and prevention of disease, or in the areas of nutrition, hygiene, safety, and the improvement of public health.

Education: foster and improve the knowledge and skills of individuals of all ages with the objective of enhancing their ability to achieve a better quality of life.

Civic Affairs: community development, ecology, public safety, justice and the law, public understanding of and participation in government and civic affairs.

Culture and the Arts: visual and performing arts and the stimulation and enrichment of the public intellectual experience, libraries, museums, artistic performances.

For What:
Annual campaigns, capital campaigns, continuing support, general purposes, operating budgets, special projects.

Financial info:
Giving: $1,000,000 for grants (high: $10,000; low: $500).

Application info:
Applications accepted. Submit letter. No deadline. Board meets 4 times yearly. Publishes application guidelines.

Recent Grants:

$5,000	Center for the Deaf & Hard of Hearing
$1,000	Hispanic Chamber of Commerce
$200	Hebron House of Hospitality
$500	Milwaukee Indian Health Board
$5,000	Urban Day School
$1,000	Waukesha County Project Head Start

Directors, Officers, Trustees:
Corby, Francis M., Jr., Director, Officer
Grade, Jeffery T., Officer
Harnischfeger Industries, Inc., Donor
Lundgren, K. Thor, Officer

Herman W. Ladish Family Foundation, Inc.

c/o Ladish Malting Company
790 N. Jackson St., 2nd Flr.
Milwaukee, WI 53202
(414) 271-4763
EIN: 396063602
Source Date: 6/94

Geographic Restrictions:
Primarily in WI.

To Whom:
Higher and secondary education, hospitals, **medical research**, health, youth, cultural programs.

Financial info:
Giving: $689,000 for 55 grants (high: $50,000; low: $1,000).

Application info:
Applications accepted. Submit letter. No deadline. Board meets twice a year.

Directors, Officers, Trustees:
Ladish, Herman W., Donor
Ladish, John H., Director, Officer
Stollenwerk, Robert T., Officer
Zarwell, Elwin J., Director

National Institute of Biogerontology

c/o Everett Smith, Ph.D., Pres.
4610 University Ave.
P.O. Box 55231
Madison, WI 53705
Source Date: 12/94

Geographic Restrictions:
Primarily in WI.

To Whom:
Medical research on aging [seniors], disuse atrophy, and osteoporosis.

For What:
Individuals, lectureships, **research**, seed money.

Financial info:
Giving: $67,100 for grants.

Application info:
Applications accepted. Submit proposal. No deadline.

Directors, Officers, Trustees:
Dodson, Vernon, Director
Ershler, William, Director
Ray, Robert O., Director, Officer
Reddan, William G., Director
Smith, Everett L., Director, Officer
Smith, Patricia, Director, Officer

Northwestern Mutual Life Foundation, Inc.

c/o James W. Ehrenstrom, Exec. VP
720 E. Wisconsin Ave.
Milwaukee, WI 53202
(414) 299-2200
EIN: 391728908
Source Date: 2/97

Geographic Restrictions:
Primarily in southeastern WI.

Restrictions:
No grants for conferences or special events.

To Whom:
Higher, elementary, business, adult, medical, and secondary education, social services, civic affairs, arts, cultural programs, visual arts, museums, performing arts, literacy, libraries, hospitals, health, drug and alcohol abuse, AIDS, **medical and cancer research**, housing, homeless, urban and community development, minorities, disabled.

For What:
Employee matching gifts, operating budgets, capital campaigns, annual campaigns, building funds, continuing support, emergency funds, general purposes, renovation projects, scholarship funds.

Financial info:
Giving: $5,500,000 for 315 grants.

Application info:
Applications accepted. Submit letter of intent. Deadline for completed applications is Mar. 15. Board meets in May.

A. O. Smith Foundation, Inc.

c/o Edward J. O'Connor, Secretary
P.O. Box 23971
Milwaukee, WI 53223-0971
(414) 359-4100
EIN: 396076924
Source Date: 12/94

Geographic Restrictions:
Primarily in areas of company operations in Granite City, Rockford, Alsip, and DeKalb, IL, Mt. Sterling and Florence, KY, Mebane, NC, Bellevue, Tipp City, and Upper Sandusky, OH, McBee, SC, Milan, TN, Seattle, WA, Belcamp, MD, El Paso and Irving, TX, Little Rock, AR, Wichita, KS, Corydon, IN, Farmington Hills, MI, and Milwaukee, WI.

Restrictions:
No grants to individuals.

To Whom:
Health and Hospitals (10% of funding): rescue squads and ambulance services, medical education, **heart research**, blood centers.

Civic & Cultural (14% of funding): youth, handicapped, leadership, museums, libraries, theater, environmental education, hunger, homeless, zoos.

Social Services (10% of funding): mental health, day care, family services, literacy, alcohol abuse, job training, housing, youth.

Education (27% of funding): public and private education, engineering.

For What:
Continuing support, annual campaigns, building funds, scholarship funds, employee matching gifts.

Financial info:
Giving: $718,200 for 210 grants (high: $100,000; low: $200).

Application info:
Applications accepted. Submit proposal. Deadline is Mar. 30 and Sept. 30. Board meets in June and Dec. Publishes annual report with application guidelines.

Recent Grants:
- Mt. Mary College. Milwaukee, Wi. Upgrading Computers For Classroom.
- National Joint Council On Economic Education. Milwaukee, Wi. Promoting Economic Literacy.
- Visiting Nurses Foundation. Milwaukee, Wi. Home Health Care And Related Services.
- Wellness Council. Milwaukee, Wi. Well Workplace Program.
- Discovery World. Milwaukee, Wi. Weekend Workshop Programs.
- Detroit Symphony Orchestra. Detroit, Mi. Symphony In Detroit.
- Hospice Of Miami County. Troy, Oh. Health Care Services To Terminally Ill.
- Lake Robinson Rescue. Mcbee, Sc. Annual Campaign Of Rescue.

Directors, Officers, Trustees:
Kita, John J., Officer
O'Connor, Edward J., Director, Officer
O'Toole, Robert J., Director, Officer
Smith, Arthur O., Director, Officer
Smith Corp., A. O., Donor

Stackner Family Foundation, Inc.

c/o John A. Treiber, Exec. Dir.
P.O. Box 597
Hartland, WI 53029
(414) 646-7040
EIN: 396097597
Source Date: 12/96

Geographic Restrictions:
Limited to Milwaukee, WI, area.

Restrictions:
No grants to individuals, deficit financing, or fellowships.

To Whom:
Higher, secondary, and elementary education, social services, youth, family services, homeless, hunger, child welfare, employment, minorities, **medical research**, health, mental health, handicapped, environment, drug and alcohol abuse, historic preservation.

For What:
Operating budgets, continuing support, annual campaigns, seed money, building funds, equipment, land acquisition, matching funds, special projects, research, scholarship funds, capital campaigns.

Financial info:
Assets: $12,753,300 (from 1995 990PF).
Giving: $545,800 for 155 grants (high: $40,000; low: $100).

Application info:
Applications accepted. Submit letter. Deadline is Dec. 15, Mar. 15, June 15, and Sept. 15. Board meets in Jan., Apr., July and Oct.

Directors, Officers, Trustees:
Cotter, Patrick W., Director, Officer
MacGregor, David L., Director, Officer
Stackner, Irene M. (d), Donor
Stackner, John S. (d), Donor
Treiber, John A., Director, Officer
Treiber, Patricia S., Director, Officer

Unicare Foundation, Inc.

105 W. Michigan Ave.
Milwaukee, WI 53203-2914
(414) 347-4221
EIN: 391549381
Source Date: 12/96

Restrictions:
No grants to individuals.

To Whom:
Alzheimer's disease research and services, care giver education, quality of life in nursing centers.

For What:
Consulting services, research, seed money, special projects, technical assistance, conferences and seminars.

Financial info:
Giving: $189,000 for 20 grants (high: $45,000; low: $2,000).

Application info:
Applications accepted. Application form required.
Deadline is end of each quarter.

Directors, Officers, Trustees:
Guilbert, Rob, Director
Gustafson, David, Director
Hastings, Margaret, Director
Hughes, John, Director
Kirk, Tom, Director
Minor, Jeff, Director
Mulligan, Bill, Director
Retzke, Ronald E., Director, Officer
Ricchio, Janice, Director
Schroeder, Colleen, Director, Officer
Smith, Guy W., Director, Officer
Wahner, Jim, Director
Wallace, Lee, Director
Wier, Nancy A., Director, Officer

Wyoming

Paul Stock Foundation

c/o Charles G. Kepler, Pres.
P.O. Box 2020
Cody, WY 82414
(307) 587-5275
EIN: 830185157
Source Date: 11/95

Geographic Restrictions:
Primarily in WY.

Restrictions:
Student aid limited to those who have resided in WY for one year or more.

To Whom:
Higher education, student aid to WY residents, civic affairs, museums, arts, hospitals, child welfare, youth, **medical research**, community development.

For What:
Student aid, annual campaigns, building funds, **research**.

Financial info:
Assets: $9,373,200.
Giving: $600,300 for 15 grants (high: $300,000; low: $1,000) and $123,700 for 75 grants to individuals (high: $3,000; low: $100).

Application info:
Applications accepted. Application form and instructions for educational grants only. Deadline is June 30 and Nov. 30 for educational grants. Board meets in July and Dec.

Directors, Officers, Trustees:
Brumage, Esther C., Officer
Kepler, Charles G., Officer
Robirds, Donald M., Officer
Stock, Eloise J., Donor
Stock, Paul (d), Donor

True Foundation

c/o True Companies
Attn: H. A. True, Jr., Trustee
P.O. Drawer 2360
Casper, WY 82602
(307) 237-9301
EIN: 836004596
Source Date: 11/95

Geographic Restrictions:
Primarily in midwest U.S., with emphasis on WY.

To Whom:
Education, community development, legal services, **medical research**, science and technology, agriculture, museums, social services.

For What:
Employee-related scholarships, special projects.

Financial info:
Assets: $2,511,800.
Giving: $254,000 for 95 grants (high: $30,000; low: $50) and $17,000 for grants to individuals (high: $3,000; low: $100).

Application info:
Applications accepted. Application form required for scholarships. Deadline is Mar. 22 for scholarships.

Directors, Officers, Trustees:
True, H. A., Jr., Donor, Trustee
True Oil Company, Donor

Section II
Federal Funders

Academic Career Leadership Award

Robin Barr
Office of Extramural Affairs
National Institute on Aging
(301)496-9322; fax, (301)402-2945
e-mail, rb42h@nih.gov
Internet: gopher://gopher.nih.gov:70/11/res/nih-guide

Geographic Restrictions:
Gives to domestic, nonfederal organizations, such as medical and nursing schools, may apply on behalf of candidates. Candidates for the academic career leadership award must have sufficient clinical training, research or teaching experience in an academic area of interest to the NIA to implement a program of curriculum development and research relevant to a program within the applicant institution; have an academic appointment at a level sufficient to enable the candidate to exert an influence on the coordination of research, teaching and clinical practice in aging; and be in a position to devote at least 25 percent effort to the program.

To Whom:
The National Institute on Aging is inviting applications for leadership activities in developing research and research training programs in aging.

The award supports senior individuals with acknowledged scientific expertise and leadership skills to improve the capacity of their institution to promote research and research training in aging.

Application info:
Deadlines are Oct. 1, 1997; Feb. 1, 1998 and June 1, 1998.

Financial info:
Up to $100,000 a year in direct costs per award. The project period is three to five years.

Adolescents and STDs Cooperative Research Centers

Penelope Hitchcock
Division of Microbiology and Infectious Diseases
National Institute of Allergy and Infectious Diseases
(301)402-0443; fax, (301)402-1456
e-mail, ph22k@nih.gov
Internet: gopher://gopher.nih.gov:70/11/res/nih-guide.

Geographic Restrictions:
Gives to domestic for-profit and nonprofit institutions, including hospitals, colleges and universities and state and local governments.

To Whom:
The National Institute of Allergy and Infectious Diseases is inviting cooperative agreement applications for an adolescents and sexually transmitted diseases (STD) cooperative research center to conduct multidisciplinary and collaborative investigations and intervention oriented research.

Research should further understanding of STDs in adolescent populations at risk and develop and evaluate effective approaches for prevention and control. Applications must include at least three research projects — one in behavioral or epidemiological research in adolescent populations of particular interest and two or more projects that link disciplines in a single scientific area and at least one that links disciplines in two different areas; research on two or more specified STD pathogens or syndromes, such as chlamydia and human papillomavirus; and a strong clinical capability in adolescent medicine.

Application info:
Deadlines are Oct. 15, 1997 for letters of intent; Jan. 8, 1998 for applications.

Financial info:
$1.2 million for first-year support of one center. The project period is up to five years.

AIDS International Training

Kenneth Bridbord
Division of International Training and Research
Fogarty Center
(301)496-2516; fax, (301)402-2056
e-mail, bridbord@nih.gov
Internet: gopher://gopher.nih.gov:70/11/res/nih-guide

Geographic Restrictions:
Gives to U.S. nonprofit and public institutions.

To Whom:
The National Institutes of Health's Fogarty International Center is inviting applications to work with foreign colleagues to build global HIV/AIDS research capacity to prevent HIV transmission through development of HIV/AIDS international training and research programs for foreign health scientists, clinicians and allied health scientists.

The goals of the program are to increase the expertise of scientists in developing countries in AIDS-related biomedical and prevention research; increase research collaboration and capacity in foreign countries on AIDS/HIV; and expand ongoing collaborative training in HIV/AIDS prevention research.

Application info:
Deadlines are Oct. 15, 1997 for letters of intent; Feb. 18, 1998 for applications.

Financial info:
$6.5 million. First-year costs must not exceed $600,000 for continuing programs or $400,000 for new programs. An additional $100,000 may be available for programs in special areas, such as training new and minority health science students.

Alcoholism Medications

Raye Litten
Division of Clinical and Prevention Research
National Institute on Alcohol Abuse and Alcoholism
(301)443-0796; fax, (301)443-8774
e-mail, rlitten@willco. niaaa.nih.gov
Internet: http://www.nih.gov/grants/guide/index.html

Geographic Restrictions:
Gives to domestic and foreign for-profit and nonprofit organizations, including colleges and universities, hospitals, laboratories, state and local government units and eligible agencies of the federal government.

To Whom:
The National Institute on Alcohol Abuse and Alcoholism is inviting applications to research the clinical use of medications to treat alcohol abuse and alcoholism.

Relevant topics include investigation of drugs to treat various aspects of alcoholism, particularly acute and protracted alcohol withdrawal, post-treatment relapse, alcohol craving, psychiatric comorbidity, alcohol-induced cognitive dysfunction, intoxication and alcohol induced organ damage.

NIAAA also seeks research on behavioral issues in the use of medications in alcoholism treatment, such as compliance to the drug regimen.

Application info:
Deadlines are Feb. 1, 1998; June 1, 1998; and Oct.1, 1998.

Financial info:
Up to $2 million for five to eight grants.

American Brain Tumor Association

Naomi Berkowitz, Executive Director
American Brain Tumor Association
2720 River Road
Suite 146
Des Plaines, IL 60018
(847)827-9910; fax, (847)827-9918
e-mail, info@abta.org.

Geographic Restrictions:
Post doctoral candidates must be citizens or permanent residents of the United States or Canada. Selection is based on the quality of the individual applicant, the program and the research being undertaken.

To Whom:
The American Brain Tumor Association offers fellowships to post doctorates to conduct brain tumor research. The ideal applicant will pursue a career in neuro-oncology research.

Application info:
Deadline is Jan. 6, 1998. Application forms are available from the association.

Financial info:
$50,000 for each fellowship ($25,000 per annum for two years).

Autoimmunity, Genetics

Elaine Collier
Division of Allergy, Immunology and Transplantation
National Institute of Allergy and Infectious Diseases
(301)496-7104; fax, (301)402-2571
e-mail, ec5x@nih.gov
Internet: gopher://gopher.nih.gov:70/11/res/nih-guide

Geographic Restrictions:
Gives to domestic and foreign for-profit and nonprofit organizations, including colleges and universities.

To Whom:
The National Institute of Allergy and Infectious Diseases and four other National Institutes of Health components are inviting applications for innovative basic and preclinical research on the immune responses underlying autoimmune disease and its regulation for preventive or treatment purposes.

Areas of particular interest are genetic susceptibility for autoimmune disease; the role and regulation of co-stimulation of T-cells in autoimmunity; and signal transduction in the autoreactive response.

Application info:
Deadlines are Oct. 1, 1997; Feb. 1, 1998 and June 1, 1998.

Basic and Clinical Research on Immune Tolerance

Helen Quill
National Institute of Allergy and Infectious Diseases
Division of Allergy, Immunology and Transplantation
(301)496-7551; fax, (301)402-2571
e-mail, hqlt@nih.gov

Lee Hall
National Institute of Allergy and Infectious Diseases
Division of Microbiology and Infectious Diseases
(301)496-2544; fax, (301)402-2508
e-mail, 1h24g@nih.gov

Scott Cairns
National Institute of Allergy and Infectious Diseases
Division of Acquired Immunodeficiency Syndrome
(301)496-8197; fax, (301)402-3211
e-mail, sc160p@nih.gov

Jessica Massicot-Fisher
National Heart, Lung and Blood Institute
(301)435-0504; fax, (301)480-1454
e-mail, jm294z@nih.gov

Anna McCormick
National Institute on Aging
(301)456-6402; fax, (301)402-0010
e-mail, am38K@nih.gov.

Allan Lock
National Institute of Child Health and Human Development
(301)496-5541; fax, (301)402-4083
e-mail, locka@hdo1.nichd.nih.gov.
gopher://gopher.nih.gov:70/11/res/nih-guide

Geographic Restrictions:
Gives to domestic and foreign for-profit and nonprofit organizations.

To Whom:
The National Institute of Allergy and Infectious Diseases, the National Heart, Lung and Blood Institute and the National Institute of Mental Health are inviting applications to clarify the basic mechanisms responsible for inducing and maintaining antigen-specific immune tolerance, that will translate experimental knowledge on immune tolerance into clinical therapies for treating and preventing immune-mediated disease or will promote more effective development of vaccines by preventing pathogen-induced immune tolerance.

Application info:
Oct. 1,1997; Feb. 1, 1998; and June 1, 1998.

Basic Biology, Immunology and Pathogenesis of Tuberculosis

Ann Ginsberg
Division of Microbiology and Infectious Diseases
National Institute of Allergy and Infectious Diseases
(301)496-5305; fax, (301)496-8030
e-mail, ag73i@nih.gov.

Hannah Peavy
Division of Lung Diseases
National Heart, Lung and Blood Institute
(301)435-0222; fax, (301)480-3557
e-mail, hannah_peavy@nih.gov.
Refer to PA 97-083
gopher://gopher.nih.gov:70/11/res/nih-guide

Geographic Restrictions:
Gives to domestic and foreign for-profit and nonprofit organizations, including colleges and universities, nationally.

To Whom:
The National Institute of Allergy and Infectious Diseases and National Heart, Lung and Blood Institute are seeking applications for research to clarify the basic biology, immunology and pathogenesis of mycobacteria and host-mycobacterial interactions.

Application info:
Deadlines are Oct. 1, 1997; Feb. 1, 1998; and June 1, 1998.

Cancer Research Network Across Healthcare Systems

Martin Brown
Applied Research Br.
National Cancer Institute
(301)496-5716
e-mail, mb53o@nih.gov
Internet: gopher://gopher. nih.gov:70/11/res/nih-guide

Geographic Restrictions:
Gives to domestic for-profit and nonprofit healthcare provider organizations, which will be network members, acting jointly as a U.S. research network. A domestic application may not include an international component. Networks must include a sufficient number of healthcare provider organization members so that total patient enrollment is at least 2 million adults. Also, network-covered populations must include diverse populations with respect to gender, race/ethnicity and, to the extent practical, rural/urban and geographic location.

To Whom:
The National Cancer Institute is inviting cooperative agreement applications to develop and support a cancer research infrastructure, consisting of one or more networks, composed of healthcare provider organization researchers able to conduct studies of cancer epidemiology, treatment, prevention and control.

The Cancer Research Network will formulate and implement a joint research agenda resulting in the conduct of three or more specified research projects in selected areas of cancer control and population studies; and develop standardized data collection instruments, surveys and analytical methods to promote the development of consistent and uniform databases and other research materials that can be shared across member institutions and utilized in joint research projects using uniform protocols when appropriate.

Broad areas of particular interest include studies that address the distribution of preventable cancer risk factors and the burden of disease in the covered population of the network; and studies of the relationship between healthcare delivery system organizational structure and patterns of cancer prevention and control service delivery associated with access to care and favorable outcomes.

Application info:
Deadlines are Oct. 17,1997 for letters of intent; Nov. 25, 1998 for applications. Applicants should demonstrate the capability of data linkages with local centralized tumor registries, pathology and radiologic facilities and state vital records. If these capabilities do not currently reside within one or more of the network members, the applicant may assemble a group with plans to develop the necessary expertise across all network members. Each network member must have access to a recourse unit that supports research data management locally or centrally.

Financial info:
$4 million for first-year funding of one or two applications. The project period is four years.

Cell Biology of the Pancreatic Beta Cell

Joan Harmon
National Institute of Diabetes and Digestive and Kidney Diseases
(301)594-8808; fax, (301)480-3503
e-mail, Joan_Harmon@nih.gov
Internet: http://www.nih.gov/grants/guide/index.html

Geographic Restrictions:
Gives to domestic and foreign for-profit and nonprofit organizations and state and local governments. Foreign institutions are not eligible for First Independent Research Support and Transition (FIRST) awards.

To Whom:
The National Institute of Diabetes and Digestive and Kidney Diseases is inviting investigator-initiated research grant applications to elucidate the pathways and factors responsible for the development and maintenance of beta cells in the pancreas.

Projects may: determine the location and identity of stem cells; establish cellular markers for isolating lineages of pancreatic stem cells; develop approaches that can be used to identify and regenerate specific populations of cells within the pancreatic islets; identify syndromes affecting the endocrine pancreas in order to identify the involved genes; explain the mechanism of "glucose toxicity" in beta cell and/or develop approaches to prevent it; elucidate the role of cell-cell interactions within the islet to explain the differences between isolated beta cells and islets; or explore other related topics.

Application info:
Deadlines are Feb. 19, 1998 for letters of intent; March 19, 1998 for applications.

Financial info:
$4 million for 12 to 16 awards. Generally, the maximum regular research grant is $160,000 in direct costs for initial funding. The project period is five years.

Centers for Behavioral Science Research in Mental Health

Mary Ellen Oliveri
Division of Mental Disorders
Behavioral Research and AIDS
National Institute of Mental Health
(301)443-3942; fax, (301)443-4822
e-mail, moliveri@nih.gov
Internet: gopher://gopher.nih.gov:70/11/res/nih-guide.

Geographic Restrictions:
Gives to domestic for-profit and nonprofit institutions, including hospitals, colleges and universities.

To Whom:
The National Institute of Mental Health is seeking grant applications for centers for behavioral science research in mental health to provide integrated multidisciplinary research environments for pursuing focused questions in basic behavioral science related to mental health and mental disorders.

The purpose is to encourage investigators from a variety of disciplines and approaches to focus the full range of expertise and advanced technologies available in basic behavioral science on unraveling mechanisms underlying mental health and mental illness and on translating basic behavioral findings and techniques into relevant clinical issues.

Applications info:
Deadlines are Oct. 1, 1997, Feb. 1, 1998 and June 1, 1998.

Financial info:
$3.3 million will be available in fiscal 1998 and 1999 for up to five new or competing centers. The project period is up to five years.

Center for Vestibular Research

Daniel Sklare
Division of Human Communication
National Institute on Deafness and Other Communication Disorders
(301)496-1804; fax, (301)402-6251
e-mail, daniel_sklare@nih.gov
Internet: gopher://gopher.nih.gov:70/11/res/nih-guide

Geographic Restrictions:
Gives to domestic and foreign for-profit and nonprofit organizations, including colleges and universities, hos-

pitals, laboratories, state and local government units and eligible agencies of the federal government.

To Whom:

The National Institute on Deafness and Other Communication Disorders and the National Aeronautics and Space Administration are inviting applications to support a center to carry out a program of ground-based research and research training in the vestibular system relevant to the research missions of both the NIDCD and NASA.

The research focus of the center will be on the role of the vestibular system in spatial cognition (spatial orientation and spatial navigation) and the role of the vestibular system in the control of balance and spatially directed motor performance. In addition to conducting research, the center will provide research training to predoctoral and postdoctoral trainees.

Application info:

Deadlines are Dec. 8, 1997 for letters of intent; Jan. 8, 1998 for applications.

Financial info:

Up to $1.2 million in total costs for initial funding of one award for up to five years.

Clinical Epidemiological Studies in Hereditary Breast/Ovarian Cancer

Susan Nayfield
Division of Cancer Epidemiology and Genetics
National Cancer Institute
(301)496-9600; fax, (301)402-4279
e-mail, nayfiels@epndc.nci.nih.gov

Geographic Restrictions:

Investigators with sufficient time left on current parent grants, nationally.

To Whom:

The National Cancer Institute is seeking applications for competing supplements to existing NIH-funded research project grants or cooperative agreements for innovative epidemiological studies on clinical issues facing women with inherited predisposition for breast and/or ovarian cancer.

NCI is seeking research on such issues as the natural history of disease associated with predisposing mutations; the efficacy of prophylactic surgery and other preventive measures; and the appropriateness of standard oncologic care for cancers developing in mutation carriers. The institute is looking for retrospective studies based on existing resources such as tissue banks and high-risk clinic registries and through concurrent studies added to ongoing clinical or epidemiologic research projects. The goal is to enhance informed decisionmaking among women at hereditary cancer risk.

Application info:

Deadlines are Feb. 1, 1998; June 1, 1998; and Oct. 1, 1998.

Clinical Trial Planning Grant

Joseph Drage
National Institute of Neurological Disorders and Stroke
(301)496-4188; fax, (301)402-0302
e-mail, jd66x@nih.gov
he solicitation is available on the National Institutes of Health homepage at gopher://gopher.nih.gov:70/11/res/nih-guide.

Geographic Restrictions:

Gives to domestic and foreign for-profit and nonprofit organizations, including colleges and universities, hospitals, laboratories, state and local government units and eligible agencies of the federal government.

To Whom:

The National Institute of Neurological Disorders and Stroke is seeking developmental planning grant applications for clinical trials to evaluate treatments for neurological disorders.

The NINDS clinical trial planning grant allows for early peer review of the rationale and design for clinical trials of treatments for neurological disorders **and provides support for development of a detailed clinical trial research plan, including a complete manual of operations and procedures.**

Application info:

Deadlines are Oct. 1, 1997; Feb. 1, 1998 and June 1, 1998. The applicant must provide detailed information regarding the rationale of the clinical trial based on adequate, preclinical science and preliminary clinical research. The purpose is not to obtain preliminary data or to conduct studies to support the rationale of the clinical trial.

Financial info:

Up to $150,000 in direct costs for one year.

Complementary and Alternative Medicine Research

Richard Nahin
Office of Alternative Medicine
(301)496-4792; fax, (301)480-3519
e-mail, NahinR@od31em1.od.nih.gov
Internet: http://www.nih.gov/grants/guide/index.html

Geographic Restrictions:
Domestic for-profit and nonprofit organizations, including hospitals, colleges and universities and state and local governments. Applications may include foreign components, but foreign organizations are not eligible to apply.

To Whom:
The Office of Alternative Medicine, National Institute of Child Health and Human Development and National Institute on Drug Abuse are inviting applications to establish centers for complementary and alternative medicine (CAM) **research on cardiovascular disease, drug abuse, HIV/AIDS and pediatric disorders.**

Centers will support basic, preclinical, clinical, epidemiologic and health services research of CAM in four areas: HIV/AIDS, emphasizing development of improved interventions to prevent and treat HIV infection and its sequelae, including cachexia, neuropathies and opportunistic infections; drug abuse and addiction, to identify potential CAM therapies to prevent or treat drug abuse and addiction, addressing both short-term and long-term therapies; pediatric research, to assess the use of CAM in the pediatric population and develop research opportunities accordingly; and cardiovascular research, to reduce mortality/morbidity associated with congestive heart failure, coronary artery disease (including myocardial infarction) artherosclerotic manifestations (including peripheral artery disease), hypertension, and prevention and treatment of cardiovascular risk factors.

CAM program areas include: alternative medical systems, manipulative and body-based systems, biofield, bioelectromagnetics, pharmacologic therapies, herbal medicine, mind-body medicine, health promotion and disease prevention and biological-based therapies.

Application info:
Deadlines are Dec. 1, 1997 for letters of intent; Jan. 13, 1998 for applications.

Financial info:
Up to $2.4 million for first-year funding of two to four centers. The project period is up to five years.

Core Support for Programs in Mental Health/AIDS Research

Dianne Raush
Office of AIDS Research
National Institute of Mental Health
(301)443-6100; fax, (301)443-9719
e-mail, dr89b@nih.gov

Geographic Restrictions:
Domestic organizations, including colleges and universities, hospitals, laboratories, state and local government units and eligible agencies of the federal government assuring adherence and compliance to drug therapy regimens.

To Whom:
The National Institute of Mental Health is inviting applications to establish Core Support for Programs in AIDS Research (CSPARs) to enhance multidisciplinary research on the mental health aspects of HIV/AIDS.

The CSPARs initiative is designed to improve and expand research by supporting infrastructure, including: subject recruitment, tracking and retention; quality control and assurance procedures; equipment; laboratories; statistical analysis; database management; and administrative coordination. Important research objectives to be served by the core support include identification of behaviors that put individuals at risk for infection and development of interventions to change risky behaviors; development of methods and strategies to aid HIV-infected individuals in coping with the disease; study of the nervous system effects of HIV infection of the central nervous system (CNS); identification of the cellular and molecular mechanisms underlying HIV-induced CNS dysfunction; development and testing of potential treatments; and studies focused on improving and

Application info:
Deadlines are Nov. 1, annually for letters of intent; Jan. 2 annually for applications.

Diabetic Nephropathy

Gladys Hirschman
Division of Kidney, Urologic and Hematologic Diseases
National Institute of Diabetes and Digestive and Kidney Diseases
(301)594-7717; fax, (301)480-3510
e-mail, gladys_hirschman@nih.gov

Lawrence Agodoa
National Institute of Diabetes and Digestive and Kidney Disease
(301)594-1932; fax, (301)480-3510
e-mail, agodoal@ep.niddk.nih.gov

Geographic Restrictions:
Domestic and foreign for-profit and nonprofit organizations, including colleges and universities, hospitals, laboratories, state and local government units and eligible agencies of the federal government. Foreign institutions are not eligible for First Independent Research Support and Transition awards.

To Whom:
The National Institute of Diabetes and Digestive and Kidney Diseases is inviting applications for basic and applied research on the pathophysiology of diabetic nephropathy.

Areas include the genetic determinants of susceptibility and cellular and molecular factors; mechanisms of glomerulosclerosis, interstitial fibrosis and scarring; development of experimental model systems; identification of markers of disease initiation and progression; identification of novel therapeutic interventions and gene targeted strategies to prevent, limit or reverse renal lesions due to the disorder.

Application info:
Deadlines are Dec. 9, 1997 for letters of intent; Jan. 9, 1998 for applications.

Financial info:
$2.5 million for 10 to 12 awards. The maximum award is $250,000 in direct costs.

Direct/Indirect Antigen Recognition in Allograft Survival

Janet Connolly
National Institute of Allergy and Infectious Diseases
(301)496-5598; fax, (301)402-2571
e-mail, jc333b@nih.gov

LeeAnn Jensen
National Heart, Lung and Blood Institute
(301)435-0066; fax, (301)480-1060
e-mail, lj15x@nih.gov

Susana Serrate-Sztein
National Institute of Arthritis and Musculoskeletal and Skin Diseases
(301)594-5032; fax, (301)480-4543
e-mail, szteins@ep.niams.nih.gov
gopher://gopher.nih.gov:70/11/res/nih-guide

Geographic Restrictions:
Domestic and foreign for-profit and nonprofit organizations, including colleges and universities, hospitals, laboratories, state and local government units and eligible agencies of the federal government. Foreign institutions are not eligible for FIRST awards.

To Whom:
The National Institute of Allergy and Infectious Diseases and three other institutes are inviting applications for basic studies to further understanding of the immune response to direct or indirect presentation of allogeneic major histocompatibility complex antigens and determine the contribution of each to acute and chronic graft rejection.

Application info:
Oct. 1, 1997; Feb. 1, 1998; and June 1, 1998.
Awards will be regular research project grants and First Independent Research Support and Transition Awards.

Drinking Water

William Stelz
U.S. Environmental Protection Agency
National Center for Environmental Research and Quality Assurance (8703R)
401 M St. SW
Washington, DC 20460
(202)564-6834
e-mail, stelz.william@epamail.epa.gov
Internet: http://www.epa.gov/ncerqa.

Geographic Restrictions:
U.S. academic and nonprofit institutions and state and local governments.

To Whom:
The Environmental Protection Agency is inviting applications under the 1998 Science to Achieve Results (STAR) program to improve the quality of

drinking water by appropriately balancing health risks caused by exposure to microbial pathogens with risks from disinfection byproducts. Funding areas include microbial pathogens in the source waters of the United States, disinfection byproducts and emerging contaminants from the contaminant candidate list.

Pathogens research should focus on developing and improving analytical methods to quantify the occurrence of such organisms as caliciviruses, adenoviruses 40,41 and 1-39, microsporidia, hepatitis A, Mycobacterium avium intracellulare, Helicobacter pylori, legionella pneumophila and toxoplasma gondii. Research also is needed to establish approaches for determining the general impact of susceptibility factors, such as age and nutrition and the role of biofilms in protecting pathogens from disinfectant residuals.

Research on disinfection byproducts should improve methods for estimating human exposures to the byproducts of different treatments in areas including ozonation byproducts, chloramination byproducts, byproduct formation and stability, treatment techniques for removing precursors of disinfection byproducts, disinfection byproduct modeling and human exposure.

Examples of health effects research needed for chemical contaminants include effects at levels likely to occur in drinking water of aluminum, vanadium and organo-tins.

Application info:
Deadline is Feb. 26, 1998.

Financial info:
$4 million for awards ranging from $250,000 to $500,000 for the two- or three-year project period.

Drug Abuse Research Development Program

Lula Beatty
Special Populations Office
National Institute on Drug Abuse
(301)443-0441; FAX, (301)480-8179
e-mail, lb75x@nih.gov

Pushpa Thadana
Division of Basic Research
NIDA
(301)443-6300; fax, (301)443-6043
e-mail, pt24e@nih.gov

Jamie Biswas
Medications Development Div.
(301)443-5280; fax, (301)443-2599
e-mail, jb168r@nih.gov

Jagjitsing Khalsa
Division of Clinical and Services Research
NIDA
(301)443-1801; fax, (301)594-6566
e-mail, jk98p@nih.gov

Arnold Mills
Division of Epidemiology and Prevention Research
NIDA
(301)443-6710; fax, (301)594-6847
e-mail, gfleming@ngmsmtp.nida.nih.gov
Internet: http://www.nih.gov/grants/guide/index.html

Geographic Restrictions:
Domestic universities and colleges that meet one of the following criteria: A public or private nonprofit university, four-year college or other institution offering undergraduate or graduate degrees with a traditionally high (more than 50 percent) minority student enrollment; an institution with a substantial enrollment of minority students, for example 25 percent in each of the previous four years, that can demonstrate a commitment to recruitment of faculty and students who are members of minorities underrepresented in biomedical and behavioral research, need for support and efforts to support minority faculty and students; or an Indian tribe that, in conjunction with one or more higher education institutions, offers undergraduate and graduate degrees in disciplines relevant to drug abuse.

Nonprofit community-based organizations that provide drug abuse treatment and services also may apply in collaboration with an eligible minority institution if they can demonstrate a research mission, service to minority populations and significant minority staff, trainees or efforts to recruit them.

To Whom:
The National Institute on Drug Abuse is inviting applications to broaden and strengthen drug abuse research in minority institutions by developing the capacity of institutions and faculty, staff and students to conduct rigorous drug abuse research in all areas supported by NIDA.

The initiative seeks to enhance the research infrastructure of minority institutions and foster increased research; to provide research development support and experiences to faculty and staff to facilitate independent drug abuse research careers; and to stimulate research interest in students and give them research experiences. **Applications must include an institutional research development plan and individual investigator research projects.**

Interest areas span neuroscience, behavioral, clinical, social science, public health, biological, HIV/AIDS and health sciences.

Application info:
Deadlines are Feb. 1, 1998; June 1, 1998; and Oct. 1, 1998.

Financial info:
There is no specific setaside. Awards will be resource-related research project grants (R24). The project period is up to five years.

Effects of Diabetes on Urinary Bladder and Erectile Function

Leroy Nyberg or Ralph Bain
Division of Kidney, Urologic and Hematologic Diseases
National Institute of Diabetes and Digestive and Kidney Diseases
(301)594-7717; fax, (301)480-3510
e-mail, leroy_nyberg@nih.gov or bainr@extra.niddk.nih.gov
Internet: http://www.nih.gov/grants/guide/index.html

Geographic Restrictions:
Domestic and foreign for-profit and nonprofit organizations, including colleges and universities, hospitals, laboratories, state and local government units and eligible agencies of the federal government.

To Whom:
The National Institute of Diabetes and Digestive and Kidney Diseases is inviting applications for research on the effects of diabetes mellitus on the lower urinary tract.

Areas include studies of urothelial cell, vascular, neurological and smooth muscle functions and interactions in the normal urinary bladder and in penile erectile function and the changes that occur with diabetes mellitus.

Application info:
Deadlines are Dec. 9, 1997 for letters of intent; Jan. 9, 1998 for applications.

Financial info:
$1.5 million for 10 to 12 awards. NIDDK will award research project grants (R01) up to five years and exploratory research grants (R21) of $75,000 a year for up to three years. The R21 mechanism is used for experienced investigators to develop pilot and feasibility studies for new and innovative research approaches.

Environmental Health

Allen Dearry
Chemical Exposures and Molecular Biology Br.
National Institute of Environmental Health Sciences
(919)541-4500; fax, (919)541-2843
e-mail dearry@niehs.nih.gov

Christopher Saint
National Center for Environmental Research and Quality Assurance
Environmental Protection Agency
(202)564-6909; fax, (202)565-2448
e-mail, saint.chris@ epamail.epa.gov.
Internet: gopher://gopher.nih.gov:70/11/res/nih-guide. Search by

Geographic Restrictions:
Public and private domestic nonprofit organizations.

To Whom:
The National Institute of Environmental Health Sciences and the Environ-mental Protection Agency are seeking applications to establish research centers dedicated to children's environmental health.

Each center must span basic, clinical and applied research and community interventions and must organize around one of the following three broad themes: respiratory diseases; childhood learning; and growth and development.

Application info:
Deadlines are Sept. 30, 1997 for letters of intent; Jan. 21, 1998 for applications.

Financial info:
$10 million for first-year funding of up to six centers. The project period is five years.

Environmental Policy Research

Robert Menzer
National Center for Environmental Research and Quality Assurance
(202)564-6849
e-mail, menzer.robert@epamail.epa.gov

Melinda McClanahan
(202)564-6851
e-mail, mcclanahan.melinda@epamail.epa.gov

James Edwards
Biological Sciences Directorate
(703)306-1400
e-mail, jledward@nsf.gov

Elbert Marsh
Engineering Directorate
(703)306-1301
e-mail, emarsh@nsf.gov

Jeff Fenstermacher
Social Behavioral and Economic Sciences Directorate
(703)306-1741
e-mail, jfenster@nsf.gov
Internet: http://es.inel.gov/ncerqa/rfa/98valrfa.html.

Geographic Restrictions:
U.S. academic and nonprofit institutions, and state and local governments.

To Whom:
The Environmental Protection Agency and the National Science Foundation are inviting applications under the Science to Achieve Results (STAR) program for projects on decisionmaking and valuation for environmental policy.

This program supports environmental policy research on valuing human health and environmental quality and economic growth; and innovations and improvements in environmental decisionmaking. Valuation topics range from economic costs and benefits of environmental policies and programs to the relationship between economic growth and environmental quality. Decisionmaking areas include methodological innovations and improvement and advances in understanding values and perceptions relevant in environmental decisionmaking.

Application info:
Deadline is Jan. 15, 1998.

Financial info:
About $2 million. Grants will range from $60,000 to $125,000 a year for two to three years.

Feline Immunodeficiency Virus As AIDS Model

Roger Miller
Targeted Interventions Br.
Division of AIDS
National Institute of Allergy and Infectious Diseases
(301)496-6430; fax, (301)402-3211
e-mail, rm42i@nih.gov
Internet: gopher://gopher.nih.gov:70/11/res/nih-guide

Geographic Restrictions:
Domestic and foreign for-profit and nonprofit organizations, including colleges and universities, hospitals, laboratories, state and local government units and eligible agencies of the federal government.

To Whom:
The National Institute of Allergy and Infectious Diseases is seeking applications on the molecular biology, immunology and host factors involved in feline immunodeficiency virus infection (FIV) of cats to advance understanding of the virus/host infection process.

The goal of the initiative is to produce a reliable, reproducible and inexpensive animal model to evaluate therapeutic compounds and strategies for HIV. Relevant studies may focus on FIV genes and their encoded proteins; host factors that interact with FIV proteins or regulatory sequences; key aspects of the biology, immunology and sanctuary sites of FIV infection of cats; and advancing the mucosal challenge model for testing potential topical microbicides and vaccines.

Application info:
Deadlines are Jan. 2, 1`997; May 1, 1998; and Sept. 1, 1998 for AIDS-related research grants.

Financial info:
NIAID will support regular research grants, small grants and First Independent Research and Transition Awards.

Genes and Mechanisms Underlying Immunodeficiency

Howard Dickler
Division of Allergy, Immunology and Transplantation
National Institute of Allergy and Infectious Diseases
(301)496-7104; fax, (301)402-2571
e-mail, hd7e@nih.gov
Internet: gopher://gopher.nih.gov:70/11/res/nih-guide

Geographic Restrictions:
Domestic and foreign for-profit and nonprofit organizations, including colleges and universities.

To Whom:
The National Institute of Allergy and Infectious Diseases and the National Institute of Child Health and Human Development are inviting applications for research on the genes and mechanisms underlying primary immunodeficiency.

Research should identify and characterize the molecular mechanisms involved in primary immunodeficiency diseases that are not the result of a single defective gene; identify the immunologic role of defective gene products and their normal counterparts; and, based on this knowledge, develop more effective approaches for the diagnosis, treatment and prevention of these disorders.

Application info:
Deadlines are Oct. 1, 1997; Feb. 1, 1998; and June 1, 1998.

Genetics Research

DeLill Nasser
Eukaryotic Genetics
e-mail, dnasser@nsf.gov

Philip Harriman
Microbial Genetics
Molecular and Cellular Biosciences Div.
National Science Foundation
(703)306-1439
pharrima@nsf.gov
Internet: http://www.nsf.gov/bio

Geographic Restrictions:
Domestic nonprofit and for-profit organizations, including higher education institutions; state and local governments; and individuals.

To Whom:
The National Science Foundation's Molecular and Cellular Biosciences Division is inviting proposals for projects in eukaryotic and microbial genetics.

NSF supports a wide range of genetics studies geared toward answering significant questions of organization, recombination, function, regulation of function and transmission of heritable function in all organisms. Specific areas range from mechanisms of gene regulation to DNA repair and recombination.

Eukaryotic genetics grants support genetic studies of eukaryotic organisms, except fungi, as experimental organisms, including studies of both organelle and nuclear genomes; viruses of the organisms as well as parasitic or symbiotic interaction at the genetic level; and epigenetic phenomena and molecular evolution. Microbial genetics projects should focus on eubacteria, archaebacteria and fungi, including yeast, as experimental organisms. This includes studies of the genetics of bacterial viruses and other infectious agents of bacteria and fungi; investigations of microbial interactions with other organisms if the emphasis is on the microbe; and studies on molecular evolution of microbial genes.

Application info:
Deadlines are Target dates are Jan. 10, 1998 and July 10, 1998.

Financial info:
In 1997, NSF awarded about 30 genetics research grants ranging from $50,000 to $400,000 a year and averaging $110,000 a year. Project periods are typically three years, but may range up to five years.

Genetic Services

Michele Lloyd-Puryear
(301)443-4427 or (888)333-HRSA
e-mail, mpuryear@hrsa.dhhs.gov
Internet: http://www.hrsa.dhhs.gov
CFDA number is 93.310.

Geographic Restrictions:
Public and nonprofit private higher education institutions and agencies engaged in research or programs relating to maternal and child health and/or services for children with special health-care needs.

To Whom:
The Health Resources and Services Administration is inviting applications under its maternal and child health programs to provide genetic services demonstrations in managed care environments; and with

sickle cell children, patients and families affected by thalassemia and for people with cultural barriers to care.

Application info:
Deadlines are April 30, 1998. Applications will be available Feb. 27, 1998.

Financial info:
$3.6 million for 25 awards.

Geriatric Pharmacology (Merck/AFAR Fellowships and Scholarships)

Office of the Dean of the Medical School or the American Federation for Aging Research
1414 Avenue of the Americas
New York, NY 10019
(212)752-2327; fax, (212)832-2298
e-mail, amfedaging@aol.com
Internet: http://www.afar.org.

Geographic Restrictions:
A fellowship candidate must be a citizen or permanent resident of the United States; board certified or eligible in a primary specialty by July 1, 1998; and within three years of having completed postdoctoral training. Previous training in geriatrics or clinical pharmacology is not required, but one or the other is highly desirable.

A scholarship applicant must be a medical or Pharm. D. student who has completed at least one year of training and must be a U.S. citizen or permanent resident. The research project must be conducted under the supervision of a faculty mentor.

To Whom:
The American Federation for Aging Research (AFAR) is accepting applications for the 1998 Merck/AFAR Fellowships in Geriatric Clinical Pharmacology and the Merck/AFAR Research Scholarships for Medical and Pharmacy Students in Geriatric Pharmacology.

The Merck/AFAR Fellowships in Geriatric Clinical Pharmacology are intended to encourage the development of a cadre of physicians with a command of the emerging field of geriatric clinical pharmacology. Selections are based on the individual candidate's ability, promise and evidence of commitment to a career in geriatric clinical pharmacology. The proposed training and research program should provide the opportunity for a Merck/AFAR Fellow to acquire experience in clinical pharmacology, geriatrics/gerontology and research.

The Merck/AFAR Research Scholarships in Geriatric Pharmacology for Medical and Pharmacy Students were created in response to the need for physicians and pharmacists with an expertise in medication use in the elderly. The scholarships offer medical and Pharm. D. students an opportunity to undertake an eight- to 12-week, full-time research project on any subject in the field of geriatric pharmacology. The subject may be drawn from the basic, clinical, behavioral or health services sciences. The research project may be carried out in any setting such as a medical school, hospital, university, pharmaceutical company, nursing home, government or non-government agency. Selection is based on the applicant's ability, promise and interest in gerontological issues; the qualifications of the designated mentor; and the merit and feasibility of the proposed research project.

Application info:
Deadline is Nov. 3, 1197 for the fellowships and Jan. 21, 1998 for the scholarships. Fellowship application forms should be filled out by the candidate and an official of the institution. Applications must be submitted by the institution on behalf of an individual candidate for the fellowship. Scholarship applications are to be completed by the applicant and the faculty mentor.

Financial info:
Two fellowships each offering $50,000 annually for two years and up to nine scholarships of $4,000 each will be awarded.

Health Effects and Exposures to Particulate Matter

U.S. Environmental Protection Agency
National Center for Environmental Research and Quality Assurance (8703R)
401 M St. SW
Washington, DC 20460
(800)490-9194

Deran Pashayan
(202)564-6913
e-mail, pashayan.deran@epamail.epa.gov
Internet http://es.inel.gov/ncerqa/rfa/982brfa.html.

Geographic Restrictions:
U.S. academic and nonprofit institutions, and state and local governments.

To Whom:
The Environmental Protection Agency is inviting applications under the Science to Achieve Results (STAR) program to research health effects and exposures to particulate matter and associated air pollutants

EPA favors research in chronic epidemiology, to investigate associations between long-term exposure to particulate matter (and other air pollutants) and adverse health effects; mechanisms of particulate matter toxicity; and exposure error, to provide information on the magnitude and variability of the errors in the assessment of exposure due to various factors.

Application info:
Deadline is Jan. 29, 1998.

Financial info:
About $2 million for awards ranging from $50,000 to $200,000 a year for up to three years.

HIV Pathogenesis In Women's Interagency HIV Study

Paolo Miotti
National Institute of Allergy and Infectious Diseases
(301)496-9176; fax, (301)402-3211
e-mail, pm122m@nih.gov.

David Burns
National Institute of Child Health and Human Development
(301)496-7339; fax, (301)496-8678
e-mail, db98d@nih.gov.

Katherine Davenny
National Institute on Drug Abuse
(301)443-1801; fax, (301)443-2317
e-mail, kd25h@nih.gov

Sandra Melnick
National Cancer Institute
(301)435-4914; fax, (301)402-4279
e-mail, sm33K@nih.gov

Maryann Redford
National Institute on Dental Research
(301)544-5588; fax, (301)480-8254
e-mail, mr48a@nih.gov

Judith Fradkin
National Institute of Diabetes and Digestive and Kidney Diseases
(301)594-8814; fax, (301)480-5303
e-mail, jf58s@nih.gov

A.P. Kerza-Kwiatecki
National Institute of Neurological Diseases and Stroke
(301)496-1431; fax, (301)402-2060
e-mail, aka45w@nih.gov

Joyce Rudick
Office of Research on Women's Health
(301)402-1770; fax, (402)402-1798
e-mail, r27q@nih.gov
Internet: gopher://gopher. nih.gov:70/11/res/nih-guide

Geographic Restrictions:
Domestic and foreign for-profit and nonprofit organizations such as colleges and universities, hospitals, laboratories and state and local government units.

To Whom:
The National Institute on Allergy and Infectious Diseases, in concert with other NIH funding components, is inviting applications for highly focused basic research to use a large research cohort of HIV-infected women to formulate specific hypotheses about HIV/AIDS pathogenesis in women.

Funders will support studies focused on basic mechanisms of HIV infection and progression in women who are part of the target cohort in the ongoing Women's Interagency HIV Study (WIHS). Research may include expansion of ongoing studies and new studies. Studies may involve one or more WIHS sites or be limited to subsets of the WIHS population. Studies may address biological aspects of HIV infection and their impact on women's health and should be hypothesis-driven.

Examples include the molecular basis of HIV infection and disease progression in women; the direct and indirect effect of drug use; surveillance of the prevalence, incidence and secular trends of cancers occurring in the WIHS cohort and the natural history of AIDS-related cancers; the in vivo role and mechanism of action of oral co-infections on HIV infection and disease pathogenesis; the pathogenesis of AIDS wasting syndrome, including the effects of HIV on endocrine and gastrointestinal function, metabolism, appetite and diet and physical activity; and the pathogenesis of central and peripheral nervous system abnormalities caused by HIV infection in HIV-positive women.

Application info:
Deadlines are Jan. 2 ,1998; May 1, 1998; and Sept. 2, 1998 for AIDS-related research grants.

Financial info:
There is no specific setaside. The initiative will support regular research project grants and First Independent Research Support and Transition grants for five years.

Improved Function of Transfused Platets

Luiz Barbosa
Division of Blood Diseases and Resources
National Heart, Lung and Blood Institute
(301)435-0075; fax, (301)480-0868
e-maillb30o@nih.gov
Internet: http://www.nih.gov/grants/guide/index.html

Geographic Restrictions:
Domestic and foreign for-profit and nonprofit organizations, including colleges and universities, hospitals, laboratories, state and local government units and eligible agencies of the federal government.

To Whom:
The National Heart, Lung and Blood Institute is seeking applications for research to improve the viability and function of transfused platelets during storage.

Research issues include storage-related changes inplatelet internal structures including the cytoskeleton and contractile proteins; the role of proteases, especially calcium-activated proteases, in causing structural alterations leading to loss of platelet function; correlations of in vitro changes with alterations in platelet viability or function in vivo; development of conditions for storing platelets int he cold without causing platelet lesion; development of conditions that would avoid storage-induced changes and improve platelet viability and/or function of stored platelets; and the effect of additives on the changes produced on the platelet surface due to collection/processing and storage.

Application info:
Deadlines are Nov. 28, 1997 for letters of intent; Jan. 22, 1998 for applications.

Financial info:
$1.2 million for first-year support of four to six research project grants. Applicants must request direct costs in modules of $25,000, up to $175,000. The project period is up to four years.

Innate Immunity

Daniel Rotrosen
Division of Allergy, Immunology and Transplantation
National Institute of Allergy and Infectious Diseases
(301)496-8974; fax, (301)402-0175
e-mail, dr17g@nih.gov

Dennis Mangan
Division of Extramural Research
National Institute of Dental Research
(301)594-2421; fax, (301)480-8318
e-mail, dennis.mangan@nih.gov.
Refer to PA 97-079
gopher://gopher.nih.gov:70/11/res/nih-guide

Geographic Restrictions:
Domestic and foreign for-profit and nonprofit organizations, including colleges and universities, hospitals, laboratories, state and local government units and eligible agencies of the federal government.

To Whom:
The National Institute of Allergy and Infectious Diseases and the National Institute on Dental Research are inviting applications for basic and preclinical research on the mechanism of innate immunity to develop new strategies to augment antimicrobial defenses, develop novel approaches for immunomodulation in chronic infectious and inflammatory disorders and identify new methods, based on mechanisms of innate immunity, to modulate acquired immune responses.

Application info:
June 1, 1998; Oct. 1, 1998; and Feb. 1, 1999.

Latent State Tuberculosis Infection

Ann Ginsberg
Division of Microbiology and Infectious Diseases
National Institute of Allergy and Infectious Diseases
(301)496-5305; fax, (301)496-8030
e-mail, ag73i@nih.gov.

Hannah Peavy
Division of Lung Diseases
National Heart, Lung and Blood Institute
(301)435-0222; fax, (301)480-3557
e-mail, hannah_peavy@nih.gov
Refer to PA 97-085.
gopher://gopher.nih.gov:70/11/res/nih-guide. Search by the PA/RFA number.

Geographic Restrictions:
Domestic and foreign for-profit and nonprofit organizations, including colleges and universities, nationally.

To Whom:
The National Institute of Allergy and Infectious Diseases and the National Heart, Lung and Blood Institute are inviting applications that propose to investigate the latent phase of infection by Mycobacterium tuberculosis and the mechanisms by which it is reactivated in some hosts.

Application info:
Deadlines are Oct. 1, 1998; Feb. 1, 1997; and June 1, 1998. **Awards will be regular research project grants and First Independent Research Support and Transition Grants.**

Long-Term Cancer Survivors

Claudette Varricchio
Division of Cancer Prevention and Control
National Cancer Institute
(301)496-8541; fax, (301)496-8667
e-mail, varriccc@dcpcepn.nci.nih.gov
Internet: gopher://gopher. nih.gov:70/11/res/nih-guide

Geographic Restrictions:
Domestic and foreign for-profit and nonprofit organizations, including colleges and universities, hospitals, laboratories, state and local government units and eligible agencies of the federal government.

To Whom:
The National Cancer Institute is seeking applications for research to identify important areas that have an impact on long-term survivors of cancer.

The RFA is not intended to explore differences between survivors and nonsurvivors that may be linked to mechanisms of disease progression or genetic predisposition. The initiative is expected to provide information about the effects of cancer and its treatment on survivors, the relationship of treatment to late effects and the measures appropriate to address potential problems and needs of survivors.

Application info:
Deadlines are Oct. 24, 1997 for letters of intent; Nov. 25, 1998 for applications.

Financial info:
$3 million for first-year funding of 12 to 15 awards. **The NCI will support regular research project grants, small grants and First Independent Research Support and Transition awards.**

Managed Care Outcomes

Global Exchange, Inc.
7910 Woodmont Ave.
Ste. 400
Bethesda, MD 20814-3015
(301)656-3100; fax, (301)652-5264
Internet: http://www.ahcpr.gov
gopher://gopher.nih.gov:70/11/res/nih-guide

To Whom:
The Agency for Health Care Policy and Research is inviting cooperative agreement applications to study the connections between features of managed care organizations, health outcomes and quality of care for patients with chronic disease.

Studies should focus on one or more conditions meeting these criteria: high prevalence; association of outcomes with quality of care, ease of severity assessment with inexpensive measures, some outcomes measurable within a two-year time frame; and adequate patient numbers across the severity spectrum.

Application info:
Deadlines are Oct. 31, 1997 for letters of intent; Jan. 6, 1998 for applications.

Financial info:
$1.5 million for first-year funding of four to seven projects co-funded with the American Association of Health Plans Foundation. The project period is three years.

Geographic Restrictions:
Domestic and foreign for-profit and nonprofit organizations, including colleges and universities, hospitals, laboratories and state and local government units.

Management of Symptoms Secondary to Treatment

June Lunney
National Institute of Nursing Research
Division of Extramural Activities
(301)594-6908; fax, (301)480-8260
e-mail, jlunney@ep.ninr.nih.gov

Claudette Varricchio
National Cancer Institute
Division of Cancer Prevention and Control
(301)496-8541; fax, (301)496-8667
e-mail, varricci@dcpcepn.nci.nih.gov

Dianne Rausch
National Institute of Mental Health
Office on AIDS
(301)443-6100; fax, (301)443-9719
e-mail, dr89b@nih.gov
gopher://gopher.nih.gov:70/11/res/nih-guide. Search by the PA/RFA number.

Geographic Restrictions:
Gives domestic and foreign for-profit and nonprofit organizations.

To Whom:
The National Institute of Nursing Research, the National Cancer Institute and the National Institute of Mental Health are inviting applications for research on clinical management of treatment-associated symptoms, which can seriously affect compliance to treatment regimens and patients' quality of life.

Application info:
Oct. 1, 997; Feb. 1, 1998; and June 1, 1998.

Maternal and Child Health Research

Gontran Lamberty
(301)443-0392 or (800)333-HRSA
e-mail, glamberty@hrsa.dhhs.gov
CFDA number is 93.110RS.

Geographic Restrictions:
Public and private nonprofit higher education institutions and nonprofits engaged in maternal and child health research, nationally.

To Whom:
The Health Resources and Services Administration is inviting applications next year for applied research in maternal and child health that has the potential for ready transfer of findings to healthcare delivery programs. (Oct. 9 Federal Register/Preview)

Areas include projects to develop measures of racism and study its consequences for health of mothers and children; investigate the role that fathers play in caring for and nurturing the health, growth and development of children; and evaluate the impact of healthcare reform and managed care on maternal and child health services.

Application info:
Deadlines are March 1, 1998 and Aug. 1, 1998. Applications are available now.

Financial info:
$1.9 million for 10 awards.

Medical Education Research 6

Deborah Kuhar, Director
National Board of Medical Examiners Office of Research Support
3750 Market St.
Philadelphia, PA 19104
(215)590-9657
e-mail, dkuhar@mail.nbme.org
Internet: www.nbme.org.

Geographic Restrictions:
Schools accredited by the Liaison Committee on Medical Education and the American Osteopathic Association are eligible to apply. Multiple investigators from the same institution may submit proposals, though individual principal investigators may submit

To Whom:
The National Board of Medical Examiners

(NBME) will fund research on innovative methods of evaluation used to measure performance in medical education or practice.

The fund is seeking innovative research on evaluation methodology in accredited medical schools to uncover new or enhanced contributions to the theory, knowledge or practice of evaluation. Projects can examine and measure educational progress or performance at any point along the continuum of medical education, from undergraduate through continuing education.

Application info:
Deadline is Nov. 14, 1997. Application booklets will be distributed to medical schools, prior applicants and recent inquiries. To be included on the mailing list, or for more information call. Grants will be made for pilot or short-term, as well as more comprehensive or long-range research projects.

Financial info:
$250,000 for grants of up to $50,000 for two years. only one proposal.

Geographic Restrictions:
Gives to domestic and foreign for-profit and nonprofit organizations.

To Whom:
The National Institute of Allergy and Infectious Diseases and three other National Institutes of Health institutes are seeking applications for studies to further understanding of the role of minor histocompatibility antigens (MiHA) in graft versus host disease following bone marrow transplantation and the possible involvement of MiHAs in chronic graft rejection of solid organ transplants.

Application info:
Deadlines are Oct. 1, 1997; Feb. 1, 1998; and June 1, 1998.

Financial info:
There is no specific setaside. **Awards will be regular research project grants and First Independent Research Support and Transition Grants.** The project period is up to five years.

Minor Histocompatibility Antigens in GVHD and Graft Rejection

Janet Connolly
National Institute of Allergy and Infectious Diseases
(301)496-5598; fax, (301)402-2571
e-mail, jc333b@nih.gov

LeeAnn Jensen
National Heart, Lung and Blood Institute
(301)435-0066; fax, (301)480-1060
e-mail, lj15x@nih.gov.

Anne Health
National Cancer Institute
(301)496-7815; fax, (301)496-8656
e-mail, ah43v@nih.gov

Lawrence Agodoa
National Institute of Diabetes and Digestive and Kidney Disease
(301)594-1932; fax, (301)480-3510
e-mail, agodoal@ep.niddk.nih.gov
Refer to PA 97-077.
gopher://gopher.nih.gov:70/11/res/nih-guide. Search by the PA/RFA number.

Minority Student Bridges to Baccalaureate Degree

Americo Rivera
National Institute of General Medical Sciences
(301)594-3900; fax, (301)480-2004
e-mail, RiveraA@nigms.nih.gov
Internet: http://www.nih.gov/grants/guide/index.html

Geographic Restrictions:
Domestic public or private educational institutions, including state or local higher education systems.

To Whom:
The National Institute of General Medical Sciences is inviting applications to and expand programs to improve the academic competitiveness of underrepresented minority students and **help them make the transition from the associate's degree to the bachelor's degree as they work toward a career in biomedical research.**

Proposals must involve a partnership between associate's and a bachelor's degree-granting institution. Transition programs should be developed to meet the special requirements of underrepresented minority students interested in science. Program areas range from establishing a mentoring program with faculty at the baccalaureate institution, to guaranteeing accep0 tance as juniors into the participating bachelor's program(s) for successful participants in the enhancement program.

Application info:
Deadlines are Nov. 21, 1997 for letters of intent; Jan. 16, 1998 for applications.

Financial info:
$9 million for 20 to 40 new and competing continuation awards.

Minority Student Bridges to Doctoral Degree

Americo Rivera
National Institute of General Medical Sciences
(301)594-3900; fax, (301)480-2004
e-mail, RiveraA@nigms.nih.gov
Internet: http://www.nih.gov/grants/guide/index.html

Geographic Restrictions:
Domestic public and private educational institutions, including state or local higher education systems.

To Whom: The National Institute of General Medical Sciences is inviting applications to develop and expand programs to improve the academic competitiveness of underrepresented minority students and **help them make the transition from the associate's degree to the bachelor's degree as they work toward a career in biomedical research.**

Application info:
Deadlines are Nov. 21, 1997 for letters of intent; Jan. 16, 1998 for applications.
Applications must include a partnership between an M.S. and a Ph.D. degree-granting institution. Program areas range from providing research opportunities for M.S. students with faculty at the Ph.D. institution, to academic counseling for M.S. students, focused on encouraging students to pursue research careers in the biomedical sciences.

Financial info:
$9 million for 20 to 40 new and competing continuation awards.

Molecular Mechanisms of Renal Injury and Recovery

James Scherbenske
Division of Kidney, Urology and Hematologic Diseases
National Institute of Diabetes and Digestive and Kidney Diseases
(301)594-7719; fax, (301)480-3510
e-mail, scherbensk@extra.niddk.nih.gov
Internet: gopher://gopher.nih.gov:70/11/res/nih-guide

To Whom:
The National Institute of Diabetes and Digestive and Kidney Diseases is inviting applications for research project grants focusing on molecular mechanisms of renal injury and recovery.

Studies may investigate the effect on function of renal cells of ischemia/hypoxia-induced alterations in cytoskeletal proteins; the role of integrins and protein kinases in events leading to acute tubular obstruction/necrosis; the role of blood pressure maintenance in recovery from acute renal failure (ARF); nephrotoxins, including antibiotics, heavy metals, oxidants and halogenated hydrocarbons; the effects of hormones and growth factors or their inhibitors on prevention and recovery from ARF; post-transplantation ARF, including protection of renal allografts and the relationship between delayed graft function and long-term outcome; the regulatory mechanisms in regeneration of the kidney following ischemic or toxic insults; evaluation of the intermittent hemodialysis and continuous hemodialysis on residual kidney function in critically ill patients with ARF; the role of ARF in multiorgan dysfunction syndrome; the appropriate nutritional support in the ARF patient; and appropriate characteristics of dialysis membranes for renal replacement in ARF. Other proposals of interest would lead to development of a cooperative multicenter database for coordinating studies in ARF; focus on developing and validating severity of illness scores in ARF patients; and lead to markers for early detection of renal injury.

Application info:
Deadlines are Oct. 1, 1997; Feb. 1, 1998; and June 1, 1998.

Financial info:
NIDDK will support research project grants and First Independent Research Support and Transition Awards. The project period is up to five years.

Geographic Restrictions:
Domestic and foreign for-profit and nonprofit organizations, including colleges and universities, hospitals, laboratories, state and local government units and eligible agencies of the federal government.

Occupational Health (CDC)

Roy Fleming
NIOSH
(404)639-3343; fax, (404)639-4616
e-mail, rmf2@cdc.gov

For application information, (404)332-4561
Refer to 811
Internet: http://www.cdc.gov
CFDA number 93.262.

To Whom:
The Centers for Disease Control and Prevention's National Institute for Occupational Safety and Health is seeking applications for research and demonstration projects on the causes and prevention of occupational diseases and injuries.

Funding categories are: disease and injury (allergic and irritant dermatitis, asthma and chronic obstructive pulmonary disease, fertility and pregnancy abnormalities, hearing loss, infectious diseases, low back disorders, musculoskeletal disorders of the upper body and traumatic injuries); work environment and workforce (emerging technologies, indoor environment, mixed exposures, organization of work and special populations at risk); research tools and approaches (cancer research methods, control technology and personal protective equipment, exposure assessment methods, health services research, intervention effectiveness research, risk assessment methods, social and economic consequences of workplace illness; and injury and surveillance research methods).

Application info:
Deadlines are Feb. 1, 1998; June 1, 1998 and Oct. 1, 1998.

Financial info:
$4.4 million for new awards.

Geographic Restrictions:
Domestic and foreign for-profit and nonprofit organizations.

Polycystic Kidney Disease

Gladys Hirschman
Division, Urologic and Hematologic Diseases
National Institute of Diabetes and Digestive and Kidney Diseases
(301)594-7717; fax, (301)480—3510
e-mail, gladys_hirschman@nih.gov
Internet: http://www.nih.gov/grants/guide/index.html

Geographic Restrictions:
Domestic and foreign for-profit and nonprofit organizations, including colleges and universities, hospitals, laboratories, state and local government units and eligible agencies of the federal government.

To Whom:
The National Institute of Diabetes and Digestive and Kidney Diseases is seeking applications for basic and applied research on the etiology and pathogenesis of polycystic kidney disease and the related cellular and molecular mechanisms that determine kidney function.

Areas include the genetic determinants and cellular and molecular mechanisms that disrupt normal kidney function, the mechanisms of cyst formation and growth at the cellular and molecular levels; development of experimental model systems; the development of imaging methods to assess cyst growth and disease progression; and research aimed at identifying therapeutic opportunities and gene targeted strategies to prevent progressive renal insufficiency due to the disorder.

Application info:
Deadlines are Feb. 1, 1998; June 1, 1998 and Oct. 1, 1998.

Financial info:
$2.5 million for 10 to 12 grants. The maximum first-year grant is $250,000 in direct costs.

Postdoctoral Research Fellowships in Environmental Biosciences

Carter Kimsey
Biological Infrastructure Div.
(703)306-1469
e-mail, ckimsey@nsf.gov
Internet: http://www.nsf.gov/home/search.html

Geographic Restrictions:
Gives to U.S. citizens, nationals or permanent residents who: have earned their doctorate no more than three years before the application deadline, or will earn this degree no later than June 15, 1998; have not been and are not at the time of application a principal investigator or co-principal investigator on a federal research grant of more than $20,000 since receiving their doctorate; have not submitted a similar proposal to NSF; and, for ongoing projects, have not been engaged in this research for more than one year at the time of application.

To Whom:
The National Science Foundation is inviting applications for fellowships in biosciences related to the environment.

The program seeks to identify and support independent scientists of extraordinary ability early in their careers who are interested in pursuing research in biological sciences related to the environment. Applicants must propose research on the basic mechanisms of interactions between organisms and the environment.

Application info:
Deadline is Nov. 7, 1997.

Financial info:
About 25 two-year and three-year fellowships. Two-year awards are $80,000, three-year awards are $120,000. Two-year fellowships may not be extended for a third year.

Postdoctoral Research Fellowships in Molecular Evolution

Carter Kimsey
Biological Infrastructure Division
(703)306-1469
e-mail, ckimsey@nsf.gov
Internet: http://www.nsf.gov/home/search.htm

Geographic Restrictions:
Gives to U.S. citizens, nationals, or permanent residents who have earned their doctoral degree no earlier than four years before the application deadline, or expect to receive it by June 30 of the following year.

To Whom:
The National Science Foundation and the Alfred P. Sloan Foundation are inviting applications for postdoctoral research fellowships in molecular evolution.

Proposals should reflect an approach to molecular biology that is interdisciplinary both conceptually and technically, identifying opportunities to broaden scientific training and experience and involving theoretical, comparative, computational and/or experimental analyses of biological patterns and processes at the molecular level, within the framework of organismic evolutionary change and adaptation. Because of the interdisciplinary nature of the program, applicants are expected to submit research and training plans that differ from their doctoral or postdoctoral plans.

Application info:
Deadline is Nov. 4, 1997.

Financial info:
Up to 18 two-year fellowships of $80,000 each in fiscal 1998.

Prevention of Disease After Liver Transplantation

Tommie Sue Tralka
Division of Digestive Diseases and Nutrition
National Institute of Diabetes and Digestive and Kidney Diseases
(301)594-8879; fax, (301)480-8300
e-mail, tralkat@ep.niddk.nih.gov

Richard Fuller
National Institute on Alcohol Abuse and Alcoholism
(301)443-1206; fax, (301)443-8744
e-mail, rfuller@niaaa.nih.gov

Leslye Johnson
Division of Microbiology and Infectious Diseases
National Institute of Allergy and Infectious Diseases
(301)496-7051; fax, (301)402-1456
e-mail, lj7m@nih.gov
Internet: gopher://gopher.nih.gov:70/11/res/nih-guide

To Whom:
The National Institute of Diabetes and Digestive and Kidney Diseases, National Institute on Alcohol Abuse and Alcoholism and National Institute of Allergy and Infectious Diseases are inviting applications for small grants to plan or research project grants to conduct full-scale multi-center clinical trials on methods for preventing recurrence of disease after liver transplantation.

Grants should focus on practical means of preventing recurrent primary disease after liver transplantation, a growing problem among recipients of liver grafts.

Application info:
Deadlines are Dec. 9, 1998 for letters of intent; Jan. 9, 1998 for applications.

Financial info:
Direct costs for small grants should not exceed $50,000 a year for two years. Direct costs should not exceed $500,000 a year for research project grants. The project period for RPGs is five years.

Geographic Restrictions:
Domestic and foreign for-profit and nonprofit organizations, including colleges and universities, hospitals, laboratories, state and local government units and eligible agencies of the federal government.

Regulation of the Immune Response

Stephen Rose
Division of Allergy, Immunology and Transplantation
National Institute of Allergy and Infectious Diseases
(301)496-5598; (301)402-2571
e-mail, srj@nih.gov
gopher://gopher.nih.gov:70/11/res/nih-guide

Geographic Restrictions:
Domestic and foreign for-profit and nonprofit organizations, including colleges and universities.

To Whom:
The National Institute of Allergy and Infectious Diseases and three other National Institutes of Health funders are inviting applications for research on the broad range of mechanisms that control the immune response, the age-related changes in the regulation of immune responses and the underlying mechanisms responsible for these changes. Funders will support basic and preclinical studies using molecular and cellular approaches to dissect the immune response.

Application info:
Deadlines are Oct. 1,1997; Feb. 1, 1998; and June 1, 1998.

Respiratory Infections in Childhood Asthma

Susan Banks-Schlegel
Division of Lung Diseases
National Heart, Lung and Blood Institute
6701 Rockledge Dr.
Ste. 10018
MSC 7952
Bethesda, MD 20892-7952
(303)435-0202; fax, (301)480-3557
e-mail, schleges@gwgate.nhlbi.nih.gov

Daniel Rotrosen
Division of Allergy, Immunology and Transplantation
National Institute of Allergy and Infectious Diseases
6003 Executive Blvd.
Room 4A24
Bethesda, MD 20892
(301)496-8974; fax, (301)402-0175
e-mail, dr17g@nih.gov

To Whom:
The National Heart, Lung and Blood Institute and National Institute of Allergy and Infectious Diseases are inviting applications for research on the cellular and molecular mechanisms by which respiratory pathogens contribute to the development of, worsening of or protection from childhood asthma.

Two major interest areas are molecular mechanisms of infection-induced airways inflammation and remodeling and the effect of pathogen-allergen interactions on sensitization, inflammation and airway wall remodeling. Investigators may submit applications on other topics. Studies involving children are desirable, but investigations with young adults or mammalian models also are suitable.

Application info:
Deadlines are Oct. 24, 1997 for letters of intent; Dec. 11, 1997 for applications.

Financial info:
$2.4 million from NHLBI and $500,000 from NIAID for first-year funding of about eight awards. Funds must be requested in $25,000 direct cost modules, up to $225,000 a year.

Geographic Restrictions:
Domestic and foreign for-profit and nonprofit organizations, including colleges and universities.

Respiratory Pathogens: Specific Research Needs

Chistopher Taylor
Division of Microbiology and Infectious Diseases
National Institute of Allergy and Infectious Diseases
(301)496-5305; fax, (301)496-8030
e-mail, ct18m@nih.gov

Hannah Peavy
Division of Lung Diseases
National Heart, Lung and Blood Institute
(301)435-0222; fax, (301)480-3557
e-mail, hannah_peavy@nih.gov

Kenneth Gruber
Division of Human Communication
National Institute on Deafness and Other Communication Disorders
(301)402-3458; fax, (301)402-6251
e-mail,kenneth_gruber @nih.gov
Internet: http://www.nih.gov/grants/guide/1997/index.html

Geographic Restrictions:
Domestic and foreign for-profit and nonprofit organizations, including colleges and universities, hospitals, laboratories, state and local government units and eligible agencies of the federal government.

To Whom:
The National Institute of Allergy and Infectious Diseases, the National Heart, Lung and Blood Institute and the National Institute on Deafness and Other Communication Disorders are inviting applications for research on selected respiratory pathogens and host responses to these pathogens.

Interest areas include projects that evaluate the unique immunogenic and pathogenic mechanisms associated with virulence and determine the role and molecular regulation of virulence factors for Mycoplasma pneumoniae, Burkholderia (Pseudomonas) cepacia and Chlamydia pneumoniae; isolate and characterize the function of novel structural and secretory proteins of human bacterial respiratory pathogens and novel host defense molecules; characterize events associated with the carriage of meningococci and pneumococci and those events that lead to invasion; determine and characterize factors involved in the progression to lower tract disease and/or complications due to infections with respiratory viruses other than influenza; and develop new vaccine approaches for parainfluenza viruses, Neisseria meningitidis group B, Pseudomonas aeruginosa, Mycoplasma pneumoniae, Chlamydia pneumoniae and Moraxella catarrhalis.

Application info:
Deadlines are Feb. 1, 1998; June 1, 1998; and Oct. 1, 1998.

Ryan White HIV Services

(888)333-HRSA
Michael Kaiser
(301)443-9051
e-mail, mkaiser@hrsa.dhhs.gov
http://www.hrsa.dhhs.gov
CFDA number is 93.153A.

Geographic Restrictions:
One competition will restrict eligibility to public and private nonprofit entities that will provide for care in the same areas being served by soon-to-expire projects; another focuses on projects in areas not currently served.

To Whom:
The Health Resources and Services Administration is inviting applications to improve

access to primary medical care, research and support services for children, youths, women and families with HIV.

Funds will be used to support programs that cross established systems of care to coordinate service delivery, HIV prevention efforts and clinical research and other research activities; and address the intensity of service needs, high costs and other complex barriers to comprehensive care and research experienced by underserved, at-risk and limited populations. Projects should emphasize enrolling and maintaining clients in HIV primary care; increasing client access to research by linking HIV/AIDS clinical research trials; fostering community-based infrastructures; and emphasizing prevention.

Application info:
Deadlines are April 1, 1998.

Financial info:
$10 million for 12 projects in geographic areas with currently funded projects; $1.2 million for four projects in unserved areas.

Social Psychology

Steven Breckler
Social Psychology Program
Ste. 995
National Science Foundation
4201 Wilson Blvd.
Arlington, VA 22230
(703)306-1728; fax, (703)306-0485
e-mail, sbreckle@nsf.gov.
Internet: http://www.nsf.gov/sbe/sber/socpsy/start.htm.

Geographic Restrictions:
Higher education institutions, nonprofit and for-profit organizations, state and local governments and individuals.

To Whom:
The National Science Foundation is inviting proposals to conduct basic research on human social behavior, including cultural differences and development over the life span. Potential research topics include attitude formation and change, social cognition, personality processes, interpersonal relations and group processes, the self, emotion and the social psychology of health.

Application info:
Deadlines are Jan. 15, 1998 and July 15, 1998 (target dates).

Financial info:
In 1997, about $4 million for 30 new and 20 continuing awards. Fiscal 1998 funding is not yet set, but the budget is expected to be similar.

Specialized Cooperative Centers Program in Reproduction Research

Louis DePaolo
Reproductive Sciences Br.
National Institute of Child Health and Human Development
(301)496-6515; fax, (301)496-0962
e-mail, depaolol@hd01.nichd.nih.gov

Geographic Restrictions:
Domestic organizations, including colleges and universities, hospitals, laboratories, state and local government units and eligible agencies of the federal government.

To Whom:
The National Institute of Child Health and Human Development is inviting cooperative agreement applications for research centers in the reproductive sciences. Center investigators will work with NICHD staff in facilitation research collaborations and interactions within and between centers.

Application info:
Deadlines are Jan. 14, 1998 for letters of intent; April 28, 1998 for applications.

Financial info:
$2.8 million for up to three cooperative specialized centers, to be funded in fiscal 1999.

Teaching and Research Capacity Building Grants

Richard Hood
Cooperative State Research, Education and Extension Service
Agriculture Department
STOP 2251
1400 Independence Ave. SW
Washington, DC 20250-2251
(202)720-1973
e-mail, rhood@reedusda.gov

McKinley Mayes
(202)720-3511
e-mail, mmayes@reedusda.gov
CFDA number 10.216.

Geographic Restrictions: :
Gives to the 16 historically black 1890 land grant-institutions and Tuskegee University.

To Whom:
The Agriculture Department's Cooperative State Research, Education and Extension Service is inviting applications to strengthen teaching and research capacity in health and other agriculture-related sciences at 1890 Institutions.

These grants are intended to strengthen programs in the food and agricultural sciences at eligible institutions. This program addresses the need to attract more minority students into the food and agricultural sciences; expand the linkages among the 1890 institutions and with other colleges and universities; and strengthen the teaching and research capacity of the 1890 institutions to establish them more firmly as full partners in the food and agricultural system. For teaching grants, target areas range from curricula design and materials development to scientific instrumentation for teaching. Research project areas range from studies and experimentation in food and agricultural sciences to technology delivery systems.

Application info:
Deadline is Jan. 26, 1998.

Financial info:
$8.8 million for project grants, including $4.45 million for teaching projects and $4.35 million for research projects. Teaching proposals may request up to $200,000; research proposals may request up to $300,000.

Urban Air Toxics

Environmental Protection Agency
National Center for Environmental Research and Quality Assurance (8703R)
401 M St. SW
Washington, DC 20460
(800)490-9194

Deran Pashayan
(202)564-6913
e-mail, pashayan.deran@epamail.epa.gov
Internet: http://es.inel.gov/ncerqa/rfa/982brfa.html.

Geographic Restrictions:
U.S. academic and nonprofit institutions and state and local governments.

To Whom:
The Environmental Protection Agency is seeking applications for research to pin down potential health effects, both cancer and noncancer related, associated with air toxics emissions from stationary and mobile sources.

Research issues include observational evidence, for example epidemiological data, linking health effects with ambient levels of exposure to hazardous air pollutants; approaches needed to identify the most toxic HAPs and HAP mixtures in urban air; identification of subpopulations at increased risk from HAPs; the most significant sources of toxic pollutants of concern in urban areas; ways that monitoring and modeling, including emissions modeling and dispersion modeling, can be linked to estimate exposure and risk; and improving current dose-response assessment methods.

Application info:
Deadlines is Feb. 12, 1998.

Financial info:
$2 million for awards ranging from $50,000 to $200,000 a year for up to three years.

Section III
Appendices

Electronic Grantseeking

Visit our Links page at http://www.grantscape.com,
under Other Sites and Services,
for a continuously updated Links page.

The *American Philanthropy Review's* site provides information on fundraising. The Review also hosts two popular discussion lists, Talk-AmPhilRev (a "Big Tent" list covering just about any topic of interest to professionals in the nonprofit sector) and PG-AmPhilRev (a planned giving discussion list).
http://www.amphilrev.com/

Association for Professional Research for Advancement
http://weber.u.washington.edu/~dlamb/apra/APRA.html

Charity Village, a Canadian-based organization, has a site that provides "news, information resources and discussion for the nonprofit community."
http://www.charityvillage.com

Conference Management Enterprises: free meeting planning services for nonprofits.
http://www.qpage.com/host/meetings.shtml

The *Contact Center's* site contains a variety of resources for nonprofits, including a searchable directory and a list of directories available on the Web.
http://www.contact.org

Council on Foundations' site provides a wealth of information for grantseekers.
http://www.cof.org

The *Foundation Center's* site provides information on its five libraries, its publications, seminars, funding trends, and other valuable information.
http://fdncenter.org

Foundations.org provides a directory of foundations and grantmakers.
http://www.foundations.org/index.html

HandsNet
http://www.handsnet.org

Hoover's is a subscription-based service that provides in-depth information on thousands of corporations worldwide. The site has a great links page for corporate Web sites.
http://www.hoovers.com

Impact Online: This site contains a listing of nonprofit organizations on the Web and in different regions. Check out the Connections page.
http://www.impactonline.org

The *Independent Sector's* site provides information on government actions that affect the industry, as well as other organizational information.
http://www.indepsec.org

Internet and Related Online Sources for Not-for-Profits
http://www.ai.mit.edu/people/ellens/Non/online.html

The *Internet Resources for Nonprofit Public Service Organizations'* site houses links and information for nonprofits.
http://www.sils.umich.edu/~nesbeitt/nonprofits/nonprofits.html

National Society of Fund Raising Executives
http://www.nsfre.org

Nonprofit Management Gateway
http://www.gspa.washington.edu/orgs/nongate.html

The Nonprofit Times' site provides monthly electronic articles on nonprofit management.
http://www.nptimes.com

The *Office of Development Research at Northwestern University's* site contains a valuable links list of prospect research and fundraising sites.
http://pubweb.acns.nwu.edu/~cap440/bookmark.html

The Parlor, at the Internet Nonprofit Center: This is a live chat page.
http://nonprofits.org/parlor/chat.html

The *Philanthropic Journal of North Carolina's* site has news, resources and links. You can subscribe to a daily philanthropy-related e-mail newsletter, too.
http://philanthropy-journal.org/

Rainforest Publications' Prospect Research Online is an online subscription service that provides information on corporate donations and sponsorships, along with news, interviews and press releases covering corporate philanthropy.
http://www.rpbooks.com/

Other Resources

Books, Directories and Guides

Corporate Foundation Profiles, 9th Edition profiles 235 of the largest corporate foundations in the United States. Features include contact information, purpose and grant restrictions, application guidelines and a list of key officials. The 778-page directory is $155 from the Foundation Center, 79 Fifth Ave., New York, NY 10003, (800)424-9836, fax (212)807-3677; http://fdncenter.org.

Corporate Giving Directory, 18th Edition contains information on the 1,000 largest corporate giving programs. Features include biographical data on corporate and foundation directors, officers and trustees; recent grants; historical data; and application information. The 1,873-page directory is $410 from The Taft Group, P.O. Box 33477, Detroit, MI 48232-5477, (800)877-TAFT; http://www.gale.com/taft/1taft.html.

Corporate Giving Yellow Pages, 12th Edition is a contact guide that lists the names, addresses, and phone and fax numbers of nearly 3,500 corporate giving programs. The 340-page book is $99 from The Taft Group, P.O. Box 33477, Detroit, MI 48232-5477, (800)877-TAFT; http://www.gale.com/taft/1taft.html.

***The Directory of Corporate and Foundation Givers** 1996* lists more than 8,000 of the leading U.S. funding sources. Features include biographical data on foundation directors, officers, trustees; recent grants; historical data; and application information. The 4,114-page directory is $235 from The Taft Group, P.O. Box 33477, Detroit, MI 48232-5477, (800)877-TAFT; http://www.gale.com/taft/1taft.html.

The Foundation Directory, 1997 Edition contains information on more than 7,900 foundations that hold assets of at least $2 million or distribute $200,000 or more in grants each year. The 2,068-page directory is $215 for hardcover or $190 for softcover from the Foundation Center, 79 Fifth Ave., New York, NY 10003, (800)424-9836, fax (212)807-3677; http://fdncenter.org.

The Foundation Grants Index, 1997 Edition lists over 70,000 recent grant descriptions from 1,000 of the largest independent, corporate and community foundations in the U.S. The 2,266-page directory is $160 from the Foundation Center, 79 Fifth Ave., New York, NY 10003, (800)424-9836, fax (212)807-3677; http://fdncenter.org.

Foundation Reporter, 29th Edition provides all the important contact, financial and grants information on the top 1,000 private foundations in the U.S. The 1,969-page directory is $390 from The Taft Group, P.O. Box 33477, Detroit, MI 48232-5477, (800)877-TAFT.

Government Online helps you access government—federal and state—information via the Internet, phone and fax. The book is $15 from HarperCollins Publishers, 10 East 53rd Street, New York, NY 10022.

Grants for At-Risk Youth contains information on approximately 200 funders of at-risk youth programs. Includes a special introduction written by Dr. Daniel Kaczyniski and Dr. John Platt and a disk containing application forms. The 342-page book is $119 from Capitol Publications Inc., P.O. Box 1453, Alexandria, VA 22313-2053, (800)655-5597; http://www.grantscape.com.

Grants for School Technology is an unique one-of-a-kind resource to assist administrators and education grantseekers tap into more than 200 public and private funding sources. The 436-page book is $99 from Capitol Publications Inc., P.O. Box 1453, Alexandria, VA 22313-2053, (800)655-5597; http://www.grantscape.com.

The Grants Development Kit. You'll use this three-ring binder over and over again as you copy the forms and checklists to streamline the grantseeking process. Includes an idea development form, grant development timeline, outline of basic proposal elements and much more. $45 per kit from Capitol Publications Inc., P.O. Box 1453, Alexandria, VA 22313-2053, (800)655-5597; http://www.grantscape.com.

The Grants Management Kit. As a companion to ***The Grants Development Kit***, this three-ring binder has forms, charts, checklists and outlines to help grantees manage a funder's money efficiently. Contains a grants management checklist, outline for preparing financial and project reports and more. $43 per kit. Both kits are available as a set for $76 from Capitol Publications Inc., P.O. Box 1453, Alexandria, VA 22313-2053, (800)655-5597; http://www.grantscape.com.

The Grantseeker's Guide to Project Evaluation. This step-by-step guide shows you how to plan and design an evaluation; collect and analyze evaluation data; manage an evaluation; and write a complete report. Contains a glossary of terms, sample evaluation plans, a description of statistical methods and a bibliography of additional resources. The book is $49 from Capitol Publications, Inc., P.O. Box 1453, Alexandria, VA 22313-2053, (800)655-5597; http://www.grantscape.com.

The Grantseeker's Handbook of Essential Internet Sites lists 250 Internet addresses for people looking to get money from corporations, foundations, associations and government agencies. Web sites for research organizations serving nonprofit groups are also included. The 163-page book is $75 from Capitol Publications Inc., P.O. Box 1453, Alexandria, VA 22313-2053, (800)655-5597; http://www.grantscape.com.

The National Directory of Corporate Givers, 4th Edition lists over 2,600 corporate foundations and direct giving programs The 1,092-page directory is $195 from the Foundation Center, 79 Fifth Ave., New York, NY 10003, (800)424-9836, fax (212)807-3677; http://fdncenter.org.

Outcome Funding: A New Approach to Targeted Grantmaking promotes a new concept for grantmakers and grantseekers—buying results with grant funds and not just services. The grant proposal thus because a targeted plan with defined outcomes for funders to invest in, and the grantwriter becomes an entrepreneur. The book is $21 from the Rensselaerville Institute, Rensselaerville, NY 12147, (518)797-3783.

Raise More Money for Your Nonprofit Organization: A Guide to Evaluating and Improving Your Fundraising contains information on the necessary first steps before launching a development campaign. The 51-page book is $14.95 from the Foundation Center, 79 Fifth Ave., New York, NY 10003, (800)424-9836, fax (212)807-3677; http://fdncenter.org.

Sources of Operating Grants. Discover more than 500 hard-to-find sources for personnel, administrative and other operating expenses. The 500-page book is $99 from Capitol Publications Inc., P.O. Box 1453, Alexandria, VA 22313-2053, (800)655-5597; http://www.grantscape.com.

Successful Grants Program Management. Learn how to evaluate your grants system, boost success rates, establish consistent district-wide policies and more. The 272-page book and CD-ROM is $24.95 from Classroom Connect, 1866 Colonial Village Lane, P.O. Box 10488, Lancaster, PA 17605-0488, (800)638-1639, fax (717)393-5752; e-mail, connect@classroom.net; http://www.classroom.net.

Writing Grant Proposals That Win, Second Edition! This step-by-step guide shows you how to assemble a winning grant proposal with concise explanations and solid examples to help you through every phase. You'll learn how to condense your entire proposal into a compelling abstract; describe project dissemination and continuation plans; write a solid boilerplate proposal first, then fit it to different situations and funders. The 200-page book is $85 from Capitol Publications Inc., P.O. Box 1453, Alexandria, VA 22313-2053, (800)655-5597; http://www.grantscape.com.

Winning Grants Step by Step: Support Center's of America's Complete Workbook for Planning, Developing, and Writing Successful Proposals. The workbook provides information on how to create a proposal that fulfills important criteria grantmakers demand from a successful request. The 127-page book is from Jossey-Bass Publishers, 350 Sansome Street, San Francisco, CA 94101, (800)956-7739, ext. 520.

Periodicals

Chronicle of Philanthropy. The Newspaper of the Non-Profit World keeps you up-to-date on the latest news, fundraising techniques, IRS regulations and recent foundation and corporate grants. Bi-monthly: $67.50 for 24 issues from The Chronicle of Philanthropy, P.O. Box 1989, Marion, OH 43306, (800)728-2819; http://www.philanthropy.com.

Corporate Giving Watch. Monthly updates on grantmakers, key trends, statistics, and recent grants of corporate givers. Monthly: $149 from Taft Group, P.O. Box 33477, Detroit, MI 48232-5477, (800)877-TAFT; http://www.gale.com/taft/1taft.html.

Federal Grants and Contracts Weekly. Helps readers find and win federal grants and contracts. It flags the latest funding opportunities in all areas across all agencies and tells how to pursue them. The newsletter alerts readers early to future funding, signaling specific solicitations often months in advance, unveiling agency grant plans in progress, tracking trends and forecasting areas of funding growth. Articles pass on advice from the experts, help readers calculate their chances and locate key prospecting resources. 50 issues per year, $389 from Capitol Publications Inc., P.O. Box 1453, Alexandria, VA 22313-2053, (800)655-5597; http://www.grantscape.com.

Foundation and Corporate Grants Alert. Foundation & Corporate Grants Alert helps grantseekers find and win private and corporate support. It provides comprehensive coverage of available national and local funding well in advance of deadlines, and reveals proven techniques and inside information on how to win more money. 12 issues per year, $289 from Capitol Publications, Inc., P.O. Box 1453, Alexandria, VA 22313-2053, (800)655-5597; http://www.grantscape.com.

Foundation Giving Watch. Monthly updates on grantmakers, key trends, statistics, and recent grants of foundations. Monthly: $149 from Taft Group, P.O. Box 33477, Detroit, MI 48232-5477, (800)877-TAFT; http://www.gale.com/taft/1taft.html.

For a list of general fundraising and grantseeking resources, go to Amazon.com's listing of books on "Fund Raising And Grants (General)" at: http://www.amazon.com/exec/obidos/subject-combination/0568-5163501-951535

Software

FC Search: The Foundation Center's Database on CD-ROM covers over 43,000 U.S. foundations and corporate givers in a fully searchable CD-ROM format. $1,195 single-user, $1,495 multi-user from the Foundation Center, 79 Fifth Ave., New York, NY 10003, (800)424-9836, fax (212)807-3677; http://fdncenter.org

Grants on Disk contains profiles of more than 250,000 recently awarded grants from more than 5,200 independent U.S. foundation and corporate funders. $695 for single-user, $895 for multi-user from The Taft Group, P.O. Box 33477, Detroit, MI 48232-5477, (800)877-TAFT; http://www.gale.com/taft/1taft.html.

GrantScape: CFDA has the most complete listings of federal funds available and how to apply to the funding agencies. Considered to be the "yellow pages of federal money," each listing includes program objectives, federal agency authorization, types of assistance and more. Updated annually. $175 from Capitol Publications Inc., P.O. Box 1453, Alexandria, VA 22313-2053, (800)655-5597; http://www.grantscape.com.

GrantScape: Corporate Foundations and Giving contains information on more than 4,000 corporate foundations and direct giving programs. Updated annually. $295 for single-user, or $395 multi-user from Capitol Publications, Inc., P.O. Box 1453, Alexandria, VA 22313-2053, (800)655-5597; http://www.grantscape.com.

GrantScape: Sources of Foundations is a national database that puts more than 13,000 private and corporate foundations at you fingertips. Features include over 63,000 names of directors, officers and trustees; contact names and numbers; application information; recent grants awarded; application forms (when available) and more. Updated annually. $495 single-user, $695 multi-user from Capitol Publications Inc., P.O. Box 1453, Alexandria, VA 22313-2053, (800)655-5597; http://www.grantscape.com.

GrantWrite: A Step-by-Step System for Writing Grant Proposals that Win walks you through the proposal-writing maze to prepare concise and compelling arguments for your projects. Available in DOS, Macintosh and Windows for $149 single-user and $199 multi-user from Capitol Publications Inc., P.O. Box 1453, Alexandria, VA 22313-2053, (800)655-5597; http://www.grantscape.com.

Prospector's Choice gives you more than 10,000 profiles of the top private foundations and corporate giving programs. Each entry provides contact information; financial summary; giving officers; application information and more. $849 for single-user, $1,045 for multi-user from The Taft Group, P.O. Box 33477, Detroit, MI 48232-5477, (800)877-TAFT; http://www.gale.com/taft/1taft.html.

Section IV
Alphabetical Index of all Funders

Index to Private Funders by Headquarters State

A

B

C

D

K

L

M

N

O

P

R

S

T

U

V

W

Z

Alphabetical Index to Federal Funders

A

B

C

D

E

F

G

H

I

L

M

O

P

R

S

T

U

Use This Form To Order Additional Copies Of

Grants For Medical Research

❑ Yes! Please send me _____ copy (copies) of *Grants For Medical Research*, at $119 per copy, plus $6 per order for postage and handling.

(District of Columbia residents, please add 5.75% sales tax. Virginia residents, please add 4.5% sales tax.)

Name ______________________________

Organization ______________________________

Street Address ______________________________

City, State, Zip ______________________________

❑ Check enclosed (payable to Capitol Publications Inc.)

❑ Purchase Order No.______________________________

❑ Charge my ❑ VISA ❑ MasterCard ❑ American Express

Account number ____________________ Expires ______________

Signature______________________________

(required for billed and charged orders)

Area Code and Telephone______________________________

Mail to: Capitol Publications Inc., P.O. Box 1453, Alexandria, VA 22313-2053.

For faster service: Call our Subscriber Services Department
toll free at (800)655-5597
or fax your order to (800)392-7886.

P00649

www.ingramcontent.com/pod-product-compliance
Lightning Source LLC
LaVergne TN
LVHW080030210926
848481LV00011B/3150